Love in the '40s
WHEN MAIL CAME TWICE A DAY

Vivian Kline

A diary and letters between a 19 year old Vassar college girl and a 26 year old PhD. student at Columbia University during World War II when a phone call from 80 miles away cost 25 more times as much as a 3 cent stamp.

Cover and interior design: Suzanne Jacobson

Copyright © 2012 Vivian Kline
All rights reserved.

ISBN-13: 978-1479337026
ISBN-10: 1479337021

1945

Dear Diary,   *September 1938*
It is my 13th birthday and I also became a woman!!! I got the curse. Guess I'll always remember this day. I also got this present from my big sister, Mard. It comes with a key so I can write stuff I don't want anyone else to see. I better not lose the key! I got a diary once before but I lost the whole diary!

I have a big brother, Walt, who is three years older than me. My dad is a famous doctor and my mother writes articles and sews. My sister, Mard, is six years older but seven years ahead of me in school as she skipped a grade as she is so smart. She married Howard last year when she was 18 and he was 21. They were both in college then. I was 12 and so fat that I had to get my dress at the chubby shop but now I've slimmed down. We live in an apartment in New York City and I go to the same school I have been at since kindergarten. I like art best and I have girl friends I have known for ages. We also have an old house in the country. We go there on weekends and in the summer. The house is on a dirt road and my family built a tennis court so I play tennis a lot. I love it there and sometimes bring my city school friends up. Now you know about me and I will write again.

Dear Diary,   *December 7, 1941*
Wow! Mom and Dad and I had gone to the botanical gardens. Since it is Sunday Dad could take some time off, for once. We were going home in the car and

Dad had the Philharmonic on, on the car radio. It suddenly got interrupted with a man's voice saying our ships had been bombed by the Japanese in a place called Pearl Harbor.

Dad said in his most somber voice, "This is a day that will change your whole life!" Will it, I wonder?

Dear Diary,   January 5, 1942
I am in the eleventh grade now. I go out with boys from school and, now Bill, who is in college. A confession: When I am with Bill I feel something that I never have felt when I go out with Bob or Marvin or when I am with Walt's friends. It's like what I sometimes feel when I go to a romantic movie. It comes from down there.

So, what I wondered is what it looked like down there and I got Walt's big round shaving mirror from the bathroom and, without any PJ's on, I looked! So interesting! Even looking brought back the feeling. So I put my finger back around and down there–amazing. Then, since I knew there was an opening I got a candle from the cupboard in the dining room, and put it in and out. Even more amazing! Things they don't teach you in school! Or at home! I suppose there are books that mention all that but I've never heard of them.
Amy gave me a book which I read–not telling my parents, of course–about a woman who loved another woman. There is much more I can learn

about life—stuff that really matters, stuff that no one talks about at home or at school!

I wonder if I will learn some of this unknown stuff at college.

Dear Diary,   April 30, 1943
Boy am I glad school is almost over. I am sick of the folks, both the kids and the teachers. I've just known them too long I guess. I do enjoy the dates with Bob. It's a platonic friendship and when we spend any money we go Dutch . . . mostly we walk, walk, and talk. He is going into the Army soon and hopes to eventually get to college that way—but who knows, he may be just a private and go overseas in the war.

I couldn't decide between college and art school. All of the girls in our class are going to college except Jean, who is going to Katie Gibbs secretarial school. I don't think I'm good enough in art to go full-time to art school, so I've applied to Pembroke (the woman's college part of Brown) where you can go part of the time down the street to the Rhode Island School of Design hat way I've covered both art school and college. My teacher thinks I'm good enough to go to art school, but I don't think so. Then there is the world news. It's so awful. The last Germans surrendered in Stalingrad—so many young men get killed. My little life doesn't seem important, sometimes.

But then again, spring has sprung and Gina and I have begun to play tennis on hard courts down the street. Allison and Joan are busy being best friends and going out with college boys—I am writing to some of Walt's friends who are training to be Marines and maybe next year when I'm a college person I will have some dates with them or others.

I took Walt's friend, Jim, as my date to the senior prom. Mrs. E. had given us a lecture on how to behave. It included that one should not be conspicuous. So my date brought me two huge white and purple orchids! Well, then, as he was such a good dancer, we waltzed and he waltzed me around and around till I got dizzy and fell down! Pretty conspicuous, I say.

My felt pins that I love to make have been selling well, so I've been able to buy another war bond.

Everyone at school was so sure I would get into Pembroke that I didn't apply anywhere else. And now I got a letter that I didn't get in!!! Mr. Moore found out they would only take one from our small school and Emmy has two brilliant sisters going there so they are taking her!

It's too late to apply to other schools, so I can only go to where my mother and Mard have gone: Vassar. They will take me (because MY family went there

I am told), but I wanted a co-ed school near a city with an art school attached. Phooey!

Dear Diary,   September 7, 1943
Interesting summer . . . Couldn't get my driver's license as there is gas rationing and there is food rationing, too. Each household gets 48 points in a ration book for meat, cheese, butter and cooking oil–sugar too.

I began going out with Dave, who is a bit older. My parents decided they didn't like him. They didn't even know him! And they tried to stop me from seeing him so often, so I saw him on the sly. I'm old enough to decide things for myself! I'm sure they were worried that I would sleep with him. I didn't– but almost. Of course they wouldn't talk about what they were worried about. Well, now he's in the Army and I'm off to college . . . And the Allied Forces have captured Naples and invaded Sicily!

September 12, 1943
Dear Parents,

    I guess you're anxious to hear all about the college girl. Things are progressing well. I've been to millions of things and my advisor is swell. My room is minute, but I've put up a bulletin board and pictures and now I feel quite at home in it. I brought Fooless from home and she sits with her stuffing coming out and her one eye looking at me fondly.

I also brought the twig from the dead apple tree in the field at Westport. Remember when we had that fire and I worked to save that tree? When I was little, I thought that God was in that tree and have kept that twig all this time– so I brought it along—guess for good luck.

The girls are from all over which makes it fun. The other day we were singing and a bunch started "Dixie," so we followed with "I'm a Yankee Doodle Dandy" all in good fun, of course.

The night before last we had the freshman/senior sing when the seniors, juniors and sophomores serenade the freshmen in each dorm. The freshman, in turn, make up songs to sing back. Barb Jerner and I, with some of the others, made up one. Someone else made another. And since no one could decide which was better, we sang both!

Afterward, everyone went to Prexy's and serenaded him. He appeared and gave a nice speech on "Unity and Adaptability."

Yesterday Amy and I went into town to get some curtains and see about a bike for me. There are no used bikes to be had and the cheapest new one is, at $35, way too expensive. So, could you send up Will's as soon as possible 'cause I really need a bike badly. I think it's silly to get one here.

Last night there was a meeting where the government etc. was discussed–speeches by the "big six" girls, and I want to be in every activity there is. Am trying out for choir tomorrow. After the meeting a bunch of us went to see "So Proudly We Hail." Don't see it! It's the saddest most depressing movie I've ever seen–all very obvious propaganda and good enough to affect one. I was a wreck! Made me want to quit college and get out to do something, but then I stop to think and guess it is best for me to stay here . . . for a while at least.

This morning went to required church. The sermon was much too long–very metaphorish and unrealistic and inapplicable (is there such a word?), but the choir was nice and the chapel is divine (right adjective, for once). Tomorrow, classes start and I will mail this now.
Love, Your Youngest
P.S. When you come up can you bring my blue chair for Amy? Also an umbrella and a Bible. Guess I should keep a list.

Dear Diary,   September 15, 1943
I arrived at college to find 35 of us assigned to live in alumnae house, which is off-campus! They took an extra 35 students as we are to go through in three years to help win the war when we get out. Obviously I am one of the extra 35.

I am on the top floor (three flights of stairs) in what they rightly call a cubicle. It is so small my desk won't fit in and it's in another room (others have the same problem).

Over my bed the ceiling slants as it's the roof! I put a picture of Bill taped on the slope so I can see him when I am lying in bed. I've had several dates with him. He's good looking and plays a mean game of ping pong, (not like me and my friends) but he stands way back and hits the ball really hard!

I really think I should quit college and go work in a factory, like Rosy the Riveter, but I don't have the guts. Can you imagine what Dad would say? I don't have Joan's nerve: she got an inheritance from her grandmother and promptly got on a plane and flew to live in Paris as an artist and she didn't even know French!!

I'm taking English, History, Economics, and Physiology. English isn't as good as ours in high school, but the history and economics are hard! Barb is just down the hall. I knew her from before and we've already decided to be roommates next year in a regular real dorm . . . if I stay! Somehow I feel I should be in a factory helping win the war, not here with all these girly–girls.

September 29, 1943
Dear Family,

It's now 10:45 p.m. and I swear this is the first chance I've had to write. Did I say something about not much work? I take it all back.

Note topic (one writes out facts on three-by-five cards) in history has taken me hours and hours and I think it is the hardest schoolwork I've ever done. Organizing it; finding the right books. It sounds easy enough, but somehow it's fiendish! Then hundreds of pages on-site reading. Another discouraging item: I had a physiology quiz and I think I was the only person who didn't cheat! It was a most disgusting demonstration! I somehow thought that college kids were different from high school, but I'm gradually seeing they are not.

But I don't mean to build up any sorrowful dramatic picture – everything is okay and I'm working hard. The greatest and wonderfulst piece of news is that Bill is now stationed at Lafayette College and is only 60 miles from New York–taking electrical engineering, and I'm going to see him!
Love, Viv

October 3, 1943 (from Mummy)
Dear Viv,

Here we are, Dad and I, rushing from vacation as fast as the train will take us. Well, we got what we wanted: fishing and walking in the woods and feel very fit. I just clipped points information from the newspaper and will presently be juggling them again. I promised my October, expiring shoe ration to our guide. And I am carrying home some slips of a heavenly begonia in hopes I can get them to grow in the apartment.

I wonder whether you did anything with your short skirt before you left?

I will miss you but no matter how we chance to be separated from one another, it will always be home for us in one another's hearts. You mean so extra special much to me. We are going to miss you fearfully, but I know you're having what you are ready for–a sort of preliminary life of your own.

Love, Mummy

October 17, 1943 (from Mummy)
Dear Viv,

The adorable card and postal came this evening bright and early–also a letter from Walt and one from Howard, just by chance. It all made a nice beginning to the day. I finished writing an article; went to Gramp's for lunch which was rather sad; came home and had visitors. I'm now at Dad's office to keep him company as he does bills.

We were going out for supper but Mard has a cold (the universal cold). Her talk last night was very successful. I could only tell it was delivered with ease as I couldn't understand a word of it. Then went home and set the table for Dr. Root and Clare, who came for drinks. We had a very pleasant time. The Chief had spoken very appreciatively about Mard and her research.

He has given her all sorts of suggestions for further work.

While we were at supper we received a phone call from Walt. He is definitely to stay at Chapel Hill another few months. He will not arrive in New York as we had hoped, so you can definitely ask someone, preferably female, to go with you to the matinee. Have you any plans for Saturday evening or we can ask someone in to dinner? Drop me a line right away.

Love, Mummy

October 18, 1943
Dear folks,

Today I went to a synagogue with someone taking a religion course. I figured that would be part of my education as we never did anything about religion when I lived at home. I was horrified! The women had to sit upstairs, separate from the men, and everyone talked during what was going on in the service. Boy! That's not for me!

And I still find the girls very wacky. Oh, well, maybe it's just my mood. Won't write till I have good news.

Love, V

October 22, 1943 (from Mummy)
Very Dear Viv,

There is so much I would like to answer in your leters— about the girls: most of them are often "wacky," but sometimes college does a lot for them and you are part of that influence. There is nothing much to do except stay friendly. I wish I had been that at college. Those wacky ones drove me into a shell, unnecessarily . . . But you are old enough and experienced enough to be yourself, calmly, firmly and smilingly.

And about religion: of course, one visit to one church, whatever the denomination, cannot give one much idea of its time. Much has gone out of the ritual for most people in most churches (how different in the Middle Ages!). To me, it is as ridiculous to go through meaningless forms in English, Latin or Hebrew, but it is the group activity that still holds them, meeting every week, getting some guidance from their leader, feeling part of a tradition and that is probably a good, though secondary, thing for us today. That thrill that is not in religion comes before a work of art, scientific experiment or in the presence of greatness of any kind – and having all that wonder.

I, for one, haven't missed conventional religion. The important thing, it seems to me, is to be lifted out of one's small concerns into a world where we can say, with Hamlet, "What a great piece of work is man" and therefore God, if you will.
Love, Mummy

October 28, 1943 (rare letter from Dad)
Dear Viv,

A sudden wave of parsimony and economy has overwhelmed me, so I find a piece of scratch paper and use it to write a letter on. In my day, we didn't take our instructors out to dinner and I think we lost out by not doing so. Now that I come to think about it, I did have a professor to dinner at my home. Of course I was not in a dormitory for

I was living at home when I went to college

Things here, like in Germany, are proceeding according to plan. WAR NEWS tonight tells of so many killed…

We are expecting company for dinner: the Langners and the Smithers, and Dr. and Mrs. Winkle to spend the evening here. Don't you wish you were home so that you could go out to escape the grown-ups?

No, Bill or Bob or Jim didn't phone or any of your other friends, but we have not forgotten you, anyway. Thanks for the offer of birthday records, but I really don't know of anything I need or want. This year, buy some more savings stamps instead. Next Sunday is Fred's 50th birthday and we are trying to get up some kind of stunt, but I find it difficult to be funny this year. Perhaps I am aging or it's the world's fault.

Yesterday, I started a new person in my office to take Dr. Parker's place, now that he is in service. She seems very nice and I think it will mean a great deal to me. Perhaps next summer I wont have to give up weeks to hospitals and illnesses. Maybe we will have a good time together. You might even catch a fish!
Well, Viv, the guests are arriving, so I must leave you:
Keep well and study hard.
Love, from Dad

Dear Diary,   December 5, 1943
Haven't written in you in ages. Between writing to Fred, Dave, Bob, Bill and the various servicemen who seem to need mail, as well as family, Walt and Howard, the diary gets left behind. How to explain

to my parents that I am not my sister! Mard got all A's and was phi beta kappa, too, and my parents seem to think I should be just like her.

College is O.K. but not really what I wanted. I wanted a co-ed school and here there are only girls. And they say I have to take French, which I'm terrible at, and I can't see the relevance of ancient history when history is being made every day (and is much more interesting!) What do I care about the past when the war is going on. But most of the girls here don't even read a newspaper. They have gone to boarding schools and I find them awfully girl-ish—many have never known any boys.

One girl actually thought you got pregnant holding hands with someone of the opposite sex!

The Cairo Declaration means the Allied Powers hope for an international organization to maintain peace. I hope that happens.

December 8, 1943 (from Mummy)
Dear Pussycat,
The other day, Ginette phoned to see if you were home by any chance because Fred was in town. And, today, Marvin phoned you. He was in town from Fort Monmouth where he may or may not stay. We chatted quite a while but he wouldn't come to dinner. He said he had been separated- from his clothes for five days and wasn't presentable.

He hadn't been able to write and said his group had been suddenly disbanded and most of the men put into the infantry. He was put into the signal corps.

Since you had measles last year, you could earn five dollars and do a good deed by donating blood when you come to town.

Dad and I, Mard and her friend Clare, from her department, went to the Boston symphony and we took them for a soda afterwards.

Your letters portray a very busy and interesting time and I can't feel at all sorry for you. We must find you that tennis racket when you come to town.

Mard and Clare are at a concert–a jazz concert in memory of Fats Faller, while Dad has been on a consultation and is now paying bills at the office.
Love, Mummy

January 12, 1944
Dear family,

I've been busy here doing various things other than just my courses. I've done some work for the Social Museum. Did some sketches. I'm not good at it, but I do enjoy it and I've taken a job three hours a week to work at the retreat (the co-op, student-run food room in Main). I decided I'd like to earn some extra money and working with the kids behind the scenes is fun. If it gets too much I can get out of it, but until then I'll stick with it.

Thursday night I went to a meeting in town. It was a

volunteer group formed out of the old citizens committee for the reelection of FDR. It was very interesting to me for its very failure! There were some eight or nine people all very willing and eager, but with little organizational ability, and it seemed, much personal animosities.

There was no one leader and their fumblings were really pitiful. It's quite a common thing in volunteer organizations, I guess. I was amazed that our democracy comes out as well as it does! It certainly was easy to see how dictatorships start! I had a terrific desire to get up myself or have someone else get up and tell them what to do. Of course the better solution is to have a leader who leads and doesn't command and yet it was a temptation to command them and get their fumblings into some order.

Friday night we heard Prof. Winspear give a talk on the sociological approach to Epicureanism, which was wonderful. Talking to him and Mr. Venable afterwards was even better! Barb and I have asked Mr. Venable, philosophy professor and his wife, to dinner again. We asked him in poetry form and he said he'd try to answer in similar form if he had time.

Other highlights of the week: we ate dinner at Palmer House with two girls and they really have an awfully good time up there. It's the one co-op house. (It's a lovely place–reminded me, more in atmosphere than physical structure, of our country place.)

What did you think of FDR's speech proposing a second bill of rights for economic security and social security?

Got a long letter from Dave which was interesting in

giving the picture of life in the Pacific. Also a letter from Barry, who is about to go overseas, and his desire to see his home again and his own plans for the future just the kind of house he's going to build etc.—quite moving, though I don't think he realizes it. Got mom's forwarded V-mail letter from Fred but he continues it on the V-mail of another for page 2. That other V-mail, apparently, hasn't arrived yet! Confusing when he left it in the middle of a sentence!
It was written December 12 and he just got my letter of September 18!! Also got a long and very nice letter from Walt in which he didn't say too much about his work, but as long as he stays there I guess he's doing all right.

   Was very excited to finally succeed in my library wanderings today I was looking for some books on the best way to put on exhibits. I never realized people wrote books about it and how to use surveys, etc. Russell Sage Foundation seems to have something to do with most of this. Exactly what is it? Any connection to a college?
Love, Viv

March 12, 1944
Dear family,
   I feel much relieved to have a physiology exam and notebook out of the way and, after working, I wrote my paper on Tolstoy's theory of history and very anxious to see Miss Russell's and mom's comments. As, like the Roger Bacon paper, I have no idea whether it makes any sense or not. It's a subject slightly above my head and I never knew whether I was interpreting what Tolstoy meant, as

he meant it, but it was very interesting and this made me more religious than I've ever been, feeling a necessity for an unseen force, a deity or any name you want to call it, with such logic that I can't find a flaw in it.

 Jo Evan, the new head of SLA (Student Liberal Association), came here to dinner. She's a swell girl – Russian, came here in 1933, majoring in Economics, History and Political Science. Had a nice long talk with her on college, Russia, and life.

 Aren't the soldiers brave to keep fighting at Anzio?

 I decided to accept the SLA chairmanship as it sounds like a well-organized group, although it hasn't been too good this year. I'm going to my first executive board meeting tomorrow. They have a new system of meeting for dinner every Tuesday evening for board meetings.

 IRG (the interracial group) has been gradually reorganized and, what with the new elections, things are changed now so that they have the secretary whose job, among other things, is to keep the file clippings. So, some of my job is taken over by her. As I get into SLA, gracefully, I will slip out of IRG. I would still be an interested member, but less of a leader. I think it's kind of a good idea to try different things. Yes?

 Played tennis match today and won 6-1. She was good enough, but her serve wasn't working and mine was, which made all the difference. I love that game!

 Still have my sunburn. Someone asked if I was sick or getting X-ray treatment! Splurged the other day on slightly above-knee-length gray flannel shorts–the only type of shorts we're allowed to wear.

Love, from your youngest

P.S. Could use some dried fruit.

P.P.S. Awful that we lost 69 planes while bombing Berlin…

P.P.P.S. What do you think about Wendell Willkie entering the race and Hitler and Mussolini meeting together? What a world!

Love, Viv

May 13, 1944

Dear Family,

    My cold is much better. In fact, after taking the medicine you so kindly offered, I decided I better get well and quickly! This has been a busy busy week so far – a good bit of work after taking off three days – plus several posters and SLA meetings to prepare for the coming conference on Congress.

    We're having four different discussions in four dorms on Friday night led by faculty members: the Dean on "The Clash between the Executive and the Legislature"; Miss Newcomer of the Economics department on "Pressure Groups"; a professor from the Sociology department and Ms. Lockwood from English on "Representation in Congress"; And Mr. Feith, from Political Science and Mr. Porter from History on "Analysis of the Present Congress." They all sound good and I only wish I could go to all of them.

    Yesterday, in some mysteriously way, I received an invitation to one of Prexy's teas. This was one given in honor of Miss Hall, who now heads Henry Street settlement. There were about 20 of us there and we asked questions and she spoke on what the settlement is and does. Impressed me as a very capable and charming person.

I went to the Vocational Bureau the other day where I filled out an application concerning what I wanted to do. I had put down social or settlement work or museum work. There is practically nothing in the latter field and plenty in the former if I wanted it. I could get jobs (working under supervision) with kids and for money; but when I come right down to it, I find I don't really want it. I seem to be drawn to helping to win the war somehow. But at this point I'm a bundle of indecision.

But now I have decided to work at one of the settlement houses in town on Friday afternoons. It's an awful time because it's my one free afternoon, and works beautifully when desiring a long weekend, but I'll probably only take one or two, anyway – will get substitutes then. It was the only time I could work it into my schedule. It's called Catherine Street and I chose it in preference to the other three because it's both Negro and white, run by a Negro couple. I've met the male half of the couple at one of the IRG meetings and he seems swell. Ought to be fun working there.

One of the southern girls who didn't come back wrote another up here saying, "Tell Viv and Barb that I shocked my family to death with a lot of racial ideas. Everyone thinks I'm going equality crazy. I guess they impressed me more than I realized." Made me feel good! And she was the one I thought was hopeless! Boy! Aren't those Soviet troops great! Did you read that Hitler said the poor Germans had to fight to the last man!

Must go to bed so as to be fresh to wait on breakfast. Saw where meat rationing is ending. Yippee!

Love, Viv

April 30, 1944

Dear Family,

Just had a very pleasant time with Mard and sending this via her because I'd like quick answers, if possible.

Have been thinking for some time that I'd like to go down to see Walt. He's been asking me to come down for over two years now. I have enough leaves left to go for a long weekend, being able to spend two nights down there with still enough left over for an emergency visit to come home.

I've thought about it a good deal and there are several disadvantages—one is the money mainly—it cost $26 train fare for the traveling. I haven't done much this year, perhaps that's only rationalization. Barb would come along with me. She got her parent's consent. (They were up this weekend.) We thought we'd like to go the weekend of June 2. We really have to decide quickly. If you say it is O.K., I will write Walt to find out if it's okay for him.

The money and traveling are the main objections. I think the fun of going is the fact that it's one of the few things Walt has asked of me. I talked to Mard about it, so if there's anything I left out she may be of help. Could you let me know right away? Isn't it great that the Allies have taken back Rome? Love, Viv

Dear Diary, (after Chapel Hill)　　June 10, 1944
Well, finally something to write about besides classes. We got the time off and Barb and I decided to visit Walt at Chapel Hill in North Carolina before he goes overseas. We took a bus down to Grand Central and got tickets even though it said civilians only can go in an emergency. We felt a bit guilty when we saw the car we chose was full of servicemen. No other civilians at all! There were a few empty seats, but they might be filled with latecomers, so we decided to sit on the floor.

There was only one light at the end of the car and it was quite dark. Pretty soon some of the men sat down on the floor with us! I could hardly see their faces. Turns out they just wanted to talk! One named Ted said he would fight so he could come back to his hometown. He would have a house with a white picket fence and three girls and three boys—had it all planned! (Sounds like a lot of kids to me!) He got out his army address and asked if I would write to him. When others heard him they proceeded to give me their addresses, too. I guess getting mail is important … that makes ten service men I have to write to! What can I possibly say they'd be interested in … Well I'll worry about that later.

We had a fine time with Walt and his friends. Unfortunately, now we are back in college.

June 9, 1944
Dear Family,

Good news about D-day! And the Nazis have pulled out of Rome! And nearly 3 million soldiers are in Normandy. Wow!

Life here is definitely fine even though I'm feeling crampy. Spoke to Mr. Lanier about majoring in Psychology and the value of occupational therapy. Also met a nice girl, a sophomore majoring in Psych—very friendly and wide awake. Then to top it off, Bill phoned that he was coming on Friday, which he did.

He was duly shown all around college and then we went into town for Chinese food for dinner. He stayed overnight at a place nearby and then visited my physiology class with me in the morning. Then we played tennis, which was loads of fun as he is very good and at ping-pong, too. He left at 3 p.m.— a very pleasant 24 hours. It gave me a taste of what college life must have been like in pre-war days with weekend dates.

I've gotten two marks: a B in psych which I'm glad since it isn't a freshman course usually and since I may major in it and a Ct in physiology . . . missed being a B by one point in the exam.

Received a letter from Bob yesterday, who is now overseas, very depressed because of a piece of rotten luck. He was accepted into OCS, even had his physical, but he'd already been assigned to a unit going overseas and they wouldn't release him. He wasn't really complaining in the letter, but it was an unenthusiastic one.

Got the laundry box last night and thanks also for the dried dates and the socks.
Love, Viv

> *Dear Diary,   June 14, 1944*
> *Oh my God! I am shocked! I think I can read people. I mean I can tell if they are sophisticated—if they will get A's and know what's what, but I am shocked! I just heard that Alice and Ann have left school. They were found by someone in bed together. Apparently they were making love and someone found them doing it. They were then asked to leave school! No one knows for sure . . . maybe they just wanted to leave.*
>
> *Now I see why some girls didn't like them. If I hadn't read that book Amy gave me I wouldn't understand about this at all.*

June 17, 1944
Dear Family

I took Amy out for her birthday to the college drug store for ice cream. Then we went to see two documentaries which were excellent. A British one called "World of Plenty," discussing distribution of food before, during and after the war. It was the most progressive movie I've have ever seen, not counting the Russian ones–really inspiring and hopeful! Another was "The Battle of the Books,"whose title speaks for itself, and yet another, an American one, "Youth in Crisis," which was like much one reads on juvenile delinquency only put into pictures. Then the last one was the most charming short ever–about children– very little plot, just showed kids in summer camp discovering life to find out things for themselves. It was done by Monro Leaf. All together a very enjoyable evening.

We wanted to have a blood donor drive, but when we went to arrange it in town they said they only did it once a month and they were very discouraging about giving blood by minors, adding red tape having to get parent' signatures etc. Certainly seems silly when they keep saying that they need blood. To lunch.
Love, Me

June 18, 1944
Dear Mom,

Yes, Mom, I beat you: I bought a dress the day before yesterday in town at half the price of the one I didn't get in New York. It's even perfect in length. I have used it already as there is a rehab center near campus and they have socials inviting us college girls, I guess, to enliven the lives of the fellows who are there. Danced with some pretty odd guys. One is a Mormon who sees nothing wrong in having many wives (he doesn't have any yet!) and one guy who was definitely strange. Guess it can be called part of my education.

Got a letter from one of the boys I met on the train. He actually wrote a cute letter – so typically American: like the phrase, "I had a grand time while on furlough. The hometown is dead; the gang is gone but I enjoyed myself immensely." I guess that must be the way a lot of the guys feel.

He also wanted a picture to show those fellows (he's in Florida) "what a swell girl comes from New York." Anyway, it was fun to get and restored my faith in human nature for this disillusioned college girl.

Barb and I will be roommates next year. Both asked for singles near each other but not in the same room. We got a double in Raymond Hall, one small room on either side of a living room on the fourth floor. Very civilized and a big improvement on this cubicle.

Our petition about education seems to have had some results: a funny letter from the Dean. It is a very poorly worded paragraph all one sentence informing us the matter was under consideration. There's to be a meeting this Friday night of faculty, students, and trustees - 20 in all - and Barb and I are invited. Of course the problem is much bigger than just four courses or five and involves all the problems of what a liberal arts education should be. The whole problem of postwar education enters in.

Did some painting at the Social Museum last week. The exhibit on the returning veteran is almost complete except for two friezes the two girls were assigned to do. It's a good exhibit as far as material, goes but the arrangement is poor – too many little pictures and not enough ideas – not much I can do about it. a good exhibit as far as material goes, but the arrangement is poor—too many little pictures and not enough ideas—not much I can do about it.

Had a long talk with a sociology professor the other morning on various matters. I suggested using our material for an exhibit instead of individual papers so that we could use a different medium to show our data. Originally he was interested, but on second thought he decided it would take too much time away from the main problem of the course, which is to work in Poughkeepsie. I also talked to him about museum work–combining sociology and exhibit work, but he wasn't very helpful and didn't seem very interested.

In economics we're now studying money and banking, bank balance sheets, etc., and it is certainly involved. Crazy when you think of it objectively. At the same time I'm reading "Grapes of Wrath" for American lit. It makes you wonder–using the bank as a super human monster pushing the people off the land and sending them to their migratory ways.

More soon and love to all,
Viv

June 20, 1944
Dear Family

Economics has been especially good of late as the discussion is on income distribution and private property. Miss Newcomer is awfully good. She's intellectual, though she does have a poor speaking voice.

Have hit on an idea that I major in Sociology and make my thesis be an exhibit in the museum, so I could get in the making and presenting of facts as the interesting problem.

Don't know if they would allow that, though.

Last few days have been pleasantly varied. I played another tennis match which I won in three sets 6-3,3-6,6-3. The first set I have lost all year, which was a good thing to take me down a peg.

Went to a Town Hall meeting on Socialized Medicine last night. The doctor who was in favor of the Wagner Bill, a surgeon from New York by the name of Koppelmann, reminded me of Dad. His opponent was an older man, a Dr. from Poughkeepsie who wasn't nearly as good a speaker. His point against the bill was not as reactionary as some I have heard, but he took up the individualist plea.

The threat of systemizing medical care seemed too much for him. He also was against the bill's idea to head the plan by one man–an appointed one– and not one elected. He thought the insurance should be voluntary insurance headed by the local counties.

Dr. K. was much more convincing in his arguments for the bill even in the question period. They went into the politics of it all about the AMA etc. Altogether it was a worthwhile evening particularly since, back at the dorm, we continued the discussion with those who are against the bill (most of whom, of course, wouldn't come to the meeting.)

Had a surprise test on the comparison of two poems and got back my paper on Tolstoy which she liked fairly will with the comment "quite a good clear account of the rather difficult subject."

Love, from Your Youngest

June 18, 1944
Dear Family,

    Only one more Sunday and I'll be home! Dad is now saying, "I think she's anxious to come home." You guessed it.

    This morning when I took a walk I suddenly bethought that two weeks from that moment I'll probably be walking around the reservoir stopping every few moments to have Dad tip his hat to a patient and Mom stopping to take a bit of gravel out of her shoe. If things go as planned, I'll be home on Friday the 17th. Until then I've got plenty of work to do with four exams thrown in for good measure.

    This week has been a good one with less homework and more reading: Freud and some short stories; went to an interesting lecture on Marxism, Ethics and Historical Inevitability by Mr. Venable, a professor in Philosophy. Barb and I went and found it was given mostly to Philosophy majors, so it was difficult to understand it all.

    Friday I got my history paper back on Roger Bacon. I was very anxious to see what I would get on it as I spent a lot of time on it and found it quite difficult. When I handed it in I wasn't sure if one word of made sense! So I felt good when I saw, "A good paper–nice work" written on it. Many people got simply horrid, really nasty, comments.

    The other night went to a dramatic production of a play written in 1819 about the war of 1812, a melodrama. The scenery and costumes were very good, but the play and acting weren't. There is a poster on the bulletin board to sign up for another play. Don't know whether to try out for it or not.

Have been put in charge of the poster committee for the Inter Racial Group. (Hereafter called the IRG.)
Love, Viv

P.S. Maybe when I am home I will have time to see "For Whom the Bell Tolled" and "Lassie Come Home." I hope. Wasn't Dad glad about Mussolini having to step down?

Dear Diary,   August 15, 1944
It's been a nice summer. Marseilles and Paris were liberated. Meat rationing has ended and the GI bill has passed. I had a volunteer job which was just okay and played a lot of tennis. Bob came home on furlough and it was good to see him. But then he wanted "to make love" as he put it. I realized I don't feel that way about him. He's just been a good friend all through high school. But somehow he got me down on the floor in the apartment and we sort of wrestled. He finally got the idea that this was not my idea of fun!

Then: MORE IMPORTANT! Mard had invited her whole department of physiology at Columbia Medical School up to our country place for a Sunday picnic August 14.

Mard and Clare and Danny are all working to get PhDs. Dr. Root, who is their advisor and another older man who is the head of the department (they call him "the Chief") and a Dr. Wang all came without wives. (Clare's husband and Howard are overseas. I don't know why the other men didn't bring their spouses. Danny and I were the only unattached ones and we really hit it off. He has a great sense of humor, not as good looking as Bill but so much fun to hang around with!)

I am sorry I must go tomorrow away to Woods Hole with my parents for two weeks and then I come home and am alone in the apartment for two nights before I go back to my second year of college. Guess I won't see him again for a while—if ever.

Dear Diary,   August 22, 1944
(writing this at Woods Hole)
Am I just boy crazy? Or did I have an especially good time at the picnic? Danny is seven years older than I am (26 to my 19). We spent the whole day together. When he saw the New York Times on the picnic table and asked if anyone minded if he did the cross word puzzle in it, I said I'd help, though I'm no good at those things, so we sat together as he did it–in ink!

At the beach we took endless trips to the water fountain so as to be away from the others and we could talk. He is so nice! He laughed when I was eating a large slice of watermelon. I sat on the porch stone step, bare foot and (as is my wont) spit out the pits–to see how far I could get them to go—not a very lady-like thing to do, I guess. Dr. Root kept making remarks about us, teasingly.

I sure hope to see him again as he is so easy to talk to, but I go off to college pretty soon after I get to leave here. It is really boring here ...

August 27, 1944
Dear Viv,
I've called at 10:30 at 12 at one 3:30 at 6:15 and eight o'clock today, but no one answered. When I suggested to Mard that she ask you to call me, Wa-3-2500 extension 384 , she thought it would not be proper for a girl to call a fellow on such short acquaintance, even if were the most sensible way for them to get together.

You may agree with her, so I'll try you tomorrow but I'd certainly be pleased to hear from you. I wouldn't think you're being forward. I've been looking forward to seeing you again. and would be really disappointed if you got back to the safety of college unmarred by my degrading company.
Danny

August 29, Tuesday, 6 P.M.,1944
Dear Danny,

Sorry you couldn't reach me – as a matter of fact I was still in Woods Hole, Massachusetts. Just got home an hour and a half ago. I doubt if that makes you feel any better but I tried to reach you at the lab, forward female that I am, but I guess you'd already left. If you somehow haven't reached me by the time you get this, call me . . . up to

10:30 AM Wednesday or Thursday, preferably around 8:30 or 9. The way the cards and plans in general are stacking up, I'm free Thursday in the day or evening.
Viv
P.S. I'd love to see you. Life is very complex and so is this letter. Hope it all straightens out.

September 3, 1944
Dear Family,

In 20 minutes I shall be leaving to meet Barb and her family for lunch before going back to college. It's been a wonderful three days. I adore living alone and I amused myself highly- talking to the walls, laughing heartily at my own jokes, etc.

Saw Bob home on leave and Danny yesterday when we played tennis with Dr. Wang and Dr. Nickerson. Fun dinner nearby and then to a movie "Hail the Conquering Hero" which is delightful. Eddie Bracken, the boy who was in "The Miracle of Morgan's Creek" is in it. This is a wonderful take-off on heroes and politics. As "Cue" says "a must". Took a ferry ride before coming home. Very Pleasant

Mom: will settle $ about the clothes that I bought and charged to you, all at Lord and Taylor (nightgown $2.95, lounging pajamas $3.95, shoes $9.95, Girdle $5.50, and pearls $2.95). "Parents Magazine" came and your article, Mom, looks great. No other important mail … also bill for the newspaper which I ignored. Will write more when back at college.
Love, V

Dear Diary,   September 4, 1944

Oh Wow! Danny and I met at 4 p.m. and played tennis before we ate at a little restaurant. (We had raisin pound cake toasted for dessert...never had that before) and then we went to a movie; but next (most important) we walked and walked and talked and talked. When he held my hand an electric shock sort-of went right thru me. We went on the ferry to Staten Island and back and walked all the way home to the apartment where I fixed eggs as, by now, it was morning! As he left (I DID have to go back to college after all and he, to work) he kissed me-.just lightly.-that was all but that was enough ! Best date of my life!

I want to tell you about him. He comes from a lower middle class family in south Philadelphia, one of seven kids and he's the first to go to college. He always knew he would go somehow. His eyes were poor and his (crazy?) eye doctor said he shouldn't read so he sat at the back of the class and listened (Of course he read on the sly too). The doctor advised him to become a chicken farmer! I laughed at that as my Dad was sickly when young.. didn't go out to school till high school. HIS doctor told him to be a chicken farmer too!!! (What's this with the chickens?)

Danny graduated from high school at 15 (he skipped two grades) and he worked at different jobs to save up money. There was no one to advise him but then he heard that at Purdue, if you got top grades, they gave you your tuition back. So he hitch hiked from Philly to Indiana; had some odd jobs to pay for haircuts etc. and did well so he got his tuition back! He's not especially close to his family. kind of outgrown them, I guess, but didn't have bad things to say about them. Then before he thought he would be drafted, he volunteered to go into the army, feeling that Hitler was bad and the state of the world needed defending. He applied and because of his eyes, he was turned down. Then he applied to grad schools to Harvard, Penn and Columbia and got the best financial deal at Columbia so that is where he is going now along with my sister Mard and another woman, Clare. He's seven years older than I am (26 to my 19) maybe that's the difference from all the other guys I've known. No, it's more than that.

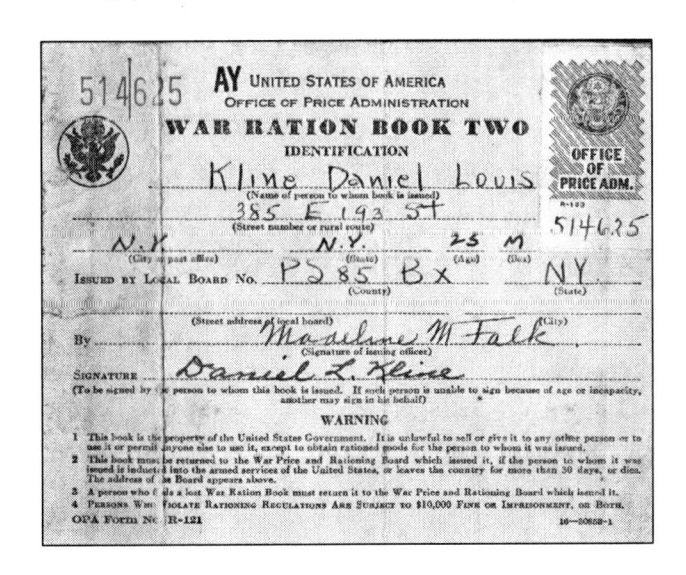

September 5, 1944

Dear Danny,

    I've got 25 minutes with nothing to do except to write to you—a thing that may not happen often in the future so tho Emily Post might not approve of my writing you but as I've said I'm in the minority in many things which gives me a few privileges, I figure.

    I'm writing you partly because there are a few things to say. This has been a great summer, a great week and even, to my surprise, a great weekend.

    Barb, my roommate here, (you'll have to meet her) and I met for lunch after you and I parted on Friday (after I had had one and a half hours of sleep interrupted by three phone calls.) We took a 4 p.m. train up to college arriving at 7 P.M..

    First job was a necessary trip to the infirmary. "How do you feel?" (chorus Barb and I) "Fine" "Got a cold?" (Barb and I in unison) "No" So they decided we didn't have polio and let us go to our dorm.

    We unpacked and then spent the rest of the evening in the traditional style. Us upper classmen serenaded the freshman going from house to house as they sing songs they have made up. When we got to the house 35 of us were stuck in last year, we re-met the young "house mother" who then took us out for drinks. (I was the lone coke drinker). We all felt a good deal better as we are now scattered around in different dorms.

    Could go on enumerating the various activities but don't want to bore you. The summary consist of surprising pleasure in being back with a feeling that I know more than when I left and a determination to make this a heck of a swell year.

Our joint living room looks like hell- nothing in it. We've each got a small room with bed and desk on either side of this center space. I've got a few pictures around and Barb has a "Men Drinking" poster and a "Proceed at your own risk," so we feel very much at home.

Big news: We are in quarantine because of POLIO and can't leave campus or have visitors until the first frost when, presumably the polio virus is killed.

By the way, when you asked me—or refrained from asking if I was "attached" did you really think I'd act the way I did if I was?

Pardon the jumble of this letter. When I'm happy I'm apt to be incoherent.

Write soon, Duchess

P.S. if I'm a Duchess are you a Duke?

September 4, 1944
Hello Viv,
"Hello" of course isn't the way I want to address you. Substitute whatever else you choose. Although I have no bank account you have my blank check.

I now know what those people who climb a fakir's rope and are left in midair must feel. All the way down to my room on the bus everything seemed surreal. I just couldn't believe it was morning. At work people were working and others arriving. They'd say good morning and I wanted to laugh. Suddenly I was extremely tired as if a spring had given way inside, and I rushed home to sleep till 6 (lucky me!) much to the astonishment of my placid landlady who barged in about noon to tidy up the room. Even now my mind wont settle down and it's impossible to study so I'll write letters and do some laundry.

I felt very sorry for you having to rush off with a train to catch and settling down in your room ahead of you before you could get much sleep. However, I'm selfish enough to realize that the same situation were repeated I'd do exactly the same thing only more so.

Eat lots of iron, Viv, one of us will have to build up his resistance. (There is your father's influence via you now coming out in me).

Study hard, monkey, but don't let your study interfere with your letter writing.
Affectionately, Danny
P.S. Parlez Vous?
>   When a Duchess
>   Does things such as
>   Kiss the way you do,
>   Tho it may sound Frenchy
>   It's clear this wench she
>   Turns VD into voodoo"
>   (P.U.)

September 4-10, 1944
Dearest You,

At the moment I'm feeling pleasantly satisfied with life–

having put in a pretty strenuous week of work. I've come to the conclusion that I'm taking about the hardest set of courses I could possibly pick. It's gotten to the stage where I'll be slaving just to keep up, and not in the least for an "A," but I'm still glad I'm taking what I am, because I've got a percentage of liking 4 out of 5 courses – a percentage higher than usual.

I'm writing this now because I've got some time-will wait and add stuff as the moments allow. It's Saturday afternoon on the still "restricted" campus, remarkably quiet due to conscientious souls bound on making an impression both on their professors and themselves. I've spent the afternoon reading Ben Franklin and finding him ""quite a guy". For REAL letters, go to him. Modern letter writing certainly has deteriorated since the invention of speedy travel, radio etc. No insults to yours so far, much appreciated one.

One of the nice things about my courses is the way they fit together. Example: studying Freedom in American Lit while studying the making of the Constitution in Polit. I can see how Polit would be a snap for those people who had had a good civics course, but as I never had any (and have always felt the grave deficiency about same) and since I sat in the row in front of a row of boys in American history, consequently learning much but not concerning American History, I find it fascinating and hard.

Philosophy continues delightful. Had a ten minute talk with Venable before class yesterday. We got outlines consisting of questions for which we had to pay 15 cents.

He asked for someone to collect said dough and I volunteered. (middle name sucker). So I came to class early ready to receive the multitudes and had a chat with him before my debtors arrived.

I read "What is Philosophy?" by Howard Selsam (Communist) this summer and was very much impressed. Another girl named Rosey had taken a course with Selsam, this summer at Jefferson School. She told me Venable and Selsam were good friends. So I talked to V. about Selsam and politics. Venerable is either a Communist or as near to one as you can be without being one. He's a very progressive teacher emphasizing the whys and reasons of things rather than the facts, which is always a welcome change, particularly when one's mind is more adapted to that way of thinking.

Am using restraint not to try out for "Soph Party," a musical show written directed and acted by sophomores as it takes up a heck of a lot of time but it would be fun, I'm sure.

Good nite for good this time. Pleasant dreams. (There was a song at camp we used to sing at taps which ended "you dream of me and I'll dream of you" which always seemed a fair proposition.

It's now Sunday 2:45 P.M.. Read the newspaper P.M. and the Times and I think I'll start on the Worker, all of which take up time but I figure tis well spent.

This afternoon we follow tradition by visiting freshman we know who have to feed us. Then tonight we sophomores take them to the Cider Mill—a famed place which I confess I've never seen.

I was going to keep writing this in installments but it's gotten to be long so I guess I'll send it " as is" even tho I may hear from you tomorrow.

To work, to work, Duchess

September 11, 1944

Dearest Duke; (As Dr. Wang would say "Hi!")

I'm not sticking to my "go slow" theme by writing you again today but I'm a gal full of exceptions (which have nothing to do with proving the rule–or don't you remember discussing that on one of our many trips to the water fountain?) But that was such a cute letter, I thought the least I could do was to abide by your words of wisdom and keep writing.

Today has been write letters day. Had my first class in French-the one class that I have the attitude of the line of least resistance to (a preposition is a bad thing to end a sentence with). I managed to comprehend about half of what went on as about the other people in the class did. The first part of the class was the usual regulation stuff: names, books, schedule. Then Mme Le Lavandier went into a great dissertation on France, her liberation, the war etc. We all listened but didn't think it vital. All were rather stunned when, as the bell rang, she cheerful told us our assignment for Wednesday was to write a resume of what she had said (in French of course).

Polit (Political Science—kindly learn the abbreviations, Professor) was next. A large lecture class (conferences smaller twice a week) when Mr. Post, head of the department and a liberal Republican (if there are such animals) spoke about various problems that will interest us during the year. While discussing taxes he said he preferred the type where everyone was taxed equally such as toll taxes etc. So little me pops up with a disagreement claiming that kind of tax is unfair with mainly poor people having the burden. To which he said, "Your point of view is perfectly legitimate. I just don't happen to agree with you". So the rest of the class was spent in his telling us that he didn't want to change our convictions etc. etc., meanwhile staring at me the entire time . . . so I wont get an A in Polit!

Next in line was Philosophy which promises to be VERY GOOD. Mostly upper classmen and people who have had more of the stuff than I (more than nothing, that is). The professor is swell . . . a vital and interest arousing approach, also male, Mr.Venable by name, and also the head of the department.

This afternoon had a two hour course in Narrative writing which I just decided to take. Quite a course! 15 in the class headed by a dynamic dame with buck teeth and a biting tongue-guaranteed to make one feel like two cents. After opening my mouth and being ripped to shreds I wrote in bold letters on my notebook SHUT UP which I proceeded to do. I ought to learn a lot though. She's up on her stuff but a bit prone to think she's the only one who is right but it will be good discipline at any rate.

Forgot to mention that the French teacher dyes her hair blue-black and has ears that are red! Honestly!!

Had to wait on dinner tonight. Last year we had only

35 people in the dorm and waiting on table was a cinch. Tonight I was definitely a novice and a heckled one at that. After dumping the soap in the wrong place, putting the butter in the wrong ice box, forgetting fruit knives and putting the soup ladle at the wrong end of the table, I caught on and came thru exhausted but triumphant. Barb and I went for a wonderful walk, then. We lay down on someone's front lawn, bought ice cream cones and raisins (ah iron!) and came back to our barnyard to study and now, write you.

My schedule is crazy: Mon. Wed. and Fri. are big days with one class on Tuesday, one on Thursday and none on Saturday, so far. Still have two unscheduled class hours and 2 gym hours. Will also have Econ (economics) which I haven't had.

I feel good. partly due to you, partly to being here and partly as it is ten minutes to the bewitching hour and soon to bed. You'll have to come up here when this darn polio ban ends. It will be fun to show you around and to see you (a major understatement).

When my typewriter arrives you wont have to deal with my awful handwriting and when the homework starts the many pages may be much reduced. Until then, let this suffice – tho I'll never be able to write such cute poetry.

As ever (such a tricky way to end this letter). Me

September 11, 1944
Darling Duchess,

Damn your hide! I've even stopped buying newspapers because reading them took too much of my time and now but that still leaves a minority who don't like the things I like. The ultimate distillation leaves a very small residue or do you object to being called a residue?

Last Sunday I was amazed to be visited by my youngest brother. I thought he was in Italy. We went back to his ship together and you can imagine my amazement when the Staten Island ferry boat passed right under the nose of his ship. It had been there Thursday night when we were right there. I got a terrific kick out of the kid who is 18 and after a two weeks training course became a pharmacist–affectionately known among sailors as a penis machinist.

His shipmates come to him with all kinds of troubles and he hands out advice like the expert doctor your father is. He has sewed up wounds, assisted in operations and even taken blood from their veins, this previously squeamish kid just out of high school. One classic case he told me was about the guy who came to him after being in the brig for 30 days. The guy complained that he had an inferiority complex and he couldn't talk to the other men as he felt they all look down on him. Without batting an eye, my brother handed him some pills and told him to swallow them and then go out and mix with the boys. As far as he knows it worked.

I think I'll clean up some odds and ends from your last letter before I forget it.

I most distinctly remember those trips to the water fountain and "exception proves the rule"

Venable, the Philosophy professor, and the liberal Republican teaching Political Science reminds me very much of the economics teacher I had at Purdue whom I mentioned to you. I'll predict right now that if you go on objecting to his illiberal ideas, your "A" is assured. I've never yet met the so-called liberal conservative who didn't have a most definite defensive attitude toward liberals. Their position is always "you radicals mean well but it's a good thing for the world we coolheaded realists are here to put the brakes on" which is another way of admitting that they are rationalizing their ungenerous feelings. Accordingly, they find themselves continually arguing on a humanitarian point of view with tripped up statistics and quote that kind of utopian thinking won't work in this realistic world. A sort of negative argument, with the net result, I have found is an A on your report card. Protestation that they, too, are generous hearted and they only argue property rights over people's rights because that is the coldly logical correct view.

Dr. Root, a very subtle man, claims to be a liberal Republican but he never talks about what he wants or favors instead of discussing the way the world is going—thereby almost, but not quite, divorcing himself from his opinions. I'd hesitate to call him a Republican at all except that he votes that way out of habit. I still don't feel that a person who sympathizes with minorities and supports the underprivileged can honestly be a conservative. (Do I sound like a pamphlet)?

You've got me between the devil and the deep blue sea: I love hot weather and here I sit praying for frost! Do you think it would be all right if I pray for just one cold week and then let it get warm again? I feel as if I could go on writing to you for days but there's a conference to prepare for at 9 AM tomorrow morning, so I'll start slowing down and hope I can wind up on this page.

Homework has suddenly assumed mountainous proportions. Thank goodness you're not in New York. Besides teaching, which takes a hell of a lot of preparation for me, there is studying to be done for my qualifying exam and a series of operations and experiments that Clare and I are starting and experiments that I'll be doing with Dr. Allison shortly. And on top of everything, the chief wants me to write up the work I've been doing for the past eight months. Of course this will get much worse when my first physical chemistry course two nights per week starts at the end of September. Classes will be over for this term, by then though.

Have you heard about the absent-minded sculptor who put his model to bed and started chiseling on his wife?

About that "attached "business -what a horrible word makes me think of a lot of octopus legs with suction pads. It seems to me that I was going to ask you that at the picnic and only drag it out now because I thought it was a very personal question. I had started to ask you and I should have been surprised if you had turned out to be attached after our date, but even so, the women I've known have changed so completely from minute to minute that I've come never to take anything for granted. Go ahead, call it an inferiority complex, you've got one too.

You're waiting on table and history instructors brought back a warm remembrance of my college days and I noticed that you had the sagacity to leave Saturday open.

**Were going to make use of that, Duchess.
So long for now. As always, love,
Danny, the Duke.**

September 8, 1944
Dear Sis, (letter from my brother)

It was swell to hear from you especially on my birthday, thanks. The brownies were delicious although I don't see how you found time to slave over a hot stove. I'm really glad you did! They were good.

Boot training is drawing to a close slowly but surely. Not fast enough for me, though. It is interesting learning about all the weapons here. A week from Tuesday we fire for record with the M-1, which is the main object of being at the range. The other weapons we fire here are just for familiarization like the 22 rifle, the Browning Automatic Rifle, the Reising sub Machine Gun and the Grenade Launcher.

It is now a day and a half later so you see how much time I have to write. Nothing much has happened except we're a day closer to leaving here. We fired the Browning auto Rifle today for the first time. It's a lot of fun and that weapon is a honey.

I was filling out my score book yesterday and put down the date and I then remembered it was Mom and Dad's wedding anniversary. I had sent a letter the day before but didn't mention it. I forgot it completely. Tell them when you see them.

Thanks for the check. It was a swell gift. When I'll cash it, I don't know for you have to go thru a lot of red

tape here to cash one. On furlough tho, I can.
Thanks again and don't work too hard.
Love, Walt

September 9, 1944
Dearest Duchess in blue jeans,

It's not easy to put into words how I feel when coming up the steps after convincing myself that there couldn't be a letter from you since you had just written, I walk in and find one there. I'll pause while you figure out that labyrinthine sentence. Last night, for instance, I got back from Ben Franklin's old hangout; there she was, two letters . . . Being the kind of guy who eats the icing last, I quickly skimmed the other (had to reread it later to see what it said) then came yours with two stamps–hotdog! I thought, maybe they haven't canceled one of them.
I'll apologize for this crack later.

Now to settle down in comfort and read your missive–but no, that guy across the hall always hops into the bathroom just about the time I've got to go. (Comfort loving me)

Now we're all set. I'm on the rocker, which not only falls over backwards cause half of one leg is missing, but also throws the unwary under the table with a tricky sideways motion. So I prop myself against the window sill and pull out the bureau drawer for my feet. Now we're all set except that your letter is on the bed, far out of reach, forgive me for taking such liberties with you on such short acquaintance . . . But I did get your letter read.

If Barb is still interested, you might tell her that I not

only thoroughly approve your making suggestions for dates but would like you much less if you weren't that kind of girl. I've often heard the argument that no matter how much a fellow talks about equality of the sexes etc. the wise girl knows that he likes to feel himself boss and even subconsciously resents the girl who acts as his equal, regarding her as less feminine and desirable because she has a cortex and uses it. I can only speak for myself, but my answer is a violent shucks.. If the only way I can prove my masculinity is by insisting that you play the mouse, I better unpack my marbles and start setting up house.

Or was her objection around the going Dutch suggestion? Since my income for now is definitely limited, it seems obvious to me that we can do twice as much that way though please understand that I realize your finances are in better shape than mine. Many girls don't have your consideration and goodwill. I've always preferred a kiss that came from the heart to one which comes from the gratitude factor, which I'm assured is located somewhere near the base of the spine.

Josh White isn't the kind of guy you get tired of.. The only drawback to our seeing him is the stiff minimum. I've been there only on weekdays and even then it's about $2.50 per person. I don't see why we couldn't stand at the bar and take in the floor show without sitting down. We can settle these things when I see you. I hope to hell there isn't a room full of people present.

I'd be inclined to agree that men don't remember as many of the little things as women do. You'll find that I forget many of the motifs though I'll surprise you with some of the things that stick in my mind. For instance, the delightful way you attacked the watermelon at the picnic- with bare feet straddled, head in and seeds flying in all directions! I'll bet you had no idea how such an earthy picture appeals to me. Or the way you looked at breakfast with hair mussed, explaining to me that it was sweat that made your eyes shine so. Before I forget, Viv, how about rooting through your stock and digging out a picture. I'd love to have it.

 Your courses seem to be shaping up toward an interesting term. It wasn't until my junior year that I had gotten rid of enough of the crappy required courses to really enjoy the stuff I wanted. In grammar school we had daily assemblies. Each class appointed somebody who would glibly reel off some adage- mostly by Ben Franklin-such as "Keep thy shop and thy shop will keep thee." "A stitch in time saves nine" and similar homilies. He impressed me as being an exceedingly sharp and versatile guy. Course in Philadelphia, we all had to read his autobiography many years before we could possibly understand it. I had thought of the first Frost as something off in the dismal future. You make it sound as a matter of a week or two. Does the weather really turn that fast? Though it's only been two weeks since you were here, I'd swear it's two months instead.

 My God! It's 9:15 Does your letter take as long to write? I started this about 7:30. The trouble is that I go daydreaming about you, I'll admit, right in the middle of a sentence. So long Duchess, but not for too long. Love, Danny

P.S. "Constant employment is a great preservative of the morals." B. Franklin. When visiting New York leave thy employment at Vassar.

September 11, 1944, 5:30 p.m.–8:30 p.m.
Dearest Professor,

So I says to myself as I soberly walks out of a conference with the head of the economics department, why go look for mail. You know an empty mailbox is a gruesome sight and a mailbox jammed full of letters for your blessed roommate ain't much better. (I always say ain't when I talk to myself) but hope springs eternal in all adolescents so I wended my way to box 436. Upon seeing in the 2 inches of glass constructed to arouse one's curiosity to the bursting point, a letter, I thought well Barb got a letter. How nice! Then secretly promising to cut her throat when I first saw her again–but no! That Zeus, Woden, or Torah must have been in a good mood for it was for me and from the right you. Being of the species who likes to eat her icing all the time, I tore it open and read it all the way home stopping only long enough to read it again. No one was around but I ain't the one who needs company to laugh with, so I plunged myself on the floor- the only alternative to the bed which was piled high with gush, and laughed straight for 8 minutes. I counted them, honestly. What a wonderful letter and I loved it. I had also figured on not getting one today as I figured with Philadelphia and all . . .

10 min. of laughing, I suddenly realized I must look awfully silly. I've been thinking of you remembering the

watermelon etc. and then tried to see what I remember about you. I got all sorts of interesting results but suddenly came back to life with the vision of myself gazing at the sky with a dazed expression, back to your letter.

Your masculinity femininity boss analysis I couldn't decide whether you thought there weren't people like that or that you were one of them. If the former, you're wrong: there are girls who want to be beaten or think they do and guys who want their women helpless. I've run into both. (Woman of experience that l am). I'm not thoroughly convinced they'd like it for long though. It's funny, I've been criticized for the exact things you like about me
but then it's a strange world.

Glad we see eye to eye on the going Dutch angle. Sorry I didn't realize that it was so expensive and seeing it doesn't make much difference to me.

Only one thing at the moment (my father in me or something anyway) I would prefer you limit things like the note on the outside of the envelope and preferably on the inside Maybe it's a silly request and shows I think too much of what other people think, but I honestly don't think it's a necessity.

I'm sending three snaps none of which are very good but they're all I possess. The other gal on the fireplace is Barb.

For next week we have to read Ben Franklin's autobiography. Do you think I'm too young to understand it? Don't know about this first frost business: it was cold up here for a couple of days and we all got hopeful . . .
Now with two solid days of rain, it's gotten warmer again.

Yes, letters to you take up a heck of a lot of time, too.

My conference with Ms. Newcomer was good. I dreamed up a lovely schedule which I showed her and she okayed with the minor change then I got up to go. I asked her if she remembered Mard and from there we talked for half an hour about the war, college, returning servicemen's problems, working while at college, etc. I was standing all the time – couldn't exactly sit down again, but it was most pleasant. If I had time I could write it up much more humorously but with this time of night, writing to you is beginning to lengthen and not good for my work. If that stamp was uncanceled use it to write again
Love, V

September 10, 1944
Dear V,

An exciting event happened in pharmacology today. Last year the entire Department went into the Army or left. Physiology took over and the students were sure there was going to be a hashed up course. Instead it turned out to be really good and today at the first lecture they presented Dr. Gelfand, the guy in charge, with a pen and pencil set–an unprecedented event.

Today also Mard gave her lecture on the cerebellum and I slept right through it at home. They tell me it was one of the best of the year and I can easily believe it. Am I mortified! I went to bed especially early as Clare and I had two dog operations to do today but some dope (me) seems to have shut off my alarm before I woke up.

I hope the heck you're kidding with that professor

stuff. The least thing in the world I want to become is one of those hams who gives immense air of profundity to every inanity he believes. If I get like that please kick me hard or at least kiss me and tell me so. Love, D

September 11, 1944
Darling Duchess,

    I just rushed a letter to the mailbox to try and catch the last mail. If they come together, read the other one first.

    I should be going to bed now but I feel like talking to you a little longer. Dammit! I wish you were here so I could talk to you and look at you and kiss you too. I've been very careful to go out occasionally on dates just to make sure my feeling for you is not mere loneliness and it still come out the same. Do you think they'd let me visit you if we both got polio?

    Learn some French, Duchess. I have to pass an exam in French sometime during the year and it's been 11 years since I had the stuff in high school!

    I'm trying hard not to say things that should better be left for some future occasion even as it is, if I wait till morning I probably won't mail this.

    "If a light sleeper sleeps with the light on, does a hard sleeper sleep with the windows open?" If you don't get this don't ask anybody else what it means.
Good night again, Duchess. Will go to sleep this time.
Love, Danny
Your impetus, impatient, impractical and passionate but not impossible impeccable and impersonal or impotent imp.

September 11, 1944
My Dear Lord,
(I've been reading more Ben Franklin and his influence seem to have crept into this letter)

I don't owe you a letter, I've got piles of work. I should be asleep but . . .

Delightfully silly day. 1) My trunk etc came and the room is now furnished with the addition of a clock and a rug. (The rest arrives on Sunday via my family and thru Barb's family when they send it. But it was such a vast improvement everyone passing admired and exclaimed. They were drawn to our humble abode, I must admit, by the enticing smell of camphor and perfume mixed as only I can mix it. The perfume odor was due to bad packing on my part causing a bottle of same to spill and give forth its evanescence.

Went to "Philosopher's Holiday" a student Philosophy club. It has informal meetings in a wonderful room with comfortable chairs, ash trays and an all open fireplace (in use!). The procedure at these meetings is to have a faculty member speak for half an hour and then have open discussion. It wasn't very good tonight–should have been but the speaker neither said what she had to say well or had much to say. Just as the discussion period got under way, we received word to return to our dorms. All day we've been hearing about the hurricane and what to do if it comes, and whether it was coming etc.

We ran home in the teaming rain. Barb and I claiming what fun it would be to be out while branches fell on all sides. Just as we'd said that and were laughing at the idea, a branch 3 feet long fell in front of us. We jumped, screamed and made a bee-line for the dorm. It isn't a hurricane at the moment but it's expected to be. We can't congregate in large groups, smoke in our rooms etc. but outside it's only mildly turbulent, quite black, beautiful but comparatively tame.

Am glad to say I'm meeting more people who are intellectual minorities, nice, progressive, interesting kids. I said "intellectual" minorities as I can't tell as yet about their emotional status.

You've got strong competition: I'm wild about Mr. Venable (Philosophy teacher). I asked him for a pencil to take notes at the meeting tonite. "I only have a red one" says he, and smiles." I guess you don't mind" referring to our political discussion last week. We laughed and joked over that and other things.
P.S. He's a nice guy, 35 approx. and married to a member of the French dept.

I'm tired and I love to sleep and it brings tomorrow close and I love tomorrows.

It's now almost the day after tomorrow being the next day 8:30 P.M. Have the day divided between Econ and Amer. Lit. the former involving homework on the cotton industry, a class including a quiz and a wonderful lecture (optional series called Town Hall lectures sponsored by the Polit dept and Econ.). Miss Newcomer spoke on the Breton woods plans. She's an excellent speaker, knows how to tell both facts and incidents well, keeping the audience interested every minute.

It's now 11:10 and I've spent the last 2 hours in Recreation with a capital letter. i.e. Faculty presented a revival: "Destry Rides Again" . . . had never seen it. Barb came away from it very blue as Jimmy Stuart and the character he portrayed reminded her of her brother who was killed in Africa one and a half years ago. I knew him slightly and from his pictures I could see the resemblance, too. She's really wonderful about it tho in general. No more tonite due to resulting circumstances of above.

Anyway, I'll mail this mess as I'd rather not have it cluttering up my room. Let it clutter up yours.
Polio, oh polio where fore art thou???? Viv

September 12, 1944
Dear Duke,

10 min. before Political Science. Started this letter to you yesterday while on message center but after two pages tore it up in disgust. It's raining like mad which is never conducive to work- only sleep.

Yesterday also decided not to try out for the editorial staff of one the two college papers. I think I would've made it and it would've been fun but somehow I can't get as much into 24 hours as some. Thought it better to keep my thumbs out of couple more pies. It's now 7:20 P.M. — time for all chickens to be studying but I can't get myself to do it. Decided I possess no mental self-disciplin. Does that imply I think I possess physical self-disciplin? (Spelling of that looks definitely strange but the dictionary is way across the room and it's so comfortable here.)

Had a good afternoon today: 1:30 political conference section with a woman called Miss McAllen–have her twice a week (Mr. Post once a week for a lecture). She's pretty, well groomed, about 30 and a conventional sort of teacher–stays very close to the syllabus which is good seeing as I need what's in the syllabus. But today she digressed a bit. We've got several texts to use: one is a compilation of different authors, short essays on various subjects. We discussed one by Harold Lasky and she really went to town on it. I don't know whether she's a Democrat or Republican, but I got the kind of feeling she's not too pro–Russian! She was amazed to find how little American government we all had had–didn't discover it from our lack of knowledge, but thought all of what we were doing today would be review for us not something new.

1:30 talked to her about lack of civics in most people's education 2:40–American lit taught by Mrs. Ellis–excellent class, much discussion without any limits as to subject matter. That was till 4:30 At 6:15 to a special college showing of "And the Angel Sings" which if you haven't seen, continue on the same status. I heard it was good and it wasn't!

6:12 to 6:15 came back to change from wet clothes to dry–went to supper 6:15–6:45 supper; 6:45 to 6:55 smoked a cigarette, 6:55 to 7:20 economics reading on production; reviewed economic reading on production and markets etc. of steel and iron for quiz tomorrow.

7:20 to 7:35 been writing this! In other words a quiet Vassar day! Could go on into similar details about this morning but will spare you. Did have archery. I used to take it at camp seven or eight years ago and taking it is a sport this fall (as I couldn't take tennis). It ought to be fun and I'll have you to know I was the only one in the class to hit the target !! Not the Bull's-eye just the target. We only shot one arrow each as the rest of the class was an explanation of the fundamentals of archery (also called how not to hit a passing Prof. in the seat-of-the-pants).

Guess I haven't answered your last letter. Will reread it. I do not have the feeling there's always a letter of yours hanging over my head. That's one complaint, fear, or what have you, you don't have to worry about. Loved your analysis of your problems about me. Shall I try saying good night at the door next time to let you see how you feel? What DID I say? I do agree with you, though, seriously, about it being mixed up with flattery and that one of the two many reasons for going slow until you know that it isn't flattery is why build something up that doesn't exist?. Oh nuts I didn't mean it to sound that way. Let's drop it for the present. I may be of help to you in some ways but don't count on the French. To put it politely it isn't one of my assets.

Got your postal today which was a pleasant surprise and though I found the X, I couldn't quite make you out. Time out to find a cigarette. Okay Dr., tell me I'm smoking too much. I was but I've cut down.

I got an appointment with the head of the economics department tomorrow to make official my change of majors from psych to economics. She's quite an authority on money and banking and was the only woman to attend the Breton Woods monetary conference this summer. She looks like Mrs. Roosevelt, is a staunch New Dealer will tell you more of same after I've met her in person. Her name is Mabel Newcomer.

Your adolescent college girl

P.S. On rereading this letter, it sounds definitely strange. Well, three hours of French will cure that. It cures anything except a better understanding of French.

Thy disillusioned youth speaking . . .

September 15, 1944

Dear Dearest Duke

    Have just supposedly consumed 4 hours of study. Read some French "La Chanson de Roland". Ever read it? (11 years ago?) It's a very old anonymous ballad about Charlemagne, a saint. Quite good tho very repetitious in theme. Have also been reading Philos . . . most of the AM and I had been wondering how long it would take before the reading caught up to my IQ or rather got ahead of it. Well, it took exactly 2 weeks. It's intriguing stuff tho requiring certain tenacity but worth it in the end (I hope). As we study, talk in class trying to define things, I realize more and more how undefined most of my ideas are. But I suppose that's better than having them so well defined that nothing contrary to them can penetrate thru the cerebellum. OK so I'm using physiological terms incorrectly.

    By the way, the hurricane turned out to be a mild wind storm up around these parts sending down millions of leaves, twigs but few branches of any considerable size.

    I wonder if before the war the same feeling prevailed

on campus, or anyway whether I'd have felt the way I do now. There's a certain hurried feeling…almost as if you can't take time out to think. There are so many things to do, deadlines to meet, you feel as if you live for a goal only in order to pass it. Guess I don't always feel that way and usually do when I haven't been doing enough work… soooo to work.

Well . . . I just worked so damn hard I completely forgot to do message center. I merrily went to the library and came back to find my sweet roommate doing it for me. I get a warning tho which if I do that again I get black listed . . . an ominous sounding thing meaning 2 hours extra and a heck of a nuisance. Also if you're black listed more than 8 times during the year, it is not good and much complicated restrictions ensue. Duchess

September 18, 1944
Dearest Duchess,

What a set back! I was going to say hello on the phone, ask you how you are and then as a joke tell you it was me. Instead you didn't recognize my voice. Am I mortified! I guess it can't be true love after all. I don't know if you like me in shorts, but this will have to be a short one!
Love, Danny
P.S. The duchess readily agrees
    That A's her family would please
    But she and her Duke,
    agree that it's AOK
    if DK, not decay, causes B's

September 18, 1944

My Darling Lady, keep smiling!

When you address me as Dearest Duke I always wonder who the other one is.

You always do the right thing. I was hoping you'd write even tho I hadn't but I'd easily understand if you didn't. Friday Clare and I did the first experiment in our new series. It turned out beautifully and I worked till late that night getting the samples ready for analysis. Maybe your letter didn't hit the spot that nite! I was all in and wished to hell you were in NYC. But that letter of yours made you seem so close as you could possibly be without being here yourself. It was the warmest friendliest you-ist thing I've ever enjoyed and with pictures and comments!

It's a good thing your dear mother wasn't nearby just then. Saturday I quit at 9 p.m. and thought I'd write you the next day since it wouldn't reach you till Monday. On Sunday I wrote about 2 pages and had to leave it in the middle to meet an ex-Purdue friend of mine who is an ensign stationed nearby. He, his cousin and I stood at the bar at the Martinique to hear Jackie Miles. (Ever heard of him?) Had something to eat and dropped in at the 2.3 Room to hear Dorothy Ross 'Freudian ballads." (Don't worry, it was on them) About 1:30 I got back to the room and sat down to finish your letter but after reading what I'd already written, I tore it up and so here I am starting over.

There are times such as Sunday, when I'm just not in the mood to write, and I've decided not to force a letter rather than take a chance that a sensitive relationship like ours, a carefree alone living individual who has forgotten what it is to have people around whose opinion must be considered.

Now for the pictures, and comments…I like the one by the fireplace the best. Not only because of the legs. It recalls for me better than the others that special warmth and friendliness. (I wanted to say sweetness but thought you might not like that) that tags you as a friend of the underdog. You also look cutest to me. The dancing maiden is going right into my inside pocket as it'll make valuable ammunition some time or other.

You did mention blackmail before. I remember it quite well because I somehow got into conversation with Mard and, in an unguarded moment, mentioned that you don't sign your letters a/c blackmail. Like a flash she wanted to know what you write that leaves you open to blackmail! Frankly, the way you start or end a letter has me slightly puzzled. Sometimes it's dearest at other times dear; your first letter to me was signed but none since. One day you sign love (the letter I liked best and the next one wasn't ended at all, but I think I understand your quixotic feeling and will let actions speak.

I just looked through that darn letter of yours with the mixed up pages and no matter how I turn, I seem to come face to face with page 3 which starts "You've got strong competition. I'm wild about Mr. Venable" Will I have to demolish him?

Your classes and extras sound extremely interesting… forums, stimulating teachers, the kind of thing I sorely missed at Purdue where we were taught the subject at hand with no extras. As for the teachers, they never had any experiences in their lives that they could give us.

This morning the Chief deigned to give me an audience and promised to try to set my oral exam for the first week in October. He wanted to make it the end of the month but finally came around. I don't remember if I mentioned my sparring with him to you. He's trying to keep me doing technical work instead of my own research but after the exam this semester that will be out.

Got to get to sleep now. Two more operations on dogs tomorrow. If there are any lapses in my writing, please understand that it's only because I'm being overwhelmed with work.

Love, Danny

September 20–22, 1944
Dear You,

I'm feeling very affectionate and mellow. The latter an emotion I am capable of feeling without the aid of alcohol. I just spent several hours writing you and here I am again temptress or would it be tempter?

I'm thinking back on my letter of this afternoon and I decided my comments on your not writing might have sounded as if I were annoyed. I honestly didn't mean it—really I understand. I know just how you feel when you're too busy to write and when everything you want to say comes out wrong.

You speak about feeling like talking. Did you know I have lengthy conversations with you, sometimes we argue, sometimes agree. We usually hold these conversations while riding my bike or walking to class or from class or before going to sleep. Psychologists say all kids make up imaginary companions. I guess adolescents make up real people in imaginary circumstances!

I could write you about how good the labor book is. I could describe my trip to the apple orchard this afternoon but I'm feeling entirely too comfortable and generally good (due in large part to your letters . . . as I get a big kick out of them each time I reread them.) I should probably give this up for now.

Thy friend of the underdog
Continued:

It's now two days later and I should throw this out but you might as well get used to my various thinking processes, so I'll continue from where I left off. Have another letter of yours to answer: how pleasant!! Letters are wonderful when you're expecting them and finally get them, but they're equally good when you don't expect them!

Its fun to read your philosophical dissertations because I find myself nodding out loud so to speak in agreement i.e. one hour's work being worth 15 hours of forced labor. Sometimes not working is pure laziness and if you force yourself to start you find you like what you are doing and get a lot out of it? Or don't you agree?

Have heard "Strange Fruit" and it is pretty terrific. Have you noticed the complete silence which follows the singing of it?

No, I wasn't puzzled over the hastily scrawled second

letter of yours. I think I know just the mood you were in . . . I was in a similar one at the beginning of this letter.

Did I tell you about the pacifist (so-called)? There was a girl who lived in my dorm last year whose father is the national secretary of the Fellowship of Reconciliation, a pacifist organization which is against war - wants a negotiated peace etc. We used to argue for hours but we never got anywhere. I set out to get to know her better and get into the subject in private -even went to a meeting of her fellow thinkers. (There's a pacifist group who meet weekly on campus. The president of this great institution, Vassar, was a member of America First for a while, I just heard, also mixed up with the Oxford Group.)

At the meeting they had a speaker whose procedure was that of claiming we started the war as much as the Axis! Was terrifically anti-British, naturally anti-Russia, weakly anti-Hitler. The girl, and many of the others, are outwardly (anyway) and sincerely, I think, very liberal on things like the race problem. Of course they're violently anti-Roosevelt. When shown the facts , they claim it's all propaganda; when shown how awful the warlords in Japan are, the tortures in Germany, they simply don't believe it and remain completely unmoved. Some believe the group is definitely linked up with the fascists here in America. It really is terrifying to see people of more than average intelligence believing such stuff.

I've been writing a mile a minute because I've got to go to class but wanted to get this more down on paper to you by lunch.

    Had an interesting talk with my economics professor, Miss Wyckoff (dynamic and liberal) after class today. We've been discussing cotton and she mentioned being one of the group to go visit cotton mills in the South for the labor department in Washington. I asked her more about it after class and the facts and statistics she found were amazing! Treatment of workers: got their pay (some getting six dollars a week before anything was subtracted); the system by which they couldn't work in another place unless recommended by their present employer; absentee landlords; the control of the entire town by the landlord etc.

    In class, she had us guessing about the prices of things. Guess she wanted to see how much we knew about our economy these days. Learned that an average house costs $3,450, and average wage is $2,400 a year. I knew gas was 15 cents a gallon and that bread costs 10 cents a loaf but didn't know the others.

    I've always got French class right after Economics and I go from deep interest to deep boredom but I guess that's to be expected. Spent most of the time in the latter class wondering whether I'll get mail which is sorted by the time that class is over.

    Last night Barb and I had Mrs. Ellis over for dinner, which was fun. There's great excitement about the campus newspaper, the Miscellany News, a paper existing for about 20 years and liberal. Last year a group started the Chronicle, aided by the administration's funds, started by those members who thought the Misc. too radical. As it turns out the Chronicle is less political . . . has more humor, lighter stuff and generally less stimulating but is quite popular. This last week they had an editorial which set the faculty and others in an uproar. They claimed that the faculty didn't respect religion and those who believed in it were discriminated agains claiming that we came to college to learn from our teachers and that they are not tolerant of diverse opinion. The faculty, of course, was furious and so were lots of us. Barb and I both wrote damning letters to them asking for facts not explosive generalities which we hadn't found true. There's plenty of political stuff around here even though college is often termed an ivory tower. I don't like the ivory tower concept nor do I like the particular type of political activity, but if nothing else comes of it, it may set a few people thinking.

Well, another restricted weekend has begun but it promises to be good anyway. They've organized lots of activities on campus to entertain us–one being a starlight out-door concert tomorrow night and a special showing of "The Little Foxes" that together with work finishing the Adamic book, reading a modern fiction book which came out of the war (American-led troops) to be compared with revolutionary writing for English class that ought to be fun.

Barb and I took a wonderful combination bike ride and walked to the orchard the other day. We rode to the edge of campus, walked through the golf course and up a hill called Sunset Hill famed for its lovely view. I'd never been there and it does afford a nice sweeping picture of the houses near campus and surrounding hillside. We scrambled up tawny knee-high grass and picked wonderful apples from the ground; put them in a box which I put in my bike basket. We came back on a path of cinders and coming down hill, the bike skidded so we had to pick up apples all over again . . . Had to rush home to dinner, filthy and hot but feeling the wonderful feeling one feels after a walk in the country.

Heard the Town Hall meeting over the radio last night. Ever heard it? They're often very good . . . even if sponsored by the Reader's Digest. This was a PAC Political Action Committee with Max Lerner and Ray Walkman and Stolberg and another guy I'd never heard of. It boiled down to calling PAC a communist organization . . . Discussion with some pretty hysterical accusations. Lerner was particularly good and the audience was amazingly liberal as judged by the applause.

I could keep on writing indefinitely but my fine parents have expressed a desire for more communication from me so being a dutiful daughter I shall acquiess.

You made me so darn self-conscious of the ending of my letters that I shall for the present leave a non-committal blank.

September 20 x days to a first Frost
Dearest Duchess,

After taking time out to play tennis today I feel that I can write to you without having my conscience put up a legitimate kick. I hate the idea of the conscience: it's such a negative thing- always telling you what not to do. I rather think of myself as being guided by a positive spirit that

tells me I must study. The tennis, as I hoped, got me out of a dopey – more than usual spell, probably resulting from too much study and not enough relaxation. With the orals only a couple of weeks away, I began to get the feeling that everything away from studying meant something else I wouldn't know when I walked into the exam. One hour's work when you're in the mood is worth hours of forced cramming, don't you think?

It's really a nice feeling to get things packed away solidly in your head. I feel as if I had two dimensions about many things, now adding a third to tie things together and getting a more complete picture. As I understand it, the main purpose of this exam will be to ask me questions I don't know just to show me that I'm only beginning.

Today I learned an interesting fact about a mutual friend of ours. Did you know that Ben Franklin invented the catheter? I'd rather take a chance and not explain physiological terms.

If you can get WNEW, Josh White is on from 4:40 to 5:25 on Sundays. Last Sunday he sang "Strange Fruit", a song from the same poem. It's a chilling thing to hear. A lot of Josh White's personality doesn't come over on the radio, but he's still worth listening to.

I don't know how much of my work you already know about or are interested in, so I'm forbearing the gruesome details. In about a week this class will start down at Columbia which means on Tuesday and Thursday nights I'm busy, plus whatever studying I'll have to do but after this oral nothing will seem important enough to draw another keep smiling letter from you.

You may be a little puzzled about that hastily scrawled second letter of mine it was late and I was kind of tired and suddenly felt the need to drop my reserve a moment and tell you at least a portion of how much I realize how much I really miss you. Lord knows what went into that envelope. I hastily sealed and sent it off because I knew if I reread it I'd probably tear it up. Why I draw back from putting on paper what I'd say if we were together, I don't know, but I have a feeling you find yourself in the same position and not on account of blackmail possibilities and will understand.

The calendar says it so but I find it hard to believe that it's not even three weeks since you were here in New York and we had that long and wonderful date. It seems incredible. Suppose there isn't a Frost for another month!

Between experiments and studies there's been little time for extracurricular activities, though our lunches are considered so lively these days with hot political discussions– Roosevelt is growing far ahead and nobody has a good word for Dewey but we have a few anti–Roosevelts at any price.

Argument the other day (when I was out with that ensign friend of mine and his cousin). We got into an argument. He's okay, but she's a singer fresh from the Midwest–really amazed me with the stuff she pulled a la Chicago Tribune. Roosevelt started this war by being too tough with the Japs, for instance, and he could end it in a minute. Yes, she wants a negotiated peace, but he's afraid of the unemployment that will follow and also wants to please the armament manufacturers. It really makes me sick to hear that stuff because she is not stupid or naturally mean and has honestly swallowed the line verbatim. I shudder when I think of how many more there are like her and it does absolutely no good to point out where they're wrong. All we can do is hope there aren't enough of them to defeat Roosevelt or make another world war inevitable.

I've got a feeling that this letter will cross one of yours. In any case, don't write less often.
Love, Danny

> *Dear Diary,　　　　　　　September 20, 1944*
> *Today Barb and I went shopping. I tried on a coat dress, so called as it opens down the front. With, I think, a twinkle in my eye, I said to her I will get it as it is a perfect "date dress". She looked puzzled, so I had to explain it opened down the front. She looked shocked: I hadn't realized she was so innocent. Her John, that she says she's in love with, has been overseas for two years. So I guess she hasn't had much "experience." Or am I sex crazy?*

September 22, 1944
Hello Duchess,

I've decided not to start or end your letters the way I've been doing. This doesn't mean any change in the way I feel about you. It's just that you are either forced to follow suit or else feel awkward because you don't. We'll know each other so much better after our next date that the right words will come naturally.

It's exceedingly good of you to go slow on my behalf. You might feel better if you know exactly where I stand. As you've probably gathered by now, I move slowly until I am sure of myself.
When I say "darling" and "love," I mean you were something special on our date, that I'm anxious to see you again and that you attract me more than just mentally. I'm not saying I have gone head over heels for you, have planned our marriage and the number of kids we would have or that I will plunge myself in the Harlem River if you should find you've over estimated your feeling. (And I most definitely am not excluding that this may happen.). It irks me to mention that I've known for many years (giving you ammunition to dig me) but I know that a) you've grown on me the longer I know you and with this start you've already gotten, it scares me to think of where I may land and b) there's enuf of a reserve somewhere in my viscera (helped enormously by the fascination that Physiology has for me) so that no matter how much my feeling for you may grow, if you should cool off, it wont crack me up enuf to disrupt the course I've planned for myself.

All this sounds kinda stuffy to me, Duchess, but I want you to know all about me (as much as I dare tell, and I don't think it's right that you should worry about both our futures.

You seem able to write your letters piecemeal but I've got to sit down, read your last letter, look at your pictures smoke a cigarette, then write the whole thing (except for sky-gazing lapses). If I don't feel in the mood with you as clearly in my mind as if I'm talking to you, it just doesn't come out right and around the lab, I try my best to dismiss you when you put in your all too frequent appearance.

    I've said very little to Mard or anyone else about you. To say nothing at all would be as damning as to talk too much. She has the general impression that we talked a great deal on our date and that we write to each other fairly frequently.

    Whenever I get too pompous about the physiology, I know you can smash me with economics. I haven't read any of the books you mention, tho I'll argue economic theory with you at the drop of a hat.

    Tomorrow is registration day for that night course and Monday I'll fork over for some research points. I just can't wait till Feb. when I can register for all the remaining points needed for the PhD.

    I've got to stop now and send this off. You'll get no excuses from me to write less often.
Goodnite.
As always, Danny
A firm believer that those who have it should share with those who want it.

September 24, 1944
Dearest Danny,
    I'm sitting on the stone steps as the warmest place I can find, balancing the typewriter on my lap to write to you. If you think that's easy, try it!
Spent a very emotional 24 hours Friday and Saturday,

which wasn't conducive to letter writing. First I saw "The Little Foxes" which is anything but pleasant, well acted tho. For American Lit we had to read some revolutionary drama and compare it with modern drama, a modern war piece of fiction, so Friday night I read "A Walk in the Sun" about the landing of a platoon in Italy, very little plot but it seemed a realistic picture of the group of men, their thoughts and reactions to wartime. You feel it's very honest and yet if you're an idealist, you hate every minute as the men have no conception of the war as a whole, their reasons for fighting for it etc. The humor is strictly G.I. and strikes us civilians not humorously but horrible. They make a joke out of everything and anything, including death. I guess you have to just keep going but it seems impossible for those men to return to any kind of normalcy, good or bad, At any rate, it left me with the usual civilian feeling of immediate uselessness and smallness.

Saturday morning I read a modern drama. There was considerable choice but as I had never read "The Moon is Down," I picked that. After I read things like that, I go through various stages of first, a vacuum; second, revulsion at the smallness of life; third, an acceptance of it and with an added desire to make more of it than that.
Love, Me

September 23-25, 1944
Hello, Cute One,
So much to say since both Friday and Sat letters arrived this AM. I went for the mail before French class in hopes

that for a change, it might be sorted by then and out of curiosity and hope that Barb would get the letter she wanted and with, I must confess, a tiny hope I might too. But God (or whatever makes people write letters and send them in order to arrive on Monday mornings) was smiling only on me and neglected poor Barb. I guess that God can't do everything at once.

Can't quite figure out the motive of changing the beginning and ending of your letters. It's just that you're forced to follow suit or else feel awkward because you don't switch. I gather this means you want me to do likewise. Why, is the next question. If it was because you've seen I was sort of hesitant about it and did it for me, I thank you. And I thank you for an analogy of your feeling which didn't sound in the least bit "stuffy." I think I knew most of it but was glad to hear you say it. As to teasing you about your many years of experience:, I undoubtedly will . . . but not seriously. I like your being older. Maybe it's the age old notion (of male dominance?) but I like the idea that in certain realms of thought, you ARE older. I could use "mature" but dislike the word. As for what your "many years" have taught you, I like it. Part of it you told me at some time on our long date between 3 and 6 AM on a certain morning – about having the reserve in your viscera not to let anything upset your goal. I liked that at the time and still do. As for the other half of the statement, I don't see how your experience can predict that I'll grow on you, cause I'm sure you've never met anyone like me (no matter how great your experience) to be able to guarantee anything but shall let it go.

It'll be a long time before I'll be able to smash you with economics but I shall bide my time preparing for it

I'm now at message center and female conversation is blaring all around me making concentration difficult.

No, I've never heard of "Thunder Rock." It sounds as if it ought to be good. Will put "Turn of the Screw" on my reading list.

Didn't mean to end the discussion on beginnings of letters till I'd explained how I felt. (Pardon the back track.) I don't want to force anything. I don't want to fall in love with love etc which I think you know. As for the word "darling," I'm fond of it and don't ever want to "waste" it or use it unless I'm 100% sure of it. Is that crazy?

I WAS going to ask you for a picture. In fact I mentioned it the other night to Barb, but I thought maybe it would be better to wait and ask in person. Males sometimes react strangely to something like that. But now you've brought it up, send me any or all you can spare and let me choose. I'll return the ones I like least, so I shan't be hoarding. OK? Also, it would be wonderful to save the film till you can come up here. Film is impossible to get here in town.

Apropos your question on discerning your moods: If I understand your question correctly, you want to know if I realized, a) I was the kind of person you like, b) you had a definite feeling that I'd like you. I guess I knew the former but not the latter. I knew I liked you but not that you thought I'd like you.

About the letter you wrote to the Purdue paper. Who was taking advantage: the boys or the girls? It could be either. But knowing men, you're probably blaming the women.

You put it mildly saying "it's cold." We're freezing here. It's against their policy to turn on the heat until everyone has reached the blue stage. So we freeze indoors and out. Am only glad cause if we freeze, the polio germs are freezing too. I figure we ought to "get out" by Oct 7, but that's just guesswork.

Venable has us going around in circles in Philosophy class. Besides which he gives us much too much reading, but I love him dearly anyhow (stubborn female that I am). The first excitement of new courses has worn off and it now consists of a hell of a lot of work, but interesting, for the most part. Your comment on laziness is good. The only trouble with me is that I don't have or haven't yet found your complete absorption in a field of work. I know I can feel that way about certain things. I do with certain books I read that I can't put down but, in general, it hasn't as yet formed itself into a field of work. And I don't think it will while at college. I like action more than study. (Is that a form of laziness?) I find the things I become absorbed in are those which bear more immediate results. For a while I was beginning to feel I just didn't like to work, period . . . which was a horrible conclusion to come to, but working on the magazine this past summer proved that not true. I'm such a damnable mixture of things though. My interests are so varied. My abilities not concentrated in one field or even one type of field that it affords much speculation on what the heck I'll turn out to be like.

I guess I'm kind of impatient with college and preparing for the future. It seems to me, grammar school you prepared for junior high; in junior high for high school and then for college and I feel the need for DOING something instead of preparing for it. Part of my impatience is due to the war and the rather abnormal life of living among so many females in war time. Pardon all this: it just hits me from time to time.

Ten minutes have elapsed as I've been lying here thinking how nice it would be to be curled up in front of a fire with a cup of coffee in one hand and a cigarette in the other with a certain party alongside, which is telling me to stop griping and get the hell to work. Oh well, it was nice while it lasted.

"She had a heart. how shall I say? Too soon made glad, too easily impressed," from My Last Duchess by Browning. Your Duchess

September 26, 1944
Darling,

Picked up a shine on the seat of my pants today dragging myself home from work. Clare and I did an experiment on an angrostomy dog (canula samples to her portal vein). Full details will follow as per your dare. Unfortunately, Clare came up with a severe intestinal attack of some sort, gradually feeling worse during the day. She finally had to lie down while we were waiting to get terminal samples. She forgot to tell me where she was going so when the dog started to go, I had to run up and down the hall yelling for her. I could hear her answering me in a feeble voice, but she was too spent to realize that final sample is touch and go and can easily be missed by a minute's delay. It is also happened to be the most important one for me. We finally got our samples by the skin of our teeth. Then since it was only four o'clock, I was dopey enough to go out and play three sets of tennis. We had a terrific game- lost two sets to one but nearly every game going to deuce at least a couple of times.

    Now I'm fighting off the lure of a very soft looking bed alongside. I know if I lie down it'll be morning before I get up and there is some work to go over. The Chief still hasn't set a date and he wants to see me tomorrow. Damn his hide.

    I'll stop now partly because I'm tired and partly to await your next letter so that we can get back in phase and stop crossing each other's mail. You can expect a lengthy but not polysyllabic treatise on my work almost any letter now.
Danny

September 27, 1944
Dear Duchess,
What a Day! This A.M. I went to see the Chief to get his OK on the courses I'll be taking this semester. He says he's very busy grading the final exams, sent word he couldn't see me; finally consented to give me a minute. (The Chief isn't a bad guy, he's pretty straight and very generous. The reason we

have so much trouble with him is because he's subject to sudden ideas and changes his mind without warning so that he may sweep away all your plans without a moment's notice.)

As I walked in, he said brusquely, waving his hand at the pile of exam books, "I'm in a lousy mood. Look at all this work I have piled up. I don't have time to be pleasant." I said, "I don't give a damn how you feel. I'm not feeling very pleasant toward you right now so let's not start an argument. Just sign these papers." (He's the kind of guy you can talk to like that.) He looked at me for a second, than broke into a big smile and we shook hands warmly.

I had found a note in small print in the school catalog, that under certain conditions, they will set a flat fee of $190 a semester and you can take up to 19 points, which ordinarily would be $237.50. I had figured on taking 15 points until I found this. Then I added a 4 point reading course that the Chief gives and it was for that that I came to him. I had expected that he'd try to dissuade me since it means extra work for him. Instead he launched into a long talk about the value of the course, what he wanted me to read and so forth (during which he hastily OK'd my research problem about which I had expected a future argument.) Then he sulkily said, "Wait a minute. I can get you out of all the rest of your tuition fees ($400 worth).

He called Doris in and told her to call the necessary people to have me classified as an assistant instructor which would mean I could take courses, get credit for them and not have to pay any tuition. As you can imagine, I went down the hall to tell Clare without once touch-

ing the floor. About 15 minutes later Doris calls me in and says the Chief wants to see you. In I go and he tells me that because I've been paid up to now from the War Research funds, a lot of complications have arisen and there's so much red tape (he used a more virile word) that I couldn't be appointed an assistant instructor until next spring (when the $400 would already be paid out). However, he felt badly about it since it was thru an oversight on his part that I wasn't made an instructor when I started teaching last spring, so he is giving me an increase in salary which will make up about half the tuition and if I take 8 points next summer, after the appointment, I'll save another $100. Since I don't expect to be ready for my degree until next August, that's probably the way it'll work out. As I've said, "What a day!"
Love, Danny

September 29, 1944
Dearest One;

I'm in a foul mood. My parents think I should drop extra-curricular stuff and just study. And I'm not even sure I should be in college. Maybe they are right though and I should try studying harder . . . Won't write more and maybe not even send this.
Me

>*Dear Diary*   *September 30, 1 944*
>*Wow! We got permission to have guests on campus, though we cant leave yet. And Danny came! Before he did, when I was waiting for him I was as tense*

as I've ever been . . . suppose I didn't like him after all these letters! It was awful . . . I was so nervous!!! Supposing he was disappointed in me? He'd have to feel he had to stay around and see it thru. What had I done?? I was shaking inside and almost ready to throw up. Then the bus came from the station. He was the only one to get off. The first time I heard his Philly accent was when he thanked the bus driver. He turned and saw me. We were about 20 feet apart and we both just froze! We stared. It was like time stopped. But then we both moved toward each other. He put his arms out wide and suddenly I was in them.

It was going to be alright. Dumb me, I cried. I guess it was from relief, I don't know. We just stood there like that for I don't know how long and then we were both laughing. Don't know why but it felt good. Thank goodness he had a handkerchief which he produced and I sure needed it.

Finally we found our voices. I don't know who said hello first since we were laughing again. We stopped when he kissed me—first on the cheek and then on my mouth. What a relief! It was going to be alright.

We walked back to the dorm holding hands and didn't stop talking and holding hands all weekend, I think, except when we were eating or he was at the place off campus overnight, we were touching the whole time. mostly holding hands. I felt as if we were drinking each other in. How odd!

October 1, 1944

Danny Dear,

    I am very tempted to use a certain word right now but decided to wait until my feet touch the ground again and I can see where I stand. After you left one hour ago, I walked back- at least I must have- I got back to the dorm thinking the kind of thoughts one doesn't think just any day of the week. As I got near the dorm I found myself in the midst of millions of people all of whom had just come from seeing Soph Party. Barb liked it as well as we did. She got a copy of the songs, which I'll send you when I get time to copy them out. I discovered I'd missed many of the lines which were quite appropriate for the weekend and us in general.

    I want to write you and describe how I feel but my mind won't detach itself to the paper. I'm tired but not the kind of tiredness that comes from five hours straight at the library rather a delicious, fluffy cloud tiredness.

    Barb and I talked and from the look on my face she kept saying " I'm glad you had such a nice time," to which I could only say that would be a gross understatement, and continue having that jerky, out-of-this-world look on my face.

    I hope I can somehow get down to work. I hope you keep on wanting me and I hope my black sweater keeps the wonderful good luck that it has had these last two times.

    I don't sign my letter with my name as the name belongs to the world in general. Duchess belongs to you. I like that and that way if you want any of my public names you can always get them.

XXX so I'm an adolescent! Duchess

October 2, 1944

Dearest Danny,

    I can't get you out of my mind so I might as well do the next best thing to seeing you.

    After I'd scrawled the letter last night I went to sleep waking up every hour turning over and went back to one of the most pleasant sleeps ever… no dreams, which you may find disappointing but I think is good

    Worked every minute of the morning at least I had a book in front of me. I really got a lot done once I'd chased you out of every leaf I turned.

    Been getting a good many compliments on my taste in males from those innumerable side glances, which of course doesn't help concentration much.

    I've just eaten a tremendous lunch and gone for my mail now. Didn't even stop working this morning (that's to impress you). Got a letter from one of the guys I was telling you about who it took two years for me to conquer. (mean that in that sense I hate the idea of women conquering men or vice versa Only mention it because I remember saying I always heard from him when things were going good) When I saw it today, I just left thinking it as funny. I also heard from Jane who has quit college for this semester and she seems much happier having done so.

    And now I'm at message center. Will look over your last two letters to see if there's anything I haven't answered. No, I guess we covered everything. I still do expect an explanation of what your PhD is on. I probably reminded you of it on Sunday so you could write it out for your benefit and mine.

Philosophy class fun, as usual- discussed dialectics as seen in Greek Philosophy and in 19th century. Talked after class as Barb and I couldn't figure something out that Venable discussed in class and I wanted a re-explanation. Then we talked about the Galileo mass he had discovered, what it said, he affirmed that it said what I thought it did and said I had definitely put a dent in his scholarship to which I claimed he could put a dent into mine much more easily.

Read one of Wallace's old speeches for American lit this morning. It was one of the most famous ones given in May '42. I guess it was the first common man with a nice last line quote "When you're fighting in the people's cause you cannot stop until that cause is won."

Everyone including me have been singing the Soph Party songs. Old lavender, as you called her, as usual came in 10 min. late. Someday we really are going to walk out, but each time we're about to, she comes…this time to find us all singing "Raise the Dukes" from Soph Party.

At 4:30 am going to hear a history professor discuss Dumbarton Oaks which ought to be good.

Would you rather I wrote shorter letters more often and went broke from three cent stamps or longer ones less often?

Just got a letter from mom which starts: I've been thinking what a lovely day you had in which to show Danny the campus. I'm sure it was wonderful to have a guest from the outside world. She also mentions that Dr. and Mrs. Root are coming to dinner next weekend. (You may make use of the information in any way you see fit.) If I slave and they lifted the ban . . . I don't even dare finish the sentence. Me

October 2, 1944

Hello again darling,

Lester Velie WQXR just sailed into Dewey for his speech on taxes earlier this evening and Buster is no Boy Scout—he really stinks. I'm really concerned about his presenter methods making a point then changing the subject without any regard as to where the truth lies. He has undoubtedly used this technique successfully on juries. I hope the American people as a whole are not as susceptible.

I'm going to try to explain what my PhD work is all about. You'll find that it surprisingly simple. As I mentioned during our all-night session, an original idea or discovery is a very rare thing. Most researchers work follow up a few lines unearthed by a handful of the top man. Of course I hope to find something eventually but for my PhD work I've chosen a very limited objective to be sure that I don't get mixed and mired for years on some difficult maybe undiscoverable problem.

About a year ago some guy discovered a number of changes that take place in the blood of animals that have large hemorrhages. This was a big discovery and set off a lot less illustrious people like me to follow-up these changes; find out more about them and what they need- what causes them- how important they are and so forth. He reported a rise in the amino acids in rats which are the breakdown products of protein.

Well, first I have to find out just what the amino acid content of the blood of a normal dog is and then see what happened after a hemorrhage. After I collected this information on about 25 dogs (three months work), I looked over the data and decided that both were different from rats. I decided to try and find out where the amino acids were coming from.

First I took simultaneous samples from an artery that carries blood to the leg and from the vein that drains that way. Before bleeding they were identical; after bleeding, the venous blood was higher. This means amino acids were coming from the tissues in the leg and were thrown into the venous blood or the proteins in the blood were breaking down the amino acids (that are breakdown products of proteins) were appearing in the blood or both of these processes were going on. I also noticed that right after leaving, the difference between the arterial and venous samples was small—later it got large and finally got small again.

At the same time Clare was measuring glucose the same way and she found the same thing. This suggested a tie between global glucose and protein metabolism. Now it is known that proteins can be broken down into amino acids and these acids can be converted into sugar. In the process some of the amino acids cannot be used so that an increase in amino acids can be expected. This process is going on at an accelerated rate under the stress of the hemorrhage, so it is logical to suppose that the body will get sugar from every possible source especially since the lack of oxygen due to loss of blood may interfere with the normal processes of which the animal draws sugar from its stores in the liver and uses it.

Therefore the liver was the next place to be investigated.

Ordinarily the liver very efficiently regulates the level of amino acids in the blood by destroying excesses promptly and in some unknown way supplying them when the blood is low in amino acids. The liver is also believed to be one of the main sites for sugar formation from protein (I was actually anxious to find out if a widely amino acid level in the blood rose after hemorrhage when the liver normally can easily be a much higher level back to where it belongs in 10 or 15 min. and is there any evidence to study what happens in the liver without anesthetic which changes conditions.

    Clare and I devised a method of getting blood from the portal vein which goes into the liver and from the attic vein which leaves the liver. In a previous operation we fastened a cannula to the portal vein. On the day of the experiment I get samples from the cannula while she puts a rubber tube over the neck on the jugular vein down passed the heart and into the liver. This doesn't hurt them at all and we get our samples that way. Neither idea is original but I don't think anybody has tried both at the same time. We also collect blood from the artery and vein of leg for comparison and other reasons that are too detailed to go into now.

    From these data I have found that the liver removes amino acids from the blood but does not bring it back to the normal level as on a good dog would do. This can mean that a deliverer suffers from oxygen lack and cannot destroy amino acids as efficiently as it did but is also manufacturing sugar from proteins in excess amino acids which are thrown into the bloodstream or both of these are going on. For a while it had me stumped as to how to separate these two processes but I think I've hit on a way that may give an answer. I'm going to leave it all and have amino acids rise a little then infuse some additional amino acids. If his liver is functioning well, you should quickly remove these additions and show approximately the same rise as the other dogs after half an hour or so, that is, the rise will be due to amino acids thrown into the bloodstream not inability to remove them.

One further factor to be considered is the amount of blood that is reaching the tissues after hemorrhage. I'll have to measure the exact decrease in blood flow and compare this with the increase in amino acids. It was for this reason that I went to Philadelphia to see the setup for measuring blood flow.

The tie up between classic findings and mine and the reversal I found in the dog without adrenals strongly suggests gluconeogenisis. If I can nail this theory down with good experiments it will be the most definite evidence yet advanced that this process is going on even though we know that animals must be able to convert proteins to sugar from starvation experiments.

As you can see this is just a little bit of one corner of the work being done on hemorrhage but it is about three times the size of the job usually asked for in a thesis. If I clean it up I'll feel pretty good about the whole thing

I hope this doesn't bore you, Duchess. I've had to cut some corners but most of the picture is there. If you are puzzled anywhere along the line don't hesitate to ask but I don't feel hurt if you just ignore the whole thing.

I now have a good case of writer's cramp this is the 11th page to you tonight

This has been purely a scientific letter, Duchess. Fill in between each line with all the choice things you want me to say and add a few. Good night.
As always, Danny

Dear Diary,   October 2, 1944
Wah-hoo! I'm free!! No more polio

October 3, 1944
Postcard to D from V

I'm free no more polio. I'm coming in this weekend. I know I'll have one night with my family I don't know which one yet. I'll let you know -will be working like a fiend so I can come. Are your orals set? if so and they don't conflict with this weekend. If they do, you know how I feel about that.
Love, V

October 4, 1944
Wonderful Duke,

He neatly says" Work hard get an A" and then send letters that shoot me like a rocket into the clouds a million miles from text books. Oh well, contradiction is the essence of life, says Mr. Venable (How'd he get in here?) Keep your love life straight) or could I say "Opposites attract"? in being engrossed in work and in the clouds.

You've probably gotten my hurried post card and know

I'm trying to work a 7 day schedule into 4 and a half so as to be free this weekend with two exams coming up next week the above fact is nigh impossible and when you feel the way I do, miracles happen (so do flunking courses) the two sides of me conflict. Anyhow, have been working hard.

You weren't a heel for not writing. I figured you'd been busy and when you're in the mood and have time, you'll write. Doesn't need forgiving.

I got your letter in the second mail. I must confess I did talk to Amy about you this morning. She put her stamp of approval on your brow. (Don't you feel it?) Which is not essential but pleasant. Somehow you're not liking my friends wouldn't matter as much as visa versa. I guess partly cause as you're more important than most of them.

I can see Mard saying that about having a one track mind, she half disapproving, half curiosity. I have visions of cave man tactics in being dragged into conversations, just as long as you don't pull out my hair or dislocate your arm, I give you full permission to go right on dragging.

The Phys Chem class sounds good. What is the teacher like as a person? Or couldn't you tell yet? How many in the class?

As to my rules and an A in French. Just because I'm trying to reach up a bit to see if it's possible, must I reach all the way to the sky?

P.S. I couldn't possibly get an A in French not even if I was taking that and only that!

No, I don't think things will permanently change between us. Certainly not in the near future but they may seem changed temporarily every so often. And if they do it'll be because I'm still definitely in the formation stage, as they call it. I don't think I'm saying this as an excuse, really I don't. If you think I am, beat me.

I thought I'd hear from Mom today about the weekend plans so I could make mine, and possibly yours, but I guess I'll have to wait til tomorrow. Maybe you know more than I thru Mard than I do. I shall now return to Economics and read about "Consumer Demand" about which there is lots to be said that wont be found in books but might be in the clouds!

Will get to NYC, 7 P.M. Friday. That's just in case things are left at loose ends.
Love, Me

October 4, 1944
Darling Duchess,

Just got your card and can hardly believe it. I hate to give up either Friday or Saturday nite to your family but I guess I'll have to be reasonable. Either one will be Okay.

Study like a fiend and let me know the details.

The Chief today reversed his promise of last week. He wants me to keep up the extra technical work along with the research but I'm going to put my foot down.
Wish me luck—orals still in the indefinite future.
Love, Danny

Dear Diary,   October 7, 1944

Finally we had a date as I came to NYC for the weekend. I'd gotten Mom to agree to have him come to dinner. (They had met him in August at the picnic and knew we'd been writing.) My train was late so he was there when I arrived home. I was wearing my good luck black sweater and seeing that, he smiled.) He seemed perfectly at ease, chatting with my parents . . . guess it helps being older.

After dinner we went out and walked in the cold for a while til we went into a darkish bar which had comfy seats. We ordered gin and tonics and sat side by side talking. His arm was around behind me touching my shoulder. Then he kissed me for a long time. Suddenly I heard a man's voice asking us to leave. Not only was it the first time I was in a bar but I was getting thrown out! When we kinda slunk out and got outside we both burst out laughing.

October 8, 1944
Darling,

 I'm trying your policy of breaking rules. Accordingly I shouldn't start this letter in the above manner but I want to and I can't see that it will do anyone much harm, so . . .

 I could write you quite a letter right now. I missed you today much more than usual. I guess 'cause you were so near as we were both in NYC and all that kept me from seeing you were my other obligations . . . Not that I didn't have a wonderful weekend but still you were there and then again, you weren't there.

Perhaps I love you more right now because I love myself less. That needs a lot of explaining, even to you, I guess. And I'm not sure I can put it into words. It just seemed that all my faults showed themselves most plainly this weekend. Not to others but to myself. And the feeling which has been more latent recently of not knowing where I am going, came out again. And then, wanting to be in the city and not return to college because of you, the comfort of being there and a certain laziness or "irresponsibility" of preferring to study at my own pace, etc. rather than those of college. If I really understood all my feelings of this weekend, I'd either be a very wise gal or I'd commit hari-kari. Enuf!

Need I tell you, Mr. K. that I had a wonderful time on Friday? If I need, I shall: if I needn't, I shall!

So much to tell you but my mind seemth to wander and my eyes turn to the tenements we're passing. (P.S. I am on the train going back to college and I'm at 140th street.)

Half of the rest of the weekend was spent in playing your records. I loved your giving them to me. Two of them I'd heard before and had liked at the time and the rest are equally good. I suppose I should be more discriminating but I do like 'em all and can't pick a favorite. They are now comfortably weighing down my suitcase. I assure you they'll get plenty of use. As for what I told Mard. Nothing specific but she gets the general idea. She was very glad.

Gave you more compliments than are good for your ego and was generally swell about it all. She kept putting in little things when ever she mentioned you to my parents.
(I couldn't help talking either which helps generally.)

Mom came down with me to the train and I said she'd have to get to know you, adding a few minor details and she was definitely OK.

Last night's party at home was a good one. A Dr. who is head of the Rockefeller Institute in China for 8 years was very interesting. They were helped by the Japs for 8 months! Then Dr. and Mrs. Bing are swell. I hadn't seen them for three years and they couldn't believe I was me. Dr. Bing's first question was "Aren't you engaged?" He was both disappointed and disbelieving when I shook my head. He also spent time telling me I should go into medicine which certainly amused me. I think we have enough in the family without me. After all somebody's got to stay sane!

I was so darn sleepy that it was hard to keep a careful watch out for Dr. Root's cracks. Neither of us said much. When he was leaving he said "if I needed any advice … etc." He also subtly quizzed me to see if I knew what the dog-star technique was. I asked Mard and she finally resorted to telling me. I didn't commit myself to either but I could have said your technique was 1) more original 2) more subtle 3) more effective.

Mard and I had a wonderful time this afternoon making Howard a present but I cant tell you cause I want to make you one when next in NYC. (and it's not food) Aren't you curious? And aren't I mean not to tell you?

If my letters are cold, short or infrequent this week, don't think there's anything wrong, just a matter of 2 exams and a paper to write.

Now off the train. I went to the PAC meeting. The people were fun to talk to afterwards and a bunch of us stayed on to talk politics at a drugstore. The proprietor was voting for Dewey . . . had voted for FDR three times but wanted a change. We began arguing with him which of course didn't convince him in the least.

It's never as bad to get back once I am here but the joys of NYC are hard to leave.

You said I'd think I was in love with you long before I'd tell you. Perhaps you will be right but if you apply it to the beginning of this letter you certainly are . . . I've been calling you darling for weeks . . . only you never heard me.

I can actually hear someone snoring! Wishing you were here . . . or should I say wishing you were here physically? Goodnite, favorite one. Duchess

October 9, 1944
Darling,

I'm sending you an autobiography I wrote first in senior year in high school and revised to use for an identical assignment in sociology last year. Don't think you'll find any particularly revealing facts and you don't even have to read it. Just thought you might like to see the red pencil marks made by the sociology professor. Amusing ? Would you return it– whenever you want–but I'd like to keep it for our grandchildren. (I'm going to do you one better on a next-generation) uggled over fiendish accounting problem in economics. Finally finished it and it came out correctly but I still didn't know what it was I was proving.

I'm disgusted at this point – so darn many things to do in only 24 hours in the day – and as an added token of affection from college, I've got a third exam on Monday in political science. If I had time I could do well as it refuses to require anything but pure memorization but as it is I'd rather concentrate on one) Economics two) Philosophy three), Campaign and SLA (student liberal organization). At moments like these I wonder why the devil anyone ever thought of an accelerated program. I'd love to write more but my eyes won't stay open
XXX (three's my lucky number),
Duchess
P.S. Wasn't it awful about Willkie? The one hope in the Republican Party and it sure makes fools of those that say Roosevelt's too old – will – die argument. Only wish it had been Dewey (The love I waste on that man). Got to be careful of this love stuff, you know—can't go around wasting it.

October 10, 1944
Darling,

You're a genius, you're marvelous; you're wonderful, and I hate you less than I've ever hated anyone in this whole world including my Aunt Cele who used to buy me ice cream cones after she washed my ears. The dumps I was in when I wrote last, hung on til I read the first word of your letter. It came on me then that I had felt low since

Saturday night which I had spent alone, when you were here in N.Y. with your family.

As a matter of fact, I've done a lot of thinking about your "go slow" motif and I found myself objecting on several accounts. First of all, I felt it had something to do with our seeing each other just once when you were here for three days. There are times when I'm very much in need of encouragement from you. If this surprises you, remember that I'm not a mind reader and have just as difficult a time understanding why you like me as vice versa. In the third place, as we've already discussed, I don't think of love as an abstract nebulous thing that happens to two people or doesn't. It's compounded of mutual likes and dislikes, pleasure shared, words spoken and understood. It grows with propinquity and mutual confidences, with kisses and warm feelings. If you were to constantly suppress these things you would cause me to draw back despite my understanding of your motives. Eventually I suppose it would be quite possible to kill a love by constantly minimizing those small signs by which it reveals itself. That's why your letter gave me such a lift! The one word "darling" as little as it means in itself, showed me that you are far too human and too warm to deny your own instincts. Of course, I'm not asking you to throw away your natural caution and common sense. In fact, I don't care any longer how closely or loosely you stick to your rules—I know now that you'll be honest with you.

I hadn't intended to write till tomorrow (and then just a short note) since I'm pretty rushed right now myself, but just had to let you know how squarely you hit me between the eyes. Knowing that you have a couple of exams and a paper this week, I had resigned myself to not hearing from you at all this week though it wouldn't have been pleasant as far as I 'm concerned. I don't know but I'll have this incident for the next time you wonder why I feel as certain in placing you at the top of the number of girls I know and have known.

    Don't neglect your studies to write but it isn't right to study all the time!
Love, Danny

October 11, 1944
Dear Darling,

    At last a little time to write to you again as one out of the three remaining exams is out of the way. Nope you were wrong. Your letter, written on Monday night arrived this AM wasn't boring. In fact, I like it. Not that I like to hear you've had a stinkin day but I liked hearing you gripe for a change. Made me feel more at home. It was a nice letter anyhow in telling me what you had been doing. I guess our moods sort of paralleled in that I'd been in a rut for two days too. Ever since the weekend and added to that, the Econ exam. It's funny: my reactions to exams: It's not fear of them particularly but restlessness before I've taken them in knowing that I haven't done the work well enough. I really trace a lot back to my darn conscience. I suppose psychologists (God bless their souls) would call it guilty feeling-but it's funny that it disappears after an exam no matter whether I think I've done well or not. In fact, it disappears as soon as I'm handed the exam itself.

And as soon as I get beyond the surface up here, I begin to wonder why the heck I'm here and where the heck I'm going and what even I am getting out of all this. The exam today was hard but rather fun. 100 true/false open book questions in 50 minutes. Of course it took so long to do them that you couldn't refer to the book much. The point, I gather, is a matter of being able to organize ones knowledge. You've got to know where every fact is and how to get at it but fast! It's a much more logical exam than the usual. Of course, the fact that many of the questions couldn't be found in the book anyway complicated and increases the interest. I can't tell how I did in it as I've nothing to compare it to and since a wrong answer counts double off, to avoid guessing, I'm sure it was ok in the passing sense . . . enough!

The Philosophy exam has been postponed til Monday when I also have a Polit. exam ... two periods in a row. (It's a hard life you lead, Duchess, I can hear you saying). Did manage in the midst of it all to go to the swell Inter Racial Group meeting at which the head of the educational part of the national Urban League spoke on the Negro in the coming election. He was excellent, humorous and interesting. Ate dinner with him (one of the six select) and he proved to be as charming as his speech. He's a good looking man, born in South Carolina; went to Tuskegee and Grinnell; knows Roosevelt for a good many years and is pro FDR tho he doesn't think he's done as much for the Negro as he could have . . . thought Willkie was better on that.

Am now, as usual, on message center duty. Jobs changed this week but I seem to have a certain affinity for message center at 3:30. Only got it twice a week this round. Wait on breakfast and lunch the other days. I feel the same about working for elections as you do. I can't possibly until next Monday which wont help with registration much although I can and will do canvassing.

This weekend is a political conference (Political Association), student group, a non partisan part of which SLA (Student Liberal Association) is a branch (It can and does take sides on issues). The subject is "The Returning Serviceman" and Joe Daniels, one of FDR's aids in the labor dept in DC (and a father of one of the girls here), is speaking. Want to go to that and the Jr. Party.

Barb and I made a bet last night. I bet that she'd get married first and she bet that I would. Neither believes very strongly in either side but it caused us amusement for half an hour. The one who gets married first has to take the other one out.

Off to the SLA meeting. Gee I'm glad I know you! (effervescent affection!)
Love, Duchess

October 12, 1944
Darling,
I'm operating on the theory that you'll have time to read letters and wont feel obligated to answer at length if you're too busy. How long you can continue to hand me

such nice surprises, I don't know. Expecting a couple of abbreviated notes this week, you've made me feel like a housewife who just discovered a handful of ration stamps. (what a simile!)

When you get this, you'll be plunging into that last desperate grind before your two exams Monday. I've got a feeling you'll hit Philosophy like a ton of bricks. You've certainly got my sympathy.

As soon as I could, I rushed to Mard to find out in my most recent manner what she and you had cooked up (not literally) for Howard before you could head her off. Unfortunately she was wiser and forewarned. Anyhow this usually reliable source remained reliable but proved a poor source.

One thing: haven't talked about much is your feeling that you don't know where you're heading and so forth. I hate to drag you back among mortals, but that state of affairs is very common to all reasoning people. If not satisfied sooner, it is said to disappear at the age of 65, coincidently with the first pension payment. It is probably bothering you more often and deeply than most because you have such a strong moral sense. I know a fellow your age who has an IQ of 186. He is extremely well-balanced, happily engaged guy but his problem is the same as yours. When I was 20 (here he goes again) I was a $10 a week Dental Mechanic who knew that some day he'd go to college but had no idea why or in what field he was interested. Those things have a way of evolving. Meanwhile I'm sure a background of Econ, History, Philosophy will be useful to you.

My Phys Chem prof believes that life is earnest. We

have an exam for next Thursday and she's really pounding away. In a way, I like the way she's teaching: a minimum of explanation in class. She expects us to go dig out the stuff and learn it whole while she pulls everything together. It's a challenge and I'm sorry I haven't the time to take it up and do a complete job. She read off the names of 8 people who had flunked that "quiz" that I mentioned in my gripe letter and recommended that they give up the course. When some of them decided not to take her recommendation, she told them flatly that they had to. Thru some oversight I wasn't on the list. From somewhere (who can understand a woman) she's got the idea I know something and she chides me when I get a little hunk of a problem wrong. I'm amazed at how I get any of it right.

You've got me puzzled about your visits. Will you be in for only one day to see family? If that's your plan, you'd better make room for me at the dorm cause I'll be coming up there.

Had quite a time this A.M. Got up, collected soap, towel, comb, toothbrush, shaving kit and stepped into the bathroom. There, scattered among paper, water closets, a bath tub were three plumbers. There was nothing to do except go to work unwashed and unshaven. (I took along my razor) I didn't think I looked so bad, but the first guy I met asked me why I don't sleep in bed. Oh well, you'll see me with that morning-after look one of these days.

Not knowing Barb, I can't make any predictions on your bet but my ideas on how to influence the outcome are getting more definite every day. (Does that scare you?). I made lots of wagers with my high school and college friends and have won very one. The interesting thought struck me the other day, how opposite we are in our attitude toward falling in love. You are afraid of falling in love with love, of imagining that it's the real thing THIS time when it may not be (I'll take bets on that) while I, a hardened (in the head and arteries) bachelor must be careful that I realize and admit it when the real thing does (has) hit. You're probably noticed my tendency to think things thru aloud just so that I can't kid myself. All of this is really needless though, since when I'm with you no amount of rationalizing seems to be able to distort or hide how you affect me. I must be careful that you don't get drunk with power!

Stopped for a minute to think of some things I've been meaning to write and found I had dozed off! It's now 2:15 A.M. Better see a bed about some sleep. Another experiment tomorrow. G'nite Duchess and good luck.
Love, Danny
P.S. Just occurred to me sleepy as I am, that you like things about me (griping, for instance) that nobody else does. It's wonderful to know you after having to invent you all these years.

October 12, 1944
Darling,

Just a line to surprise you and because I need a pleasant change from Polit reading. And to tell you again I loved that last letter which was a reply to mine – "hit you between the eyes". (I hope it didn't hurt) As to my doing the right thing: you flatter me. The letter just happened to come at the right time I'm not psychic. Luck just worked things out that way. (I'm not a fatalist either). So I can still go happily wondering why you like me. See, you can't solve everything quite so easily.

Didn't mean this to sound so flippant. Did I tell you Jane couldn't get over the glow in my eyes? She had us all married before we finished lunch.

Had an amusing time refuting our Polit conference leader's damning ideas on Russia's one party system. Got myself into deep water and couldn't help smiling at it all with the rest of the class looking bewildered and bored (with the exception of one girl who backed me up).

By the way, would you consider letting me be one of the privileged few to enter your sanctum sanctorum, your domicile, or what have you?

A flighty Disney-ite sat at dinner with us last nite. She asked if I was an Econ major when I said yes, she said, "I knew it. I can always spot them!" continuing, she said they were all intelligent, intense and knew "what was going on" Only she said it so you couldn't tell if it was a compliment or an insult. (As a matter of fact I'm not sure I am an Econ major after that exam.)

How about getting someone to use that role of film on you? Have to go to dinner, and as usual didn't get all I wanted done. And I want to go to the "Marxist Study Group" tonight. Why don't I just not take any courses and major in extra curricular activities??? I'd have a wonderful time. (Of course I would include you in extra activities.)

It's funny what little things keep us apart: exams, papers, 80 miles. For once in my life, I know what I want: I want to see you and I can't. Frustrating world we live in.

Keep me posted on you, your work, your love and the pursuit of happiness (not interested in your liberty)
As always, Duchess

October 14, 1944
Hello Darling.

My beloved roommate has lured me from studying and we're now listening to Brahms 4th. Somehow when I listen to classical music everything seems to relax within and without me. Beautiful music sweeps away all the petty trivial things and they're replaced by the movement of something bigger and unexplainable. It always amazes me that man can have created something so magnificent.

And along with nice things, I think of you which led me to take out my trusty pen and paper.

As for hitting things right: your letter sure did this morning. I'd been studying Polit which actually isn't so bad as one anticipates it to be, but my mind began to wander until I looked for the mail and then the problem was how to get back to work after having gotten it. I solved it by safely tucking your letter underneath the pillow and leaning on it

As to what I've cooked up, I thought I will try to use, make, get, not giving you any hints, for you just for the fun of it.

You hit the nail on the head in regards to the "not knowing where I'm going". You're very logical and sane about it all and in my more rational mood, I agree with you and thus am still in college, majoring in economics but other times I get hellishly impatient for the dawning moment to arrive. It's sort of a vicious circle. I'd get so much more out of college if I knew more about what I wanted to do. etc. and yet I've got to be here in order to find out.

I guess you feel about your Phys chem. class the way I did about ancient history last year. She was a wonderful teacher and expected you to know the fundamentals (which since I never had had the history I didn't know) took a while to learn and she kept things together which left me not a clue. I guess I should take the course over every three years.

As to my visits:
They've got me puzzled too. Will give you complete data on the next three weekends and get your ideas on the subject: Oct 21 my brother may come home on furlough in which case I want to see him. He may come in the middle of the week however in which case I'd come home either then or on the 28th. THAT weekend Mard might be planning to come here.

Then there's Nov 4th. I guess this one should be put in the form of an invitation. THERE'S a PROM. It's called Soph Prom which at first I thought I wouldn't go to but there's a conspiracy to get me to go as there is a rumor there may not BE a junior prom since we are being pushed to graduate in three years. Get to the point, Duchess . . . OK but hurry up (go slow?)… anyhow … How would you like to come? It ought to be fun. We can stay at the dance for a while and if we don't like it, leave. (It's formal for the women but not necessarily for the men). Big weekends always have their amusements. I had decided I wouldn't bother going unless Barb went (It doesn't mean that much to me) as the problem was to get her a date. She knows plenty of people but they have a habit of being scattered over the globe … so I thought of a guy I know (vaguely) who's a second year med school at P and S and have written him. I haven't the least idea if he'll come. I'm not sure I would if I were in his place but we figure he could only say no … If he can't come, we'll have to think of something else. So if your orals aren't in that vicinity and you're interested …

Depending on Walt, I shall decide whether to come in on Friday or Saturday.

As for your ideas on Barb and my bet: no, it doesn't scare me and the fact that it doesn't, surprises me. I've thought a good bit about it and can't think of any reason why it should scare me. I can't see that our attitude on love is so different. We both want to be sure that we recognize it for what it is when the time comes which is the important thing.

We're now playing Beethoven's seventh which is slow "good stuff".

Another thing: I've been meaning to say, and don't think I have is about sex. My views on the subject (written partly to clarify it for myself) as long as I know what it means both for myself and the guy, I don't much care about the speed of things. Most people (girls anyway) think that if it takes the guy five dates before he kisses a girl, it means more than after the first one. I think it depends on the guy, the girl and their relationship. I guess my feeling is there are kisses and then there are kisses and more than kisses. Looking back on things, I'm not sorry I've done anything I have done; tho probably in some cases it might have been wiser at the time, not to have done them. You learn a lot about people and yourself in the process (I'm smiling at that statement). But what amuses me, is that subconsciously or consciously I don't feel that way all the way thru—or I wouldn't still be a virgin. Do I make sense at all, darling or do I end up in the usual psychological muddle?

By the way, Barb's camera is for film is 118 A or V. It would be swell if you ever COULD get a hold of some. Guarantee a reward!

Did you notice the position of the stamp in the last letter or don't you know what that means? Or has it been since your time? (Upside down means it stands for a kiss).

We got the Econ exams back. The marks were said to be very low so a B- wasn't too bad. On the other hand it wasn't spectacular. You'll just have to take me as I am or not at all. (Does that present problems?)

Finally after many playings, I like "Foggy Foggy Dew" the best with a good many others tying for second place. I like to think of them as a start to our record collection (and an expense account, I fear).

To bed, to bed not having studied enough to get an "A" but very glad to substitute a D.K.
Love,
Duchess.

October 15, 1944

Darling,

I've got to write to you before I start studying or you and hunks of your letter would keep getting into the Phys Chem formulas.

Your autobiography (to 18) is fascinating for me. I've only read it twice and will need a couple of days to let it percolate. There are some things tho, that stuck me forcibly and with immediacy. Your comment that I wouldn't find much that was new is quite true but while I felt that I knew you, I wasn't sure how conscious you are of what you've developed into and are becoming. I owe you a deep apology for underestimating you so grossly-even tho, you continually put out a picture of yourself as not being pretty, not an A student and so forth, there shouldn't have been the slightest question in my mind that not only are you all the things I thought I saw in you, but you've become such a wonderful person consciously and intelligently. (At the moment, if I didn't know your I.Q., my guess would be distinctly on the high side). Probably for all your self-belittlement, you are well aware that your sensitivity, freshness without naiveté, sincerity and innate good taste are all contained within that rag doll head of yours, and much of your earlier frustration must have come from knowing this and realizing that it wasn't appreciated. That I've had the same feeling goes without saying. Our mutual recognition of this underlying unity between us, I'm sure, plays a large part in our love for each other. Of course this isn't the complete story with me and I hope it isn't with you. There are undoubtedly other girls in existence to whom the above description would apply but it is you, Duchess, the girl who likes and talks and walks and kisses the way you do, whom I want.

I couldn't have done nearly the job you did if I tried to fathom the influences on my life. It amuses me and confounds the psychological school which places such overwhelming emphasis on environment rather than heredity that the biggest guide to my development is enormous comfort tho I don't see eye to eye with the extremists on this subject.

We'll have to take in a football game soon. Perhaps you don't know that I'm a sport fan. I've never yet found any sport (indoors or out) that I don't like. If I can't get in it myself, I like to watch, if that's impossible, I'll listen on the radio. My favorites are basketball and football. If you don't like either of those, you'd better keep it a secret for 10 years or so until it's too late for me to leave you.

You say it's funny what little things keep us apart. It seems funny to me now, but I saw little humor in it a week ago when exams and papers were left at school, the 80 miles didn't exist, and yet Saturday and Sunday saw us not seeing each other. At that time, though, I suspected what the motive might be, it seemed much more logical that you were simply doing what you proposed. Hence my let down, and the wonderful lift from your next letter. You may think I was unreasonable, but I've had such a hard fight for the things I've wanted that it takes an effort for me to see the sense in turning down a hand because of some abstruse fear of the future. I understand exactly how you felt at the time and

admire your will-power in sticking by your principles even tho I wouldn't see the situation in the same way. D

October 16, 1944
Darling,

You're wonderful! You somehow manage to get your feelings on paper so that I can really tell what you're thinking. I never feel as if I've said what I meant to and that's partly why I'm amazed at how well you know me, my thoughts etc. That letter (Oct 15) had an awful lot in it and I'm still walking on air (try that when you're sitting on a bed, it's quite a feat!)

Your analysis of my autobiography has me going around in circles. If I say I still think of myself as I did (or rather as you thought I did) you'll say it's disproved by what I've written. I gather you think that before I've played myself down and that since you've read my great manuscript, you see that I don't really feel that way. All I can say is that in certain respects I pass on my own marking system, in other respects I don't. I don't agree with you on the idea that I've known all along how good I was and having my frustration come from not being appreciated. I assure you I haven't that much self confidence. I think it's truer that upon appreciation I realize that I have more than I thought I had.

As for the underlying unity between us: I think it is more than appreciation but I'm not sure of anything at this point. I wonder what will make me sure. I know I want you; I miss and I need you. Perhaps right now I am in love with you and don't recognize it. Maybe I should drop the whole subject till I know what I'm talking about?

I'm a sports fiend too but you can have the dubious pleasure of initiating me into the arts of watching football. (I used to play it with much gusto up at our country place with the gang) but watching requires an intimate knowledge of where the ball is and when. The one time I've seen the game I found I ardently followed the guy who I thought had the ball, only to find several minutes later that he really had nothing to do with anything. But I'm a willing student (when I like the teacher).

I don't want to see your room for the pennants etc. but mainly so I can picture you in it later, tho it isn't vitally important if your landlady has other plans for you. Are you a hen-pecked tenant?

Your ideas on using a Mrs. as an excuse for not graduating sure hit home! Although I'll have to defend myself and say I knew that "Mrs. wouldn't solve all the problems and I do realize I'll have to graduate, only sometimes I really wonder why and whether it is worth it. The things that make me wonder are that I've always heard about college being the best years etc and when I disagree and talk about quitting, it's always put on as a responsibility basis. Who am I responsible to? Myself? Then if I thought I could be happier and useful not graduating, why shouldn't I just quit? As a matter of fact right now, it's probably the best thing to do for all concerned. Sometimes I feel so rushed and feel guilty going out for a walk or reading something not on the curriculum. or going to NYC for a weekend!!!

No, I didn't know you glanced around in the movie till you told me. And I haven't the least idea what I looked like, so I'll have to watch myself (or watch you) in the future.

That sketchily finishes answering your letter though I know it hasn't really answered it.

I'm glad Friday the 13th was good for you. It didn't affect me one way or the other but that's too obvious to be a superstition to believe in.

As for my exams: I haven't the least idea of the outcome. I studied just about the right things for both except that the Polit turned out to be tricky little things which is sort of silly I've since heard that he usually has to raise all the grades ten points or everyone would fail. It seems silly to make exams so much above the heads of your students. 'There were 50 true/false and four short essays and two long ones. You fit that into 50 minutes!

The Philosophy was hard. About what I expected and the only trouble was how to decide what of all the many things to say, to put down. Pretty much a case of organization rather than knowledge. None of it made much difference tho, after I'd gone, at the end of the second exam, to the mail box and found your letter. Barb got two from "the man" after not hearing from him in 8 days. We're going to celebrate by going into Poughkeepsie to dinner. I'll drink to you, even tho it may only be water.

Don't think I mentioned the Polit Conference this past weekend. Was determined to go to it despite the two exams coming up and did, tho it wasn't worth the effort. Friday night Jonathan Daniels spoke. He didn't say anything but said it very well. Saturday afternoon Hindricks, of the Bureau of Labor spoke and had a lot to say and said it poorly! Sunday afternoon a woman from the personal staff of Nahims in Brooklyn spoke, who was the best of them all. (Aren't women superior creatures?) She didn't offer any particular solution (all were talking on the returning servicemen) but stated problems very well. Also a guy from the A F of L who thought the solution was for women to stay in the home and men to get higher wages from then on. Let the union get men higher wages and keep the women at home. (Nuts) All in all, it wasn't very successful.

Have been reading Emerson by the ton and much is good tho much of it is repetitious. He says: "What I must do is all that concerns me, not what the people think" and "It is easy in the world to live after the world's opinion, it is easy in solitude to live after our own; but the great man is he who in the midst of the crowd keeps with perfect sweetness the independence of solitude."

"Men imagine that they communicate their virtue or vice only by overt actions, and do not see that virtue or vice isn't a breath every moment."

This weekend is still undecided. If Mard can make it on the 28th to come here, I'll come this weekend; if not I'll come on the 28th depends on my brother's plans.

Sorry the letter I wrote on Saturday didn't get mailed til this morning, no stamp.

Have to go celebrate. Wish I could do it with you.
As ever,
Duchess.

October 17, 1944

Darling,

On the way home tonite it was apparent that it would have to be short on account of Thursday nite's exam. Then I found your two letters waiting and now it is apparent that if I don't say what's on my mind to you right now there wont be any use pretending to study.

Right now I 'm as rich as a munitions maker-figuratively and literally. Two letters from you and, after the whole matter had been dropped, the appointment as an Assistant Instructor came thru. I rushed to the Registrar's office and made arrangements to get back the $200 I paid last month and in addition I'll save $200 more this February. From now on my entire salary is mine with no tuition to save for. Dollars, they're wonderful!

Your letters are so full of stuff to talk about, I don't know where to begin. I'll try running right down the line and see how far I can get.

Classical music-I love it. Especially Beethoven, Bach, Mozart and Brahms in about that order. I have a passionate and sentimental attachment to the Eroica – tho I think the 5th and 9th are greater, mostly because it was also one of the first pieces I consciously enjoyed. Cesar Frank's D minor also means something special to me. My one favorite movement is the second of Beethoven 7th-especially the part when the violins form a background to the dominant theme, then gradually come forward and finally blend in a way that knocks me out. Do you know the part I mean? Bach, of course is unique with everyone – I guess a next addition for our collection will be his little fugue. Altho I've come to like a wide number of composers and many different types (symphonies, string quartets, sonatas etc.— there are certain favorites which I can trace back to the Academy of Music in Philly. We used to stand in line from 6:30 to 8 for gallery seats; rush up to cover a seat and then run out for free pie and coffee to unfreeze ourselves before the performances started at 8:30. These were extremely happy times for me and hearing again the music that I first heard there, brings back a glow.

When you think of all the possible fields in which you'd like to work, don't you feel that a solid background of History, Econ, Polit and Philosophy is absolutely essential? While you haven't localized the field in which you'll remake the creaking world, I have little doubt that in general you'll need the stuff you're learning now. I just can't picture you far removed from people and social economic problems.

You may call me wonderful or anything else you please, as long as you remember that beauty is in the mind of the beholder. Your feeling that I get my thoughts down the way I want them while you don't is exactly the reverse of how I feel about our letters. The truth is probably neither of us says what is he or she really has in mind–we fill in the gaps when we read them. You seem to think I know you pretty well don't you feel that you also know me?

I'd love to come for the sophomore Prom but if the Chief sticks to his plan to set the orals date at the end of the month, it may or may not interfere. As far as I'm concerned if I can make it, I'd like to come up Nov 4th whether or not you decide to go to the Prom. I think I've warned you that although I danced a lot between high school and college, that was some time ago and I've got very rusty since. You'll have to promise not to sue me for any damages inflicted.

One thing we didn't click on was your interpretation of my analysis of your autobiography. I don't think that you've gone around feeling brilliant but unappreciated. I do feel that you realize and still realize that you haven't found the field which best brings out what you are and that is a sense of frustration come out of this minority feeling. Also your happiness and expression of your self confidence in a group such as at the camp where you were in your true milieu. Incidentally, your interpretation made it seem as if I have been going around feeling un appreciated. Do you think I'm such a smug ass?

We've talked a lot about the subject of love. Is it or is it ain't (a famous line from burlesque). I've been concerned mainly with why it bothers you some much more than me. The best I can make out of the whole business is the old story that time only will bring the answer. It's true that you are much more concerned than I-that you may be wishing so hard, that you may mistake the dream for reality. I'm not wishing anything (except that you make up your mind on my side). At the time we met, marriage plans were a very hazy part of my future. What I do know is that no matter what the future brings, nothing can change that fact that I do love you now. In a way I sometimes suspect that despite all our forewarning, our ideas of love are still influenced far too much by the idealized love epics written not as they happened to the authors, but written to tickle the romantic day dreaming public. After 20 years of absence Heathcliff returns to claim Kathy and we vicariously enjoy the sharing of an undying love . . . I've mentioned this before but I've got to repeat that for Hollywood to the contrary, love for me is a living dynamic thing and not a special spot in your heart that is entered by one man who thenceforth is your mate. There will be plenty of times; times when we'll feel jealous or maybe even attracted temporarily to someone else. Give us time, darling, we'll know.

I've got to stop now or I'll flunk my exam cold. Wont be able to write till Thursday nite though I'll write mentally many times before then. Goodnite, Duchess.
Love, Danny
P.S. I've got an idea you'll find me a little difficult to boss. We'll have a dog that we can both order around.

October 17, 1944
Darling,

This has been one heck of a day. I guess I've been lower today than I have been for a year. And the things that have caused it are comparatively minor that I'm ashamed at letting them bother me so much.

The major lack of joy was losing (there's still a chance I might get it back) $35. I went to the bank and cashed checks for both Barb and me and then proceeded to leave the money in Polit class. It annoyed me partly cause it was a heck of a lot of money but mainly because it was such a dumb thing to do. I've never lost anything like that before and I suppose there always has to be a "first" to teach me a lesson, but the rush of classes were over for the day etc. etc. just added to the general rush of things. Then little other things went wrong. It's good to write to you cause it makes me realize how insignificant it all is/was.

In the midst of rereading your letters: the first one I read was one of yours which you said didn't mean to start it "hello" that I could fill in anything I wanted-that you had no bank account but that I had a blank check for it.

That hit home ironically enough. But then I read your most recent letter which should have boosted my morale but only made things more ironic than ever. I had a long moment's pity for you, having fallen for a jerk like me but then snapped out of it, winked at you and went to the library for two hours. I'm still not really over it yet but at least I can cover it up better than before.

Before I forget: Are you busy this Saturday night? If not, and you're still interested in seeing a certain dim-wit who goes to college, it's a date. I'm coming in Sat. AM. Can't afford to come in on Friday but just have to come in this weekend. I'm sick of living with myself and magnifying my little egotistical thoughts to mountainous proportions and am in need of civilization and you (or you and civilization- or just you).

Barb and I had a very good time last night when we celebrated 1) our tests were over for the moment 2) she'd heard from "the" man 3) I'd heard from you 4) it was exactly one year since her man was up here for a weekend so we had a steak dinner in town. You did too only you didn't know it. You see, you and Barb's man came with us. We introduced the two of you and you hit if off quite well. You didn't get much to eat but we played "Sweet and Lovely" on the Nickelodeon and we danced. The two of you came back to the dorm with us. People really must have thought us completely nutty. There we sat talking to air, sitting in a corner so as to give you and him plenty of room, flirting with imaginative creatures, but we got a big kick out of it.

Then I discovered that the gift I was planning to create which I thought I could only be made in NYC was make-able in town here . . . the present you probably have received by now. If you haven't found a place to play it, bring it on Saturday nite . . . only I'll leave the room while you listen.

How about coming to dinner? It just struck me, and you're not being asked out of kindness. I haven't the least idea who'll be home except I know Dad wont be since he's going away for a conference in Rochester. Mom may be there, as may Mard. So I'm not writing you for any ulterior motives of meeting the family. Just thought you might like a home cooked meal and (maybe?) a chance to see me at dinner.

It's approaching the bewitching hour of midnight and this has been a heck of a long day (up at 6:30 to do Polit) so Good nite- pleasant dreams. Include me in them.
XXX Duchess

October 17, 1944
Dear family, (post card)
  Am sick of work and am chucking it all to come in this

weekend. I will be home Saturday early morning. Invited Danny to dinner. Hope it's OK. If it isn't for any reason, phone me . Glad Mom had fun on her vacation. Hope my coming in doesn't disrupt anyone's plans. Don't let it.
Love, me

October 19, 1944
Dear Darling,
1) This may not reach you before I do but
2) I gotta explain
3) When I received your call I had just sent the telegram so I wasn't expecting your call.
4) The girl who called me to the phone said "Don't get exited. It's only from Poughkeepsie" so I did as I was bid.
5) So I thought it might be from the PAC in Poughkeepsie.
6) Then with the formal pronouncing of my name it confirmed the fact that it wasn't you.
7) I thought it was you anyway because of your voice but particularly didn't want to make a mistake.
8) Therefore, am I excused?

Yes, the convertible thing came this morning and I love it!!! Couldn't have chosen anything better. I put it on immediately though it wasn't on something black. Everyone notices it, admires it, desires an explanation which is not forthcoming. Am intrigued and curious how you made it. Haven't decided whether the "Liberty "on the head side is significant of what you are taking with me or not! How did you melt the plastic and get it to harden? I've never seen anything like it and get the dime inside?

Well, if we're ever broke!!!

Am sitting in Polit class in the front row. Its two minutes before class starts and everyone is looking over my shoulder . . . oops! Class has begun.
Love, Me

October 20, 1944
Hello Darling,

What a day, what a week what a world or as Dr. Wang says "What a hell". For the next ten days my program will be home and to Philly and this weekend to see friend Harry who is coming down from Washington, my sister and her husband also from DC and the family. I haven't been home for about four months except for dropping in briefly the weekend I went to Penn. Next Thursday I have a Red Cross appointment; the weekend of the fourth I go upstate on some business the details of which I cant recall at the moment and Tuesday, the seventh the election and exam day at the same time.

After the whole business about getting my tuition back had been stopped as my being paid from clerical and technical fund, instead as it is, I'd only be paid once a month the way teachers are paid from now on instead of twice as technicians. Some reason this got under my skin and I wanted to know why. I should be paid as an instructor but not get tuition free. The upshot of the matter was that thewhole thing was rehashed. The difficulties disappeared–the proper papers were signed and approved and now it is practically certain . . . tho it won't be till I see the check . . .

and I not only get back the $18.75 I paid out last month but $75 for the additional four courses last summer. My appointment as instructor and dated back to July 1 tosses in the courses I had taken during the summer. It was approved. In case you still think of your $35 darling, forget it! We're way ahead of the game.

Now to get my friends straight: Harry is a guy I met in high school. He hitch hiked with me out to Purdue and we were roommates. He's now in Washington DC working as a physicist with the Bureau of Standards. You're going to meet him one of these days and find him a dignified looking, shy at first, extremely likeable guy. once he gets over his reserve.

Dave is an ensign at Princeton, taking a radar course. We met at Purdue and became extremely close friends – is sharp and bright-very lively and friendly. He and I hitch-hiked from Purdue to Philadelphia and back one summer. His girl friend, Connie, is like him in her appearance, shrewdness and the way she thinks. She's about 21 and is a senior at Wellesley.

Gene and Leon are two other close friends of mine who are now overseas. Until I went to Purdue they were my closest friends.

Just remembered FDR is on . . . May I stop for a few minutes? Have to resume this letter or, Duchess, you wont get it till Monday. How can anyone vote for Dewey?

Clare has had a talk with the Chief and he advised her to go ahead write up her second paper and take her final exam in June. Since I'm filing right behind her, it looks as if I get there by next June – two years and two months from when I began. Since the end is coming into view I've started thinking about the next big object of my life . . . getting married. You want to know what kind of girl I want? Someone with dark curly hair . . . five feet three, around 120 pounds and sincere, with a good sense of humor – you know in addition she must be stubbornly idealistic and take a vital interest in the world around her. It would help if she was pretty and had a way of looking at me that makes me want to put her under my coat and take her home with me. Do you know of anyone who might fit the bill? I thought you might discover such a girl in your class at college since I'm partial to college sophomores.

    Your Polit test really gave me a lift. You'd think I got it instead of you. I can smell an A in the making. I'd much rather talk to you about your new resolutions than try to write about it but don't hesitate to tell me what ever is on your mind. I want to feel that nothing enters your mind that you don't feel free to discuss with me

Goodnite, Duchess . . . don't forget I love you.

Danny

October 23, 1944

Dear Darling,

    I started a letter yesterday on NYC yellow paper full of yellow sentiment but I was ruthlessly interrupted by my beloved father who took me on a healthful airing around the reservoir. Actually did some work on the train coming back here, so couldn't write you then. All this is leading up to the fact that tho I haven't sent you a letter, you've been right beside me for the 41 hours since I saw you. It was good to see you (major understatement) and feel at peace with myself and the world.

Sunday was a weird sort of day-partly cause I was sort of drunk on the luxury of you, partly cause I was so tired that I went around in a fog.

Read FDR's speech and it was a beaut! Barb said it was extremely thrilling to hear the delivery as I can imagine it must have been. Played Brahms first while reading "TWA Democracy on the March" (for Econ) and went for a walk with Dad. We discussed me and college and he thought I ought to give up extra-curricular things and just concentrate on my classes. I disagree with it on many points but I do see that I'm spreading myself too thin in too many directions now which isn't exactly successful. Also Mom's point was that one can always hear extra lectures, do political work after college but can't get degrees and a thorough background in the courses I'm taking. My contention is that a college education should include "other things" too and that they are equally important. But with the accelerated program, I guess, one's got to cut out those other things. So I've decided to give it a try.

Then today, I got pleas to try out for the editorial board of the Misc. (They said no one any good had tried out) and do an extra poster for someone, do some AYD work. Then I spent the day sadly shaking my head. (Don't mean to sound bragging, it's just no one has the time or interest to do the things like that). Anywhooo . . . will try to keep things down to a stricter minimum and work harder on courses with the theory that I'll be getting ground work 2) the courses will improve when more effort is put into them. Not being the purely academic type, like Mard, I'm dubious of the outcome but will give it a try. Means giving up trying out for head of SLA-oh well- Started off well by working ten hours today. They were preceded by waiting on table and only woke up in time to rush like mad so missed my own breakfast. A brilliant way to start off the week!

No Philosophy today as Venable is sick. Good lecture in Polit on Congress.

If this sounds cold, don't let it disturb you. It's only that the material world is coating over the emotional or the emotional needs rejuvenation with the aid of sleep.
See you in my dreams.
Love, Your Duchess

October 23, 1944
Darling Duchess,

Didn't we have a good time yesterday! I had expected that you and Connie would get along ok since you both are so natural and lively but I was really amazed at how quickly you took to each other. (She just loved you, she told me about 3 times while your back was turned. I knew you'd like Dave too and that he'd give you an enthusiastic ok. Those pictures of herself that Connie showed us at the Commodore were alright but our kids will have better pictures than that. Don't you think Dave's Aunt and Uncle are nice? I got a real kick our of the way she decided to vote for FDR on account of one of Lipmann's columns and then had to send him a letter to tell him all about it. She must be O.K. as she must be the only Bronxvillette who reads P.M.

Our dinner at the Boar's head was lots of fun for me. I thought you wouldn't mind if I ordered veal cutlet for us both. You didn't, did you? We went to hear Dorothy Ross more because Dave wanted Connie to hear her than for any other reason but from the way you carried on, I don't think you missed many of her double entendres or was it the daiquiris that went to your head?

The only flaw in the whole day was the drunk I met after I had dropped you off and was waiting for the subway to take me home. Why he picked on me I don't know, but he kept picking on me trying to cheer me up, told me not to worry and not to look so sad and lonesome. People say drunks are psychic but any sober person would have left me alone after I insisted I wasn't lonesome-just tired. Love, Danny

October 24, 1944
Dearest,

I'm so glad you felt you had cause to be proud of me. I hadn't thought about your noticing the way I was acting ... Didn't think about poise, dignity or anything. Just felt they were 1) your friends 2) young and engaged 3) looked like nice people and didn't feel the least apprehensive about it.

Just finished Moby Dick and the fact that I'm looking forward to some explanation of its symbolism in class may indicate I'd feel kind of lost in the lack of the conference system at any other school.

I love you whether your tie matches or not, whether you've shaved or not. I can't decide whether you are serious or kidding about criticizing you. Don't you know, you delightful goon, that I don't give a hang what color combinations you wear and certainly haven't meant that to have any affect on you momentarily or otherwise.
Off to study. Love, V

October 25 1944
Darling,

God, how I miss you, darling. Dave and Connie hadn't seen each other for three weeks and kind as they were, it didn't help any to be with two people so evidently in love. Connie is determined that the four of us get together and have some real times. She knows girls who are at your dorm and has a million things she wants to talk to you about. Raised in a snotty village (her family used to have money) she is simple and natural—loads of fun and as liberal as could be.

I'll have to tell you what a great effort it is for me to write this letter. Tonite just before class, I picked up a one and a half inch splinter right where I sit down. I got an inch of it out but am itching to get the rest of it before gangrene sets in and they have to amputate, but if I don't finish this letter, it wont get out til Tuesday, so here I sit, slightly on a slant suffering. It suddenly occurred to me that Dave knows a bunch of nice guys one of whom might like to come to Vassar for the Prom. He's going to ask a guy named Lou Rambo if he'd be interested. Lou is no Clark Gable but he's pleasant, funny, slightly heavy–set, who, I think, would do admirably. Let me know if I should close the sale in case he's willing.

Just stopped to probe and I can feel the damn thing sitting there smug and contaminating. It's in a spot that I can't see without making a pretzel of myself. Gosh! I wish you were here!

Tomorrow Clare and I do an experiment which if it turns out alright will finish up this series for us. We'll do a couple more to clean up some olds and ends and then I'll start on the last set of experiments-an easy set that shouldn't take more than a month. I've got an appointment with the Chief tomorrow A.M. If he sets my exam date so if it interferes with the Prom, so help me I'll have his liver on the end of my knife.

It was with mixed feelings that I read your letter. In a way I'm glad you've become more or less reconciled to the situation as it exists and have decided to knuckle down. But as you know, I am very much in sympathy with the way you feel toward the part of extra-curricula work should play in your activities at college. In ordinary times, the contribution is probably more balanced, but with the accelerated program it's impossible to keep up the pace without something being left out. The trouble is that your attitude is entirely right, it's the set–up at college that's wrong but since leaving school would be essentially unsatisfying you've just got to arrive at a compromise between idealism and practicality.

I feel that I'm on the wrong side of the fence in

congratulating you for compromising with your idealism. Yet this isn't an ideal world and like it or lump it, sometimes we've got to be "reasonable" (ugly word). In a way, it's part of growing up. I remember how (many years ago) I thought it was possible to have everybody like me. All I had to do was to be reasonable and thoughtful of others and automatically I would be everybody's friend. Than I learned that it not only was impossible but that I didn't want to be a friend to certain people! The disillusionment was just as shattering as when I learned that truth isn't always rewarded and evil punished.

The world is instantly knocking into the corners of us that don't fit into the mold, trying to round us off into a single likeness, and I'm proud of you and love you for every unrounded corner you possess (this is not to be confused with your anatomy. Unfortunately we're not independent. To get to a goal we've got to reach a certain understanding with ourselves and the world or else our rebellion ends in a complete neurosis. While it hurts me to see you forced into such an understanding, it is an important and necessary step for you to take. It means that you and I will have a happier and fuller life together for Lord knows, I'm not an ideal and in accepting me with your eyes wide open to this fact, you make it possible for us to be a couple of humans with strong idealistic tendencies having one hell of a good time together.

At our first date (real) you liked the fact that I know and can plow on with my work no matter what happens. Do you think there weren't hundreds of times when I battled with myself to stay in school-times when it seemed as if so many of the things I wanted from life would pass me by while I slaved over books? Now that the end is in sight, I feel strong and confident. I know what I can do and that I can do those things that I don't like but must get done.

You may feel that you'll be the same way if your goal was as clear cut as mine is, but there was a long time when I wasn't sure when I was young. All I wanted was embodied somewhere in the word "sciences". I think you feel just about the same way except that yours is social science. So ends the lecture. I think it stinks as a sermon. What I really wanted to say in the above paragraphs is that I love you and want you to be happy. I feel that you'll eventually increase your chances for happiness by doing what you've decided to do and I hope you can reach a state of mind where these intervening times will be bearable.
Love, love love, Danny

October 25, 1944
Darling,

Am now on message center and since I can't possibly do any work I will write a letter to you and one to my family.

Nothing much has happened except work which doesn't count (oh yes it does, Vivian. Oh where did you get the idea it didn't? OK, it counts but I give you permission to write to a certain guy who you've always got your mind on anyhow. Thanks).

Life continues to be full of little things. As one of Dad's patients in the Bronx once said to him "Docktah, I don't

see how you manage with so many dinks on your head."
It's become a saying in our family. Have you famous family quotations, or have you been away from home so long that things like that have melted away?

Spent an hour getting you and "whosit" (which we call Barb's date since she didn't get his name over the phone) a room. Finally got one. It's near the Arlington firehouse so if you're hot you can run around the corner and get cooled off. (Aren't I considerate?)

Been concentrating on Econ in hopes of getting two of the many outside reading books out of the way and so write the book reports by Saturday. Just finished the TVA book by Lilienthal, the director of same. He makes the whole project sound a bit too good to be true and when one knows so little on the subject, it's sort of dangerous just to read one side that one takes his word on face value, reinforced with the attitudes given, it really sounds like it is a wonderful thing.

French was a joyous mess. She announced the fact that she would spring an hour written in the near future. This is against the rules of the college, i.e. you're allowed to spring short quizzes but not hour ones, certainly not a mid – semester exam the way this will eventually be. When this little fact was called to the lady's attention she replies (in French of course) "It's not one of MY rules" So I guess we get a sprung hour written. Oh la la! Among other things the assignment for Friday includes memorizing a poem by Villon (14th century) 2 pages long. Poems are stupid to memorize and stupider to memorize in French! People who memorize poems so often do it just for the culture with a capital "C". The real purpose has been sort of lost on me.

    I like to remember things that "hit home" but just to memorize "To be or not to be" etc so that you can spiel it off in an exam or in front of a literary person is a waste of valuable time. But if I were writing this to my father, he's say, "forget your principles for a while and learn something."

    If you make it up here on the 4th, bring the camera again and this time we'll see that someone's around to take pictures.

    Philosophy was funny today. Mr. Venable used some particular apt analogy that struck one girl so funny that she was crying with laughter. She couldn't stop and finally left the class early practically in contortions. We all started to laugh with her but suppressed it as Mr. V. continued the discussion. Just as she'd left the room, HE began to laugh.

    Just a line to surprise you and because I need a pleasant change from Polit reading. And to tell you again I loved that last letter which was a reply to mine that "hit you between your eyes". (I hope it didn't hurt) As to my doing the right thing, you flatter me. The letter just happened to come at the right time. I'm not psychic. Luck just worked things out that way. (I'm not a fatalist, however, either). So I can still go happily wondering why you like me. See, you can't solve everything quite so easily.

Love,

V

October 26, 1944

Dear Darling,

    Tomorrow as a special treat I've promised myself the pleasure of writing before I'm so tired I can't think, write or see straight. But tonite must be a late one. Yes, I did have a good time with Connie and Dave. As for the splinter, I sympathize but can't help laughing. Were you walking or sitting slantwise? What WERE you doing to attain such a thing?

    As to Lou and the prom: was all set to write you to check the matter when Barb got a phone call from some guy in Monmouth. A blind date via her sister's husband (you figure that out) and all unexpected like, he's coming! So that takes a load off up your mind, my mind and hers' too. Thanks anyhoo, darling. Now I've just got to be sure I have date! But if your orals do come then, it won't really matter. I just want that stated for the record. We'll make it another weekend.

    Am coming in Nov.18th weekend. Am apparently going to be busy one night with my parents.

    You may think this paper very appropriate but you're wrong. At the moment Barb and I are luxuriating lying on a wide clean bed in a clean room in the infirmary. Both of us discovered the other wasn't feeling well ... hadn't all afternoon when it got to the point where I couldn't stand up and Barb hardly could, we called the infirmary. We both had important classes tomorrow but since we obviously couldn't work tonight we decided it was better to go to the infirmary rather than take tests unprepared. We thought it awfully strange that only us two were sick. It was obviously something in the food. So when we arrived here and found over 50 people have it and are in the infirmary too, it made more sense. And there are 25 more who can't get in! So we're not in the least original!

They have a word for this delightful disease which is famous, tho I've never heard of it before. They call it "the plague". This place is quite a social institution with the poor nurse running from room to room but a clean room with much noise is a welcome change.

As usual, you're right here with me. In fact, you're continually grabbing the pillow away! But I'm glad you're here–you and your letter which I received today.

It's a beautiful letter, darling. The discussion on college plans plus in essence what Dad said only he antagonized me and you didn't. You're going to make some curly headed kid (they'll surely have curly hair) a wonderful father.

As for the orals: It's wonderful you got a chance to have a say about the board. Do you know yet who they will be? As for being on election day, isn't that going to be hard to vote? The prom is unimportant. I wouldn't go with anyone else if you couldn't come. I'll work. It's naturally up to you to decide. You know I'd love you to come, but you know, also, how I feel about me and your work. So whatever you decide will be swell with me!

Of course, dopey me, dear, I'll understand if you don't want to write and I assure you it'll need more than that to get me to stop writing you. Just let me know what's doing about the 4th for sure and if it's that you're coming, at what time.

You say you're not "ideal". Of course not. If that word has a universal connotation but I can consider you ideal for me, cant I? I can even think your faults may be the ideal ones for you to have! What I'm trying to say is that I think you're wonderful and I'm falling very much in love with you. In a way, it's probably too bad it didn't happen one year later. It would have made practical things simpler and possibly ideal things too. But believe me, I don't regret a thing!

I'm a little weak from the joys of "the Plague" and shall take advantage of the hour and get a real nite's sleep. Your future wife.

October 27, 1944 Friday thru Sunday
Good morning, Darling,

Here I am having slept ten and a half hours, having read your letter for the nth time and dreamt about you and feeling fine.

At this moment I'm probably missing a French exam but 1) I love you 2). I'm in a very comfortable bed and 3) I've had all that sleep . . . all important counter balances to missing the exam.

The last time I was in the infirmary I had measles, freshman year. Barb was getting proposed to by mail and had to be stuck in here. She gave me permission to tell you of same . . . which my darling is quite an honor since her man's family doesn't yet know. (Her parents do. They and I and now you are the only ones.) So now we're both in here.

It's now 6:30 and have spent a lovely day here. Heard

that 200 kids have come down with the plague and lots of people in town, too. We've had some state doctor down to trace where it came from or rather what's causing it.

It's funny what you grab to put into a suitcase when you are sick and in a hurry on the way to the infirmary. Only work I brought was for American Lit: Hawthorne. Have read a bunch of his stories and one of three novels–had read two of them and wanted to reread "The House of Seven Gables" anyway. So have been doing same this afternoon. It's very dated, wordy and still promises lot of truth and charm. It's the kind of thing that couldn't possibly be written today in an age of rush where not one excess word is included and I suppose many people would get very impatient reading it. But, as you say, I've got something of the old-fashioned in me.

Don't work too hard and take care of yourself and don't worry about me (am feeling fine and will leave here tomorrow AM). I'll always be in that room of yours anyway, leaning over your shoulder, winking at you or saying "hello" so don't worry.

XXX

Good morning again: this is Saturday. Just woke up from a divine sleep only my feet were cold – so I was dreaming I was rescued by brother from a snow storm and that he was eleven years old. Barb and I both feel fine . . . will leave after breakfast. They just stuck thermometers in our mouths as we continued to sing the Burl Ives repertoire. Ever sing with your mouth full of a thermometer? We ended in surprised laughter (since we couldn't open our mouths) and prayers that we wouldn't break the darn things.

Am assuming you're coming next weekend but you can always change your mind at the last minute if there's more studying than you anticipated.

This evening Mard is coming up. Haven't really seen her alone for any length of time in ages. Will have to try not to talk about you ALL the time. The poor thing will go mad hearing it from both of us.

Am giving this to her to give to you as I forgot to finish it and mail it and wanted you to get it on Monday.

It's now 5 P.M. on Sunday and I've exhausted my sister who is now peacefully asleep. We've had a nice time and tho I didn't talk about you ALL the time, you somehow managed to wedge your way into conversations. In fact she's up to date on events. Said she:" I can't think of a brother-in-law I'd rather have". All in all she was very pleased, amused, and cute.

Barb and I since took a walk and had a lovely time at the Cider Mill near where we discovered millions of sheep . . . fed one some grass so I could feel its wool. Finally got the bright idea of plucking some of the wool and the dumb thing didn't even know the difference. I'm amazed they can make anything out of the knotted grey burr-infested coat–a wonderful inventor they tell me.

Study hard, my Duke, and remember a weekend is coming. Guess you'll take the 9:30 that gets here at 11:14, yes? Better look it up again. I ain't so bright at such things.

Took an hour off this afternoon to go to Poughkeepsie

and buy curtain rods. We forgot to measure the windows (thinking the rods would be the adjustable kind) and had to return and get something else.

Hope the experiment went right and that the Chief and you were appropriately mad at one another since things seem to work out best that way.

Pleasant surprise today: Miss McGown entered Polit class with our exams of last Monday in hand. Said they were disappointing on the whole and proceeded to return them. A B↑! Maybe there's something in this idea of work!

They cut the metal strip when we got the second pair of curtains, the couch cover and pillows etc. Once finished, the room may even look like a room!

Am trying to be less introspective, partly it takes up a lot of time and partly cause it doesn't seem to get me anywhere so if my letters sound bleak or lacking my usual circumscribed reasoning you'll know why.

Dewey's answer to queries on his coming action regarding Senator Bell, the matter of congressional approval of use of arms etc. were priceless in today's paper. He's really been put on the spot but good!

Polly came in today all excited because her mother has finally decided to vote for FDR says Polly in typical Pollyanna manner. "I knew underneath it all, her heart's in the right place".

Must get some sleep. Am learning to live on 7 hours or less as opposed to the 8 or 9 previously consumed. (Am I preparing correctly for married life?) I can repeat your last words:" study hard, sleep well, and don't forget me" tho I think they're equally unnecessarily said to you as to me. (signed) "the girl you're going to marry" Viv

October 30, 1944
Darling,

Having spoken to you on the phone about thirty minutes ago I figure it's about time to talk to you again. Of course, as usual, I didn't say all I wanted to, nor would I if we'd had all of the three minutes, 15 minutes or hours. But should enlarge on what I DID say at any rate.

I didn't realize it (getting Barb a date) would entail so much on your part. It's a little mean when I wanted to do something nice for her to have the burden of it shifted to you. The point was she got a telegram this afternoon from the guy saying his father had just died and he'd been called home. She was feeling blue about it not that it is so important but she had been looking forward to it and we'd made some plans. So I felt sorry for her.

I asked if Mard gave you the letter partly to know if you'd gotten it and partly to know if she was o.k. She had a sore throat all weekend and I figured I'd know how she was or if she'd stayed home.

Have been thinking of you so much that you're never far away from me. Instead of growing less with getting used to the idea of it all, it grows, becomes more important and wonderful. as it should.

While waiting for you to call this evening I was reading Polit. Read for half an hour before I realized I was re reading last week's assignment. How to concentrate!

Work continues at its usual pace, interest, etc. Election debates, poster etc have everyone keyed up. Some pretty rotten mud slinging going on around here but will tell you about that when I see you. So much to talk about when we get together. Do you think we will ever run out of things to say? I remember when I was little thinking that married people would run out of conversation. But it is one of my childhood fears I have managed to conquer!

Wonder how your weekend home was. Didn't get your letter you mentioned on the phone on Saturday but this A.M. which was better. Starts the week right.

Certainly am glad the tuition worked out right. It's too bad it took so much back and forthing but as long as it ended on the "forth" and not on the "back", it's swell. Thanks for the fill in on your friends.

Love you,

V

October 30, 1944
Hello Darling,

Since the phone call I've been trying to get satisfaction out of this partially spoiled pomegranate that my mother gave me in Philly. I've just dumped the damn thing in the waste paper basket.

My visit home was a lot of fun. My sister and husband were in from Washington DC. She's expecting in Feb. and looked very odd in her condition as she is small and rather delicately built. She's going to send me a picture of herself and Ed (her husband) so you'll soon be able to

visualize them better. I introduced you to everyone and they all seemed pleased from my description, (I left them no choice) and from snapshots. The chief reaction was surprise as they had me ticketed as a perennial bachelor. Of course, this in no way binding on you.

It seems to me that I never gave you a positive answer on your visiting my room here (or did I?) I half expected to move closer to school if my finances permitted, but now that they do, I don't think I will after all. It's quiet, clean, and cheap here and I don't feel like making a change so you'll have to come up and have a look over my shoulder (unless my back is in the middle of the room, and are on the wall, floor, half out the window, I'm afraid.

Your comment that my reasoning was the same as your father intrigued me. I hope you don't think that our arguments were basically alike except that mine was more diplomatically couched, It seems to me that your father, after a hard and triumphant life, feels that nothing succeeds like success. In college success is measured in marks therefore you must get good ones or you are a failure. I may be wrong, but I don't think he believes (as I do) that it is wrong to have to give up extra curricular activities but came to the conclusion regrettably that it is the only sensible things that can be done. Perhaps I'm wrong about your Pop's but I have a feel the "practical" comes largely from him and the idealistic feelings from your mother.

While in Philly I got something for you. You'll see it this Saturday. I'm new at giving things to people and don't know if you will like this or not. It its not, you can hide it somewhere as soon as I leave the campus.

I was amused at a new reaction I discovered in myself tonight. There's a girl in our Phys chem. class, fairly pretty but not too bright who is one of those who was asked to quit the course but is sticking it out. After class, on the way to the subway, she remarked that she wished she had someone to explain some of the stuff to her. She looks like a nice kid and so I offered to work on this week's assignment with her. I suggested a nearby drug store and she very sensibly invited me to her apartment (shared with three girls). The funny thing is that she was obviously being a little more than nice and three months ago (and the previous ten years) would have leaped at the opportunity. Instead (darn you) I told her I was practically engaged and we went to the drug store.

As I told you over the phone, I'll try to get Lou for Barb since the other guy can't come. As far as I'm concerned, I really don't care whether we go to the prom or not, except that if it'll make you happier, then I want to go.

This is the last sheet of paper I've got, so I'll have to stop now. Some time you'll have to explain what you meant about wishing we had met a year later. I don't care if the reasons are practical or idealistic, I wouldn't consider trading a year knowing you for anything I can think of.

Good nite, darling. You have wonderful times ahead. I'm no longer "falling in love" and know what you have in store when you finally get there.
Love, (never thought this would be inadequate to say everything I think). Danny

October 31, 1944

Darling,

Am now recuperating from a wild and wholly satisfactory Halloween party. It 's this dorms' tradition that freshmen scare and feed upper classmen on the nite of the witch's delight. We were led in groups of 4 up to the blacked out 5th floor thru a maze of wet string hung from the ceiling so as to tickle the face, stuffed pillows for dead bodies, people pouncing unexpectedly etc. Recuperated with cider and donuts. Then someone brought forth a Ouija (weegee? Spelling?) board. I'd never seen one before tho I d heard endless tales of them. In case you haven't, they are supposed to answer any question you ask. They're wooden boards with the alphabet, numbers from one to nine and no and yes written on them. There's a small wooden block which rests on three felt feet on the main board and which two people sitting opposite each other could rest their fingers on. Both wish the same wish and the board moves by itself, supposedly. You don't consciously move it but you must semi-consciously. Barb and I tried it. Question one: Will Barb marry Johnny? answer: "yes" Nov. 1995. Next: "Will I marry you? answer "Yes" (see you even have my subconscious having opinions) When? Oct 1945. So get ready for a fall wedding. Hadn't planned it that way but what can you do when the supernatural so wills?

We just got a hold of the darn board again and after disproving it by making it spell the name of Barb's husband "truer," we amused ourselves with all sorts of questions. Pat (a swell girl tho not highly attractive) was trying it.

She's going to get married in the year 2006! To the man of her choice but, thank God, she's going to have 2 love affairs–the first in 1945 with 8 illegitimate children so things worked out better than the first gruesome moment. We were all hysterical over the answers and looking at ourselves objectively in the middle of the night sitting cross-legged on the floor "concentrating". Other important facts about us: We will have 2 children and I will be a virgin on marriage and my family will approve of you. Make of it what you will.

Not much happening today. Mom sent up my evening dress which siteth in my closet, making the Prom weekend ever present in my mind (as if I needed an evening dress to remind me!) It's 12:10 and time to dream about you in the less conscious state.
Love, Duchess

November 1, 1944
Hello Darling,

Have just spent a most amusing hour. Tried your unfavorite but sometimes necessary occupation of being a salesman. I got some very cute wooden earrings with FDR painted on them from the AYD to be sold for 25 cents a pair. Went from room to room and sold all, just in the dorm! (20 pair). We really should have ordered more. But what was so funny was the varied reactions to 1) the facts 2) my salesmanship. The technique was to knock on an occupied dorm room (which didn't have a huge Dewey sign on it) and ask if they were for FDR or Dewey. Then display the earrings with myself as model. Sales talk varied with the individual but darned if one of my side remarks meaning to be funny, didn't do best! The background of the earring is navy and when people said "when would you wear them?" I said I'd just discovered they matched the color of our blue jeans. (the cleaner pairs!) which worked on three people to clinch the sale. Things got a bit more involved when someone asked who got the money, so I had to explain AYD which I did in very general terms. None were interested to probe behind my glib answers so I didn't push things. (P.S What was that about quitting all extra curricular activities?)

    Even if Barb's date doesn't work out, let's go to the prom for a while anyhow ... partly as my cute mother spent hours remaking my dress and I'd hate to disappoint her by not wearing it and also it might be fun. It's a program Dance.-something I've never experienced. There are a certain number of dances and the girls fill the guy's cards trading dances with their friends. Since lots of the nicest kids aren't going and since I'm conceited enough to think you're coming up to see me and not Vassar Sophomores at large, I figured we wouldn't go for all the Dance and have only arranged 2 changes for you. One with Amy and one with Bobby Green. The rest of the time you'll have to dance with me!

    Member when you said you'd remember me as an end-of-the-month-er and I said I might fool you? Well, consider yourself fooled. If you don't know what I'm talking about: I haven't gotten the G.D. curse yet though I'll probably be blessed with the same by tomorrow . . . which is another reason I've been hesitant on the dance (i.e. look like hell and mightn't feel like going to a formal dance).

In the excitement of the phone call I didn't ask how your work was coming, which should not indicate disinterest or lack of sympathy. Hope all is going well though I'm not worried over it and hope you are not.

Only 60 hours til I see you. It seems like much more than only 2 weeks ago since last time. As for the more controversial things in your letter like the conclusion on my staying at college compared to Dad's reasoning, that will have to wait til I see you.

Hoping its warm this weekend and that you are fine and that 60 hours passes fast.

Love, Duchess

Dear Diary,   *November 8, 1944*
He is right: he is not a good dancer–but so what. Once you are grown up you don't go dancing much, I've noticed.

He told me how great Dr. Root had been. Since his orals are next week he thought he ought to stay home and study but Dr. Root not only said he should come but gave him money to buy a new suit. (I do wish it was navy instead of brown as it kind of made us stand out at the dance...but so what.

November 5, 1944
Dear Family,

    The prom weekend is now over with the beginning of a tough week ahead. The former was wonderful: the evening dress was perfect, admired and appreciated by all. The prom itself was loads of fun. Amusing to see people you've seen in blue jeans for one and a half years suddenly blossom forth in luxury attire. They fixed the Student building very cutely with decorations of colored paper and there was a big crowd to be held in its four walls. I've never been to a program dance before and they're really funny! You keep switching and what with trying to meet people at designated spots, it's a little like the game "pussy in the corner." Saw some men from junior high dancing class … was amazed to find them ensigns and grown up!

    Friday nite was a political rally at which Miss Newcomer spoke for Roosevelt – very good. Mr. Post spoke for Dewey. He wasn't nearly as good as I expected as he harped on the fourth term at great length and summed up his speech in a tone which sounded as though he knew Dewey didn't have a chance-and that if Dewey didn't get in that they'd have to pull together for unity in America, etc. It seemed to me that there are some valid points against the Democrats and that he didn't pick them but they are less important ones and he was less dramatic than usual. Usually his speeches and lectures contain a good deal of Mr. Post which is enlightening and amusing in its own way. Mr. Porter spoke for the Socialists but I've heard him last year and other times informally on the subject so I left before he attacked all existing institutions.

Have an American Lit. paper to write this week and I'm going to hear FDR tomorrow plus lots of little things to do. To bed, to bed.

Love from your youngest.

November 6, 1940 (midnight after the prom weekend)
Dearest Darling,

I love you and I miss you. In fact both facts hit me with an increased suddenness the minute I left on the train which hadn't yet left the station. It was a wonderful weekend. At the time I agreed with you about the fact that we didn't learn anything new about each other this time … and tho I still think it true in comparison with other times, I think the Prom taught us some things.

I got the bus after seeing you get on the train and found myself sitting next to Miss Drinkwater, last year's history teacher whom I've mentioned as a brilliant, strange individual. I guess it was good I met her tonite as it snapped me out of the mood I was approaching. We talked college politics. She is also for FDR as I'd thought and everything was fine – sort of took me out of myself (was gong to say "and you" but could guess what remarks you'd make to that!).

Have been reading the French like a dutiful girl friend (will I always obey you so obediently?). I got the English translation and the regular French one we're supposed to read. In comparing the two it is immediately evident our English edition is decidedly cut. And what people are missing! I thought I'd read some filthy literature but WOW! I can't imagine anything filthier or more graphic (Maybe you knew all along and that was why you told me to go back and do my French!)

Am a little worried about Barb as it's 11 P.M. and she hasn't come back yet-must have missed the train. Hate to ask if there's been a message since if she's trying to get away with something it would just bring attention to it.

Why do I write all this unimportant stuff when my heart and mind are so full of you, the weekend, and us in general. I feel all engrossed in you and everything else has the same appearance as people's conversation as when you're dropping off to sleep: blurred and far away. But I'll be good and after a few more hours, once again become a college girl.

Hope the trip back wasn't too bad; that the pin kept you company and that you have a happy studying time. Just put me in the corner during your exam: one of the corners where I can wink at you and your teacher won't be able to see.

Love from your Tigress

November 8, 1944
Dear folks,

Now I have something to write about which isn't just about classes and college life. It was election night and a bunch of us decided to leave Poughkeepsie and take a bus to nearby Hyde Park to see if we could see Mr. Roosevelt.

By the time we got there it was dark. We ran through a field and I lost a shoe! Silly me, I had got dressed up and wore shoes that just slip on and have heels.

So I was standing in the dark, one shoe on, one shoe lost.

    We could see the back porch light on and soon, sure enough, Eleanor came out (so funny: she was in the light and we in the dark. The first thing she did standing there was to pull down her girdle!—first one side than the other). She said her husband would come out to greet us—and he did! He was wheeled out in his chair. His voice is just like on the radio. He said predictions were good but he would not declare victory yet . . . then he thanked us for coming!
It was so great even though I lost the shoe.
Love, V

November 8, 1944, Tuesday
Dearest Darling,

    When you get this you'll probably have a combination of a hangover or (can't think of the word that is the opposite of a hangover) to express your relief and gladness that the exam is over. The hangover will be from all the champagne you'll be drinking to celebrate a) your exam b) the election. I expected having met a bunch of kids who needed help carrying their posters. So I went in blue jeans with 10 cents in my pocket and no gloves.

    We got there before much of a crowd had assembled and got up front. As it became jammed someone else was taking pictures said it would be better if all the college girls who had banners and posters didn't stand together and he took me along the front lines and installed me in the front row. All the kids began to object, little brats who'd been waiting even longer than we for which I can't blame them . . . and everyone objected to the banner obstructing their view. So I was one unpopular gal for a while.

Saw Amy at some length and she liked Peter (the guy at the Prom) and is going to NYC this weekend to see him. I'm awfully glad something has come up for her even if it isn't lasting- and it isn't, I'm sure. He's a glamorous type with a fast reputation merrily preceding him but he'll fill the bill for now, I guess. (God, I sound condescending, don't I?).

Must get back to work tho I'd rather write more to you. No wonder I feel complete when I'm with you as when we're not, you've got half of me in your room, at the lab; the other half which I keep is decidedly less interesting and I've got to live with it!

Bye now, almost PhD avec beaucoup d'affection and love.
Duchess

November 8, 1944, 8 AM
Darling,

Congrats! Of course I can turn up my nose and say I knew it all along but it's nicer now when you know too. I loved the telegram and you for sending it (made me know you'd passed). I tried to send you one but the woman at the desk was very nasty and said it sounded too much like congratulation and they couldn't take it. So the practical prohibited the idealist from acting. The sentiment was there tho the telegram wasn't.

Am listening to election returns which at this point 10 P.M. there is a trend for FDR but not definite. We thought we were going to Hyde Park to hear the returns and see FDR who comes out every so often but things prevented it. (1) Mix-up in bus space 2) I fell down running down the dorm steps running in the dark to Main for your telegram. It's the first time I've done that in years and just after I told you how I used to make it a daily routine when I was little. I turned my ankle ... not serious but I figured it wouldn't help to stand on it for 3 hours.

7:10 P.M Just after I'd finished writing the above sentence, a girl came screaming that another bus was going and that we should come immediately. Without time to think, we dashed out. We got to Hyde Park at 11 P.M. and joined the torch light parade right up with the band. We walked for miles to the main gate, midst red flares giving a horrible gas-y smell, sang a war song and it was a wonderful atmosphere of excitement, awe, faith, and fun all mixed together.

When we got inside the gate there was a mad scramble like you've never seen in your life — people tripping over each other taking detours into the underbrush etc and by luck I got in the very front of the mob and within ten feet of FDR. He came out on the porch looking wonderful. You probably read the speech ... very informal, making him seem more of a man and less an idol than ever before. By the time he spoke, the Times claimed us victory but it wasn't absolutely sure. After he went inside with a bunch of celebrities who were standing behind him. None of the crowd moved.

Betts and I were talking to the Secret Service man in

front of us. He was very nice, seemed intelligent until we hit on the Negro problem. (He was from Virginia). It added to the fun of the evening. Eleanor came out to give the news of the Times and said "aren't you cold?" in a pointed hint for us to go away, which we did. When we got back here a bunch of us celebrated by listening to further returns and eating food. It's now 7:30 and only paper around doesn't give anything at all final on other elections so I don't know more than I did at 2:30 in the morning but the general trend and the number of Democrats elected is OK. It was really a night to remember and to tell our children about.

It was quite a lesson in mob psychology ... a fascinating thing. The singing and the surging of the crowd, yelling down in front.. Americans seem to make a football game out of everything; the band playing- the way each person keeps his own individuality while at the same time becoming part of the crowd–quite different from Germany!— the critical eagerness of everyone to know who the celebrities were, gaping and worshipping yet ever critical in their hero worship, in short the American spirit so often talked about and scorned by cynics.

I kept wishing you were there and wondering where you were hearing the returns and how you were celebrating your exam day . . . more soon.
Love you, V

November 10, 1944
Dearest,

I've been walking around in the clouds after having received 2 letters in one day from you. It's the strangest thing the way I know there's a letter waiting for me. I've only been wrong once. I just have a certain feeling that there'll be one from you in the box — even illogical times like the second one today. But whether I expect them or not, they're still wonderful to get. (Oh! the inadequacy of words!)

Much as I agree with you on your dislike of a double standard, I guess I do think of the differentiation as far as sex goes. I don't think of it in terms of virginity or brains but I thought in a purely physiological sense. Isn't it true that a guy needs sex more than a girl? Not needs sex, but satisfaction, I guess is what I mean. If that supposition's wrong then my idea is wrong. But it is that reason I said I wouldn't mind your going out as long as it was only for sex. I wasn't saying it being noble or sophisticated but as a result of what I thought were physiological (or maybe psychological?) facts. I got that idea from a guy (Bill, if that helps you to understand). If you do go out with other females I may show you how jealous I can be!!! But as to my going out: I think I should for several reasons. Firstly I'm convinced it will make me just that much surer that you're for me; secondly, there are people I still want to see – not other than platonically but when you live with 1500 women, it's nice to get a male's company. It's not sex that makes it fun to go out with guys but a whole different slant of looking at things. (p.s. there are very few males around that I COULD go out with in any case). Also there will be occasionally times when I have to go out whether I like it not. I suppose one calls it social obligations. But all in all, darling, I wouldn't say you had to worry about competition! If this has left you dissatisfied, we'll talk about it this weekend.

Were you really cynical about love and marriage before the August 14 picnic??? It is hard to believe.

After these last experiments of yours, what happens? Writing them up? Or are there other experiments?

If you ever had the least thought that you were checking up on me on my Saturday nite activities when you phoned, it was the farthest thing on my mind. Don't ever feel you need to check up on me. If I haven't told you what I was doing and you want to know, ask me and of course I'll tell you.

I'd love to see you Saturday all afternoon too but Mom has requested there is some kind of party she wants me to attend but we can see each other in the early afternoon, have a recuperation spell and then see each other around 8:30. Yes? And how about seeing your room? I'd love to or we can wait til Christmas for that?

Have just written my family…Better not get the two envelopes mixed up!
Love, Me

November 15, 1944
Dearest,
You were wondering about your position with my parents. As I see things now I'm not going to say anything specific to them for a while, at least until Christmas when

it may become necessary. I think it will help for them to get "used to you" not only you but the idea of you, if you know that I mean. They'd be very apt to object over the short length of time and, so we might as well let them think it's taken until Christmas for me to feel the way I've felt for some time already.

As to the problem about reaction to our enemies' "civilian populations"– it's a tough one. I started out a few years ago being much more soft hearted toward them than I am now. It's going to be a heck of a problem to determine who are leaders and have helped initiate the war and who have been innocent victims of circumstance... and should one wholly forgive those who were following the leader when the leader was wrong? In American courts we don't let a murderer go scot free just because they've been brought up in the slums and "haven't been given a chance." The rules would become arbitrary among many objections. Of course the thing to do is to get rid of the slums; but being realistic, what can you do immediately to those affected by the way the slums have been?

You were worried about your responsibility: how much you affect my school work and preventing me from marrying someone who could offer me more in the way of material things. The first of the two will come into the discussion to be held this weekend; the latter doesn't bother me. I'm not an expensive object. Money is important; I won't pretend it isn't, but it isn't THAT important. Not having it will make some things harder to do but I don't think the difference worth serious worry.

Today I am a new woman: I have flunked a test.! It's kind of a shame as I worked for it, trying to understand the darn stuff and it is in my major field…But it doesn't really worry me too much.

Today I learned something I've learned very often but each time I find it startling: that people one admires and that seem to have an extra amount of "good" have also equal amounts of less desirable attributes. I become more and more convinced that for every good there is a bad. Particularly in regard to people. The admired famous people have an equal proportion of worries and obsessions The geniuses are often the most miserable of people. There's sort of a parallel of opposites: good/bad; life and death and yet they don't remain opposites in the sense of wide differentiation between them. Does the good influence and help create the bad and vice versa? The eternal dynamism of action and reaction, the dialectic in Marxian terms . . . and I suppose then that life creates death and death, life.

Pardon all this but what brought all this on was on quite a different plane: It involves an insight into a character . . . a realization that a girl up here whose brain I have admired for a long time and envied, is quite immature emotionally. I hadn't thought so before but do now. Among other things we were discussing love and marriage, Rosey, Mary (the girl in question) Betts and I. Mary is rationalizing the fact that she doesn't think she'll ever get married by saying she thinks she'll lead a very happy life single. She doesn't think she'll get married because her ideals are too high and her specifications too great. She doesn't care about money or looks but has great ideas on his occupation, specifically stating that he be a teacher of social sciences, an anthropologist or a psychologist. She says she has never been in love but knows just what it's like thru a dream she had which she apparently puts implicit faith in.

She dreamt she was married and went thru all the emotional qualities of love; that he died and she experienced the emptiness of life without him. The last seems to have given her a fear of love in that she rebels against giving herself up to something bigger than herself. Fear of losing herself in it and the possibility of having the props knocked out from under her in the event that he should die. It's most obvious and illuminating psychological data! And yet I don't think it's serious cause she's fairly conscious of the loop holes in her thought, is intelligent and realizes she may change her mind. It ended up amusingly: Betts doesn't think she'll get married either and she turned to me in typical Rosey-esque manner and said, "Do you think you'll get married?" To which I answered, "I most certainly do!" It's funny; it's one of the few fears I've never had.

Tonight went to an Econ meeting just for those majoring in it, to hear Mrs. Norris, a former member of the faculty who's been in Hawaii with the OPA ever since 1942. She talked about her work and most of it was pretty dry stuff but she's such a wonderful person that she made the stuff come alive, vital and challenging. Much of it was over my head but I got enough to know that she's a real person and to add something to my meager knowledge of Econ. I'd heard a great deal about her thru Mard whose roommate was an Econ major and they both knew her pretty well. It's too bad she's returning to Hawaii as the dept. needs more with her humor and vitality.

Member when I said I loved you as much as was possible? As time goes by it increases. Don't think I'm building something up. I've tried every criterion I can think of and, like a mathematical problem, it comes out the same. I don't doubt it anymore – just continue to be amazed by it, at the idea of being in love … of it happening so smoothly so rightly and I never cease to be amazed at you. It's so nice to have fallen in love with such a terrific guy!!!

Hey! Would this be called a love letter? If it isn't so in a majority sense, it's in a minority one. So, being as I'm a minority, that I think the minority way is the best way, and that you are a minority, too, I send a major amount of love in a minority manner.

XXX A mixture of the tigress and the kitten.
P.S. And I'm not getting the curse!
Have been working 10 hours a day so as to ease my conscience in taking 2 and a half days off this weekend. Am reading "Moby Dick" and find it both good and bad, quite spotty and overlong … only two more days" Oh joy!! God, it'll be good to see you!
A sleepy warm passionate g'nite.
Your sleepy Tigress.
Duchess
P.S. too bad about Luce, n'est-ce pas?
P.P.S pleasant about Fish. Took long enough to do it but at least it's done now.

November 11, 1944
Very dearest darling,

There are so many things I want to say that they are all knocking against each other and the result is I've been seen sitting here staring at nothing, writing nothing.

Remember when we were talking about feeling sad without any real cause ... just certain sadness over life. I've felt it often and before I knew you but never as strongly as today. Part of it wasn't sadness over life in general but, first, no mail from you ... and that just shows how greedy I've gotten. I'd gotten one letter and a wonderful telegram and had no cause to complain. Then when your letter came this noon, I felt badly that you hadn't gotten any of mine. Don't understand it as I wrote to you before I wrote my family on Sunday night and twice since then. But I guess it's all straightened out by now. Just the same I felt badly that you hadn't gotten a letter Tuesday when of course you wanted it most that day, particularly after my attempts to send a telegram were frustrated.

About your telegrams for any future reference: the procedure is that I get a message saying there's a telegram at Main for me. I can either phone them for it or get it in person.

Anyway, feeling very lonely for you, I walked in the rain to Philosophy where I heard one of the best lectures I've ever heard in a class at college. It was Mr. V's last one to us (On Monday we get a new instructor who was out to have a baby). No matter how good she is she wont be Mr. V! He's been one of the best teachers I've ever had with the point of view I like and the obvious love of his subject and of teaching it, that inspires students. Mard had him when she was here and thought so too.

I came out of class feeling like a wet rag (literally as it was raining). Walked over to the book shop to buy Howard a book ... started reading a cartoon book and found myself laughing and feeling the better for it. Came back and dutifully wrote my parents and now here I am feeling ok but with the horrible desire to board a train and spend the weekend in a certain room on 193rd street. (But what would the poorly assimilated landlady say to that?) and anyway you've go an exam to study for and I have that American Lit Paper to write. So, let's be realistic and realize you miss him and want him but that you've got to do certain things you don't want to do so that you can do things you DO want.

Glad you had company to listen to the returns with.

Five weeks from now vacation starts; exams will be over and, God is my witness, I'll never look at another French book again! Do you get any Christmas vacation? If so, how much?
Love, love, love (three is my lucky number)
Duchess

November 11, 1944
Dear D.

I'm so mad and disappointed now, that all I can do is write you which is, to put it mildly, inadequate. After trying to write a lousy paper all day and having contemplated coming to NYC (I would have kept topic of finances and logic gone to the wind). Before dinner I had a sudden thought that you might call but put it out of my mind as wishful daydreaming. So Barb and I escaped all and went to the movies. It wasn't a successful escape as we both came out feeling incompleteness especially strong. Then to come back and find the message that you HAD phoned. I'm in quite a mood and only a certain something, called by some, "common sense" keeps me from hopping a train, leaving this place and marrying you. (Of course I knew you wouldn't have me now ... maybe that's where the common sense fits in. Is it going to be like this for one and a half years?)

Are we going to drive ourselves crazy the weekends we don't see each other? Darling, for Pete's sake, shut me up! I'm a selfish glutton and I'm being exceedingly greedy and unrealistic and stupid. OK feel better now. It's just that your phoning must have meant you felt the same way and the idea of both of us ... oh SHUT UP!

Got your letter and the pictures. I didn't like the x'd one, but both Barb and Rosey did and, as we agreed, you can't tell with pictures of yourself; maybe they and you are right. Sure, you can do anything you want with it. Can I have the negative temporarily, of the one of us full face. I like it of you the best I've seen and except for the sweater, it is passable of me. (Slips do not keep out the cold but they do prevent sweaters looking like that!) Do you want them back? Barb wants a copy of the x'd one so when you're thru can I have the negative of that, yes?

Don't worry about falling asleep in the middle of writing tho I do . . . cause it means you must be tired. As for my minding if you fall asleep, I certainly don't unless you do when I'm acting the part of the tigress (in which case, I'll continue the simile and bite your head off.) As for what we learned about each other at the Prom. Perhaps you didn't learn anything (not meant to sound derogatory) but I learned that being minorities we still could have fun in a strictly majority setting. It's one of those things I learn but have to repeat about myself or things involving myself. It's not that one learns slowly but the lesson has to be repeated over and over before its taken for granted. I thought you'd felt and learned the same thing at the Prom when we both decided we hadn't wanted to come and now were glad we had.

Nice news: for the next 5 weeks I'm a "sub" which means I don't have any regular co-op jobs but have to be ready to do jobs when people go to the infirmary. Not bad tho, as since most people are quite healthy ... will be nice around exam time, too. By the way, what's your phone number at the lab ... just in case I ever want to phone you during the day. I seem to remember the main number as being Wa-2000 but if I'm wrong, correct me. And what's the extension? (And don't give me Dr. Root's by mistake!)

Did I tell you Walt has now gone to Officer Candidate School? It's really wonderful as it's the first thing he's ever really tried hard to get and wanted very much. My family is so pleased. He's now at Quantico, VA.

Ellie told me Connie was getting A's at Wellesley until she met your friend Dave and now she's getting D's! What will I do?. starting with a good deal below an A average?

Barb and I took a walk in the afternoon and discovered

a new second hand book shop. We went in and had a long talk with the guy who runs it who's 1) intelligent and widely read 2) not only a liberal but a radical! Greatest surprise of my life!! He's had a bookstore in NYC and has just moved up here. He buys books in NY and around and resells them here. Wonderful assortment with lots that are now out of print. You'll have to meet him; he's quite a person and a "good thing" for the college and her humble surroundings.

If I ever remember it, I'll send you a copy of the "Misc" which is a good one and includes a discussion of the accelerated program and the Prom.

Heard tell of a girl who entered a friend's room Sunday afternoon after the Prom to find the friend in bed with her date. What doesn't go on (or come off) at this institution! (Was about to say we were wise to take precautions but that could easily be misconstrued!
Better just get some sleep before my mind sinks any further.)
All my Love, Duchess

November 13, 1944
Dear Family,

Have been engrossed in "Character types in Hawthorne" and "long run adjustment curves" in preparation for an Econ hour written on Wednesday. Last night was fun when the Econ dept. had a meeting in the living room of the Alumnae House for all Econ majors to hear Ruby Norris talk about her job on the OPA in Hawaii. She's just here for a short time and is planning to go back there. Her talk was very technical . . . Econ stuff . . . on the methods of price control, how they'd worked it out in Hawaii, the difficulties and problems but she made it fascinating. If most people talking on the same subject it would have been very dry but her personality and humor made it very enjoyable. I introduced myself to her and she wanted to know all about Mard, remembered Howard—that he was a doctor now and had taken her exam when he visited.

Other than that, the weekend wasn't much differentiated from the other days. Finally sent Howard a present. Looked thru millions of books and finally decided he'd like the "War Atlas" best. Hope no one has had the same idea . . . took the chance.

We had our new Philosophy teacher today. She's not bad but definitely not in Mr. Venable's class. I guess extra good teachers are pretty rare. The poor woman was so obviously nervous that she made me so in sympathy. We'll learn a lot from her, in a more cut and dried manner tho and minus the inspirational quality. The end of the term is not far off in weeks but there's an amazing amount to cover until then. "Moby Dick" (to be read in two weeks for Amer. Lit) a book report on "The Genesis of Plato's Thought" by Winspear for Philosophy and an extra Econ book we're responsible for, to mention only a few items.

Got a letter from Fred which took a month to reach me, as did my letter to him. It makes correspondence rather strange to be answering questions related to my summer job! Got missives from Bob and Dave both from overseas.

Did you receive my laundry box with my evening dress,

coat and spread in it? I sent it several days ago and it should have arrived. Let me know.

What's the news from Quantico? And Trinidad and NYC?

Love, from your youngest

November 16, 1944

Hello Darling,

I guess you'll receive this Sat. A.M. after I will have talked to you, so it'll be kind of stale. But there's nothing like stale cake when you're hungry except, of course, fresh cake . . . so you can see I'm sleepy and if you were here right now you'd say I lisped ... or shouldn't you give me chance to?

It's now 11 p.m. and for the first time I can really begin to think of this weekend as a reality. Every time I've started to before I've thought of the stacks of things to be done first and tried to concentrate on them.

Don't tempt me with "Look Homeward Angel." Let me luxuriate over Xmas with it.

I wanted to see your room but now that you've got me plastered all over it, I'm not nearly as intrigued. After all, if I have to look at me I can always use a lake or a mirror.

It IS hard to tell when someone's joking in a letter and I always figure it's better when in doubt to take someone seriously than to laugh when they're in earnest. I read somewhere one of the differences between white men and negroes was that when the former indicates humor in writing he writes (ha ha); the negro writes (smile).

Tres affectionately and impatiently! Your Duchess

November 22, 1944

Hello wonderful one . . .

I've been looking forward to this time all day as it's the time I allotted to write to a certain guy who bears a strong similarity—in fact is identical- with the guy I'm in love with.

6 minutes of the allotted time has been spent in day-dreaming.

Several amusing bits of news. What you do to me, Mr. K! I was so darn stiff all Monday and Tuesday and it wasn't from playing pool! I kept laughing about it partly cause it wasn't the kind of stiffness one can complain or explain to others and partly cause it reminded me of what had created it. (laughing isn't the right word . . . but I think you understand)

Then today we got our Econ exam back, and I'll never give my opinion of my own rating until I see the mark again. I could have sworn I'd flunked it. To prove my surprise I let out a shriek in class when I saw a B- on my paper. The teacher wanted to know what was the matter. I said I thought I'd flunked and she smiled tolerantly. Really it was a pleasant surprise.

Took bowling for my winter sport and had it for the first time. Did better than I have done in years. We didn't play any games, just practiced combinations but at one point I got a certain combination down four times in a row and I tried for hours last year to get it 3 out of 5 times. Out-of-practice luck, I guess.

Did you get the proofs of the pictures of me? Like any? Do you care what size? Do you want more than one pose?

Do you know I love you? Hey, how did that get in here?

Polly got head of SLA and Rosey vice pres. Which is good. I declined from running as they'll do as good , if not better job than I could and can still keep up with their work (and I probably wouldn't have gotten it anyway).

Been toying with the idea of calling you up and telling you to come tomorrow and it'll be much better in the long run if you don't, I keep telling myself.
Barb left this afternoon and will be away until tomorrow night so this place is all quiet and there's nothing to stop me from working, except you, darn you.

Am still undecided on the weighty matter of my academic future tho I've got an idea which will either wither or bear fruit soon. Don't want to say too much about it all, any one way or the other, til I know myself what's possible and what I feel.

Darling: you mentioned several times during the weekend that you didn't think I was sure that what I wanted was you . . . and I don't think I gave a wholly satisfying answer. All I can tell you is that every time I see you I love you more, and become surer you are what I want. You are the man to be my husband and the father of my children. I think we both agree I'm not ready to get married yet, tho I become less convinced (or more ready?) every day but I know that as time passes I love you more and more. (I wonder if I'll ever burst?)

Have a wonderful Thanksgiving. I know I wont be able to resist you if you call up tonite and still want me to come, but I've managed to control myself enough to keep away from the phone now for several hours. so I guess I'll be OK. We've got a heck of a lot to give thanks for … and I do. XXXOOO, Your Kitten

November 23, 1944
Dearest Darling,

    Every day proves something new. And today thru your absence I learned that you mean more to me than anyone else ever has or does. If you really thought that the next weekend apart after the last one would be less lonely, you were wrong. It's funny that tho I've always been very close to my family I've never been very homesick when away from them. Of course there have been times when I've wanted my mother, or Mard, around but never anything like the way I feel now in missing you.

    Part of it, I guess, has been the irony of your not being here (tho a good part of it was just the usual incompleteness.). The irony comes in the fact that it would have been just as good for my work and much better for everything else. I mainly didn't call up yesterday to ask if you still wanted to come because (I can tell you now as it's no longer existent) I had a bad sore throat which a) I didn't want you to get b) I thought it might get worse. I went to the infirmary where they scared the life out of me when they thought it was trench mouth. But they took a test on it and decided it wasn't. Got swabbed with some sulfur stuff and either that or 13 hours of sleep did the trick. It's almost gone today. So that was irony number one.

    Then dinner up here was wonderful and there was one

vacant seat which was next to me. (We had place cards!) All I could do was look at the empty seat, my food and shake my head. I did some work but no colossal amount and anyway, my work from now on is secondary to you. So it doesn't do any good to lament over the past. I do wish you'd been here and in the future shall remember this day as an example.

While I've still got the moral of the above lesson well in mind, can you come up the weekend of the first? Tho I'll be getting the curse and Walt will be home? I may have some work to do but will try not to and even if I do, I know it wont take all weekend ... And I can't wait till Xmas. (Take it easy — that's me talking to I or I talking to me, if you prefer).

The more I think about it, the more the New School is out. I'll probably stay here "b' term (the one following Xmas) and try taking 4 courses. That's today's decision.

After dinner today we had/gave some entertainment. A bunch of kids had made up a song for the occasion and I helped sing it...quite cute. A girl's father played some Bach. You'll have to teach me what to look for while listening to Bach. He's quite beyond me. And a girl did a hula-hula dance. (She's famed for same)- is quite an exhibitionist which you'd have to be to get up in front of a bunch of people scantily clad and wiggle. I got more amusement out of the 2 boys who were in the audience (we all sat around in the living room- she in the middle) who blushed the most beautiful blushes! The rosy hue started from their hair-line and crept over their ears to their cheeks and finally met in the middle of their faces.)

Can't I keep a little of my modesty, pride, in reserve? Just a little? I knew you had the brakes on in certain ways the last time I saw you and I mentally and at the time, silently thanked you.

Was a bit confused on your comments on your one and a half days of doubt. It was "a good thing" I guess. It was the Christmas business at home that confused you. I was much amused at your interpretation seeing as I'm usually having to tell myself that "we do have families to whom we're very attached and whom we like to see at times." I certainly didn't mean it that way (I'm laughing) and thought as I was daydreaming about vacation … and I guess I didn't express what I meant in lucid terms, should we say? I told my family I was coming in this weekend (just remembered in the middle of this sentence I'd said that already was reminded of it on rereading your letter).

Darling, you ARE cute. I'm going to feel a great gap in our correspondence when you finally stop writing about your choice of pictures.

For Pete's sake don't worry about Xmas presents and $ as far as I'm concerned. I've got your pictures, the pin and most important you and I don't need anything else.

I did have fun just now. I bought a bond (pledged at the bond rally mentioned in my last letter) and was sorely tempted to make it payable to Mr. and Mrs. K but I refrained …This is the first time in buying a bond that I've had selfish reasons along with patriotic.

Love, love, love you.

From Me

November 24, 1944

My most favorite one:

    I feel good. I've felt good ever since you phoned. I guess I'm still up in the clouds and being there everything looks in a different light. (celestial glow?) It seems strange to be writing you in the day time but I can't resist telling you I love you. I had taken time out just before starting this letter and was sitting in the living room luxuriously inhaling poisonous tobacco when I bethunk of all the different ways I love you: mentally, physically, spiritually, culturally, ethically, increasingly and absorbingly. I was so amused at me just sitting there alone searching for the right adjectives, that I had to write you. It's amazing how each time I think I can't love you more than I did an hour ago, I find I do. Methinks, my darling, that you've got a girl in love with you and that you'd have a heck of a time if you wanted to get rid of her. Gee, it must be hellish to be in love with someone who isn't in love back.

    Every once in a while I think of my letters objectively and smile at me: the girl who thought it would be years before I was in love enough to sincerely write the kind of letters I do write now.

    I've just read "Shipyard Diary" an auto biographical story of a female welder. Had to read it for Econ. It's a nice little piece of work; nothing sensational ... gives one a nice feeling of America the melting pot ... full of idealized but comforting types of people. Anyone with half a brain could have written it tho it's enjoyable. I can't figure out why they gave it to us to read for Econ. Not the usual assignment.

Barb had a fine time in NYC. I told her to call my family and say hello. Dad asked if I'd decided my future plans and Barb told him she thought I'd definitely decided to go to Sarah Lawrence, which I haven't.

Love, love, love.

Thy Kitten

Thanksgiving, 1944
Darling,

Just got back from the movies and guess what I saw: "Top Hat"! I know I'm in a hyper-susceptible mood because I enjoyed the picture tremendously. I had forgotten most of it and tonight it seemed the most perfect escape movie I've ever seen. I was Fred Astaire tossing off brilliantly nonchalant remarks, dancing on ball bearings. We sat at a table and sang and then suddenly magically we were on stage dancing together, the center of everything. It's only rarely that I completely lose myself that way but tonite after talking to you, the lonesomeness seemed less weighty and it was almost as if we were together doing these wonderful things.

About two days ago I had my first (and I think my last) moment of doubt about you. For about a day and a half I wondered if I'm really in love with you. Are you the girl I want to marry? Will I feel like this always? For a day and a half it lasted, then I came home Wednesday nite and found your letters and the pictures. I was a little afraid to look at them; I was scared that they'd be good, they look just like you and I wouldn't like them. Then suddenly the whole feeling vanished. The pictures look like you, smiling, trying to look flirty, and looking straight at me-deeply, sweetly. I felt like crying almost for there you were, and I loved you. Than I thought of that day and a half and realized how I had been talking to you, looking at you, thinking of you and now I'm sure, darling. I know that I love you and will forever. All this was in my mind while we talked over the phone but I didn't want to say anything, I just wanted to feel that we were together again and bathe in the warmth of the feeling.

There was a scene in "Top Hat" that struck me terrifically. They are dancing in a crowd-the song is "Cheek to Cheek". They look at each other, say little things and dance straight. Then wondrously they are alone on a big balcony. As if they've been pent-up with their feelings and now find themselves alone and free, they break into a swirling, twisting dance that somehow gives one the same tremendous release that I felt when we found ourselves alone last in your apartment. I felt ashamed to watch them as if I were intruding in a passionate love scene tho they were only dancing. I don't know if I've got across to you the emotion that drowned me for a minute, but my sensibilities are exceedingly heightened right now, and even tho I quickly realized that I was being absurdly sentimental, it was an experience that is only possible because of you. and I had to tell you about it.

Just stopped to re-read your letter to bring me back to earth.

I'm not going to offer advice or suggestions about your studies. You know the advantages and disadvantages of each place and you also know which no one else does how much each of theses factors mean. If you want to know anything in particular about Sara Lawrence I can find out from Clare who went there.

Right now I'm going to choose which of the pictures I like best. A is not one of my favorites; B has an expression but it is unflattering around the mouth. C. ummm. D, OK but not the best; E were you trying to look flirty? Can't decide between E and G for my non-smiling favorite this one and for C for smiling F ditto for H first and last one go together. Winners: C and F both smiling . . . there won't be much to choose between the two, but if the budget is tight, I'll settle for either one.

I'm sending my pictures under separate cover. (They should be kept that way.)

No, dear, I wasn't kidding about the necktie episode, but it's terribly unimportant. Remind me about it and I'll tell you why I mentioned it at all.

I know you were not consciously poised or dignified to impress Connie and Dave and that's just why I was so pleased. Perhaps unconsciously your upbringing and natural charm have made you an excellent hostess. I was proud because the fact that you're a wonderful person just sticks out all over you (couldn't resist that one).

I'll say good nite now with the tenderest but not the vaguest thoughts about you.
All my love,
Danny
P.S. Don't do anything rash unless it's with me!

November 25, 1944 (after Thanksgiving)
Dear family,

Another week and weekend gone and I don't seem to know where they fly to. Spent the day today mixing letter writing, studying for a polit test, and writing a Philosophy paper. I hope I don't somehow get them intermingled: writing about the Pythagorean theory of numbers, overseas describing my weekend in New York on the Polit exam, talking of joint resolutions and closures in the Philosophy paper!

Yesterday afternoon I went out sketching by myself and I would say it was more fun than fruitful. In my zeal I forgot the fact that my fingers would get numb which might hinder the great artist from giving her all but it was a beautiful day and the poor attempts, though poor, were fun. Tomorrow night Barb, Rosey, and I are taking Mrs. Ellis out to dinner in town which will be fun, I'm sure.

Thanksgiving was really nice here. They fixed the tables banquet style with place cards and the privilege of smoking at the table even supplied the cigarettes! (which is quite a feat these days.) The food was really tops with turkey and trimmings. Some of us sang songs and did skits afterwards. Only two more weeks of classes; one week of exams and then 18 days in New York!

Two things before I forget: could you send back my dry box so I can send a few things home for Christmas without having to carry everything on the train—and two, can you return the proofs of my pictures soon so I can have any you like made up and ready by Christmas. Hope you like at least one.

Unpleasant business going on around here. There have been too many losses of late to continue calling them losses. Barb had five dollars gone from her wallet. Today another girl had $3.50 gone; and today I too lost the green jacket which goes to my suit disappear. There is always the possibility that we might have carelessly misplaced them and I'd hate to call it stealing without direct evidence but the circumstances of these three cases do make it look suspicious. It's a pretty nasty business but I guess I shouldn't be surprised that hasn't happened more often. Some kids have had fur coats disappear and even things like perfume mysteriously disappear Shoes and tweed suits, too. Apparently the culprits aren't only short of cash.
Love, Me

November 26, 1944
Hello Dearest,
    You'd think that after just having talked to you I'd be doing something else rather than immediately starting this, but as you know, my appetite in regard to food and you is entirely unpredictable and hunger pains may arise at the most ungodly times.
    Your letters ARE becoming models for the French school-in your own restrained way, and the number of times I re-read them seems to vary directly with their warmth. (How much of love is egotism???)
    We used to indulge in such deep discussions and now our letters are full of us. Are we not as interesting to each other mentally or are mental considerations being

over-shadowed by emotional ones? (A round about way of saying I love you darling, let's TALK about it later!)

A minor confession is in order. The desire to call you came from the feeling that it's been two week ends but the means to call you twice within a week came from the fact that the operator on Thursday tried to give me 5 cents change and instead returned the entire 75 cents I had put in. This is just so you wont get spoiled and expect me to call as often in the future. With this admonition off my chest, I'll probably call just as often in the future.

With the orals behind me I'm beginning to breathe easier but there is next Thursday's exam. By next weekend it is going to be wonderful with nothing on my mind but you and I'll be with you.

You mentioned you may have homework to do. Don't hesitate to let me know if you do. I can read something while you study. You'd be surprised how well you can concentrate just knowing that the other person is right there. (This is from other people's experience, not mine). Mard and I have been discussing what I have chosen to give you for Christmas. She didn't think you'd like what I had chosen but in your family's tradition indicated her disapproval but left it up to me to decide. It was a pretty goofy idea in the first place and I wasn't much sold on it myself but I pretended my mind was made up just to tease her. When I finally told her I'd changed my mind, she was vastly relieved and said one test of compatibility was in choosing a gift the girl would like. I claimed that if a girl liked you enough she'd like your gift. The truth, as usual lies somewhere between the two arguments. Still I think that once you got used to it you'd enjoy a hookah.

Clare and I had a good experiment Friday and it may be the last of this series. The only hitch is that my determinations have gone screwy and I'll have to get it straightened out before I know the results of the experiment.

You'll get this around Tuesday which will mean only 4 days more til the visit and only 3 weeks to Xmas holidays. So long, darling, can you find a private room at college or will we have to send Barb to the movies?
All my esteem, affection, love, admiration, adulation, adoration, approbation, backed up by a healthy appetite.
Danny

November 27, 1944
Hello Darling,

So now I'm a wildcat (in bed)! I certainly am a menagerie! But I love it and I'll promise to be any animal you so desire. The appellation referred to above comes from your letter of today which had me squirming and laughing. (the squirming is in reference to your needling remarks about my shyness)

Ordered the pictures today but will let which ones be a surprise. As for yours: they came today and I disagree with Mard and Clare (It's their taste in men that is unaccountable for) i.e. I like the smiling one better. The serious one doesn't really look like you. I guess it's cause your face is rarely that expressionless. But I like them both just cause of the subject matter! I sacrilegiously cut your friend Harry off in the non-serious one and will return him to you if you want him. Do you consider it a good picture of him? It looks so very different from the snaps of him.

Glad you talked to Clare about Sarah Lawrence. I still have no definite plans except not to go to the New School which means I'll be back here for one more term anyway. Will visit Sarah Lawrence during vacation— or at least talk to some people that go there. I think as far as college for college goes I'd get more at S.L. but other things are involved such as I'd live at home. How that would work, I'm not sure. In some ways I think it would be better than here, not because of my family but for the change of scene aspect of things. Then there is the problem of being so near you. I know darn well it would accelerate our marriage date . . . which is something to consider.

Of your three reasons to wait about marriage: I think the first one still holds the most weight: being more sure of my vocation . . . not that it would make any difference to us what I decided to do but I think I ought to solve this before I take on more responsibility. It's a debatable point tho . . . as for your second point, waiting until I know exactly what I want: if you mean other than my own vocation and refer to the kind of guy etc I can't see how waiting would change me much on that score.

Today was a very long day. Every three weeks we have an extra hour of French and it came today. So had two hours of the stuff in a row with the Polit exam directly following that. The latter was a very nasty test full of little picky things. Everyone seems to feel the same way about it, even the girl who sits next to me in class who never gets below an "A" in anything.

Have written the Philosophy paper . . . just have to type it. When Barb and I went into town to return the proofs we did some window shopping for Xmas but as we had exactly 11 cents between us besides carfare back, it remained in the window. Haven't found what I'm looking for, you.

There's been an awful lot of stealing going on around here of late. It's disgusting but I suppose one should expect it in such a large group of people. And I don't see how it can be stopped other than locks for every door. It would be a shame if it really came to that.
Nighty–night my smiling chipmunk.
Love, V

November 28, 1944
Dear Family,
Here I sit, very Sunday afternoon-ish, listening to the concert—have been working and am now writing letters. Friday nite went to an interesting lecture at the Aula on race riots. Mrs. Kennedy of the sociology department gave the back ground, the psychology of it, which was interesting to me as we've just been studying attitudes and prejudices in Psyc. Then a Baptist pastor from N.Y. Mr. Powell spoke and was fascinating. I didn't agree with him on a good many points but he was an intriguing character anyway and did have some interesting ideas and statistics. He was part Jewish, part Negro, very egotistic, vehemently CIO—quite dynamic.

Amy's parents came up yesterday and we went to a delightful place–a private house where they have tables in the living room and the porch with a fire in the fireplace . . .

good food too. From there to a Spanish fiesta given by the Spanish Club which wasn't very good. Bagpipes supposedly are from Spain.

Thanks Pop, for the check. Glad my stay was worth the $100.

I didn't tell you the newest episode did I? The day before yesterday I received a small alligator in the mail from Dave! When I opened it up, it reminded me of the chameleon episode when I was young. Remember Mom? I had thought to send for one as advertised on the back of a comic book but had decided against it. You, Mom, found my letter and thought I had not sent it because it asked for a bit of money, so you kindly put that in and lo and behold, it arrived but I had forgotten all about it. I about had hysterics when I opened it up! This time the alligator was about 8 inches long and really quite cute. It said it lived on ground meat, fresh fish and required a cage the size of my room (which would necessitate my moving out!) I decided to donate him (her?) to the Zoology department. After deciding he looked a bit undernourished, they took him with plans to feed him up and then preserve him for posterity. Bet he shall go down in historic journals as being (I think) the first alligator to ride on a bicycle.

Between coconuts and alligators, I'm almost scared to ask for my mail. Hope everything is OK.
Love to all, Me

November 29, 1944
Dear Chipmunk,

Am torn between two desires: you and bed. Wont it benice when I can combine the two! Like correlating courses. But I figure right now I need you more than bed. I've gotten myself into such a darn muddle over myself and I don't know how to get out of it. I know perfectly well this college mess is much more than what it seems on the surface. It isn't good having so many courses etc but it isn't that that makes it so complex. It's mostly me and my preoccupation with where I'm headed. If I were sure of that, college as a necessary preparation would be more reconcilable. But I am not. I 've decided I'm right in the middle in regard to any categories I set up; between the factual and the creative; between the intellectual and the nit-wit. I'm a dabbler. I like to know a little of everything and never feel inspired to dig down deeper into one field and then on top of that I've got some of the most ridiculous complexes on social (more intellectual) scale and a deep feeling that I'm more suited to do things usually considered on a lower scale than I am the higher. And yet knowing they're lower makes me dissatisfied. I've got a concrete example of it in making a choice of courses for next term. I can take a sociology course or Econ course. The former I think is lower on the scale in factual material, the tone of the course intellectually; the Econ is superior. Yet I don't feel I'm fully suited to either . . . and I drive myself crazy trying to decide. I wish like hell I had your faculty for quick decisive decisions . . . this stuff is what I usually write to myself in Diary form. Don't know why I should bother you or send it on to you. But you might as

well get a fuller idea of the type of girl you've fallen in love with . . . You've still got time to back out. (That sentence is using the same psychology on myself as you use when you make cracks about my having other dates.
P.S. I really do wonder what you've fallen in love with. There must be plenty of wide-eyed adults much less mixed up than this one.

 I had been thinking in the above vein all day until I got your letter which made me feel very humble and unworthy of you. Decided then and there to go to NYC this weekend; partly to get away from here and partly so I could see you later . . . and if you tell me getting away from here is getting away from myself you're perfectly right. What keeps amazing me is that during all this uncertainty I still know you're right for me. So anyway: called you up which helped some. Then called home to a) wish Dad happy birthday b) tell them my plans. They're leaving at 3 P.M. to visit Walt and I cheerfully lied that I wasn't coming in til after then, so that I could see you and not them.

 For pete's sake don't worry about xmas presents and $$$ as far as I'm concerned. I've got your pictures and most important you and I don't need anything else. I did have fun just now. I bought a bond (pledged at the bond rally) and was sorely tempted to make it payable to Mr. and Mrs. K., but I refrained. This is the first time in buying a bond that I've had selfish reasons along with patriotic ones: I figured I'd rather save on things now so we'd have something extra when we might need it more than we do now.

 I'm awfully glad you feel that way about giving up your

independence et al. It makes things that much easier for me. I don't think you'll have much trouble with my independence either.

Sleep has conquered me...

XXX Duchess

Dearest,

Enclosing this letter from a friend of the family . . . received 10/8

After all the months of fooling around I've finally had some real work to do here in the Philippines. By a curious coincidence my Navy Civil Affairs Unit has been attached to the 96th Infantry Division for the past two months. After a long voyage out we hit this island on Oct 20th. Our unit landed on D-Day and there was a lot of work from the beginning. We found a group of bombed-out, hungry and almost naked group of a few hundred civilians on landing and it grew rapidly into the thousands. There were many casualties among them, mostly shrapnel and bullet wounds. So there was a lot of work for my four corpsmen and me under the primitive conditions. You can imagine that our surgical aseptic technique was hardly up to standard. However, thanks to sulfadiazine, the remarkable endurance and fortitude of the people, and luck, we lost very few of the wounded and have had no deaths from epidemic disease despite the worst possible living conditions and sanitation. I have never before seen such ability to stand up under mental and physical trauma, in all ages and both sexes. Now that things have quieted down, I'm getting a chance to learn a little tropical medicine.

Fortunately for us the Japanese failed completely in their attempt to put over their Asia for Asiatic propaganda. Officially they tried to befriend the Filipinos, in actual fact they despoiled them of all they ever had and maltreated them severely. We were welcomed with more enthusiasm than I think even the most optimistic expected. The guerillas particularly have assisted the campaign tremendously.

Our personal lives are easier than during that first period. We are however still living in dug-outs, under canvas. The mud, dust and especially the flies present a real problem. To think I joined the Navy to avoid all this! However we are now eating cooked food again, Filipino girls do our laundry and the scenery is of real tropical beauty.

I've had no mail for weeks so write whenever you can and tell me news of you all and of the world.
As ever, David

December 4, 1944
Dear Family,

Sounds as though you had a highly satisfactory time in our fair capital with our fair brother when he could get away and that you had a nice room and all.

I also had a highly satisfactory weekend . It was fun to be with Mard now that she is living in the apartment with you both. I think she misses Howard though.. I talked to Jane who applied to Barnard. Went to her house for a very nice party- Saw her parents– good to see them again.

If you are missing a loaf of rye bread, I stole it. It's such a luxury I couldn't resist. Barb and I devoured the whole thing yesterday. We only had a very dull knife so tore into it literally- tearing it apart.

Received a letter from Bill yesterday who is in New Guinea-very depressed because of a piece of rotten luck. He was accepted into OCS-even had his physical, but he'd already been assigned to a unit going overseas and they wouldn't release him. He wasn't really complaining in the letter but it was an unenthusiastic one.

I can't wait to come home –as for my Christmas presents I bought another war bond so I'm trying to save money therefore I shall be extremely happy if you would make your gift three pairs of underwear pants (I don't know whether I'm kidding or not). Really doesn't seem Christmas-y so much going on in the world.

Did you see that Glenn Miller was reported missing? Maybe you don't even know who he is. He was a bandleader and played some of my favorite songs.
This war is the pits.
Thanks for my laundry box. I will return it in a few days.
Love, me
P.S. Did you see that the Metropolitan Opera House hosted a jazz concert for the first time with all the great performers: Benny Goodman, Louis Armstrong,
Lionel Hampton, and Artie Shaw.
Has Dad ever heard of them??

Dear Diary;   December 4, 1945
Wow! What a wonderful date we have had.!!!!!!!!!!!!!!
By the time we got back to the apartment, I lit the gas fireplace and we were lying on the floor in front of it. We kissed and then his hand went under my sweater and he undid his belt and pulled his pants down… and my pants down. In a soft voice he said "spread your legs" and I did. Then he was inside of me! It didn't hurt (as it does in some stories I've read) and when he moved back and forth, I felt like a kind of explosion!

So that was what it's all about. I suddenly remembered when I was 13, I got my period for the first time and thought "so now I am a woman," but now I really am!

We lay there for a while and whispered. Then suddenly I was terrifically hungry. We went into the kitchen and raided the ice box . . . and giggled. Eventually he slept on the sofa and I went to bed one happy camper.

December 6, 1944
Dearest Cute One,

Before my eyes give out completely, I want to write you. First relaxation of the day. 9 P.M. and we're listening to Brahms 4th. Even with a scratchy needle, a lousy Vic, with a lot of dumb things on my mind, it still serves as an excellent "soother" and general relaxer.

Started reviewing (?) for French today. (felt my wings sprouting) I count the days, not only them but the hours, too.

My mother wrote me a much funnier letter than she knew. She said that when she came home she looked all around the apartment for signs of me. Finally found them in 1) hairs in the sink 2) two towels and 3) concluded I'd washed my hair in the sink. Boy!! Was she off track! I guess Mard didn't tell her you stayed over . . . all she said was that Mard had said I'd had a good time laughing. Kind of a one-sided comment as, after all, I didn't laugh ALL weekend, did I?

I'm still living in the glow of the weekend. For one and a half days I've been up in the air. Now I'm gradually coming down enough to see the future 9 days ahead and to continue to wonder about the future 2 -3 years. But the glow is definitely still there.

Got a letter from my dentist today in answer to my sending him the information on the Reader's Digest. He claimed to have been previously convinced of the appropriate opinion but said he'd be doubly careful from now on. Barb was all excited. She'd seen the letter in the box and rushed up in great curiosity to know who the mysterious male was that I'd kept secret from her.

We got our Polit exams back. I didn't do spectacularly: a B-. Had our last American Lit class before next year. That's going to be one of those distinctly sloppy exams: a one hour essay question so broad you swim around in it for 20 minutes trying to decide what it means b) what you think of it—agree or disagree c) why d) what you're supposed to think e) plus some shorter questions.

Music is so darn beautiful. It must be very satisfying to be able to create it. It's even satisfying to be able to put on one record after another.

Did I tell you that Barb and I devoured the bread in one sitting. It tasted wonderful.

Mard is right. We will have to see that Mom and Dad get to know you better and you can get more home cooked meals in the bargain. And anyway, I'm feeling generous and want to share you tho I'll only rent out small portions and for a short length of time (don't ask which portions!) (Who's dragging who down?)

Darling: what should we do about Friday? I wont get in til around 8 I guess and I wont be able to stay awake very long and I should get home…at least the first night… but I want to see you. I can think of nothing nicer than being sleepy in your arms. (Just then the music soared in triumph and the house bell rang calling one and all to a house meeting. Ah! the reality of life.

Pardon. Don't know what I was going to say but it's an hour later and I've just had thousands of instructions poured into my ears which have left the general impression that college life is definitely crazy, abnormal and nuts. I love you muchly.
XXX Me or Thy future wife.

December 7, 1944
Danny, my Darling,

Two important things to tell you: 1) in 187 hours I will

have finished exams, my college career in the year 1944 and will be free to think of you 100% of the time for days and days and days. 2) Second but by no means less important, I love you.

As you can see I'm in a better mood than I have been. Nothing has happened to change anything but the fact remains I'm less despondent-enuf- (Have you gotten used to my abbreviations yet? If you've managed these so far, perhaps I can advance to trickier ones. But I guess it's a lot to expect you to understand me AND my hieroglyphics (hierogliphyics? Last time I try.)

Have been feeling very near you all evening. Would have called you if I could. Think I will tomorrow.

Thinking over your comment that you would have felt as if we'd been married for a weekend, I decided I couldn't see how on earth you thought I was serious about maybe having to sell corsets in a department store if we could be. It was an exaggerated alternative and not meant seriously and I thought I had forgotten it. Then last night, for the first time I dreamt about changing colleges. There was much confusion and the scene switched and I was sorting laundry with my mother and that followed a long debate about a corset, who it belonged to, etc. The linking of the two things didn't strike me until noon today. What a sub-conscious you're marrying!

Did I tell you we'd gotten locks for our doors? There's been more stealing so they advised us to get them but gave us only one key for two people . . . as if we were Siamese twins! We haven't used it yet but will the next time you come up! The first question I asked when I heard about them was "Do they lock from the inside too?" (Always thinking of you, darling).

Three years ago America got a rude awakening. I'll never forget hearing the news of Pearl Harbor, being completely stunned and wondering just what living in a country that was at war would be like. And I feel very small and a little ashamed when I realize how little affected I have been. Sure there are less dateable men around and I have less sugar and I can pride myself on buying and selling war stamps, but actually my life hasn't been directly marred by it. It's caused some psychological changes, some mental thought about world affairs and many intangible things but I've made mighty few sacrifices and I feel pretty selfish (and just that much worse over not getting what I should out of college when so many people are just dying for one. Meant that figuratively but it's true literally, I guess. Three years . . . It's seemed much longer. I can't seem to remember a world without war; from Manchuria when I was 8, thru Ethiopia at 11 and England at 14. Darn it, we're going to do our utmost not to have a record like that for our kids. Tho it hasn't affected me that much, there are plenty to whom it has. I've lost some of my very idealism in thinking this will be the last war but I do think still, that it's possible for us to learn from our experiences and keep learning so that maybe in a thousand years, if there's still a world left, children will read about wars not in newspapers but only in history books. And yet the paradoxes of life! In the midst of so much horror, destruction and sadness, we, you and I, fall in love, be happy and experience some of the finest of basic emotions. I'm not ashamed that we can and do, rather proud of it and thank 1944, being me and you being you so I can so sincerely say I love you.

Duchess

December 10, 1944

Dearest Darling,

    Too bad you can't take the exam for me seeing as you're constantly first in my mind. I live mainly in dreams of the future, disgust at most everything in the present. Barb and I went to the movies for escape last night and it helped quite a lot. Didn't help her as it was "The Seventh Cross" and usually considered depressing.

But it was just the kick I needed to get me out of myself and to realize what a spoilt selfish brat I am. So I really came out feeling much better tho it was quite a movie! I read the book this summer and found it stuck quite closely to it tho it left out many of the finer touches.

Typical: some one just ran down the hall shouting joyfully: "I'm up to the the third century!" It's a stupid week and everyone gets on each others nerves. The atmosphere distinctly strained and the silly part of it is, its' all so unimportant and unnecessary! In fact, it's all so ridiculous that I can't get down to work. My mind wanders and time passes. I guess I shouldn't write to you at a time like this; I'm so empty of emotion except to get over the present and into the future and life shouldn't be like that

I smile at your picture, wink at you, try to make you smile and turn back to my book. Can't wait to see you; talk to you and kiss you. Would love to go on writing but must get back to my bed-lam. P.S. If you should just happen to phone any time this week, I may be out Tues. and getting another "kick" I doubt it but I'd hate you to phone and me to miss you and you to miss me.

Unless I hear otherwise, I'll phone you when I get to the station in Poughkeepsie at 5:15 ish on Friday.

All my love and most of my thoughts. V

December 11, 1944
Danny Darling,

Well, now that I've lived thru this day, I feel I can live thru anything. Of course that's exaggerated but it HAS been rather hellish. I got the curse this A.M. which you may think is a mere nothing and compared to some things I guess it is, but after you've once seen me in said state you'll know more what I mean. I couldn't study. I couldn't eat and I was afraid I couldn't take the exam. After consuming a cup of tea and a couple of bottles of drugs, I crawled over to the building to do my best. I knew I couldn't take the make-up exam as it conflicts with others and I'd tried to reach my Prof. before but she was away. So 10 minutes before the exam started I went up to some unknown woman who was the proctor and asked what I should do in case I collapsed in the middle of it. She advised taking it in the infirmary so I crawled to the infirmary. They took one look at me and filled me full of another bottle or two of drugs and I took the exam in peace, quiet, bed and drugs. Luckily it wasn't very hard nor a very good exam and I can't remember one single thing I wrote. Just praying I passed it. The system in the infirmary is wonderful for honest people: quiet, peace and for dishonest people? They just put the exam down and shut the door without once looking to see if I had any books with me. After two hours and five minutes I rang the bell saying I'd finished. Of course I could have had more time. I could have kept it for 6 hours and no one would have known the difference. I've since heard that many people make use of this craziness and pretty awful things go on.

    I left after the exam still feeling pretty lousy but there was a required chapel to go to. And what a chapel service it was! They've found two of the girls doing the stealing... not only stealing on campus but forging checks in town etc. and they were 2 girls I knew. Both were Phi Bate, brilliant, radical on the Misc board (newspaper) and a good friend of some of my friends. They were both due to graduate next week. Of course, they wont now. As a matter of fact, I think I mentioned them to you in a letter once. They'd come to dinner and I'd commented that tho brilliant etc. they lacked warmth and charm. I think I wrote about them as examples of "brains aren't everything." Well, they aren't! But tho I hadn't liked them much, it was still quite a shock and particularly as they were good friends of Rosey's and Pat's.

    The best part about today was the MALE box. Barb got

two letters from Johnny and I got two from you. One I got via Rosey who brought it to me this morning midst my groans and the other came after I'd just left the infirmary. So once again, your timing has been so right. I love writing to love-sick puppies but I've got to get at that darn Polit. No one will know how I'll bless 4:30 Friday. It's just so stupid and such a bother and there are so many things I'd rather be doing.

All my love, respect, honor, kisses, and thoughts.

Your crampy kitten

December.14, 1944
Dearest,

Don't know if this will reach you before 4:30 Friday. We'll have enuf time to discuss our problems to our hearts content so I'll make this a newsy letter.

Last nite Clare spoke and did very well. A typical incident near the beginning of her talk put everyone in a sympathetic mood and it went over fine. She had finished explaining her first slide, turned toward the back of the room and asked for the next one. It was thrown on quickly and silently. She waited a few seconds then repeated her request for the next slide. There were a few second of silence and we all waited to see her reaction when she realized it had already changed. She turned to the screen again, Clare- style said "Oh dear, I'm wrong again". Everyone laughed good-naturally especially our Physiology Dept's cheering section.

We then moved to your folk's apartment for beer and

pretzels. Your mother was at a concert and came in later and your Dad followed shortly after from a Phi Beta Kappa meeting where he had heard Rumble speak. I pulled the second boner of the evening (before your parents were around) by mentioning one of the women who had been at the meeting only to find that she had also come up to join us as she went to school with Mard. We gathered round the table and were joined shortly by your Mom and Pop where the following impressions and incidents were noted:

I would occasionally think of previous events that had occurred in the apt and smile to myself wondering if the same thoughts might be passing thru Dr. Root's and Mard's fertile brains. Most of the time I had to keep a close eye on Clare and steer away quickly when she seemed on the verge of a not-too-happy comment, tho she manfully succeeded in not alluding to us. I heard the story of the fire once more, only this time from the point of view of your father discussing butterflies at 2 A.M. with a curious fireman, and being reminded very much of the lovely walk down a country road one sunny Sunday morning. These are the events noted. The impressions are much more subjective and consequently more liable to error. It seemed to me that your mother's eye was upon me a rather large percentage of the time. She is always charming and very kindly mannered, but it seemed to me last nite she was unusually so.

As we broke up and prepared to leave, I somehow found myself alongside of her, discussing etchings in general, the ones on your walls in particular and a search

I've been making to re-discover a certain etcher whose work I had once seen in a book years ago and have been unable to locate since. Afterward it occurred to me that besides being friendly and trying to put me at my ease, your mother may have been interested in a closer look at a rather familiar pin which I was proudly wearing in my lapel. Your Pop was his usual self - friendly, full of anecdotes and entirely un self conscious, accepting me very casually (in the nicer sense of the word) as an old friend of the family's.

This may be an old story or quite fresh depending on when you receive this letter, but it was certainly foul of the curse to wait till your finals began. I wonder what our anti-love Rosey thought as she played the role of cupid in delivering my letter to you. I'm afraid her love of people as well as of THE people doesn't favor a long bachelorhood for her. I wonder if the idea that love is sufficiently strong to break down a person's independence doesn't tempt her to investigate the matter. If her independence means so much to her, she should be eager to discover something that may mean even more.

Tomorrow I will wait for your call or if it doesn't come by 5:30 assume that you caught the train around 5:10 or thereabouts. One day for me—only hours for you
(if this arrives tomorrow).
See you soon,
ALL my love,
D.

Dear Diary,   January 5, 1945

Well Xmas was different this year. Since Howard is away in the Navy and Walt is away in the Marines we felt their absence greatly. We usually celebrate Xmas eve with a great meal followed by Mom playing "Oh Tannenbaum" on the piano when we then open presents. Dad gets the most as they are from many "grateful patients." (Parents of kids he has healed during the year). Of course I wish Danny was here but he never has celebrated holidays at all. When he was little his grand father gave each child pennies for each nite of Chanukah but they were never religious or anything. After Christmas, Barb, Danny and Joe,(fellow D got for Barb) and I went for three days to Bridgeport, CT to Barb's father's wonderful big house on a lake. He is divorced and lives there alone with a zillion books and a frozen lake! There were lots of ice skates available and we all skated on this big lake for hours. D later told me he's never skated before in his life but he was determined to do it and he did. (I did notice his ankles were not straight up and I bet they were sore afterwards but he never said a word about that.)

We read and sang and cooked and made "s'mores" by the fire and had sex . . . on a bed this time!!!! Now back at college which is an anti-climax to be sure.

January 3, 1945

My darling,

Back in my sloppiest clothes in my little room, writing to you. But as yet I'm not in my college slump—partly, I think cause I feel as if I'm still with you. You're so much a part of me now, so much in my thoughts and yet I'm still greedy in preferring you "in the flesh".

It's been a terrific 18 days and I'm so happy about us and that you love me that all else seems unimportant. Every so often I feel my ring and smile. If I'm alone I wink at Fooless; blow a kiss in the direction of your picture and generally feel good all over.

Life goes on; they pile on the homework; I've been to 4 classes in one morning; I listen to tales of vacation; cheerily greet people and yet I feel incased in a glow which no one can touch, except you.

I'm so sure we're right that what we've got is something to be prized for ever and tho it's still a bit terrifying, it gives me confidence-confidence in me and the world as a whole. It wasn't so bad last night after you left. And you are so sweet to come all the way here and then have to take the train all the way back right away. I had a lot to do in fixing up the place and talking to kids . . . couldn't squeeze in a letter to you tho I wanted to. When I started to, it was midnight and I thought I'd rather wait til today when I was a little more awake.

Classes so far are good. 8:15 Econ and we have Miss Newcomer for the next 5 weeks which is swell. She wasn't teaching #105 last term so I thought I wouldn't get her.

We got our Econ mid-years back and I got a B which was OK too. It was good to hear Mr. V. again. Sociology promises to be amusing-taught by a new man, Mr. Serjimaki who is young and egotistical with a love of trying to shock us college girls – continually making cracks at the leisure wealthy class etc. I can't tell whether it's a good idea or not. Our Psyc. Prof used to do it, but more subtly and humorously. I think this man does it more in a show off way. But I wont condemn him for that. The class promises to be quite easy, informal and possibly interesting . . . all about city planning. Have a book report due in two weeks. Also included in the course is a week of field work in town which sounds as if Miss Newcomer's ideas may be put into action sooner than expected. 4th class was an Econ lecture on Social Security.

Amusing if crushing incident: when we were trying to get Barb a date for the prom we asked Bob S. He made up a fancy excuse of having to go to a wedding but it sounded like a nice letter, member? Barb just learned today he was AT the Prom with another girl from this house too! A rather raw and dangerous trick.

I try to write little things that are going on but my mind just keeps running right back to you and how wonderful you are; how you smile; how cute you were ice-skating- kidding with Barb's father, how we went to Princeton , ripped the couch—how beautifully you handle me and life in general. (Get your mind up to my level!) - how cute you looked asleep; how we made use of the living room pillows; how we laughed, flirted, talked, kissed. For some strange

reason, darling, I think of you. We're going to have a terrific life together. You're IT! And I'm so glad to have found you. I knew what I was looking for—only you're better than I imagined. All of me except one corner of a lobe of my brain belongs to you, my heart, my soul and certain anatomical details which you can always look up in a certain book in a library. I must come down to earth ... and go bowling!
Your fiancée, V

January 4, 1945 on yellow paper!
V. Darling,

It would be crazy for me to even attempt to put our vacation into words. If that other weekend (when your parents were in Washington) had continuity about it that we'd never had reached before, these past two weeks seemed to start at that level where we left off and hit an entirely new plane. Up until now we've talked about marriage pretty definitely but now it seems so much more concrete-so real that I can almost reach out and touch it. This may be a funny analogy but I feel like someone who has suddenly bridged a gap between a civilian and a soldier at the front. I'm LIVING our life together now where before it was a mental, tho vivid, and now is a real picture. How we'll ever reach such heights again is beyond me but I know that we'll exceed them.

The hell with these formal words. Darling, I love you completely, entirely and finally. You constantly reinforce all of my feeling in so many ways-love is made up of such little things. You could be everything that you are and I would like you exceedingly, but it's because of your look at certain odd moments, a smile or a softness in your eyes, a tilt of your face or a lovely wicked thought you get- it's for these things and many more that I love you and could not love anyone but you no matter how many of your qualities he, she or it possessed.

The train pulled out about 11 on Tues. nite and I got home about 2 A.M., but I slept late and wasn't bothered in the least. I spent all the next day getting ready for the first blood flow measurement but, as always, a little bug crept into the works and it took all day to work it out. The measuring device is in a glass bulb through which water flows from out the tap which can be regulated to stay right around 39 degrees, so I hooked it up to see that everything was OK. Soon bubbles started to come out of the water and fill up the glass bulb so that I couldn't time how long it would take the blood to flow through it. Then I tried hooking up a trap so that the water would flow thru the top and out at the bottom but still bubbles came. I tried a larger trap, then both together. Still bubbles. Finally at 6:30 I took out all the traps, hooked it back up directly to the tap and let the bubbles collect. After a while a larger layer of air collected in the glass and it suddenly dawned on me that it was perfect just like that!
Love, Danny

January 5, 1945
Dearest Darlingest,
   "It's getting so that I don't know how to start these letters

or what to say-no words seem adequate: "Dearest, darling, I love you, I miss you, I think of you constantly-how far they fall below my thoughts! I don't even want to use superlatives to describe you-even they are too defining because you're you, which to me means more than words or sentences can describe. Shall I say simply that you are a part of me as much as my eyes and hands or beard, but I am free to love you completely and unashamedly in a way that I dare not love myself. (Thank God you're a woman!) I just stopped to re-read that last sentence. I don't like it. I just can't compare my love for you to anything else, least of all to myself.

I've been home a half an hour now, re-read your last two letters and am beginning to feel less tired. It was amusing and significant to see how much alike our first letters were this week. Especially all the small things that we remembered about each other-and how we both signed our letters "fiancé". Informal engagements are fun. Let's do it more often.

Today was a hectic maddening day as was to be expected when something new is tried. I was careless in picking out a dog and didn't notice till he was on the board that he was so tiny. The poor thing weighed only 11 pounds–about half the size of what you would call a small dog. Consequently, tho I had avoided the most obvious troubles by planning ahead, we ran into unexpected difficulties such as the dog's arteries being so small and not long enuf. In addition he was one of those kinds we meet occasionally on whom Novocain doesn't have the usual effect so that he squirmed maddeningly every time I touched him. Despite these "added attractions" the experiment was a three quarters success since we got the flow meter on him and ran a control series. After bleeding, however, the blood clotted and we got no post hemorrhage data. All in all it wasn't too bad especially for the first time and it seems certain that there won't be any insurmountable obstacles to this method. Working with a dog who acts as if he's in pain is extremely wearing on me–somewhat the same as hearing a baby crying.

Got a letter from my sister Ruth today in which she asks me to forward her thanks for the book from you. What did you mean by that crack of Barb's about my dancing? I know a) Barb was cock-eyed b) I know I'm not a good dancer, But I love you for disagreeing with her. I'd love you if you HAD agreed. I'd love you even if you didn't. I'd love you if you were flat cheated, I'd love you if you snored. (I doubt if I'd love you if you were fat).

I mentioned a Boston trip to Mard and invited her along, (suppose she said yes?). Harry called up unexpectedly yesterday. He was in N.Y. on business but hadn't time to drop in Friday night. For a minute I thought he was trying to get transferred here but he said he can't get released from his present job for the duration. I think I mentioned to you our long conversation, how he's in the doldrums etc. and I think change of scenery (meaning a chance to meet some girls he'd like) would do him worlds of good.

I spoke to Joe on the phone yesterday. Was kind of worried because he hadn't shown up for work at all. He said he has a touch of grippe and I think he's still bothered by a headache. He sounded OK and said he feels all right but is going to rest up the balance of the week. I wish I'd known about his headache before. He asked for Barb's address and while I was musing on the thought he said something about writing her a thank you note. So I don't know if that was the only reason he wanted it. He also said several nice things about you or rather I said them and he added "and how!"

Last nite our Phys Chem. Mourning society got together to do this week's problems. The Dutch fellow had a sad story to relate. They are just getting news out of Holland and practically all of his family is either underground or unaccounted for which he thinks means concentrations camps. We're having an exam Monday for which I'll have to prepare mightily since I can't seem to recall anything I knew before Dec. 15th. Our final exam for this term will be Monday Jan 22 but fortunately it's all problems so that it won't interfere with any week-end plans. It's not the kind of stuff you have to memorize at the last minute for later regurgitation.

I investigated opening a bank account and have vetoed the idea-at least as far as the Corn Exchange is concerned. Unless you have a balance of $100, they charge something like $2.50 per month which is absurd. Instead I've decided to separate my "cash reserve" from the salary checks and so if I can keep it intact and add $10 per month. I need a suit and some other clothes (besides shirts) so I doubt if I'll be able to save much for a couple of months, but I'll see what I can do. I think I can regulate myself enuf not to have to have a bank account to keep me in line.

Haven't received a letter from you yet, so I don't know how the impact of school has hit you this time. (I'm trying to be prosaic as I can about not seeing you for 18 days, but no matter how lucky we are compared to other people, its still hell.

I've read over the Misc newspaper and the Lampoon of P.M.–also showed the latter to Clare. Do you want the Misc back or shall I throw it out? The book went back to the library without incident.

I guess that will be all for now except that even if you already know it, I must tell you that I love you and think of you all the time and would now consider the Harlem River if anything ever happened to you. So long dearest one.
p.s. I dreamt that I was a murderer. What does that mean?

There's about to be a round table discussion on Greece over WHN. I'll see if they say anything worth noting. Alfange, George Hamilton, Coombs, Sidney Walton and some other guy talked but I didn't hear them. I looked at your picture, started to day dream a bit, and the first thing I knew the program was over and I hadn't heard a word! Sorry, darling. What a cockeyed world. That fiend, my Phys chem. Prof (of all people) is coming between us. I have to stop now and study for her exam due Monday nite. But I'll show her—all the time she thinks I'm studying Phys Chem the better part of me is really with you.
Good nite my love, love, love, love,
Your Fiancé
P.S. I cant resist these PS's to you. It's like just one more good nite kiss.

January 6, 1945

Danny darling,

    I feel a little the way you must feel when you sit down to write. The place is quiet and the ticking of the clock reminds me of the passage of time. Am snuggled in a blanket and smoking a cigarette.

    I got your yellow letter yesterday and was again surprised at 1) how many of our reactions are the same and 2) how much better you state them than I. I'd hate to admit to anyone else how often I've read that first page! And to let them see it! Goodness, someone might think we were in love!

    No matter how often I reread the back page of one, I don't follow exactly this blood flow business. Was the diagram the whole measuring device or only part of the "little bug" messed up? I'm only half teasing you-I can see now the layer of air would solve the seeing part but I still don't know where, in the diagram, the bubbles collected. Aren't you glad you don't have me as a student? Or do you? But seriously, I hope the following experiments are working as they should . . . Hoping it selfishly and otherwise. The otherwise is cause I want what you want and the selfishly is if we get what we want, we" get other things we want all the sooner.

    Gee, that's a shame about Joe. I hope he's really OK now. The amusing side of it is that it will be forever debatable as to who gave which to whom. i.e. Barb being sick too. At present she's in the infirmary tho I just spoke to her and she said she's better. I loved the idea of your saying nice things about me and his "And how." It's sort of like asking a question and then giving alternatives of "yes" and "yes".

Was trying to picture what you're doing right now. Thought of the "Arrowsmith" conception of you pondering over blood flows in a very romantic white lab coat . . . but thinking it over, you're probably unromantically engrossed in Phys Chem.

You know, one of the few things I can think of that we may disagree on will be the matter of money. I think I've got a much stronger idea of rainy day money than you do. Maybe it's my natural inclination toward worry. But I guess we can work that out. I don't mean guess, I KNOW we can. That all came from your comments re bank accounts. I think you're perfectly right in not starting one. Only I don't quite understand the "cash reserve" you mentioned.

I wasn't being as nice or prosaic to you when I wrote of how I missed you—only I think at the time I wrote I mentioned that it wasn't to make you more lonely. Nope, it didn't. If it did, from now on I'll tell you I don't miss you in the least and you can call me a liar in exchange.

It's probably just as well you don't talk of me so much to Mard. Even without the Root business it's probably a bit wearing for her.

You can throw away all the Misc newspapers. How do they compare with Purdue or any other college papers you've seen? After years of French, what do I do but spell fiance wrong. Almost did it again, by Gosh! But as you say spelling isn't important. There are other things more important about that word!

Last nite I finished "The Turn of the Screw" and tho I found it fascinating, I'll confess I'm quite lost. I think I got some of its implication but I'm sure much of it went over my head. I found it confusing partly cause there's no strict dividing line between its face value and its psychological one. Often there are two interpretations that the author gives you and the line between is quite indistinct. In this way it reminds me of "Thunder on the Left" by Christopher Morley which I think you'd like, if you haven't read it. I read it first on my 15th birthday out West and again on my 18th in CT so have decided to make it a tradition to read it every three years on July 3! I wonder if I'll remember on my 21st.

Did some Philosophy in the libe this morning and suddenly found I'd been thinking most intriguing thoughts while supposedly reading Descartes. I was making all sorts of plans for a stolen weekend . . . that we'd meet somewhere and spend the weekend together. What thinkest thou? Also . . . I guess I should only come in for one night Jan 20th much as I hate to make it that short. If I take 2 for Connie and Dave's wedding and one for the next weekend for Mom's birthday, I'll be going over my quota. Could always cheat but I hate to do that.

Have been reading Simon's Strunsky's "Mean City" for a Soc. Report and it's certainly a funny book about NY . . . in such a chatty conversational style that it's hard to know what to make of it. I don't know whether he means it ironically or shows naiveté. Oh well.

Finally got my Philosophy paper back from last term: a

B which is better than I expected. I don't know whether it's being away from you or what, but I find myself continually starving! Prophetic note: slept with Fooless again and dimly recall giving him a shove in the wee hours of the dawn, found him on the floor in a most uncomfortable position in the morning. Need I say more?

When anyone asked me who gave me the divine locket I say some cheap skate and refrain from making all sorts of possible puns. Sadly enough for them, I don't mention that he's a terrific guy who I'm in love with-who writes wonderful letters full of diagrams, rides with me back to college, buys me cigarettes I'm smoking, looks at me and the world the way he does, has a delightful curl I love to twist and smooth and irresistible ears . . . and other things.

Rosey has been here talking. Among other things about how she gets no pleasure out of kissing a guy. What would the world be like without individual differences?
All my love–V. Only 14 days til I give it to you in person.

January 8, 1945
Darling,
From what you say, I guess this weekend has hit us both the same. It's not a general "missing you" feeling, but a definite concrete idea not only of wishing you were here but also why I wish you here. The idea of a stolen weekend is something I've been pushing to the back of my mind ever since we talked about the Boston weekend. I don't quite see how the heck we ever could make it, with the watch they keep on you. Surely your family must know

how many leaves you have. It'll be a disappointment if you can only come in for one nite the weekend of the 20th. The way I had figured, you'd use 2 leaves a month, 3 in February, 2 in March and one in April since you'll have exams in April and probably couldn't get away if you wanted to. I had figured on coming up at least twice-the end of Feb and March. Of course those visits mean early hours and not being alone, but I just won't consider more than three weeks between seeing you. (Even two weeks seems too long when we're only 80 miles apart.)

There was an interval of 20 minutes between the last sentence and this one. I reached for a cigarette and discovered I had none here while two full packs repose in my desk at the lab. Then I found there wasn't even a scrap of tobacco in the room to put in my pipe, so out I zoomed to try the neighborhood stores. It was just about eleven and 3 of them closed in my face. I finally found one open and settled for tobacco and paper so now I'm smoking a homemade thing that isn't half bad considering that I have rolled one since 1937 when I lived in Washington with my sister Ruth (and burnt a hole in her sofa).

To get to writing: I've been thinking of some of the ways in which you've proved to me that you are ready for marriage. (I don't mean to sound as if I've been carrying a list around checking off requirements as we go.) These things occurred to me only after I realized that you had done them. First of all, the realization that you are ready to settle down, have had enuf "glamour" and experimenting with different types of guys, and have decided that you don't want what I'm not which is almost as important as wanting what I am. Then you've blossomed so beautifully sexually(!). I know you're waiting for me to say I expected this to happen so I'll say it, but the intimacy we've found physically is such a warm binding thing that it's wonderful to know that we share it. Finally, it's nice to know that there won't be a tug of war between your family ties and your feeling for me. It may surprise you that this angle ever occurred to me, but when you think of it, there's a might big T.L. to your parents and your own mental balance that you could shift so smoothly to give me a high spot in your loyalty without disturbing your close relationship to your family. All these may be somewhat boring and old stuff to you, darling, but I like to think of how true your deepest instincts correspond to my idea of a perfect wife, besides all the little things, besides your imagination and your zest for living, laughing and loving.

    I was disappointed that my letters to you were slow in arriving this week. I wrote one on yellow paper Wed. afternoon and it hadn't arrived on Friday but I guess we're caught up. I'm having a heck of a time keeping the days straight this month as I haven't got a 1945 calendar yet so I wrote in the day of the week on top of December's calendar to make it right for the month. The only trouble is that I can't get used to having Sunday appear where Thursday usually is. Confused? So am I.

    This has been a working week-end. Did great heaps of laundry all this morning. I'd been washing from day to day these past couple of weeks. It's amazing to see the number of crumpled but otherwise clean-looking handkerchiefs that have piled up. From now on I think Ill send the darn stuff to a laundry. The small expense involved is worth the time and trouble.

Yesterday, the rest of today and tomorrow are strictly reserved for tomorrow nite's Phys Chem exam. I'm completely lost since the last examine- have lots of catching up to do. That so and so of a teacher not only lectured ten minutes over-time on Thursday and included the lecture in the exams but also included the rest of the chapter which she hadn't had time to cover!

You may be amused or at least pleased by a little drama that's being enacted around the place these days. Roughton is back for a stay of several months. Have you ever met the guy? He's close to being the least self-conscious and most self-centered guy I've ever met. I suppose you've heard about him from Mard. He is subject to heart attacks which is why he was sent from England for the duration. He has a special cot in his lab and in addition demands constant attention. Well, he's picked Root as his nursemaid! Root tells the wonderful story of how last year Roughton was lying down, recovering from an attack when he called Root in and informed him that he had to urinate and Root finally came up with a liter graduate cylinder-an enormous thing about twice as long as a milk bottle with the diameter of the largest part of the bottle. Roughton looked at it skeptically and said it wouldn't do. Root said he thought it was big enuf and Roughton shouted back with his rich British accent," It isn't the volume, that's too small, its' the bore!"

To get back to the main story since Roughton is back, Root hasn't had two minutes to himself and is he burning! Anybody else would see that Root and Mard were engaged in conversation but Roughton walks right in and just stands around without saying a word, all of which is terribly sad especially since Roughton demands company practically every evening. Since Mard told me this without any embarrassment, I assume her relations with Root are entirely on a companionship basis and would be nothing to be concerned about if they stay that way. Mrs. Root was in the other day, and I had my first close look at her. It wasn't hard to see why he isn't completely satisfied with her. Gee, it's wonderful to know that the girl I love is so completely just exactly what I want.

Still haven't heard from Dave but I'm sure he hasn't changed his plans. I doubt if the fellow for whom Dave was best man will be able to come in from Missouri to return the compliment which leaves it strictly up to me. What does a best man do and what does that make you? At least I'll be able to get a close up of the routine.

From now on I'm going to try writing from the lab when ever I can. At first there may be a difference but I guess I'll soon get used to it. I do as much dreaming and cigarette smoking while writing to you that it just eats into my evenings when I'm supposed to be studying. Next to getting your letters (when we're not together) the best part of my day is when I write to you. I've just got to figure a way so I can write and study.

By the way, what did Rogers and Clark stand for on the

outside of the envelope? All I know about them is that they explored the virgin forests of the Great Northwest. Or are you getting me used to a couple of your favorite names for our children? I guess that's the way things will be with us: you'll be busy laying foundations and I'll try to take care of the other things around the house.

For the last half hour I've been dragging along, hating to get to the end of this letter, but I've got to leave you now. So long, darling. Don't forget that I love you: Impatiently, Lovingly, Opinionatedly, Violently, Erotically, Emotionally, Yearningly, Osculating. Urs D.

January 9, 1945
D. Darling,
I love you. Words are inadequate and still I love you. Reasons for same: the usual and important one, plus an unexpected letter today. I thought that the Phys Chem would deplete the postman's pile today but as usual you (and he) out-did yourselves.

Sometimes when I get your letter I feel like I do about exams or papers when after I've written mine and read someone else's who's gotten an "A" I feel, "Why didn't I say that? I meant to." But the nice thing about it is I don't feel any jealousy in your "case" just lucky to be at the receiving end.

Nobody can compare one's love to someone else's or with something else. Perhaps that's why everyone thinks their love is different from others . . . and yet once you've been in love, you can understand other people's so much better. This is apropos to your comment that you can't compare your love to me with/to anything else. (In case you were lost in transitions). If I'm honest I realize I love you very much and yet there are still some things that keep it from being completely complete. It's nothing specific and I'm convinced it's not important and probably doesn't surprise you. It's just that I don't think I'll feel completely complete until we're married. I don't feel it when we're alone and when I think of you, so I know it's just certain social consciousness which I'd like to think I have less of, than I do. Does that make sense, darling? If it doesn't, please don't worry about it. I think for once it's one of the things about me that doesn't worry me. I know that it's natural for being me to feel this way on occasion and I know also that it will change. I'd be sorry I wrote it all if I though it would bother you. Not only was it amusing how similar our first letters were, but it was amusing that we both commented on how amusing it was! As for fiancé: I feel very very small knowing my great disability in spelling. I've come to watch others and take the cue from them. (Never use a dictionary as if I can't spell it how can I find it?) When I wrote you I put fiancé. Then I saw your letter with two e's for me and I wrote you that way but I forgot the little matter of your being male! (Well I never did like French!)

    Do you ever remember in the past few months what FDR said that the Atlantic Charter was just a piece of paper? Barb said he did and I can't believe it. (Just recall he DID say it was not binding, guess that is what she meant.
Yes, I had heard about Dr. Roughton and his rumbling from Mard and Dr. Root. Your anecdote topped them all, tho.

Mard would have told me it was none of my business when I asked about the sex nor would she have acted the way she had that night if there wasn't something more than a platonic friendship. But my faith in my sister not to do something silly is great. I am surprised at Mard's telling you in an unembarrassed way she did, which may indicate that things are on a different plane than before. I've met Mrs. Root several times and they certainly don't seem well matched-which didn't help my feeling of comfort in the situation. And yet Dr. Root seems to me quite a conventional man in that even (just supposing) Mard were to fall in love with him and she not be married, he wouldn't get a divorce. I just have that feeling somehow. Am I wrong do you think?

How many weddings have you been to before? I've just been to a second cousins (when I was about 10) and my sister's. A best man loses the ring, dear. He stands by the groom and consoles him when he stands alone and consoles him later. OK? Rogers and Clark were the twins we are going to have,
or were you really too drunk New Year's Eve to remember?

I'd like nothing better than to go on writing, laughing and loving you even tho indirectly, but my responsibilities call (sounds important, doesn't it?) Had meant to comment on our Christmas "activity" didn't seem to affects cramps. I had some wishful thinking dream that it might prove a remedy for same (in which case we'd just do it more often...for medical reasons!!!!)

Got my marks: B in Philosophy and one in Polit and a C+ in Amer Lit which I ought to be able to raise as it is only a provisional mark but a really low mark in French (quelle surprise!)

Yesterday I also worked in the Retreat for the first time-rather fun to ring up the cash register tho it will soon be dull, I guess. Also got the social museum work straightened out and I go to work there tomorrow. Don't know if I'm going to get snowed under by this extra stuff but I'm giving it a try.

Last night, to celebrate Barb's return, we went to the movies (spending the $ I'd so diligently earned in the afternoon.) It was "Mrs. Parkington." We arrived about 15 min. after the beginning and they were already married so we HAD to stay thru Laurel and Hardy to see the preliminaries and the love scene (a la Laura) and like Laura, there was exactly one embrace. I guess it's just better to do it oneself. At least you can plan the experience! There was one scene in Laurel and Hardy" where they, plus a drunk, go to bed in an upper berth. It was quite beyond the usual Hays Office idea and semi-revolting as Hardy is a little too fat to be attractive from a rear view in pajamas. (I doubt if I'd love you if YOU were fat). But we giggled muchly and the evening was well spent. You, meanwhile, poor darling were in the throws of your Phys Chem which I trust wasn't too bad.

Today in Polit class we have been studying taxation and got talking about our ideas of a" a good tax" the ones of us that talked were all pro income tax over sales tax and Miss McCowan kept making comments on how interesting it was that we were all for the more progressive views etc. Of course, she's new and doesn't know that half the class was having internal boiling fits in disagreement but they are too scared to disagree. It happens so often in classes or lectures and debates that I'm almost used to it. It is silly of them and a really good teacher could get them to talk . . . at least it would help discussions and clarify their own views if they really had to defend them.

XXX as many X's as dollars in our national debt-Whew! All my love. Yep! Every bit of it and a terrific kiss (even if it meant I never breathed for ten minutes after it!

Your fiancée.

January 9, 1945

Dearest Darlingest,

Today was my most class-less day, with only one class, Polit at 1:40. Worked all morning except to pay a visit to the Dean. I decided since I may be asking for my record if I switch colleges, that it would be diplomatic to tell her the possibilities of my leaving. She didn't seem very interested or curious to know the whys and wherefores which rather surprised me but I don't much care what she thinks.

Got my Polit mark and was a bit amazed by it. Not that it makes any difference except in the eyes of another school. I got a B1. From 4:30 on I made something: Got out my pile of scraps of junk and "created". Can't decide whether you'd be amused or bewildered at the result. May send it to you just for a laugh and to confuse the landlady.

I'm learning what it is to really miss someone. I physically ache in missing you. (Perhaps yesterday's bowling has something to do with it?) But seriously, this incomplete business is distinctly acute. It's there all the time but sometimes little indescribable things give an added pang to it. I'm not telling you this to make you feel sad. It doesn't really make me sad, but just to let you know that I love you, that I think of you and want you like I've never wanted anything before.

I'm practicing on having a double bed in my future. Fooless slept with me last night . . . the whole night. I usually push her out at some point. Is Joe ok? Send him my regards but my love is strictly for you.
Passionately, provocatively, perpetually yours. V

January 11, 1945
D. Dearest,

While you were in Phys Chem tonite, discussing your exams, seeing that you did better than most, growling at the demos, I was seeing democracy in action, God bless it. There was a Citizens committee in town which had worked for the election of FDR. When it disbanded a group within it decided to form an educational group, thru discussion groups, to stimulate a liberal view. At least I guess that was its purpose. This was a meeting of that group. Mary M, the girl we met at the station, and who had the ideas on love, had been on the previous committee and was to be on this one. She told me of it and that they want college girls to come so six of us, Barb and I among them, did so. It was about the most confused meeting possible-much personal bickering, hazy ideas and general lack of organization . . . fairly typical of such, I'm learning. It's easy to see how dictators get started when people mess around the way they did tonight. And I'm not saying dictators are good, but a little organization wouldn't hurt this free country of ours. It's going in all directions at once and at the same time, in no directions at all . . . enuf!

Good Philosophy today and did some sketches for the Soc Museum. I am no artist but I do like doing it. Went to dinner with the pacifist and roommate . . . unexceptional

Did a girls' lunch job so now I have 5 people owing me so all ready for the curse and weekends away.

Such was my day except for all the little things and my inner thoughts which are growing increasingly more about you and less about me. I keep wanting you around to make comments to, to talk to and to love. I want to walk hand-in-hand or stare into those deep eyes of yours. I want to laugh with you and rub my hand against the grain of your cheeks or again, after we've been on the floor for a while . . . I want to hear your "ouch!" as you lie on you keys. In other words, darling, I want you. Right Now. This minute. I'd like just to be near you—not sex with a capital "S" but just nearness that comes at time like our "intermissions". Gosh tho, we're lucky!

Barb got a letter from Johnny today. He's in the Philippines and his pessimistic view of his next seeing her is in 1948. The girl's going slightly crazy-not only the long wait ahead but the present set-up which isn't good. She hasn't seen him in a year. He was in California for 4 months and he's been overseas for 8 months. They've built a lot of their love since he left, thru the mail which certainly isn't the best way and she's feeling it now. Not that she doubts her love for him, just so much frustration. It's good she hadn't "gone very far" sexually or she'd really be knowing what she's missing! She also has recently gotten the feeling that she's not as attractive to men in general. It's not a serious feeling, just that in general . . . just that she's not met new people and these that she has, have not especially clicked.

When Dave calls, will you find out if he really expects me at the wedding? It was all so casually mentioned.

Guess I'll be taking to rolling my own cigarette shortly when I run out of the ones you so kindly gave me. There are none to be had in town or here. Do you realize in three days it will be our 5 month anniversary (since the picnic)?

Dearest, I've passed the bewitching hour and I don't feel much bewitched, just incomplete and sleepy (sounds like the title of a song or book). Since I can satisfy the second objective and lessen the first by solving the second, I shall do so, with hopes that thou art fine, happy and love me as I do you.

Your fiancée, your future wife, your weekend exercise, your increased laundry, your pupil, your admirer, yours . . . V

January 12, 1945
Hello Darling,

What a goofy up and down then up again day. Let's start at the beginning—the least part of it makes sense.

The postman was on time for a change so I got your letter early in the morning. It was a pleasant surprise since that made two in a row, and I had been preparing myself for less frequent letters from you on account of all your increased activity at school. Do I still have a priority on your extra curricular program? That made a good start of the day-an important day since a highly crucial attempt to measure blood flow from the venous side was on schedule. Then comes the "down". It proved to be the worst dog I've ever tried to work on. He jumped and heaved without any reason until he worked himself into such frenzy that it was impossible to do anything at all. In desperation I gave him an operative dose of Nembutal. Then we got the flow meter hooked up to his vein, and it worked! Since the dog was under an anesthesia I can't use the experiment, but I took out blood gradually and got good readings right to his last breath-readings which are in line with what Clare got and what other people have reported. So it looks as if I can go ahead now with all objections met. It's very puzzling to try to explain why I couldn't measure flow up thru the artery yesterday but could measure it coming back thru the vein today. Of course one experiment doesn't prove anything but today's showed that there is enuf pressure in the veins to push the blood thru the machine in spite of the dire predictions of Wang and Noble. So the day ended up fine after all, especially when I decided that a series of 6 dogs would prove my point (instead of the 10 I was going to do) and Clare agreed heartily. Another good point that came out today was that I'll only have to teach lab this term-no classes. I like teaching but I'm very happy to skip this year and have that much more time for my own work-and us.

Now to go thru your last two letters and pick up the points that need answering (or that) I can't resist commenting on. On more careful reading. I see that the "not quite" complete completeness "business was not related to your family at all. I'm puzzled by this." I know it's just a certain social consciousness which I'd like to think I have less of than I do" If you want to add to this it may help me to understand what you mean but if you'd rather , we can just let it stay till we can talk it over together.

I guess there'd be an end of our commenting on our commenting on how similar our reactions are etc etc. Darling, you can call yourself fiancé fiancee or anything you damn please, as long as the ring is on the right (left) finger and WE know what we mean.

The shirts arrived and they are beautiful. Three grey ones and six white ones. You'll like them.

Roosevelt did not say in so many words that the Atlantic Charter is just a piece of paper, but his (and Churchill's reactions) are such that you can interpret his latest attitude to mean just about anything. Actually, of course, the Charter is a statement of principles, not a work sheet and I believe FDR is convinced of these principles tho I have doubts about Winnie.

You hadn't mentioned the Retreat before. Or the Social Museum. How about some details, especially about the museum which sounds highly interesting. Also I consider myself lucky, I can count my friends on one hand and have lots of acquaintances. I think the "crowd" idea sort of disintegrates after high school days, tho my experience is far from representative in this case.

I am no longer jealous of Fooless tho I'm still extremely envious. I loved "Fooless is but a mere substitute for the better life" which is exactly how I feel about it . . .
Tho I may believe you are ready for marriage now (and I'm not yet ready to admit that I think so) that doesn't mean that we are. I'm only trying to keep my mind clear in this constantly changing world so that reasons which were more important and have dis-appeared won't interfere when the time comes for us to make a decision. I still have a feeling that you're going to think we should begin it all before I think we're ready.

In regard to Root, I wouldn't care to decide how closely he'd stick to conventions, tho I'm inclined to agree with your opinion. Anyhow, this will remain pure speculation since Mard is very much in love with Howard, is simply lonesome (unfortunately we make it worse) and wouldn't consider Root seriously for two minutes.
I went to many weddings for the food and dancing but paid no attention to the solemnities since it was so obvious that I'd never be up there. How about that "then he leaves and consoles himself" Do I have to console myself alone? And when do I kiss the bride?
Just can't recall Rogers and Clark at all. Are you sure you had the conversation with me?
Letter #2

Depend on you to know how I feel even about words. I like superlatives (connected to you) like darling and don't like "sweetheart" and hate "honeybunch, baby etc"

You sound so- busy so happily busy- these days. I'm convinced that what you needed was more activity and less book work. This doesn't settle the basic problem, but it seems to me that you feel closer to your goal now than you did the term you tried to concentrate on studies. I can see a small cloud on our horizon. You run about 30 days per period. This one is the 11th-exactly one month before the Boston trip.

You mention: "I was thinking of sex today." Well, I was so busy today that I didn't think of it (hardly).

I'm mixed up as to when you expect to come in (tho we'll probably settle it over the phone before you get this). You say that you'll come in the 20th for 2 nights. The 20th is a Saturday also I presume you mean Friday the 19th since you don't have classes on Sat. I can arrange my work to be free all day Friday since Clare has finished her work and my plans take precedence. Today Mard asked me when you're coming in and I said I wasn't sure-either Fri or Sat. Then she asked me which week I meant, which was surprising.

You hit the nail on the head about being interested in how we figure out ways to test our ideas. The ingenuity that goes into an experiment is the whole difference between success and failure and the improvisations that have to be made on the spot are what really make the work interesting. For instance, yesterday somebody suggested that my values were so low because blood was streaming past the air bubble so that timing how long it took the bubble to travel between the marks didn't show how much blood was actually passing. To test this, I put in an air bubble and shoved some blood dye in right behind it. None of the dye appeared ahead of the bubble and I felt prouder of this little improvisation than anything I had done all day. So don't ever think that you'll bore me with talk of your craftwork. No, I haven't read "Thunder on the Left" but will as soon as my conscience will spare the time. Also- No. I didn't mean you have to love a person to enjoy a kiss. Know better from my own experience these past years.

This letter has been full of facts and leaves unsaid many more facts about you and me and us. Perhaps I'll be able to say some of them over the phone. Perhaps you can guess what I would say. In just one week I'll be able to say them in person.

Good nite, darling, I love you fiercely, not only there and there and there but everywhere.

Your fiancé, D.

January 15, 1945
Dearest, Realest, Duchess,

Even tho I know much of what was in your letter, I enjoyed reading it this A.M. especially because I wanted to see if you'll sound any different now that I'm back to earth (or rather now that I'm no longer back to earth), and I decided that it was a darn good thing that I had gone up to see you, as I expected the letter sounded fun and wonderful and just like you which made me feel so happy. All day the minute Mard saw me she said "You look as if you're been to some college this weekend" and I nodded happily, kind of dopily.

So much for ancient history. The train pulled in at 11:20 which wasn't too bad and I talked to the guy who was in the library when we were there, all the way home. He's a funny guy-far more naïve than he'll ever suspect and is worried because the girl said she's crazy about him and it was only their second date. He said she came from a wealthy family ("out of my class") and he didn't like the suddenness of it, ("she's probably hard up for a man" but he decided he'd "kick it around a bit" just to see what happens …. sounding all the time like a scared kid trying to appear suave and sophisticated. I didn't ask the girl's name for which I'm sure you'll be grateful.

A letter from Dave came in the morning mail and the poor guy is having his troubles. Altho Connie's father likes him, he is against their getting married in Feb. And refused to attend the wedding, so Dave and Connie have decided to have just a simple ceremony in the presence of two witnesses. Accordingly, he regretfully withdrew his invitation for us to attend but invites us to come up to their three room apt which they have already rented and will occupy Feb 3rd. The worst angle of his present trouble is that Dave will have to pay Connie's tuition for the last half year which I think is a dirty trick for the old man to play. I'm hoping he'll soften after they're married.

Today I talked to little Joe about the Waltz from Tchaikovsky's sixth and the Shostakovich's Age of Gold waltz and learned in an off hand manner that he'd be delighted to come up to see Barb. He really had a good time at the lake over New Years with her (and us) and he sounded quite pleased about a repeat week-end.

We got the Phys Chem papers back and she hadn't deducted as much for my errors as I had anticipated so I got an 82 which would be O.K. if I wasn't trying to raise my previous low average. I figured out that my average for the term is 67 and the highest in the room is 73 which isn't as bad as I'd expected

How did you make out with the Galileo, Epicurus, Venable and the falling weights? I'm expecting to see a note on first page of the second edition of the N.Y.Times any day now.

For some unaccountable reason I was dead tired this A.M. and didn't get to the lab til about 10:30 so tomorrow will be the first attempt at a real <u>venus</u> (veinus?) flow in an anaesthetized dog. Clare said Friday that she wouldn't be doing any experiments this week but exercised her prerogative and is doing one tomorrow. I don't like two dogs in the same room and it would be crowded so I shifted the flow-meter to another room which is no trouble at all, but found that the water there is too hot and is so full of bubbles that I can't see the inside the flow-meter. Luckily both problems solved themselves when I let the water run into a large tank and drew water from the bottom of the tank where there weren't any bubbles. It came out at just the right temperature.

With luck I can be all through the research in two weeks except for one test that I want to run. I've got an itch to measure the actual flow again and when it stops, cut the vein and see if anything flows out. This ought to show conclusively whether it's the machine that is blocking flow

**up the artery or if not, will pose a neat problem to whose blood that's in the vein. I haven't said much about us in this letter because I'm still a little self conscious but you are now near again, I know how much I love you and how sure I am of my feelings and I know that in only 3 1/2 days you'll be here in N.Y. and I'm very happy.
Love, D.
P.S. Your idea of coming here to my room Sat. nite sounds fine. I'm a lousy host not to have thought of it myself!**

January 15, 1945
Oh Darling!
I'm up in the air! I'm floating. I'm full of mental energy. PS I've read a terrific book. I guess that will hit you as an anti-climax but it shouldn't. The book is Margaret Halsey's "Some of My Best Friends Are Soldiers" and it's so full of wit, depth and zest for living that I'm bubbling over vicariously. Darling, I wish I could write you like that. (It's all in the form of letters) and reading it makes me feel like a lump-on-a-log but it is great enough to be filled with things that remind one of oneself and it also somehow, strangely enough made me love you so darn much that I wanted to yell from the roof tops.
Really got the curse today and groaned for two hours before I could down enuf of the contents of my meds to put me to sleep. (Am I building immunity with taking the stuff?) But tho I felt like hell I found myself missing you in even greater degree—which is a superlative in its own little way. Yes, I missed you just as much as I ever have and a little more.

You coming here yesterday was a wonderful idea (it was also good that providence didn't decree to make today of yesterday).and even the curse can't diminish my appreciation of you and my eternal blessings to some unknown force for having brought us within reach of each other. Also thought of our various conversations and kicked myself for being a darn fool regarding such vanities as social consciousness. It was a very stray remnant of a very foolish adolescence and God knows how or why I dragged it out of the closet. It was definitely minor but the more we talked of it, the worse mess I made of it although trying to do the opposite. It was so childish and you're so gosh darn patient with me and I love you so (this exuberance is partly the feeling that I've gotten over the worst of the curse which, by mere process of contrast always improves morale and partly the book which in itself made me love you and mostly just an accumulation of today's missing you and thought of you.) Rabbit dearest, I feel like calling you from 80 miles away to wait for mc.
Love, love, V.

January 16, 1945
Darling,

I didn't expect to have time to write today but even tho having the time means that today's experiment was no good, I'm just as glad it worked out that way because your letter hit the nail so neatly on the head that I wanted to add me too. The especially apt sentence (which once again proves your ability to get right to the heart of a situation) was the one in which you've noted that we are both the kind of people who try to and want to understand the other person. That's why I knew everything would be O.K. as soon as we started laughing together and you threw me a wink and I realized that our love for each other is strong enuf in itself to with stand almost any temporary awkwardness. I feel now that if we can't be happy together the rest of our lives, then nobody in the world can.

Talked to Joe today but said nothing about the Barb incident, in a month or so it'll probably seem much less important to Barb and a great deal funnier than she now thinks it, but I wonder if she and Joe would have a good time together again before it has all died down. Personally I think we're darn lucky that we take our sex so casually and as good fun.

Mard says your parents won't be home for dinner Friday nite and your mother suggested you invite me to eat with you.
(This is certainly a round about way of getting myself invited to your place for a meal!) Mard also thought your parents wouldn't be home for dinner Sat. so we could make it either nite. I don't know when your mother and father are going away or where they are going but will try to find out.

This should reach you Wed. or Thurs. which will leave just a day or two before you're here. If you can figure out any way to let me know which train to meet I'd much rather be at the station when you come-otherwise, call me from Grand Central and I'll come down as fast as I can push the subway.

All my love, D.

P.S. Today's experiment was no good on account of a sick dog. The method still seems to be OK.

P.P.S Nearly forgot to tell you that I love you or did you guess that on Sunday?

January 16, 1945
Nicest One,

So it's been blizzarding out, a 50 mile gale since last nite. It's been so terrific that the poor men who spend their entire lives shoveling paths finally gave up and took a much needed day off with the Missus. It was so blustery we embarked on a pilgrimage to the drug store to get yours truly some tampax. Who could complain about such a needy cause? We bundled up like germs in a worm (so much more descriptive than a bug in a rug, no?) and daringly exited from the warm dorm. So then I says to myself can Barb have gotten all outfitted like a germ in a worm for nothing? No, she must receive some satisfaction for her efforts and I pushed her into a passing snow drift. Then she pushed me, then I pushed her, she's up, I'm down, I'm up, she's down. A giggle a scream, a tussle, a scream, a scramble, a few choice remarks, a misguided push. A last gasp, an increased effort for the last 10 feet and we're there! The haven for all poor crampy desperate females and fate has dealt us a blow. Transfixed in disappointment, anguish , chagrin, we stood gazing upon a closed, abandoned, empty, dark drugstore . . . a tussle, a scream, a yell, a stumble, a push. Well, here I am again.

Your insane, happy, and adoring fiancée (misspelled?) Had a good time tonight reading Soc. A book on a section of Chicago where the "gold coast" the area of residents of the 400 is directly opposed to the slums with only a few disconnecting blocks between. The factual material is greatly enlivened by actual documents written by inhabitants of both extremes: the stupid society life where all is a matter of keeping up with the Joneses and climbing into the Social Register and the lonely anonymous life in a 10th rate rooming house. All descriptions made me bless you and realize what a full life we can, do and will have. Loved you so much today. And hate the English language or my own lack of ingenuity in not being able to tell you so in different ways each time.

    Ellie and I had a pact that the first one to hear news of Dave and Connie would inform the other. So I told her that as far as you and I were concerned the wedding was off. I imagine that it is for her too. She feels they shouldn't get married due to their financial status. I disagreed idealistically but wavered when she told me Connie's father had had to help them out last summer. It seems to me it's one thing to be scattered brained about cash-it's ok to have a philosophy of independence, if you can somehow manage to keep that independence but when you've spent the money, it's a little like the grasshopper and the ant . . . but maybe I'm being too cruel. According to Ellie, from what I can gather, it doesn't seem to bother them much when they go their merry ways but are helpless when something goes wrong. You probably wont like these sentiments and somehow they sound harsher than I meant or mean them to sound. And it does seem mean of her father to be as stubborn as he sounds…unless he really expected them to give in to the threat. In any case, we've no plans to attend a wedding on the 18th! Are we going up to visit them? Or should we take a stolen weekend somewhere, or what? I'm open to suggestions. I guess neither of us are the concealing type. What would my sister say about a stolen weekend?

Got a letter from home and they asked which weekend I was coming in. Our letters crossed-really just innocent confusion. Now they know it's this weekend. I wrote a hurried postal saying I'd be in on Friday for dinner and that I wanted you to come for dinner either Fri or Sat and to tell Mard which so she can tell you whichever is decided and not to have oysters or spinach on the nite you will be there. They mentioned that all would be out Saturday eve-Mard too. (at a cocktail party I think.)

Got a letter from Bob; the first since he went overseas and tho he's no idealist he's not as bitter as some I've gotten. He's in England living quite a soft life, I take it. I don't tell you all the mail I get except I like you to know of the people I have known. If it ever bothers you that I write to those of "the past" too much let me know and I'll shut up.

No Polit class today as Miss McC got snowed in. It's really quite a blizzard . . . but lovely with the wind blowing the drifts into very graceful mounds and curves. The trees moan and the cheeks get red. Love the idea of you entertaining me in your room. In fact it's wonderful that you are you. It's wonderful that in less than three days I'll

see you…see you alone too! It's wonderful to be alive and living and it's wonderful to feel that its wonderful!
All my love, sex, tight sweaters, gleams in my eyes
and etceteras.
Me.

January 18, 1945
Darling,

    Tonite's exam was just like all the others. I got about a 75 which stinks but will probably be above the average. She gave us a stiff lecture Thursday and not only included it in the exam, but also a problem on the rest of the chapter which we didn't have time to cover yet. And at the end of the exam she asked us if it was too easy! Charming bitch. (Time out while I roll another one. I would get lumpy tobacco so not quite as good a job as the other one. If you see holes in the paper, it's just me losing the end of the cigarette.

    It's true that we'll disagree about rainy day money, but I had long ago realized how you feel about it and that I need someone like you to keep me in line. I'm an absolute baby when it comes to money matters, but I promise to see your point of view often, if you occasionally see mine. While we're on money matters (like a married couple will often be) let me explain my cash reserve angle. I got $180 back on tuition. Of this I spent 70 to repay a couple of debts and 40 over Xmas which includes all the train rides, your present and all the extras. Now I have $80 which I call my cash reserve. If possible I want to keep this in tact and add all I can to it each month. Unfortunately I have to get some odd and ends so this it will be difficult to keep the $80 in tact let alone add to it. With modest living I can start saving at least 10 a month starting in March. What does my financial advisor advise?

Don't worry about making me more lonely-it would be almost impossible to add to what I feel now and I'm insecure enuf to want to hear that you love me and miss me as much as I do you. If you started not missing me, then I'd really be lonely.

It wouldn't be fair to compare your campus paper with either of Purdue's two. The most charitable things that one could say about those that they were brief and dealt mostly with Sorority and Fraternity news. Neither paper dreamed of venturing off the campus with one exception: Washington Merry-Go-Round was carried by one and so startled everyone that it was permitted to run for only a full term. The one you showed me compares well with others I have seen and is far less provincial than most . . . much more adult and less full of gossip.

I was amused to see you "make a tradition" of reading "Thunder On the Left" every three years. The amusement goes back to my Purdue days when Harry and I looked on while the school tried to establish traditions in vain imitation of the older schools tho they pretended to sneer at the Ivy covered colleges. There isn't any connection between your "tradition" and Purdue's except for the word itself so don't get the idea of your re- reading it seems silly since that's what I've been doing with Hans-Christophe ever since I first read it in 1935. From the sound of your marks, I should think you'll get mostly B's and possibly all B's this term. Isn't that good?

Rosey's attitude on kissing is nothing unusual even in girls older than she. There isn't any intrinsic pleasure in it like there is in eating candy. It's more the feeling of closeness to someone you love and the return of that feeling. Wait til she meets someone she likes.

Forgive me, Darling . . . all this time and I haven't said that I love you. I'm not going to start enumerating why just now or I'd never get to sleep. All I can say is that I've never been in love before because I've never felt for anyone the love that you've created in me.

All my love, D.

January 22, 1945
D. darling,

An eventful and incomplete 26 hours since we parted in the dreary station after a wonderful weekend. I don't think I'll ever forget these past few days . . . the bus ride, seeing you at Columbia in the seminar room, lunch of peanut butter etc dinner of apple pie . . . movies in empty balconies . . . herring a la Vienna, testing your stubbornness, museum, being tired, being in love, food in the kitchen. ETC.

Do you think we'll ever reach a point where each time won't be better than the last? I don't think so, as you so wisely said, people are always changing and one is always making new discoveries about one's self and the other person (On an intellectual plane of course!!! Ha!)

The train ride back was pretty gruesome. I sat with a girl I knew slightly before and we talked part of the time– Econ major, conservative, friendly, not too deep, engaged for a year, marriage planned for after the war, doesn't seem to have too much understanding of people or her fiancé but that may not be a fair statement.

The train stopped for half an hour because a man died of a heart attack in the car behind us. (Like a fool I looked out of the window as they carried the body away and felt rather sick. First time I've ever seen a dead person except for the med school dissections (when I visited Mard) which somehow don't have the same reality.) The train got in 40 minutes late. Innocent Nanette came in to my room and wanted to know what I did. I told her as much as was logical to tell and she beamed and glowed saying "I get so much pleasure hearing about it as you did doing it" I choked slightly but refrained from any comment.

No Philosophy class this A.M. for some unknown reason. Spent the time reading "Walden" which is interesting stuff, more for the character of the author than the actual contents . . . a plea for the simple life, living on the bare necessities, living with Nature and disregarding society, material possession, competition etc. Not wholly logical but a good attempt at finding a satisfactory philosophy of life.

Played tennis with Thea, the girl I told you about…my doubles partner in last year's tryout. First time I've played since I played with you, Dr. Nemerson and Dr. Wang up at school on our first date! Today we played on the indoor court (naturally . . . give him a little credit for brains!) And I talked to you thru out the two sets. It was fairly good tennis tho I got sloppy at which point you bawled me out and I improved. The first set I took easily at 6-4. It sounds close but really-wasn't.

The second set I found myself after merrily day-dreaming and wasting points, behind at 0-3. Then made it 3-1, 4-1, -5-2. So it was 5-2 against me in the second set when I mentally slapped myself in the rear and told myself to get to work. She (Thea) was very persistent which is bad for me who relaxes, but I was determined and I wasn't going to let you slap me on the rear and lose! So I beat her 7-5. See what power you have over me darling? Well, you do.

Today I had 4 girls over for dinner which was pleasant. Friends are nice to have and not to have too much of, but to have available. Barb sent a telegram saying she wasn't coming back til tomorrow . . . don't know what's up. She's taking 4 leaves at once! Tho I have a hunch it may be connected with the cocktail party she went to Sunday afternoon that I wasn't invited to . . . which would be swell for her if that's really it.

That darn tennis match threw my work schedule off and the fact that my eyes wont focus anymore has further turned it off.

I'll probably come in for the party if they don't announce a Polit exam for Monday but I don't think they will "And what did you learn at college, Mummy?" Well dear, you see your father . . . "Future conversation ???

I have your new picture up and I can't decide how

it compares with the old one except that you've gotten thinner. I hope that isn't my influence! Do you burn your caloric intake faster these days? Seriously, tho, I love both and like having choice to look at, particularly as the choice is you or you.

Good nite, my husband . . . some day, I'll be able to say that and not have to just write it. Me.

January 23, 1945
Darling,

What a good for nothing dope you're going to marry. Altho this was the first free night I've had in a long time to do all those things that have been piling up to be done, I've just spent 2 hours messing with a piece of oil cloth, a cardboard box and two glass rods, trying to "invent" a cigarette rolling machine. I finally stopped when I rolled one that is kind of loose and thick but which CAN be smoked by a determined person (who doesn't mind spitting out hunks of tobacco).

The exam last night, as I had feared, was plenty tough. Even for her it was really bitchy. It ran from 7 to 9. About 8:30 I had gotten thru the last question (there were six) and realized that I hadn't been able to do a single one of them completely. I glanced around the class and everybody else was looking kind of dazed-like at the walls or at each other. Luckily, I got some inspirations at the last minute and with the help of some of the luckiest guesses I've made in years, it now appears that I probably passed the damn thing. If everybody else did as badly as they claimed my B ought to be forthcoming.

Poor Dottie. We had studied the medium hard stuff figuring that we knew the easier parts and would never know the tougher things. So she was lost from the start and I would have been too except that I can't learn anything unless I know where it comes from and this exam took more than just knowing the formulas. Anyhow, the first term is now over–a good thing– and there are no classes until Feb 5, also a good thing; but it's not definite that we'll have the she-demon again...a not so good thing.

Today was one of mixed blessings. They came in the form of a whole gang of good dogs which Dr. Allison and Gelfand turned over to me as they've finished their research for a while. Also good was my decision and Allison's approval that I drop blood flows after this week and start writing up my paper. He is writing up a series of experiments of which mine and Clare's are a part, and wants me to get mine thru so that he can refer to it in his paper-a less than nice guy than Allison would have written his paper using the part of my data that he needed and would have left me a few scraps to write up which would have meant additional research to bring my paper up to thesis requirements. The Chief has also asked me to gather my data together and show it to him. Since it fits in so well with Allison's, he'll have to accept it and could hardly fail to take it as my PhD thesis.

Now for the blows which aren't too crippling. Last Fall I signed up for a reading course with the Chief. It's a haphazard affair. We're supposed to read articles and report to the Chief. Clare took it last year, never did a thing about it and got a passing grade. Well, when I went to the Chief to get his necessary approval for this terms courses, he suddenly came out with the fact that he has giving me an incomplete in his reading courses. When I had caught my breath (there was a pause while I rolled a cigarette in his machine), I suggested that he pass me in the course on my word that I'd do the reading this term. After some discussion which brought out that I had been doing loads of research, he decided to transfer the points from the reading course and credit me with them in research which is just fine with me.

So now I'm signed up for his reading course for this term which means more work. Then the second blow: He said that since I'll have a heavy teaching schedule he wouldn't let me take 8 hours of research this term-only 3. I couldn't budge him from this and so I'll have to take my last 5 hours of research this summer. Actually, there's not much difference as far as I'm (or we're) concerned. It wont hold up my degree as the Chief promised to let me take my final exam as soon as I'm ready for it whether I have all my points by then or not.

I'd like to know that I have all my requirements finished by June instead of Sept. but it wont make any difference (a) in the time I get my degree or (b) in my salary. Actually the only damage from the conference was that I'll have to do the reading for the Chief. He certainly is a weird guy. Clare has been trying to see him for 5 minutes but he is always busy all day, scratching numbers on glass tubes-a child with a toy! Then I said I wanted to see him about my courses and five minutes later he came down the hall personally to tell me had time to see me then ! I was ungracious enuf to complain to him that he had interrupted us while I was rolling a cigarette-and we talked for half an hour. As soon as I got back to the room, Clare rushed up to his office to see him, but he was too busy-scratching numbers on glass!

After the conference I went to see Bill Walcott who is in charge of the course this year to find out what the Chief meant by "heavy teaching schedule" and found I was down to teach a lot every Monday (all day) every Wed afternoon, every Thurs afternoon and conferences practically every Thursday. This was more than twice the load everybody else had, so I put in a kick and Bill is fixing it up. Would that have put a strangle hold on my plans!

Are you still with me, darling? I've been ranting and raving about myself for 2 whole pages. This is a fine time to tell you that I love you. "I love you" And just because I've waited till page 3 to tell you again, "I love you" attach unseemly number of kisses to each of those (in a number of unseemly places) and you'll have a faint idea how near I am to you (It's a good thing I had Dottie to keep me studying on Monday. Alone I would have passed ¾ of the day dreaming in Phys Chemistry, dreams that would not have passed that exam.

Have you decided about this Saturday nite: the answer to this question will probably be in your letter tomorrow if such is on the way. I asked Joe today about coming up to college Feb 3 but he is leaving Feb 1 and wont be around NY after that. His classes start Feb 9 in Rochester. I suspect (he didn't say) that his ex? girl friend in Mass. is in some way involved. This will amuse you, I'm sure--and you wont be able to tell Barb why the wicked laugh! Last nite I experimented with myself to see where my "timing" etc. stood. As I had expected everything was back on schedule. I have some more practice sessions in mind, the results of which will please you, I hope. Don't worry, I wont wear myself out and you are still a very necessary part of my plans!

Oops, it's 10:30. I don't think mail is collected after 10:30 tho it says 10:45 on the mail box, but I still rush these out, hoping. So long, darling. . . . soooolong.
Love, D.

January 23, 1945-midnight
Dearest,

Thou puttest me to shame! i.e. writing me so that I'd get a letter today while you wont get one from me until tomorrow. And you had an exam besides. Oh well, I DO love you even if I went to sleep instead of writing.

I kept thinking of you during the time when you were taking the exam. Thought of you hard, so what if you were too busy to clutch the pin, I was there anyway. I trust it wasn't too hard and that your studying and eggs (the way you like them!) improved life generally.

Today has not been a long day. Tuesdays usually are. Did some studying this A.M. until Barb returned from her vacation. I was right in surmising she'd stayed on to see Carl. She had a gay time. It was his last leave before going West and overseas so they both were in the mood to do the town up right Was glad she had such a good time. I have a hunch if Johnny happens to come back a while after Carl is back, enough of a while later for Barb to see enough of Carl, that she'll marry him and not Johnny. I think her family and his would both like him and in general it would seem likely . . . tho she's still sold on Johnny. If you recall, he is the boy I went out with a bit two years ago who tried to talk me into seduction (he should only know!) and I kept thinking him of an awfully nice guy, just young. Just found out he was twenty last week. No wonder I thought he was young!

Paragraphs without saying I'm terrifically glad you're you and that you love me and vice versa. I keep thinking we are so far ahead of others in our knowing each other so well . . . or does each person think so when in a relationship?

I've got an Econ test tomorrow for which I've done practically no studying, and it doesn't bother me, which is amazing!

Class meeting today in which I decided to buy a class ring. I'm optimistic enough to think I'd wear it only a short time before it had to be supplanted and I think you might be interested in my giving it to you . . . or would you?

Have decided we knew I would come in for the party. Will try to get the train in some time Sat. afternoon but wont know which or when til I see how they're running. I'll call. I haven't decided what to do about Sunday. If I told my family I was taking a train back Sat nite, they probably wouldn't believe me and get most suspicious as to where I spent the night. There wouldn't be much point to staying over Sunday at home. Oh, I'm too sleepy to decide which/what to do. If I don't go home at all, my family will definitely be suspicious. I tell them I am taking the train Saturday nite it might dawn on them that they wouldn't let me in at college-which they wouldn't!

I read somewhere once, that one thing bad about our current social customs is we (people in general that is) have intercourse before going to sleep after a long day when we're tired. I started mentioning it as an analogy to the fact that I feel the same toward my letter writing to you (It's now after midnight).

Darling, this is a very sloppy letter. I'm tempted to tear it up because it doesn't say what I want it to. It doesn't say that I miss you, my Duke, that I've felt incomplete particularly muchly today, that I'm waiting eagerly, impatiently for the weekend-in short tho it may be, and in inadequate language, that I love you.

Read between the lines, behind and above them too and you'll see what I really have to say.
All my emotions, V.

January 24, 1945-midnite
Dearest Wabbit,

I love you; I did laugh wickedly and I was with you all the way. O.K. You don't remember what I'm talking about. All comments except the first caused by your letter of the 23rd, the first, caused by you and life in general.

It's the good-for-nothing in you that I love, darling. i.e. the part that makes you "convert" a cigarette rolling machine when you've a thousand other things to do. It's just what I would have done and so there we are back at loving each other and being alike. Machines are so scarce around here that I haven't even had the chance to see how they work or I'd try my own powers too.

That reading course sounds like an unfortunate thing and the teaching schedule even worse. Hope you can get the latter straightened out. How do they work hours of credit in research? Do they have any check-up on the number you do? You'd told me about Allison's paper and its swell that the Chief will have to rush yours thru accordingly.

Can you write up the paper minus blood flows and add that later? Or forget about them?

I was amused at your timing experiment and at your approach to same. I'm very happy to know that I'm still necessary part of your plans. May it be always so. As a matter of fact (and interest) I did more or less the same experimentation not on the basis of timing but merely for exploration and curiosity. Found the scenery much changed. (I'm laughing at us and life and at my eternal conclusion that we're awfully cute people).

The Econ test wasn't too bad and didn't require any studying or at least the studying wouldn't have done any help: 4 essays and could have written several hours but was given 50 minutes.

Began bowling with a beautiful game; had 72 at half way but messed it up and ended with a stupid 113.

Decided to work again for the IRG (inter racial group). They had several nebulous plans: one among which I was particularly interested in. We've collected a bit of material on the subject and have now acquired space in the library for it. Part of the group is working with kids in town on discussion groups, story telling etc destined to un-bias some of their present bias. For that purpose, and for possible use as a campus exhibit, they (we) want to convert some of the factual material into graphic displays and posters. Another girl and I have set to work on that.

Went to see Martha Graham and her dance group. Ever seen them? I hadn't before and they're quite terrific. Use the Dance form for psychological interpretations and do a beautiful job. I don't usually like dance stuff unless it's something special and this would come under that heading. One "scene" concerned the circus as you'll see in the program that I'll probably forget to enclose. A beautiful job of showing a woman always conscious of her self as being her favorite admirer. In the background is a "spectator" who continually tries on hats and admires herself. It's done with a great deal of humor and portrays such universal feeling that one can't help but laugh and enjoy it. The other two scenes were more serious but equally effective.

Just thought after writing all this that maybe we are past the stage where our letters are solely about us. As you've said, we're sure of a certain base and maybe now we're able to widen our range of topics. Not that "us" has ceased to be the most fascinating subject ever created and not that it all shall be forever forgotten in the cob webs of our minds. Just a progression in the stage of "our love affair". (I don't like the sound of that "passé" phrase…sorry).

I'll call you from the station. Probably take the 2:47

Fooless and I are very tired, darling. So with many fond thoughts about cute things (you in general and you in particular) I bid you an affectionate good nite.
Votre, fiancée

January 25, 1945
Dearest Aphrodisiac,

If someone hadn't just yelled, "Hey you, get up!" on the radio, I'd probably have slept till morning. A faint recollection of what I'd been dreaming plus more visible evidence prompted the above salvation.

As much as I missed much this week-end and not being with you means missing you, no matter how short the interval, the week has passed fairly quickly, helped along by the exam and daily experiments (in the lab, I mean). For some unknown reason (tho it may be better dogs) the experiments have started to click and the last two seem to be O.K. We switched back to measuring arterial flows, removing the objection that the pulse is lost with the flow meter by making a slight alteration so that the pulse remains. I don't know why the earlier arterial flows wouldn't work but they do now. There is still one big headache to the problem of my arterial measurements don't check with the ones Clare made. She simply let the blood flow out of a vein and measured it in a graduate. After hemorrhage her dogs showed a decrease flow to

1/4 of the control while mine drop down to 1/12.

This makes a tremendous difference in how we interpret the data and so we've got to find out who is right. The question is: does the machine measure the real flow or does it in some way slow it down or are Clare's measurements too high because she bleeds into an open graduate which permits a faster flow than really occurs when the blood remains in the blood vessels. To settle this point we're going to try to make our measurements simultaneously on the same dog. If my results are still lower than hers on the same dog, it probably means that mine are right-if the machine interfered with the flow, it should show up on her side as well. If we're both the same, that may mean a) the machine slows up the flow or b) my readings are correct and the ones she made may have been correct for the dogs she used.

Anyhow, we may be able to settle something. For instance, if my reading speeds up, WHILE she is letting blood flow out of the vein, it means that bleeding into an open vessel does change conditions. It's going to be very difficult technically but we've both vowed to keep trying till we get proof, one way or another. It would be nice for both of us if her results prove right as our data is easier to interpret with her figures, but we've got to get at the truth no matter which it ends up.

Some guy on WQXR just said, "The glow worm glows and glows and glows, cause that's the only thing it knows." Is that why we glow when we're together? Which reminds me that you haven't told me how happy I am this week. I can't remember your mentioning anything that took place in your classes tho you did mention a couple of classes that didn't take place. I've been trying to think of what we can do about Sat. nite, too, but I'm afraid you've got to be home that nite. I wish your parents would get an urge to go see Walt again, but I suppose that's asking too much.

You're right about how unsensible it is to have intercourse at night when you're too tired, but that doesn't apply entirely. After an evening of being together, holding hands, looking at each other, and waiting . . . you'd certainly think people would be in a more romantic mood than they are on waking up in the bright morning. But we'll find out in true scientific way–by experiment!.

I don't know why I'm writing all this since I'll be seeing you (in person!) in less than 48 hours. I wont be fit for much in the way of work, Saturday, so come in as soon as you can tear yourself away from your books-tho not if you have studying to do. We might be able to come up here to my place Sat. afternoon if that has any attraction for you.. I mentioned this to give you a chance to decide whether to get off at 125th street or Grand Central.

It was nice to hear that Barb had such a good time with Carl. I'm glad he was very nice but too young when he made his indecent advances to you. How could anybody think of such a sweet sincere thing like you in such a vulgar physical way?
Good nite, my love. Be good, my financee, and get plenty of sleep . . . with violent affection.
Love, D.

P.S. Ambrose Bierce said: "Administration: our polite recognition of another's resemblance to ourselves." Would he call love: the exciting recognition of the resemblance of another's desires of our own?

January 29, 1945
Dearest darlingest D. (alliteration . . . I just noticed it)

Getting drunk was a good idea. No one else mattered except you. I felt very close to you-just as close as I do in our "intermishes" when we share a cigarette and purr together. The unimportant things slipped away and I never felt more yours. that I belong with you. It wasn't something that lasted only while I was reeling but continued on the train and is in the act of continuing right now. Darling, I'm so very in love with you.

And I saw another side of you too, this weekend. I don't know if you were conscious of my noticing or not, but I admired you so much in the discussion with Jane. You not only handle me well but other people too. You got at the points very quickly and knew what to say to sound her out. I think we'll always keep learning about each other. I know I've still got a lot to learn about you and I love learning it.

The party wasn't a very good test of us together among other people, I thought, and that is why I wasn't disappointed in it, more than any other reason. It was, I think, because of the situation of my parents being there and the mess with Howard being sick. I felt a little drawn in all directions and a little as if I was letting you down. But we'll have other chances to show how wonderful we are among people as well as by ourselves. We've got so darn much, darling. Pardon if I'm repetitious; its just like poetry, emphasizing the important phrase with repetition for the pure joy of the sound of the words.

Well, well, all these paragraphs about us. I thought we'd gotten beyond or above such things.

Who am I kidding? I'm terribly tired which means you must be even more so. I can't get myself to go to the library so I'm writing you and then going to sleep . . . "And what did you get out of your college education, mommy?"

Had a good Philosophy class as usual tho Mr. V. kept interrupting himself with "I smell smoke." There'd be a silence and then the whole class could be heard to simultaneously inhale. Then he rushed out of the room in search of fire but come back disappointed. Perhaps it was only the flames of our enthusiasm that he smelled.

Polit was quite amusing with Post (the liberal Republican???) giving a lecture on Rockefeller and the fact that outsmarting other people was not bad…claimed it was human nature which wouldn't change in 3 million years. I attacked some points but retreated in disgust as I saw we weren't getting anywhere and that the class wasn't interested in it except to hear Mr. Post "be funny". He takes important subjects and makes a joke of them, which is difficult to combat in a large lecture hall. If he's not playing to the audience, one might get somewhere.

Had a conference with Mrs. Ellis (Amer. Lit) which was very pleasant. Talked about the course and why it wasn't better than it is. It's a large class and she wants more discussion which is a difficult thing in itself. I said I thought having it only once a week wasn't too good an idea when it was so large, as people didn't think about the work during the week and just began to get ideas as the 2 hour session was over. Then they had to wait a whole week before we could discuss again. It's different in a seminar when you presume everyone is interested and stimulated to work with only a few people. She agreed and told me I was a smart girl which of course I denied (Are you laughing?)

Decided on my term paper which is what the conference was really for. I wanted to do something on museums and she liked my idea on narrowing it to propaganda museums. We decided to make it fit the form of an American Lit course, I'd take it from the angle of seeing the relationship of the actual exhibits, types of exhibits to the social trends at the time they took place—correlating the two. I don't know how quite it'll work out but it ought to be good.

Don't bother to send up Henry James, which (whom?) I presume you have. It will be OK if I can get it by the 10th. Sorry I made you give it back-We sure do live in a dream world for two sensible people!

Tonight am going to an SLA meeting shortly and working on the IRG (inter racial group) display thing I told you about. So no homework but OK.

Betts thought sending the magazine on to Bill was a poor idea . . . said she'd heard that that sort of thing was the worst kind of thing to send to a guy who couldn't get sex. I hadn't thought of it that way at all and perhaps she's right. I don't think he'd take it that way but passing it among the guys might not help them. What do you think?

I want to get this off to you so you'll get it Wed. so I'll quit this tho I could add 10 pages. All of them would say I miss you like anything and love you even more.
All my love, V.

January 30, 1945
Dearest Pickled One,

So it's with a drunkard I am in love! Before I marry you, my inebriate, you are going to have to promise to stay on the wagon at least for 3 months before our children are born. And I want it in writing . . . God were you cute! I was not too sober myself-just enuf to get a huge kick out of you and wish we had been alone. Did you have a hangover you'd promised yourself? Or am I digging up an episode that's been forgotten among the welter of things that happened this weekend?

The trip home was quite an affair tho there were no ill affects and most certainly no regrets. (Just remember you were just unsobered enuf five or six times to tell me how much you appreciated my going up to college and I was stewed enuf to insist five or six times just as seriously that as long as you loved me I wasn't interested in your appreciation-we were doing fine!

I just missed a bus and waited 15 minutes for the next. It wasn't cold and I walked to where they turn and listened to a nite watchman at the town's business section. I started walking to the station but after a couple of blocks another bus came along and took me to about 5 blocks from the train. That pulled in about a quarter to 12 and I was home by 2:45. For some strange reason I didn't feel tired Monday till about 4 tho the Chief talked to the new class all morning and I sat up in front yawning prodigiously. I came home about 7 with every intention of writing to you but suddenly discovered it was morning. I was in pajamas which surprised me greatly.

As you no doubt know, I love you. Hey! What I meant to say was as you no doubt know, I have your book. You said you were reading for an advance assignment so I didn't know if you want me to mail it back to you. (I'm hoping to have finished it by the time I get your answer.)

Altho I'm supposed to drop the blood flows, I just had some new tubes made and had to try them out today. For a while my result checked out perfectly with what Clare got tho later they didn't. Friday we're hoping to do an experiment together and no matter what the result, it'll be my last till the paper is written up. From all appearances her results are O.K. and I'll either run some more later if anyone insists or use her values since the few times my machine worked right, I got the same results as she did.

If there are any scraps of tobacco on this letter, you can probably guess why. I've remodeled the "rolling machine" and tried out the new model today with terrible results, tho I think I'm on the track of a workable model now. Don't worry about my not having cigarettes: I picked up a pack of Raleigh's and one of Chesterfield's this A.M. I'm learning when the local stores give out. I'd probably never use a cigarette machine if I had one (that worked!), it's just, well, like solving a word puzzle.

Do you remember anything we talked about in the Western? It seemed to me we had a fascinating conversation. All I can remember is that I decided you're undependable. I'd like to be able to put some more of the pieces together.

News items:

Mard heard from Howard and he is now all right. His pneumonia responded slowly to penicillin as they thought it was a virus type which isn't as dangerous but lasts longer, but the penicillin suddenly got to work and he's now well past the virus.

We wont have dental conferences till a week from Thursday but I'll take care to look over at Stern's lab tomorrow and Thursday.

I love you terribly but you crept right into my heart when you pillowed your head on my shoulder and said "I've never been so drunk!" and I was so proud when you greeted your friends so soberly on the train (not staggering til we were safely out of their sight.)

It's been a busy two days for me and will be even be busier after Phys. Chem starts again. I thought with less time to think, I wouldn't miss you so much, but when I sat down to this letter, it came over me in a flood and I realized that I had been thinking of you just below the surface since Sunday nite. There's no use in my looking for a solution, darling. I'm going to feel incomplete whenever we're not together.

Got letters from both my Mom and Pop yesterday. My father had a cyst removed last week and is resting up at a convalescent home. It was just a minor operation, but my mother predicts it'll be the topic of conversation and weapon to evoke sympathy for the next ten years. She also reports that my youngest brother, Morrie is expected in New York almost any day.

The radio has just announced that the Russians are 73 miles from Berlin, less than from here to you. Wow! Wonder if Stalin will feel incomplete til he gets together with Hitler! Good nite, keeper of my dreams. Good nite my ethereal darling. Good nite my solid stimulant.
All my love, D.

January 30, 1945
D. Darling,

I could have written you a good letter this afternoon. I felt all stirred up and at the same time lyrical. I'm still missing you as much as I did then but the ability to write it down has fled along with my energy.

I've missed you so much these past 2 days. I was and am very glad that I don't dislike college so heartily since vacation because before I always might have wondered if my loving you could be some sort of rationalization and escape from college but now that I feel better about up here I can completely discount any such nutty ideas. And I miss you even more since I'm happier here. Everything I do and see or think asks to be shared with you. I try to pretend you're here or to write my thoughts in letters but seeing you, being near you, is non-reproducible.

Yesterday afternoon I went to the first SLA meeting

with the newly elected officers. It's going to be more of a discussion group than formerly with more frequent meetings about current issues with the hope that we can reach conclusive decision enough to take some sort of action. We discussed the Wallace Commerce George Bill affair yesterday and I wrote Senator Mead this A.M to keep plugging.

Went to dinner at Main with Sara G, the new gal from Soph party et al. She's all excited about a blind date next weekend for Dartmouth Carnival. I hope nothing happens to her as I've heard the Carnival parties can be pretty bawdy which would not be good as she is about the most innocent girl I've ever met.

After dinner I had an IRG meeting to discuss our proposed exhibit on minority groups. .Had some difficulties as we had to define for ourselves our purpose, aim and means, starting with rather vague views and gradually coming around to more concrete ones. We're making this a more or less exhibit on the One Race One Nation idea with use of painted posters to show scientific facts and photos for different minority groups in action. We had had more complex ideas of showing education differences in the South etc but when it came to before –and- after or right and wrong pictures we suddenly realized since the exhibit is destined to be used at a town center, the audience would be much more likely to be comprised of the "before" and see only those pictures of the "wrong" as real and familiar. It's fascinating about obvious things one can forget in a thing like this. It's much more complex than it looks on the surface.

This A.M. wrote my senator as I've said and a couple of organizations for minority group photos, plus a little "work".

Polit: had a sprung quiz which was NOT a good idea. Read some Hamlin Garland short stories which was what got me stirred up. I'd read a novel of his several years ago and hadn't thought much of it, but these stories, in a collection called "Main Traveled Roads" are terrific . . . about the West, simple wonderful people with simple situations and beautifully, feelingly done. They give so much truer a picture of America than Whitman.

Got the book out tonight which has the Polit questions for our local government term papers: 90 questions each about 4 sub-divisions-some short answers. none hard if you know the material, not thought questions, just research. The dumb thing is that many kids send their mothers to look for the answers or, if it's a small town, write their friend, the mayor, who gives them the dope.

Last night from 10 to midnight Barb finally told me about a problem, a family problem, which I'd known was on her mind. It's a pretty awful mess and of course I couldn't help–except to listen. I guess everyone has his, her, their problems, but any problem that is even remotely comparable to us makes me realize how wonderful our lives are and will be.

Hope to get a letter from you tomorrow but if not I'll be patient and only mildly curse the medical and dental students for usurping your time.

Got an interesting and amusing 10 page letter from Dick including rather vivid descriptions of his friends and his own escapades involving talking himself out of a court martial-in front of a colonel and a major. He honestly gets away with murder.

Also got a letter from Walt who was in D.C. waiting to meet your friend Harry for lunch! When he was in NYC two weeks ago he saw a girl who has since come down with mumps. Just hope he doesn't get that as I don't think Officers Training camp waits for you.

Two weeks is going to seem hellishly long, darling, but I'll use your "lucky Philosophy" and all will be O.K., I'm sure. A tremendous hug, kiss with all the trimmings,
Yours,
V

January 31, 1945, 4-11 P.M.
Dear Darling,

I'm sprawled on the Soc. Museum floor waiting to be given instructions. Am to meet some kids here in about 10 minutes. Meanwhile I write to thee.

Got your letter today- this afternoon to be exact. Must I really stay sober three months before our children are born? I don't see why I have to. I want to initiate them early into the pleasures of drink now that I've learned!

Mary M. had a guy up here last weekend and she knew the train back didn't get to town until 11:50 so I felt most sorry for you. The bus ride or lack of same must have been a darn nuisance. How you got thru Monday, I don't understand. And who has been putting you into pajamas without your knowing it?

Are you really reading "Portrait of a Lady" and are you enjoying it?

Guess I'll learn your saying "last experiment" business sooner or later tho certainly can't blame you for wanting to tie everything together. (Just kidding you about the fact that you've said this was the last experiment several times.

I still have two full packs of cigarettes...am smoking less or have decided to do so in the future. I realized comparing when I have them and when I don't, that many times I start to smoke one when I really don't want one, really from habit.

No. I can't say I remember an awful lot of the conversation when we were at the Western. I do remember the one about analyzing people and I remember getting very serious and recall your comment in return. Do you remember?

Thanks for news of Howard. I got a postal from Mom today. It was good enuf news to warrant plenty of repetition.

You know, I could see how some day I could get jealous of your busyness. God! What things I do think of to worry about! But it is true in the sense that I know you're absorbed in your work and you should be! And I haven't found one equally absorbing field (besides you!)

That's swell about Morrie. I'd love to meet him. But maybe he's only in for a short time?

Had an interesting report for Sociology about a town in N.J. called Radlawn. Stop me, if you've read about it. It's a new 1929 development, experimental. A small group (1000) of people whose average age is men 35, women 33 with one or two kids. 77% Protestant, no exclusions. 87% college graduates with incomes must be between $2,000-3,000. Occupations are salesmen, engineers, teachers and Jr. executives. 88% work in NYC; the rest in Newark or N.J. Planned as a residential community with modern low cost housing with a tricky street and park layout. It's administered by a group of citizens who run it as a non profit organization.

This group thru questionnaires found varieties of activities were started: music, theater, all sorts of recreational stuff, forums, discussion groups, nurseries, courses in cooking. They have statistics of attendance which are quite remarkable. It seems a bit like an adult college campus with the advantage of housing and living planned for a certain standard. Couldn't help thinking of us and how it isn't going to be hard when modern living makes advances like this one.

Darn it, darling. Can't stop missing you for a minute. You probably say, "Why darn it?" but it is so difficult to think of it being like this for one and a half years. Perhaps I'd miss you less if I go to bed . . . but who am I kidding? Good nite, my wonderful one.
Your pickled Puss.

Febuary 2, 1945
Precious Pickled Puss,
(I don't care much for Precious but I had to match your alliteration)

I'm trying not to comment on how I feel about you and how much I'm missing you-we've said it so often before but I'll have to risk your getting bored since I enjoy telling you about you far more than telling anyone else.

Some of your reaction still catches me unaware. I had no idea you'd be enthusiastic about your drinking session. Instead I expected you to be slightly abashed at being so uninhibited in public. I'm glad tho that you feel the way you do about it-in an abstract way. I feel flattered that you trust me as completely (mentally that is). I seem to remember that you got serious at one point but I don't remember what my answer was and I'm anxious to know what I did say.

I don't see how you can criticize the girl who put on my pajamas. It seems to me a certain girl I know did some maneuvering while I was asleep without letting me know-she, too could have had MUCH more fun.

It's a good thing that I only glanced thru "The Portrait of a Lady" before reading it. The last page was 400 and something and I figured I'd finish it in a couple of days. It wasn't till I had read a couple of hundred pages that I found our there were two volumes and over 400 pages. By then it was impossible to stop. It's a fascinating book and I love his precise crisp prose. Each word is just THE word, with connotations and inner meanings that keep the mind jumping from one rich allusion to the next.

Every once in a while there's a sentence that reminds me of a piece of meat from which all the fat has been trimmed-It's lean and lithe and all meat. One of the beauties of James' characters is that you don't know what he himself thinks of them. I don't think you've met Merle and Desmond yet-it's an intriguing event worth looking forward to. And as for Isabel, well, I won't try to influence you before you decide about her yourself.

It's funny that just before you mentioned how many times I've done the "last" experiment and kept on doing just one more, I decided that enuf was enuf, cancelled today's "last" one and started getting my data together. I've got a book full of determinations done on one point but I don't remember what my answer was and I am anxious to know what I did say. About various dogs. I've got to make up talks for each type of experiment, calculate the changes that took place during each experiment, put it into percentages and draw the graphs for each dog. After that's done, Dr. Allison and I will sit down and go over the whole thing after which I'll start writing it up.

The cigarette machine is not beautiful but it makes cigarettes that aren't too far from the store bought variety. I haven't decided whether to bring it up to you or bring up a couple of packs of cigarettes. If I can pick up enuf "to keep you supplied." I'd rather give you them since you'd probably have trouble getting the tobacco and paper and the bought ones are better.

You might feel jealous of my busyness if we weren't together and it kept me from writing, but when we're together you'd want me to be busy-or did you mean envious rather than jealous? I wonder if we're the kind of people who want to own each other's minds as that while in all outward respects you could serve as the definition of loyal, I still think of you as "undependable" and while I'm not interested in other girls, you can still be jealous, sometimes. I think that we are starting on a plane of love and understanding that most other people are trying to reach and that any misunderstanding we will have will be in a very illusive kind of stratosphere level concerned with those vague feelings and emotions that don't quite reach consciousness-or am I being swayed by a fresh contact with our astute psychologist, Henry James?

Today was registration day and I found out that I'd passed Phys Chem O.K. We started with a class of 23. Four were asked to leave the course and 5 flunked- 9 out of 23, a pretty high percentage. We only get a "passed' mark so I don't know if it was an A or a B and don't much care. Poor Dottie flunked out.

You certainly sound as if you're doing a wide variety of interesting things, and I don't suppose your marks will be any the worse for it.

I haven't spoken to Peter yet, tho I think I know who he is. If Amy hasn't already said anything to him, I'd prefer that he doesn't know that I know her. It cant be terribly important but I think he'd be less self-conscious and I prefer a normal teacher-student relationship.One of the guys in the class took histology and bio-chem with me a couple of years ago. It seems funny to be his instructor now.

I feel in the mood to go on writing and writing to you. It's as if I end this letter it means that the week-end away from you is beginning but I'd like this to reach you tomorrow so I'd better quit now.

Good nite, darling. One week-end oughtn't to be so bad –but it is.. It is frustrating to love you so much, and I AM

thankful that it's you. I wouldn't go back to my old "incomplete completeness for anything in the world."
XXX—D

Febuary 2, 1945—late
Darling,

When I haven't written to you for 2 days I miss you just that much more. I guess it's because when I write, I feel the nearest to you possible without actually seeing you tho there have been moments when I've felt equally close if not closer when not writing. You're just suddenly here, very close if not closer and you console me, comfort me or give me an often much needed kick. Nice to have you around, dear.

I've been having a minor battle with a cold since Wednesday which I wouldn't mention except that you'd suspect me of even greater than usual laziness. One minute I give in to it and patronize its every wish, feed it drugs and give in to sleep and the next minute I completely lose my temper with it and tell it to promptly go to hell. I'm not kind to my colds:- particularly when I have to wash the handkerchiefs that my damn nose insists on needing. A whole paragraph about a cold, how dull!

Wed. I went to classes, except that Mr. V was sick so no Philosophy. Skipped bowling and slept and pampered "it". Thursday skipped my one class of Polit but when by 4:30 I found that pampering it was merely spoiling it, I went over to the Soc. Museum and then out to dinner.

I've been helping a girl at the museum working on a large frieze which is loads of fun. She's an art major and quite good . . . definitely out of my class and I distinctly play laborer to her role of master but I enjoy that too. This is an interesting girl. The same one who played the female lead in soph party though you probably don't recall her. She comes from Pittsburgh. Her family WAS wealthy and isn't now.

At any rate, she was brought up by governesses and went to high school in an extremely strict boarding school in Maryland, St. Timothy's. She's majoring in art, tho her family disapproves. She wants to live in Greenwich Village this summer and go to art school in NYC. Is more or less engaged to a guy at Harvard, a civilian who is majoring in English. These are merely facts. As to personality, she strikes one as rather delightfully naïve- no, not really naïve, but as if nothing really bothers her.

We discussed boarding schools and she said the shock of coming into the world, upon graduating, was terrific. But taken all in all, she'd send her own children there. I brought up the point that one didn't have very close family ties when one was away so much, which she agreed with ... said she didn't know her parents at all and she didn't think it right and yet she thought the "discipline" of boarding school was a good thing . . . good even enough and important enough apparently to surpass parental affection. Enuf about her, tho these are interesting points to think about.

Went out to dinner with a girl who used to go to my school and whose family I know. She's a smart girl, going to be Phi Bate and yet I can never seem to get beyond the mere essentials of conversation with her.

"How's your sister?"etc. I always have an insane desire to shock her for a reaction . . .

Miss Newcomer in Econ is really awfully good. Today: We've started on money and banking and she can even make THAT good. Unfortunately she's leaving for the west tonight for a couple of weeks stay so I don't know what will happen to money and banking.

No Philosophy again today. I wonder if Mr. V caught my cold or I caught his (p.s. joke)

Typed out the myriad questions for the Polit paper. There are 78 large questions and about 4 sub questions with each. They think up the darndest things!

Have been deeply engrossed in "Portrait of a Lady" and love it dearly. It's quite possibly too long but so terrifically superior to modern novels, don't you think? One feels as if you know the people so well . . . in fact, I dreamt about them last nite. I like reading it knowing you're reading it at the same time, sort of enjoying a movie seen with someone beside you.

Mr. Post isn't really as bad as I said. He agreed one shouldn't squash other people in desiring success but he did so with such a glint of humor that he twisted his own meanings whether purposely or not, I don't know. He's a young guy. Probably not too bad if he once just got over looking at himself in an imaginary mirror and stopped saying things only for their affect/effect.

My mother would call me impatient and intense, but I can't wait to be married to you. There are so many things, I want to be near you and to talk over the little things along with the big, that come up during each day. Just to know you're around would be awfully nice.

Only seven days plus one night before I'll see you. How delightful and how spoiled I am with the past consecutive weekends.

Does Mard know anything about Howard's leave? He'll probably get sent back here, at least temporarily, wont he?

I've done just about what you were doing with my picture: facing you while I am writing . . . only knowing certain things, I've grown greedy knowing the real McCoy. In other words, I want you . . . modern female subtly. What would James say?

All of me, my love and all my other things. V

February 3, 1945
Hello Darling,

Isn't life complex tho! I've finished "the Portrait" an hour ago. Couldn't stop reading it all day. I thought it comprehensive, complete and very engrossing. I live with those people and having finished it, I feel as if I've lost a group of friends. Or doesn't this happen to you when you read a good novel? I was really very wrapped up in it and life at college seemed very incongruous. I feel exhausted and sort of empty upon finishing it but I hadn't looked at the late mail so I trudged over tho the results were negligible.

I promised to wait dinner for someone so I couldn't see Peter as planned before dinner. Therefore I walked over to Amy's to see him earlier. I found her amidst scores of females trying on everyone's clothes and squealing Amy-ishly. Peter came and tho it was a bit awkward standing in the hallway, we talked for a few minutes. Got a general impression which was so hastily received it wasn't really fair. He seemed quite ill at ease, showing it being quiet rather than noisy which is something.

He wanted to know who you were. Apparently Amy had mentioned you; which course you taught. I asked him what he thought of physiology. He thought it wouldn't be tough which I said you thought he'd think. I mentioned that you said about being more interested in the way people got their answers than if they were right but I got the impression he either wasn't mature enough or didn't think enough of his brain capacity to exactly love the idea. Tho I may be misjudging him. Was really amused at the whole picture of Amy getting dressed and then this discussion.

Between it and feelings generated by "The Portrait", I came away feeling much older than the group I just left. Barb and I were talking of just that feeling last night. We've really made very few friends up here; just shut ourselves from them. It isn't a new thing for me; I've done it with girls for as long as I can remember. I never know how much of my thoughts on the subject are just rationalizations- such as I don't need female society en mass and that having you, I don't find the need for a great number of friends etc. And yet I think liking people, I'm missing something. I have so often been told I give the impression among women of my own age, of acting as tho I felt superior and to be honest, I DO in many ways, and yet I naturally want to be liked by them. But it certainly bothers me less than before, partly cause I consider my stay here as temporary and not my whole life. And I'm not the type to know a lot of people at once. Not even among boys. I guess I require a lot from my friends—perhaps too much when I think how few I have here that are really close.

It's also partly that I don't want what many of them want right now. I don't seem to require parties and their ideas of excitement.

Very often, darling, you make me feel like a very selfish heel. Not that YOU MAKE me. It's just that I realize it thru you ... in little things. I realize how often I've just thought about myself and my own reactions. As usual I don't see why you love me ... and I suppose we'll go on wondering that into eternity.

It's Saturday night-ish and my arms feel unaccustomedly empty; my head is in search of a shoulder, a very certain shoulder. I could continue enumerations but propriety, the thing everyone was so concerned about in "The Portrait" bids me stop. It is a gross understatement if I say I can't think of anything I'd rather do tonight than be alone with you. Gee, aren't we going to have fun when it gets warm!

I just phoned home because I hadn't heard about Howard since Mom wrote on Wednesday. There was nothing bad. I didn't think there would be but I didn't think they'd write if there was, tho I think they would tell me over the phone.

They were waiting to hear from Walt any minute. I should learn never to phone home when/if I need cheering up. It always makes me feel somehow as if I should be at home.

I hate to see my parents getting old. It makes me feel

so darn inadequate. I haven't been as good a daughter as I ought to have been. Tho why I should cast regrets about my family feeling onto you, I don't know.

   Barb and I have taken the night off to write letters and play records. For a change we're playing a bunch of old jazz. Teddy Wilson, Duke Ellington, etc which is fun. It's amazing how I don't care about swing the way I used to. I never was a "fiend" on the subject but I used to go out of my way to listen rather without discrimination to the stuff. In fact I used to treat myself when I was alone in the house, to playing records or the radio while I enacted stories I made up. I'd get into some glamorous outfit (I thought) and depending on the mood; I lived a life of bright lights or Salvation Army girl. If I made up a story tonight, it would take place at our country place, time: soon, characters you and me . . . no coffee, not even a cigarette; sound effects: low voices, purring, sighs, and panting.

   Don't ever forget I want you, darling. I hope I don't disappoint you. I'm not very pleased with myself. The best thing I've done was to fall in love with you. V

Febuary 4, 1945
Very Dearest most missed one,
   It's much earlier than I usually start Sunday's letter, but I just can't wait any longer to say hello to you. I've been spoiled by being with you so many weekends since Dec 15 that even a single one seems interminable.

   It wouldn't be an exaggeration to say that I'm been thinking of you 99% of the time since Friday eve tho I've done lots of work at the lab and have read the last volume of the "Portrait the Lady." The feeling has probably been accentuated by not having a letter from you since Friday morning (written Wednesday) tho you may have written since then. You said then that it's difficult to think of this going on for one and a half years-difficult is a vast understatement-when I'm not with you, I just don't seem to be anywhere.

Good news arrived in the mail on Saturday. On Jan 31 Ruth gave birth to a boy, Stephen and mother and child are fine, doing well, I presume since the postal was in her handwriting. This reminds me that I never found out what we'd decided about calling our (when they arrive) that wozzy New Year' eve at Bridgeport. I'm starting to think you can hold your liquor better than I since you remember more details of those times than I do.

Also got a card from my mother that Morrie had been in to Philly. The mystery of why no Xmas and birthday present from her this year is now cleared up.
(You remember I passed up the lapse quite casually but I had been disappointed) She and Morrie had gotten together and bought me a wrist watch. He gets them half price in the Navy stores. I don't suppose Morrie will stop in here at all as they are mailing the watch to me. His ship usually put in at N.Y., tho sometimes at Norfolk, Va. There's a certain young lady he rushes to see in Philly and I don't think he'd be such a dope as to come up here on one of his rare chance to see her. How well I understand!

Worked til 5 o'clock yesterday organizing the data. It's amazing how much work I've done in the past year and a half. Working close with the numerous figures, numerous "misfit ting" determinations seem to stand out all over the place calling attention to themselves loudly tho these exceptions are hardly noticeable. It's a lot of fun trying to find the best way to present the stuff as it'll bring out the important points most clearly. For instance the amino acids rise after hemorrhage and keep rising till death. I made columns of the control values, I, 2, 3, 4, hours after bleeding and terminal figuring that the averages of these columns would show the rise. Instead, it shows just the opposite because dogs with the highest values died the soonest as that the first two columns had some high values that didn't appear in the 3rd and 4th hours as the dogs had died before then. To get around this I'm going to graph each dog, divide the time from bleeding till death into 4 parts and see if the average of each quarter doesn't show the rise better. Is this confusing?

On Friday afternoon Clare, Dr. Allison and I went over her paper. It was valuable experience for me and Clare remarked (and I incline to agree) that I should have less trouble with mine than she had with hers. She has a remarkable knack of not being able to say what she means!

Yesterday Mard, Clare and I had lunch together. Clare had a funny story to tell about a used rubber that someone had tossed into the girl's living room at Bard. It was found by the house mother, and she's now interviewing each of the girls. Altho the girls are pretty sure some fellow had done the dirty deed, they're getting huge enjoyment out of the woman's search for the guilty girl and have even suggested a general meeting if the individual questioning doesn't produce any results and the poor lady gratefully accepted the helpful suggestion. All the girls are future M.D.s and quite blasé about sex which the poor house mother isn't and I'm afraid she's in for some nasty ribbing.

We also got around to Jane and I was a little surprised and delighted by your mother's attitude toward it. In a long talk with Mard she didn't think Jane should sleep with the guy but her reasons (at least her spoken ones) were based on Jane's future happiness and not on abstract issues of morality. I'm quite sure that her upbringing would cause her always to come to the same conclusion no matter what the circumstance, but I'm glad she realizes that conventions and ingrown concepts of morality are not virtues per se. Can't you just picture her saying to us "YOU two are in love and would get married immediately except for financial and school reasons so I don't see why you shouldn't sleep together?" Or doesn't she think we've known each other long enuf to be sure?

The Portrait of a Lady is a wonderful exciting thought provoking story. After I'd started the second part I couldn't put it down tho it was 4:30 AM when I'd finished. As entrancing and absorbing as it was, still my thought of you were mingled thru out the book. Each chapter had some mental link with you in one way or another, and I kept wondering how you'd react to the people involved; tho I have no doubt what your general reaction will be. You'll love the book and I honestly envy you for not having already had the experience of having finished it. His style is very reminiscent of Conrad's tho on a more detailed basis. Whenever Conrad deals with the same intangible motivations of will, conscience, duty and love, he paints in only the good and background leaving you to interpret the actions of the characters while James suggests his interpretation much more concretely. But each is a master in his own field and both manage to make their people "felt" rather than just understood.

The cigarette machine is working OK. The ends aren't as nice as the bought ones and tend to fall out when I carry them around in the case, but they're fine for smoking here in the room. I bought a package of general papers and found they're wheat papers and tend to go out when you're not puffing on them.-which isn't a bad thing.

It's about 35 degrees today and the ice is melting rapidly. There was a solid 3 inch sheet covering 193rd St. but now you can see it disappearing hourly. Every time I see how much is gone, I think of Leon and his receding hairline which was the butt of our jokes for years (and bothered Ruth's as much as our cracks about her recessive bust line annoyed Leon.) It also makes me think of the approach of Spring-of warm, balmy, looking forward days to be spent out doors. This in turn reminded me of out last warm Sunday together when we sat on a wooden bridge watching leaves and froze and talked of life while the idly drifting leaves whirled underneath. We bathed in the deeper currents of the unity we were beginning to recognize.

I seem to be in a sentimental mood so I might as well continue. Last nite I heard a popular (?) song called,

"My Heart Sings". Ever heard it? It's a very rare occasion when the words of a popular song mean anything to me, but this one so fit my mood that it affected me strongly. Let me know if you've heard it.

In one of your letters this week you remarked that you could have written me a good letter earlier but by the time you sat down to write it, you were tired and weren't feeling so lyrical. Of course I love to hear from you when you are not only feeling close to me but are also in the mood to put it into words, but I also want to hear from you during the other times. A peak would no longer be outstanding if we were on it all the time and many times even while we capture that elusive feeling, it's impossible to put it into words. While I'm conscious of the desire and need to hear occasionally that you love me, miss me and feel close, I wouldn't want you to think that I expect you to have your deepest emotions on tap every hour of every day. Forgive me if I'm laboring an obvious point, darling.

That newspaper clipping was very interesting to me, It's nice to have guys put in a good word for the superiority of PhD's as instructors over MD's but the most interesting thing was that this is about the fifth of a series of letters from different top men over the past couple of months on the subject of raising the salaries of people like me. They disagree on different points but they're all agreed that PhD's who are doing research work and teaching should get better pay. Eventually I hope (and think) something will come out of that. I had figured that the most conservative top salary I could count on was about $4,000-enuf, I figure ell, if not luxuriously. If this is upped by 1,000 we can live well beyond any financial worries.

It's impossible for me to end this letter without telling you (and myself) again how much-how terribly much I've missed you this week, how much I love you-how happy I'm going to be some day even these separations are no longer necessary. So long, my love–I'll be seeing you in 5 days–1220 hours. X's from here to infinity.

All my love, your fiancé, D.

Febuary 4, 1945

Dearest,

I've always thought myself quite self sufficient not wholly so naturally, but fairly so. But I've missed you so darn much this weekend that I haven't been good for much work-which fact both pleases and displeases me. I found myself thinking some rather wild thought such as how silly it was for me to be here when you are there but as my father would say "we must be practical" and so here I am and there you are.

What have I done in the valuable time in which I'm supposed to be receiving my education? Last night I wrote letters; finished the one to you and then ripped off three more: one to Ruth and I felt distinctly awkward in everything I had to say and yet I wanted to write it.

This morning I read the paper thoroughly for the first time in weeks (really read it tho there wasn't much new to read. You realize how little the poor correspondents know: they try to throw together an article and so often either they can't or don't have the knowledge to say anything illuminating; washed my hair and "I can't do a thing with it" is true this time. It needs your mussing it up! Darlingest, did I ever tell you I love you? Well, I do. I love you when you're cute and when you're not; when you talk and when you're silent; when you're near me and when you're 80 miles away. So I washed my hair.

Went to the libe and hunted down books for my Amer. Lit paper. I'm going to have troubles. Partly cause I don't know exactly what I'm doing and partly cause the books that would help me aren't books but magazine articles which few libraries keep-much less have copies dating to 1902.

Came back after dinner feeling awfully restless and continuing my "wild thoughts'. So Barb and I went to the movies. Saw "The Very Thought of You" which has more kisses in it than any Hollywood movie I've seen. It didn't help missing you less but it was pleasant tho definitely no great picture.
Laughed heartily at the silliness of the second feature and here I am.

When can you come up this weekend? Early or not? Oh hell, darling, I find that whatever I start to write I find myself saying and wanting to write "I want you, I love you and I want to be with you" but I imagine that gets a little tiresome after a while even if you like to hear it. So instead I could write you how Barb and I giggle foolishly while tripping the light (?) fantastic over the ice on the way to the movie. What a pleasant sign it had been to hear the icicles melting in the sun today. Spring is just 6 months around the corner, thought. So we come out of the move and find an inch and a half more snow under foot and God's dandruff still shaking down to earth.

I could tell you how I love to wander around the library finding strange and wonderful books-sprawling myself on the floor between the stacks and rummaging thru old papers. Or I can tell you what infinite pleasure I get in thinking of myself as a "bad woman" and how nice it is to be "bad" with you.

It's funny how my thoughts of you "hit" me. You're there, just underneath the surface as you call it, all the time, but there are certain unpredictable moments when you, your kindness and your masculinity or various other qualities, suddenly flashes very clearly, deeply across my mind and it's at those moments that I want to run to you, or when I'm not very fond of myself and I want to be soothed and pampered back to "normalcy" or shouldn't I be so honest?

All my tenderest, deepest passionest—

That's a heck of an abrupt ending. For once, I reread over this letter and once again I wonder at your love for me. V

Febuary 5, 1945

Dearest Duchess,

Thank god this weekend is over. From your two letters that came today I gather that by Friday one didn't arrive till today either.

What a day Friday was! An inexcusably table of the dentals kept me in the lab til 6:30 tho I'd warned them that

I had to leave at 6. From 6 to 6:30 I tried to show them why you had to have marks showing where the writing levels and the signal magnet were at the beginning of the experiment if you wanted to figure the latest period-the time between the shooting of the impulse and the twitch of the muscle. Is that so very difficult to understand, darling? Anyhow I had no time for dinner before our first Phys Chem. class of the new semester. The guy (we're not having the demon after all) kept us overtime and so it wasn't til 9:30 that I could read your letters and then get something to eat.

I waited for the mail til 8:30 this morning, and then had to leave. The postman was working his way down the street and tho he was nice about it, wouldn't give me my mail as it was near the bottom of the bag.

Don't be too much bothered that Peter knows that I know Amy though I rather that he didn't. It was unimportant and won't be unless he acts "familiarly". You might not approve, but I've found that things go best when the instructor is friendly with the fellows and still think of them as my "fellows' more than anything else-but some of the guys got slipshod and expect me to wink at it. I finally had to freeze a bit toward them (tho often makes me laugh inside) and from there on things went much better. I'm sure whether you would or wouldn't be surprised at how stern I can be when I think the situation calls for it. It's always my desire to have the fellows respect me because of how I teach and act but in any case there are some who mistake friendship for weakness and I step on them hard.

I had no idea you were reading "The Portrait of a Lady" too. Our comments on the worth of the story pretty well agree tho I didn't feel as if I were losing any particular friends at the end of it. Ralph, Henrietta and Casper were "on my side" but I had no love for the rest of them, especially Desmond and Isabel-especially Isabel who sacrificed many other people's happiness for her sense of duty which to my mind seemed like intelligence without understanding-tho of course women were much more bound in those days. I agree that no modern writers measure up to James but then he'll stand out in any period..

Are you trying to wear me down with this talk of marriage? If you're not, I'm highly disappointed in you. After this past weekend, I'm in a highly receptive mood. Every time I looked at your picture, I regretted every second that I hadn't looked at you while you were here-and for every second that I did look, I regretted that I hadn't kissed you. If you were here now and felt kittenish, I'm afraid that I'd just go ahead and rape you.

I hope you're over the low you were in when you wrote on Saturday's letter. (Saturday nites are by far the worst of the week-ends.) When you start in on how unworthy you are for noble me, I know you are in a soul-flogging mood and I just ache to be where you are. If you think these tactics are going to break my lease on you, you are pursuing exactly that wrong course. (Need I say P.S. joke?).

I'm a little surprised at your attitude toward the girl who is a good artist.-how superior she is to you. Do you expect to be as skillful as an art major? And remember that skill and technique and craftsmanship reach a level of development-after that its ideas, imagination and soul that counts and if you're lacking in any of these, I'll eat my proudest possession, the lapel pin.

Tomorrow I'm going to look at a room near school that was advertised in Saturday's Times. It's probably taken by now, but if it isn't and if it is clean and if it's cheap enuf, I may take it. It would be nice to be near school-especially since I'll be doing lots of library work and who knows there might be a phone in the house!

The new Phys Chem instructor seems much nicer than-the demon was, but he's a young guy and 4 times tonite had to go back and put something in that he'd forgotten. It's easy enuf to do this on the board, but it messes up your notes and leaves you feeling confused at the end of the period. I must say that the demon knew her stuff andI'm even missing her challenging attitude a little (a very little).
The class has shrunk to about 8 this term-ample comment on what they thought of her!

There are about ten girls in this year's medical class at P. and S. but tho some of them are cute, they all seem very young. (You are mature for your age, darling. You're mature and still young, a combination I knew I wouldn't be able to resist if I ever met you) but don't worry about my happiness–there will be 40 girls in the next class when I'll be finished with my studying and you'll still be in school! Aren't I farsighted, Kitten?

It is exactly 12 o'clock and for the past 5 minutes I've

been thinking such thoughts so-suppose you came in Friday evening, the weekend of your mother's birthday and we spent the nite here and had half of Saturday to ourselves. It would be within a week of your period- the safest time- but why should I torture myself like this. I'm so hungry for you, darling, that I'm ready to get into bed with your picture and my thoughts.
Good nite, you very special you
All of my love, D. your fiancé.

Febuary 5, 1945 (6 mo and 9 days)
Darlingest,

    Part of my despondency over the weekend was the fact that I hadn't heard from you since Thurs. And now all is wonderful having received 2 glorious letters in one day- one written Fri. and one written yesterday (Sun.). They were such nice letters too, in fact I've been going around with even more of a glow than usual. I was again amused at our overlapping ideas—how we both say the same things in our letters which cross: i.e. missing each other and risking boring the other by saying so. Aren't we dopes!

    I'm awfully glad a few of my reactions catch you unawares tho I must confess I don't plan them to. You didn't think I'd be proud of my drunken stupor, did you? I guess it's just a feeling of being glad it all comes down to not always being the dependable woman. Who for instance would have guessed my joys at being a bad woman? But I guess it all comes down to being proud of whatever we do together. Discriminating, aren't I? I'm glad anyway I have the sense to have independently or dependently fallen in love with you. I'm also glad you don't remember your answer when I got "Serious" when we were at the Weston. I was sort of hoping you wouldn't remember. You might feel funny hearing it repeated and I loved it so much at the time that I just want to save it the way it was. May I?

You keep mentioning the Portrait of a Lady as tho I hadn't read it but I guess by now you've heard that I was probably turning the pages the same days you were. I think we enjoyed it equally and for the same reasons. They were such real people and had so many universal traits as can be seen by Barb, your and my thoughts of them. For both Barb and myself, it brought out many of our own foibles and experiences and in the relationships between people it made me think of us.

I'm sorry I mentioned you to Peter tho I couldn't have helped it seeing as Amy had already mentioned you. It was silly of me not to think that it would put you in an awkward position.

Now to rereading (for about the 6th time) your Sunday letter. It brings you especially close and I'm in the mood for closeness. Queen Victoria must really turn in her grave at the modern (forward) girl.

That's terrific about Ruth and "it". I'm so glad it is now named Stephen as I felt foolish when I wrote to her when he was only 4 days old and unnamed. I wanted to write even so and I trust she'll understand.

After you prided me so on remembering more than you when we were in our alcoholic state, I have to confess I don't recall having come to any decision on naming our children.

Maybe we didn't come to any?

Organizing your data sounds like a big job but it must make you feel good to see how much work you've done. Must get back to studying.

love, love, love, from Me

Febuary 6, 1945
Dearest one,

It seems that all I do these days unless I'm forced to pay attention to something else, is think of you, what you've written, that I'll write. Even before you mentioned it, I was wondering what you do Sat. morning and if 10:11 would be too early for me to arrive? Don't hesitate to let me know if this is too early for you-unless I hear otherwise from you, this is the train I'll make. The way the mail is these days you'll have to write soon as you get this letter, if you'd rather I make a later train (I'd leave before Sat.'s mail gets here).

Today was decided on working on my data, doing some administrative work for the Dentals and getting side tracked for a couple of hours in a fascinating discussion of Wang's work. Taking them up in reverse order: I learned that Wang was a bad guy as a kid. Not that he takes it wrong (he seems to like the feeling of being right) but when I teased him about his experiments, he hauled me into his room and went over all that he's done and is doing and it's one of the most beautifully conceived series of experiments that I've ever seen. He's a most logical and thorough investigator and I'd be proud if some day I'd turn out some work that is as good.

As you probably know there are many kinds of shock from which animals and people may die. Wang set out to prove a) that there is a difference between hemorrhagic shock and traumatic (muscle injury) shock and to try to prove that the nervous system involvement makes up most of the difference. He proved the point brilliantly by showing that dogs that die from hemorrhage have much less blood left in them than when they die from trauma-that is, trauma is severer so that those dogs die at a certain blood level while the hemorrhage dogs coma go on living until they reach a much lower level.

Then, to show the difference is nervous, he hemorrhaged dogs then stimulated the nerve from the dog's leg and they died much sooner (just like the traumatic ones). To clinch the point he is now traumatizing dogs whose nerves from the injured leg have been cut in a previous operation-and these dogs act very much as if they were hemorrhaged! I'm sorry if I've bored you with this long recital darling, but it is such a clear-cut well planned experiment that it's a thrill for me even to write about it.

To get back to the second of my activities-administration work for the Dentals: It's beginning to look as if the running of the Dentals will be left to me (and later to Clare) despite all my efforts to dodge it. The other people are rotated almost weekly while we'll be there for two months at a time. If there's to be any continuity to the course, it's up to us to supply it, and so here I am making the necessary announcements, putting up notices, deciding who will take which conferences and what we'll cover in the conferences-an honor which leaves me completely unimpressed.

As for the last item: going over my data, this is progressing moderately well. The graphs are shaping up beautifully and I suspect it'll turn out to be rather a nice picture. I'm a bit startled at the number of dogs and mound of work that's piled up. There's to be a national meeting at Cleveland in a month or so and Root dropped in to ask me if my paper would be well enuf along to write up and short resume to be printed in the meeting's proceedings. There's no special honor involved and I don't think I'll be ready in the one week I have to get out the resume. Besides there's a good chance the meeting will be called off on account of transportation difficulties.

This afternoon Mard showed me a most intriguing picture of herself, Walt and you on a beach. It was taken about 8 years ago and you are sitting there just giggling your head off. Do you remember it? Incidentally this reminds me that I've been wanting to trade in the "sexy picture" of you that I have for one in which you are lying in snow with that irresistible laugh all over your face. Will you make the trade?

I've had some new ideas about a stolen weekend in March or early April. Remind me this weekend and we'll see how that looks to us.

After going to see the room near school that I mentioned and finding the lady out, I reconsidered and now think I'll stay here. The advantages of here are: it's cheap and kept clean and towels are supplied and it's quiet. The advantages of the other one is that it would be closer to school and possibly have a phone in the house and better arrangements for receiving visitors. Unless the last two are included, I'd rather stay here.

Nick and I had dinner together tonite. We always have interesting fairly under the surface conversations and as you might expect, when my surface is scratched you pop out. We had been talking about what we like in women and how our values had changed over the years. Then he remarked that I like you quite a bit, didn't I? Repressing an enthusiastic outburst, I quietly said yes, and he made some very lovely and not perfunctory remarks about you. He likes you and especially admired your friendliness along with a certain reserve (somewhat like poise) that we both agreed we look for in women. He was also delighted you played tennis bare foot!

This is the last letter I'll be able to write that you can possibly answer before Saturday-another milestone passed in this long week. These past nine days have been the longest that I can ever want to go thru. Unless you're prepared to overwhelm me with love, darling, you'd better be ready to be overwhelmed yourself. You'd think that somewhere among the girls I've known before, I'd be able to recall some momentary feelings that would compare with the part of how I feel about you, but I've never felt anything like this about anybody and can't even begin to compare anything else to it. I love you, completely, and absolutely. The best thing that's ever happened to me is that you love me too. Impatiently, D.

P.S. I haven't asked about your cold not because I don't care but so that you wouldn't think I too worried.

Febuary 6, 1945
Hello Darling,

    I was still living on the nearness when your 2 letters came yesterday and as always you're right beside me now. Sometimes I even feel I don't have to tell you things because you're always right there and I figure you must know them instinctively which must be a little tough on you who are, after all, but human.

    But you kept me company last night in bed while a mere onlooker might have though I was hugging Fooless in the dark – the truth of the matter: it t'weren't Fooless at all, but a certain guy. You were there when the alarm went off- in fact you pushed me out of bed and you needled me into cleaning thoroughly—cleansing the room (I forgot to clean last week ...Tuesday is cleaning day until 20 minutes before inspection time and the result was a rather make shift job.) So I attacked the matter with vengeance. When I'd completed that I started on cleaning clothes. You're right, darling, your way of washing handkerchiefs is infinitely superior to mine. The things you do teach me!

    Then you went with me to the drugstore where I bought all sort of things for the future cleanliness of myself i.e. soap, tooth paste. Then to get you a pillow on which to lay your weary head this Sat. night. The man at "the Pines" where you're staying.(I never pick the same place more than twice) was a talkative chap who explained it was a double room but the customers always found it satisfactory since he saw to it personally that admirals didn't sleep with ensigns. I explained you were a civilian. He beamed and said, "well, they mix with anybody" hmmm. I also bought two cakes or rather ordered same for a party Valentines Party which Barb and I are giving on the 4th. Just having a bunch of kids and giving them some food.

You were with me in the libe where I embarrassed you by blowing my nose in such unfemininely tones as to reverberate thru the tombs of said institution.

P.S. I still have a cold tho it's much better. I'm so used to it I don't even notice it anymore.

You went to Polit where we both slept soundly and to Amer Lit which was better than usual. Talked to Mrs. Ellis about my term paper and the troubles I was having. She suggested taking just one museum and tracing both techniques and the displays and their correspondence to social trends which is much better. We figured the Natural History Museum (79th St CPW) would be a good one as I can get data if need be right from them and from the exhibits at present. Feel better about it.

It was a celebration day for Barb: 2 years since she met Johnny. So she treated Rosey and me to a drink before dinner at Alumnae House. I'm getting to be quite an imbiber … tho I didn't much like the taste of an Old Fashioned.

Rosey asked me to eat with Mrs. Fritz whom she'd invited to dinner. (the woman who taught Philos last term for a while). She proved to be a sweet undynamic soul; went to Smith, married and just had a son who is Charles

Allen Fritz III. (We are not going to have a junior much less an III, yes?) We played records and I think Mrs. F was a little bewildered at Burl Ives and Josh White but she took it quite well. Rosey is quite a gal. Certainly not the essence of tact and I spent the dinner time playing mom's usual role of trying to play appeaser and general soother. Another girl came too. The one I spoke to in Alumnae House. She stayed after Mrs. F. left and is an entertaining soul. She's changed her major from Econ to Psyc to Anthropology so we felt rather like kindred souls. We got talking about sex via Mrs. Lee's (anthropology prof) ideas on nursing of children. Mrs. Lee has 4 children, won't have anesthesia when they are born as she likes to suffer the pain of childbirth . . . thinks nursing essential and the most wonderful act a woman can do. From there the discussion went to the number of kids people wanted. The fact that the higher income groups had less kids than the lower and they were the ones who could give their kids advantages etc. At one point we talked of the moral status of us "girls" and Joan said that 9 out of 10 kids on her corridor last year weren't virgins. Much discussion about lurid facts about said cases (which only goes to prove one should keep one's mouth shut). Rosey was delightful in appearing to take no interest in the question, tho I think she was listening intently.

 Barb and I were invited to a meeting of the curriculum committee and some of the trustees on Fri eve concerning the 4 course mess which might be entertaining.

 Wrote to Jane and am interested in what she has decided to do . . . interested both subjectively and ethically.

There are a few cases of German measles around and everyone makes great surveys of themselves and others to determine "who's next"!

Got a long and nice letter from my mother...more warm than usual. I wonder what the incident (discussions) of Jane has made her think about us.

Can't wait to see you, darling. Just about 84 hours from now. How lovely!

1 haven't planned anything but that's what's so nice. Neither of us plan anything and yet we both do what we ourselves and the other person want. Sometimes I think we're too good to be true.

Amy is definitely straight on the fact that Peter is not for her permanently. They had a "long talk" which made her realize that all Peter wants out of life is a pleasant set of friends–which his friends mean more to him than anything else. I knew he was intelligent and alive enough for her but I'm glad she realized that that wasn't enough.

Good night, my fiancé. I'm hungry both physiologically and psychologically (and that's not a misprint).

Bring an apple and yourself and satisfy my desires. Forget the apple. I can do without that!

Love, V

Febuary 7, 1945–11 p.m.
Darling,

My estimates of dental students go perceptibly down i.e. why it should take them so learn to mark the beginning of the writing lever. I remember it is quite obvious, but I guess at 6 P.M. anything takes a while to sink in. But it was a shame you had to miss dinner. You seemed a little sad at not having the demon again for Phys Chem but I can see that the shrinkage to 8 in number must be a bit forlorn . . . and, after all, what fun is a male teacher?

No, I agree with your ideas about student teacher relationship and I can see teachers here having the same attitude. The fact that I'd had Mrs. Ellis as an advisor and a friend, that Mard had known her with many mutual friends was fun for both of us but made it a bit awkward when I took Amer. Lit from her. Of course it's mostly due to the dumb system of ours: marks et al. If things were merely on an individual basis a teacher wouldn't have to be quite so on guard though I guess the problem of respect would always be there.

You can try to kid me out of my "unworthy motif" if you wish and I heartily hope you have success but its true, never-the-less. You'll just have to get used to my thinking in contrary methods of myself as inferior to other people and yet in some ways, superior.

Now to defend my attitude toward the artist and how superior she is to me–I meant regarding art, tho not particularly otherwise. She is better than I artistically with equally little training and I do admire both her skill and her ideas. I didn't mean to imply she was a skilled craftsman.

Anxious to hear about the room near school as it would be nice for you and a phone would be pleasant. tho not certainly necessity. (That's to sooth you in case it was already taken).

I thought such thoughts as you thought at 12 o'clock

writing the letter i.e. coming in Friday nite but you miscalculated, darling-and I love you for it. I should get the curse on the 16th or 17th if it's on time in which case I'm not fit for company of man or dog, much less certain types of company. But we can discuss the possibilities this weekend, Yes? How nice!

Had a different Econ Prof today as Miss Newcomer went to give some lectures out West. Miss Myers-looks old maidish except she has a lovely smile . . . was a bit surprised to learn she was married and has a son in North Africa. We're studying bank balances at the moment and it all seems very crazy as I'm reading "Grapes of Wrath" at the same time (for Amer Lit) and you see the bank as an insurmountable monster which kicks the poor tenants off the land and sends them on their migratory paths.

Started bowling beautifully today . . . had 74 at the half way but as usual messed it up.

Had an IRG meeting and the problems of organizing for the high school exhibit is a tough one. There's so much to say and between selection of material and methods of presenting it, we're running around in circles.

My new co-op job is cleaning corridors which isn't too bad and linen distribution 3 times within the next 5 Sunday evenings. It's a hard job to get subs as it comes at 9:30 Sunday eves . . . not the next two Sundays tho.

Was supposed to play in the tennis double tournament tomorrow but my partner is in the infirmary and it's been postponed for so long that I think we may have to default.

Found myself thinking a funny thought on my walk over

to bowling. I was thinking how easy it would be to slip, hurting myself, to being delirious . . . having my parents come up . . . to calling for you—to have my father call you up at school to tell you to come up. Found myself creating the whole phone conversation. You figure it out, Psychologist!

Did I tell you that Connie's friend Ellie told me she had spoken to Connie's sister and that they were going to get married Feb 3 at a moment's decision. Don't know if they did—or if it's going to be this weekend. I gather you haven't heard???

Amy's parents are coming up this weekend. They're awfully nice people and I've always been very fond of them, particularly her mother. (It's her step father. Len who has the house on the frozen lake is her real father.) I've told them a bit about you and I guess Amy's told them her version. Anyway, they'd like to meet you and I'd like to have you meet them. So we'll see them some time over the weekend if it's OK with you. (Also haven't seen them in ages and would like to).

Was thinking of asking you if you'd be interested in coming up Fri. instead of Sat but before I did, along came an invitation to a student faculty trustee meeting on the 4 course business on Friday eve which I shall have to attend.

But at any rate, I'll see you in 60 hours and what are 60 hours? (I know, don't say think what you can do in 60 hours). Boy, "Grapes of Wrath" certainly doesn't mince language, does it? Lovely train of thought, yes?

Guess what I got in the mail today? You'll die laughing or at least I did. Dave sent me a grass skirt! Which was amusing enuf but when I put it round my waist I found it only went half way around! Couldn't decide whether to be flattered or insulted! And certainly don't know what I'm going to do with the darn thing.

Conversation:

Me: "some people turn to prostitution for money; I will for cigarettes"

Barb "But think of all the social diseases."

Me: "Well I'd be discriminating."

Betts: "Choose your clientele?"

Me: "No, my brand of cigarette."

Your silly girl friend.

February 7, 1945
Hello Darling,

Tonite was to be devoted to Phys Chem but a) I discovered Dotie still had my book since the exam- just remembered that I haven't looked on the dresser and there it was. But there is still b) which is that I have a full day's teaching tomorrow followed by class and a letter to you after class might not show up till Saturday. Heck, now I have no excuse not to study Phys Chem tonite. The new guy is having us hand in problems on Monday instead of Thursday and since I'll be with you this weekend (wow!) I've got to get them done by Friday.

Discovered today that the five graduate students who are in with the dentals have another class at 9 o'clock tomorrow when the dental conference is scheduled so your soft hearted and dopey fiance offered to give them a special one at 11 tomorrow. They're pretty nice people, interested in the course, and I didn't have the heart to throw them in with the 60 medical students in what is euphemistically called a conference. This means one hour less for me, but it'll be a pleasant hour. I'll have to study up on the stuff for them as they'll probably ask much more difficult questions that the dentals do.

After I'd addressed a few remarks to the lab group today Peter came up and introduced himself. We only exchanged a few words, and he seemed like a pretty nice guy. Towards the end of the day, his table was one of the last finishing and I hurried them up. It was amusing (nasty fellow that I am) to see Peter leap to clean up their table. I've got an idea that he'll be a model student whenever I'm around! But you may have to get used to your girl friend's boy friend thinking of me as an older generation.

The Watch came this morning and it's a beauty! Sweep hand and shock proof. It has a bronze face and looks a lot like yours (your watch not your face) (I'm afraid to trust you with an analogy-you carry them so far!)

Oh yes, I made a decision for you today. I hope its O.K. with you. Mard was sending for tickets to "Dear Ruth" for Howard, herself and Clare and wanted to know if we'd join them when you'd be on vacation. I said yes and to make it early in the week of April 15th OK? We both remarked how wonderful it was to talk about April . . . made it seem closer.

Clare pulled one of her super dupers the other day which I'm sure you'll appreciate to the fullest. She and Chris were trying to bleed a dog so that it would die in about 4 hours. The dog's blood pressure went way down and she held her breath, hoping he wouldn't die too soon. After a while the dog took a big drop and Clare got ready for the final samples. Just then his blood pressure shot way up and the dog never died. When she told me about this just to be helpful, I asked whose blood pressure went up, hers or the dog's? She said, "the dog's" and then realizing that I was kidding she added entirely unintentionally," Chris and I were rolling and panting at the time!"

Gene wrote today that he's getting engaged to a London girl named Rose in February. Everybody does it except us! Talked to Mard at some length yesterday about us. I wouldn't have started but she practically put the words in my mouth and seemed anxious to talk. I'll tell you about it this weekend.

Just think-only two days til Saturday. I've looked forward to this college visit even more than any previous one. Instead of getting used to being incomplete, it gets worse with us which as you said is pleasing but not pleasant. See you Saturday morning.

Love, D.

PS. On Feb 5th you wrote 6 mo.11 days from our day. It should have been 6 mo–9 days. You're a terrible disappointment, darling. Don't you know that I'm depending on you to remember birthdays, anniversaries and so forth not only ours but all our friend's families too?

P.P.S. My God, nearly forgot to say I love you. Lord, how I do!

February 10, 1945

Dearest,

    This is being written 5 minutes after you left Sunday nite and there's not much news somehow unless you call my knowing that you're a terrific guy and that you're the guy I love and the guy for me, is news. And it is news, the best I can offer and tho its' an old report, it's still up to the minute, in fact, it's a news flash right from the scene of the action.

    Perhaps this will reach you before Wednesday, before that drag on the early-week-empty-mailbox has a chance to set in. If it does you'll know before Wed. that I miss you. (You've been gone 10 minutes now). I think you're wonderful and hard to believe.

All of my lof, love, affection, passion, admiration and please be my Valentine!

V

February 12, 1945

Dearest,

    Got home about 12:05 a good 2 and a half hours earlier than the usual time. The trip wasn't bad. I didn't get a seat at first but walked to the end of the last car and sat on my dependable weekend traveling companion suitcase. Some guy claimed he was supposed to have gotten off at Beacon just after we pulled out of the place. A conductor whose job seemed to be to wave a red lantern at the cows as we passed, told him to ride to Harmon and get a train back and that the ticket collector would give him a ticket for a free ride back. Instead the conductor made him pay 70 cents to get to Harmon and told him to buy a return ticket there. The guy griped loudly (after the conductor had gone and said a) he hadn't called out the station and b) he hadn't collected his ticket to Beacon which would have told him it was time to get off.

After he'd gone the lantern waiver sat where the fellow had been sitting. He showed me that the window shade had been all the way down and said the conductor had charged him because he suspected the guy had deliberately gone past Beacon-which shows there are two sides to many questions. We talked some more and he told me that quite a few soldiers were buying extra tickets to the stop before theirs and were then playing drunk and "accidentally" riding past their stop.

There was a letter here from Dave containing a notice of their wedding with no explanation attached. You may think we've been slighted, but knowing Dave as I do, I think it was one of their usual last minute affairs. They were supposed to have been married on the 11th but made it on the 3rd instead-probably last second compromise between a brief ceremony with witnesses and a larger affair with the notices going out a week later.

It's been too wonderful a weekend even to talk about, Darling. I've never felt so close to you so continuously—the radio just announced "My Heart Sings" with a few corny lines and some very apt ones. I may pick up a copy though it's not what I have in mind for Valentine's Day, our anniversary.

I'll never forget how you looked in town when you

d me about college vs. Sarah Lawrence. Something in your face went straight down deep inside of me. I feel loose inside just recalling it.

Good nite, darling.

I'll love you always—even if you become a punster!

As ever D.

Febuary 13, 1945

To my Dearest Darlings and Trickiest Valentine,

A happy Valentine's Day and a most enjoyable ½ a year anniversary to you–may I wish you many many more of each!

You know, darling, from the looks of things, we're going to spend a large part of the future time and energy in cooking up little surprises for each other. It was a wonderful surprise to get your note Monday and yet like all your surprises, I wondered afterward why I hadn't guessed you'd do something like that- it's so typical of you a)to be so thoughtful and b)not to let the fates doom me to a perpetual mail-less Mondays or Tuesdays.

One week is not 1/10 as bad as two weeks away from you-tho in all honesty I must admit that I continually picture a time when we can be together permanently. Without a weekend in between, it seems as if I've seen you just a short time ago (the college glow is just beginning to become distant and I'll be seeing you in only a few days after you get this letter . . . I hope!

I've been thinking of the past six months and find it difficult to put into words the vast change you've made in my life. You're such a close part of me that I can remember that but I can't recall how I once lived without you. I remember how I once thought that marriage for me was like God for some people, not necessary for a complete life if you were sure of where you were going (A confused sentence, I'll admit). Now that is all changed. You've appeared so much better, so much nicer, so much more perfect than I had ever hoped that I'll never get over the feeling that some day I'll wake up. Love you truly, darling, in every sense of the word.

Yesterday was medical lab day-all day and Phys Chem at nite. A rather pleasant event occurred in class that nite-one of those things that gives one new hope in a hard world. Dottie came back to class. She had gone to the very severe woman who passes on your qualifications for taking Phys chem. in the hope she could take the second term of Phys Chem even tho she had flunked the first. Before Dottie could say a word, the formidable woman (She's pretty deaf which makes it worse to approach her)"I hope you do better in the second semester of Phys Chem. than you did in the first" and they're also going to give her a re-exam and give her a chance to pass the first term's work. She told me after class that she hadn't yet got up the nerve to tell her family that she had flunked—Now it isn't necessary.

Spent all day today working on my data. I've finished the graphs and am now making tables of the values, at the beginning, 1/4, 1/2, 3/4 and at the end of each experiment. I'll make up a complete graph of the averages and hope it shows the points I'm trying to put across. I'll be finished this preliminary stuff early next week and can then get together with Allison for a conference before starting in on the actual writing.

It just occurred to me that if I give a talk on this work, it'll probably take place in the middle of the week and you probably won't be able to hear it–which doesn't grieve me tremendously.

I was rereading one of your letters today and noticed how much better I could picture some of your references to Mrs. Ellis now that I've seen her. I'm hoping to meet my heavy competition, Mr. Venable some day.

Told Mard today that you'll probably be in on Friday as well as Saturday and she said that's what the family had expected. I guess it wouldn't have been a good thing to have pretended that you'd be in only on Saturday-especially if I didn't show up around the lab that day, Do you have any idea when you'll get here? (I know you'll tell me even if I haven't asked, but I love to—it makes the weekend seem that much closer.

My activities are starting to press in on me from all sides. Phys Chem must be done, my data must be worked on, and conference must be prepared. Oh Well, I'll take them as they come and save my worrying for you, an infinitely more pleasant subject.

Took the watch to the jeweler today and discovered that the balance wheel was bent. The manufacturer was some little company neither of us had ever heard of, so I left it with him and should have it back by the end of February

Gee! February is half over already. In two months even you will have to admit spring is here. I thought you might not feel at home in NYC in the bare state in which I found

it yesterday so I ordered snow. It's been coming down since this afternoon and should reach 6 inches. Let me know if this isn't enuf and I'll see what can be done about it—La Guardia and my father are old friends.

It's just 9:30 so this should reach you tomorrow. If it arrives late, will you still be my Valentine?

All my love, D.

February 14, 1945
Dearest, D.

   Your letter was a lovely one today and made me very celebratory of our 6 months anniversary. Then, at this very minute 6 months ago, we had just finished a large repast and were completing a cross word puzzle. I, rolled up in a blanket, you, sitting in the old seat whose stuffing has been coming out for years. It was growing dark and Dr. Root kept a) making remarks about night blindness b) a bee line to the Punch bowl. I don't remember what we talked about except your saying you guessed it wouldn't be proper to join me in the blanket with which I concurred. And I remember how I wanted to drive to the station but there wasn't room in the car. In ways, it seems like a short time ago and yet I feel as if I've known you all my life—as you say, "You're a part of me."

   Now for a tricky question. Have I received your valentine present yet? I feel very sheepish about this. Today I received an envelope containing a very pretty hanky (looked like more than 10 cents). The envelope was in disguised handwriting which at first I thought was yours and the significance of the hanky and all . . . and then I looked at it but I looked more closely and decided maybe it was from Mom and also it was mailed from the Grand Central district which would be more apt to be Mom than you.

She knows my constant lack of same and the fact that it looked like more than 10 cents when you had explicitly mentioned that sum and in fact which I now recall your saying you would add to it and not send it thru the mail . . . all point to Mom's sending it. If she did, it would be awfully funny seeing as it's such an appropriate gift and would signify encouragement! BUT I'm not sure she'd like to have that encouraged! BUT IF you sent it, I love the thought and thank you muchly. (Boy! That was a tight spot to be in. How did I do?)

Got a big laugh this afternoon. Barb and I tried to buy some cigarettes. We couldn't, so we settled on home made stuff: a little package of tobacco and white paper and we practiced. I'll have to brag and say mine came our better, at least it was smokeable if not beautiful. Barb lit hers and the whole thing went up in a flame . . . dangerous but funny as hell to see. We were rolling on the floor in giggles. One trouble is that if you don't smoke it while the saliva is wet, the thing dries and falls apart. How do you prevent that? (Advice to the cigarette-lorn).

Some day the lack of studying is going to catch up with me but it's so much pleasanter not to work . . . Having had straight classes all morning I got back for lunch and had only a few minutes before I had bowling so I decided to skip my job of doing the corridors. But I got caught!

Which means two hours on the black list which isn't serious morally. Just means two hours extra work when, if I'd done it, it would have just taken 20 minutes (I could have lied my way out of it easily enough but just couldn't. You're saddled with an honest sucker, darling.

Pardon me while I go dribble a cigarette. Hey! It actually bears some resemblance to objectivity.

Joan came to dinner tonite with Rosey and either she's trying to get us to say something or she's awfully interested in discussing sex and people sleeping with other people. I can never decide if she's discussing it because she has or because she hasn't! But if she expects me to divulge my favorite secret, she's sadly mistaken.

Really must get to work, but before I close, may I remind you to tune in again tomorrow, every day, same station all the time and don't forget our sponsor "Cupid," the guy who makes the best article in the world: it can't be sold and it isn't rationed. Be sure you have plenty of it at all time. Happy Valentine's Day and all my love, V.

February 14th 1945–THE DAY
Wonderful, wonderful, Darling,

I've just received the best, funniest, the most touching, the nicest, most thoughtful Valentine anniversary gift that I've ever gotten. It's perfect, darling and I love it, which is another way of saying you're perfect and I love you. The words are just right, the size and blackness of certain words are just right and your choice is diabolical. I laughed so much and felt such a thrill at the re-realization

that you, who will someday be my wife, have such a good clean, wicked sense of humor-Lord, darling how I love you!!!!!!!!!!! The only thing that could have improved it would have been to have you here while I read it-and we're going over it together some day soon.

In comparison you've made my Valentine seem such a trivial thing that I'm ashamed to haul it forth. In fact I'll beg off entirely except that my gift has a certain intrinsic worth that I want you to enjoy.

I really can't get over our "Album". I'm dying to show it to somebody, but I guess I'll have to restrain my generous impulses. I may show it to Mard up to page 6 and the last page (the dirty work came on page 7, 8, and 9 and how I love it!

I've got loads of Phys Chem to do for tomorrow and two conferences to prepare so I'll have to cut off my rambling soon, but the album has brought you so close to me that I'd give 10 years of my life (the first ten preferably) just to have you here for five minutes.

Clare has passed another milestone. Today the chief OK'd her second paper and it now goes in for publication. She'll take her final exam in a month or so and then she'll be thru. She started writing up her stuff about last July so it took her about 6 or 7 months. Since I have only one paper, I may make it in even in less time. Wouldn't it be nice if I got through in time for us to have a month's vacation together in July? (Take it easy, D. let's not raise our hopes at this early date)

Got a check for $10 today from Jerry and Mitzie. The letter said simply" to be used for something special" and

they sent regards to you. I'm tempted to put it aside and try to scrape together something special- rooting for a not too distant visit to Washington. How does that strike you or do you have a better idea? Since this money was to be used for a Valentine, it really belongs more to you then to us.
I've got to stop now. Gosh! But I hate to leave you.
G'nite my valentine, my darling, my fianace...less than two days to go! D.
P.S. Did you see pictures of the Yalta Conference?

February 18, 1945—11:30 P.M.
Dearest Darling,

We haven't been separated long enuf for any news to have occurred, but I've been in such a cloud since I first realized that you not only love me but are also in love with me, that I'll feel as close as possible. The glow of this weekend is still thick around me and it seems as if all I have to do is reach out and you'll be here. Mmmm. (That wasn't a small mmm of contentment but the kind of mmm that goes with a hug.)

    Studied from 8 to 10:30 with Dottie. We finished the chapter and I think the exam won't be so tough. I had told her about a dumb girl in the class for whom I had had to explain how to use transfer on ordinate paper. Tonite I found out that she (Dottie) didn't know either. And not only that but the Dutch fellow also didn't know!

    This is only an interim to help both of us get over the Monday to Wednesday no mail let-down. I've never felt so near and close to you and so very much in love with you. I'd thought that I couldn't love you any more than I did, but now I realize that a small part of me (the part I hold back as a cushion against possible let downs) was waiting for this new phase.

Good nite, Darling and don't ever forget how much
I love you. D.

February 20, 1945
Dearest,

    Gee, you're cute! That was such lovely surprise getting a letter from you on Tuesday and as usual, such a nice one. Why is it I never like any letters after a weekend half as much as yours? But have you noticed that we often start our letter the same way? If you start Dearest, I 've inevitably started Dearest also.

    I got the strangest feeling reading that letter I had written that you enclosed. I half recognized it was from me and I felt as if I were reading a letter by a girl I vaguely knew. But as Barb said when I mentioned it, "A lot of water has flowed under the bridge since then.

(no cracks please) There certainly wasn't anything shy about me, was there? Telling you to write soon etc. but as long as "it worked," I don't mind.

Have spent the last half hour working myself out of a mild fury at the futility of life in the library. I spent the whole evening and several previous hours tracking down material for my Amer. Lit paper. I spent hours looking up stuff and following leads. Finally I found an article on just what I wanted-looked it up in the catalogue . . . Yes, they had the periodical. #370.5/vol 82. Found where the 370's were and it wasn't there. Looked around and went back to the catalog, and saw it said "basement" on the bottom of the card. Went to the basement-couldn't find it.

Was in the wrong basement-found the right basement-couldn't find the periodical-finally found the appropriate spot hidden near the floor in gobs of dust. Then . . . they didn't have the right issue!!!! 'And that was only one instance. Just wrote home asking Mom to find out specific thinking about the museum library and if they have what I want I'll come in a week from this Thursday for the day. (Don't plan on it tho.) If I do come in, maybe I can see you for early supper before your Phys Chem class . . . or maybe not.

I've narrowed down my topic and what I want to do is very simple. Tho this wouldn't seem so. I want to trace the development and growth of visual education and aids in the Museum of Natural History. The growth of school exhibits, traveling exhibits, how they've changed in form and content. The growth of new museum services. You'd think they'd be some easily attainable data somewhere! The joys of research ... You MUST have terrific patience, darling. Part of my impatience with it is the fact that I've deadlines to meet and can't take all the time I might like to doing it.

How about calling me Fri/Sat at 7 P.M.? Gosh it will be good to speak to you. I've decided there's a lot of imagination involved in this incompleteness—not that I imagine I'm incomplete and really am not but the weeks when I'm going or you're coming, I don't feel nearly as lonely as when it's a Tuesday nite of a week in which the coming weekend isn't a blaze of glory. Do you agree?

We've had more fun over the cigarette roller you gave me. At first I had a little trouble cause I'd put the paper in one way and roll it so that the gummed part would be on the outside meaning one's fingers got sticky and the cigarette splattered, popped and shredded neatly (or not so neatly) over the newly cleaned rug. But I've gotten it down to a speedy technique now. Also found that when I packed em tight, I could never smoke a whole cigarette. Now I pack them looser and pinch it. Am smoking them tho I want to save one (for the time when I'm dying for a cigarette—you understand).

In Amer Lit, we may work on a scenario for "The Portrait of a Lady" if we have time . . . taking just a few scenes, working in groups and after studying movie techniques, writing up the scenes, also designing the sets, costumes, and music, would be loads of fun if we have the time.

Working in the libe on the museum stuff this evening was the first time I've not consciously thought of you for more than an hour since I've been back. I find you in my mind when I'm not really conscious you're there. You just suddenly pop up and I realize you've been there all along. Guess maybe I'm in love with you, darling. Do you think so?

I get so impatient for the time I'll burn the toast, wear the ring and try millions of positions and see you grouchy and get you out of it and push you out of bed when I have cramps and crawl back into yours when I don't. Do you suppose those are the kinds of things most people anticipate in married life?

Well, my duke, I must leave you to join you again soon in the land of dreams, where time stands still and you're right beside me.

Every iota of love, V

February 19, 1945

My Dearest Darlingest Most Loved D.,

How I do love you! And how wonderful this weekend was! Or need I go into details. Of course I do . . . for my own pleasure and I trust yours. I loved seeing you in the lab and would really have missed something not seeing you in action as far as your work went. It is so nice to see how obviously everyone likes you (which I supposed is just flattering myself on my good taste in picking such a likeable guy) . . . and how well you get along with them . . . knowing how to approach each one from the secretary to Dr. Root. I also got a better feel of the spirit that pervades the lab and your work. Member when I told you that Mard had always said she wouldn't marry a scientist (Dr.) and she did, and how I somehow knew I would and wanted to? It wasn't pure whim. There IS something different about the way scientists act and think and work, and it's something I like.

And then there were those perfect hours in your little room feeling and being so close to you . . . and my apartment and the new position, mustn't forget that!

And Sunday, too. How I loved your casual and premeditated comments and actions when Jane and Don came over. I felt so glad and so superior in somehow having had the sense to have "picked" you.

I wrote to Sarah Lawrence today and so I'm now officially staying at Vassar. It's best I guess, but I DID enjoy the sense of freedom it gave me to even imagine the possibility of an alternative. It somehow helped me put it all into perspective.

Last night I got to the train about 5 minutes before starting time and had a bit of trouble finding a seat. Finally sat on an aisle seat. I casually glanced at my neighbor– a male about 25, dark hair, wearing a moderately loud checked suit, tan sweater and a woven unmatching tie. We said a few words about whether or not to hang my coat on the already crowded hook or to keep it behind me. I noticed he was reading "What Dumbarton Oaks Means" in the Reader's Digest.

When the conductor came by and punched our tickets we had to discuss which ticket was whose; he was going to Albany. I took out my book to read, but it was a smoker and it hurt my eyes to look at the printed page. So just for the hell of it, I asked him what the Reader's Digest had to say about Dumbarton Oaks. He said it presented it favorably and we began talking about post-war policy etc. For about 3/4 hour. He was liberal–about like you with not as much knowledge . . . pro Russia and knew a lot about that tho he didn't like the dictator angle.

We discussed Dewey and the campaign. I asked him, finally, if he was as liberal as he was, why did he read the Reader's Digest? He said he liked its condensation and that he likes its conservatism partly to see the other side and partly because, underneath it all, he thought he was fairly conservative. A contradiction I didn't get a chance to probe.

I got up to get a drink of water and stopped to talk to some others from college. Others had been saying hello as they passed and when I came back he asked how I knew so many people on the train. When I told him he said he hadn't realized Vassar was where it is! Asked about my major. I asked if he'd gone to college and he's graduated from Columbia last June. When I asked about HIS major, I somehow pictured engineering, but I almost jumped up to the ceiling when he said he was at present in Divinity school! (Episcopalian–had majored in Psyc. at college; his father was a clergyman.) Then for one hour straight we discussed religion. We both got very excited and I completely forgot I was on a train. We kept kidding when the discussion got hottest that come hell or high water (naturally not the terminology used then) we would part as friends . . . and we did. He said at one point that it had been good talking to me since he'd have to learn what to say to people like me in his congregation some day.

We parted knowing only our first names and as two folks who had enjoyed a two hour conversation. I think we both got a lot out of it having a feeling of warmth and appreciation in people as a whole (or does that sound like a sermon?)

I was so very glad that for once I hadn't just accepted life on face value. There he was a fairly uninteresting looking soul and we could have had a completely uneventful uninteresting trip, but with just a little curiosity, it was so much more.

In Sociology we discussed plans for our in-town projects and land mapping. I can't figure out Mr. Post's political philosophy. Today, discussing Social Security he expressed his opinion that Government will have to give people the jobs they won't be able to get from private enterprise. One day liberal, one day not. American Lit., reading on the period of the 1930's with special projects, i.e. tenant farmers, Tenant Farmer's Union . . . O.K., but what is fun is discovering new books on new subjects or new books on old subjects.

Darling: you say you now think I'm completely in love with you. I KNOW I am. I've never been so sure in my life of anything. I've found a very real purpose in life. If I can help make you happy and give you a fuller life, that's what I want to do–that's my purpose. And in doing so I can make other people happy, somehow, because I myself will be so happy (member the joke of Herman and Elsa?) But joking aside, I'm serious and so glad about it.
All my love, all my life.
V

February 20, 1945
Hello Darling,

I try to make the first days of our interludes seem shorter by figuring that the first ½ then ¼ of the time has passed as the days go by. Then it's the half way mark and it doesn't seem that far off but it doesn't help much. It's a good thing I'm kept that busy. Fortunately I'm getting used to the after the weekend lag, but I can't squelch that ray of hope on Tuesday nite.

It's been an interesting couple of days. Switched Monday and Tuesday afternoon teaching with Clare so that I could study for Monday's exam. It turned out to be a very easy affair as far as I know. We had three problems and a choice of between two others for our fourth. In case anybody finished early, he had one tough one for extra credit. I think we all did all six of them. Not sure I got them all. It's funny how teachers differ. As he said, anybody who could do those problems knew the chapter. Yet we all thought it was easy while we always sweated over the Demon's exams. If everybody's mark is high we won't be better off relatively, but I'd rather be low with a 90 average than high with a 50.

Haven't done my work on my paper this week but I hope to be ready for a conference with Allison by the end of the week after which comes the writing. Clare will take her final exam March 2nd which makes my final exam seem much more real and close.

I discovered that the hypodermic needles we use in the lab come in metal holders which have slits in them made to order for a cigarette machine. I bored holes in a box, screwed the ready-made metal support and, lo, I have a new machine. Have you wearied of playing around with yours? (Your machine, darling, yet?)

In the foreseeable future, I think my thoughts will constantly be on the days ahead-when I'll see you next spring, finishing Phys Chem., writing my paper and getting my degree. Summer of course, the main event that underlies all those minor waitings.

During college looked forward to graduating and really getting started in Physiology but for the year and a half after that, the days just seemed to exist for themselves. I was blissfully contented unaware of the excitement that you have given to the rest of my life-and how I hate blissful contentment!

In thinking some of the stuff we've talked about the past weekend, it seems to me that I may have given you the impression that I thought you didn't love me before this last phase set in. If so, this is far from the way I feel about it. I know we would never have reached our present intimacy if you didn't love me-tho we kid about it, I'm extremely flattered and grateful that you've made so many changes in your thinking and outlook through my influence.

Harry writes inviting us down to Washington and sending his love to you. He sounds rather depressed-probably accentuated by seeing how happy Ruth and Ed and we are while he seems to be stagnating-and so I suggested that he come up and see us. Greedy tho I am, I think he could stand a trip away from Wash. Even if it cuts into one of our days together.

No class Thursday nite tho I have classes all day. Good nite darling. I love you almost painfully.
Yours, D

February 21, 1945
Darling

It's 7:10 p.m. and I have to leave here by 7:15 if I'm not to be late for your father's talk, so this will probably be written in two sections.

It was wonderful to hear from you even if half your letter was devoted to describing another male. Guess I'll just have to get used to a wife who can't resist picking up strange men. You did have your nerve, tho, in arguing religion with him or don't you know the usual outcome of an argument on this topic? It's hard to keep emotion out of religion or politics and I hate to have anybody "throw the lord" at me in a voice filled with righteous and unhumorous indignation (tho the guy was OK). Anyhow I'm glad the trip was lively and you didn't have time to sit and mope.

If there were any doubts left in my mind about your loving me, they would have vanished completely by the picture of you wishing I were there in the middle of a hot argument on religion! It was also a pleasant surprise to know that this weekend you remembered you'd been here at my place. By the way, I don't feel that the Mona Lisa on my wall is such a dope any more She has a secret to smile!

I think I see now what Peter meant about tough questions. Today I was looking at their turtle and remarked that they had a freak. The ventricle was first and the auricle was second. They looked with me, and sure enough it went ventricle, auricle, ventricle, auricle, then one boy wised up and said it all depended when you start and to him it looked like auricle, ventricle. Then I asked them how they could tell which came first and told them I'd stop by later to see if they had figured it out. They did, observing there was a complete stop between beats and the auricle went first. Part of the experiment was to cool the heart and slow it down which brings this out even better. Do you think this is the kind of question he objected to? Is he justified? (They aren't marked on this answer.)

Time is almost up. After the talk I've got to prepare a conference and a make–up quiz (one word answers.) I'd rather not give them quizzes at all, but they feel their studying isn't appreciated unless they have marks to show for it, so quizzes they will get. It amazed me to have kids come up and ask if I wouldn't give them a quiz every week as then they'll have to study!

Have to break off now. I didn't care to mention this to Mard, but a good part of the reason why I'm going to hear your Pop talk is because it'll make me feel very near to you. Hang in there, darling, and here's a big one to keep you warm till I get back.

10:30 Hello again. Thanks for waiting. I'll use your patience as an excuse to kiss you again and pretend it's a reward for you.

The talk was excellent-one of the best I've ever heard. Even tho I don't know anything about Pediatrics, and I'm sure your Dad wasn't talking down to the audience, everything he said was plain and clear and extremely interesting. I sat next to Mard with your mother on her right-it really did bring you close. At one point when your father mentioned how serious it is (for the child) when the prospective mother gets German measles while she is in early pregnancy, Mard turned to me and whispered (don't worry she's already had it") which was exactly what I had in mind. I didn't hang around to congratulate your Pop which may have been bad psychology but I had to leave in a hurry.

   Stopped for a cup of coffee (to help me stay awake) at that place that has the wonderful signs on the table. Somebody had added to the "Please remove your hat first or else we'll take it off for you and your head along with it". Another thoughtful patron had added at the bottom "Don't whistle at any woman-it may be the boss's wife" So I guess we're not the only ones who thought the sign funny.

   Your reactions to the lab visit were along the lines I should have expected, and yet they surprised me. I had never thought of whether or if the people around like me. I suppose part of the atmosphere around the lab is due to the fact that tho we talk physiology practically all the time, there is an underlying feeling that we all like each other. It certainly is the best for co-operative work that I've ever been in. I wonder if a certain type of person drifts into scientific work or if science trains a person to be reasonable, open-minded and co-operative. I suspect the former is the main explanation.

   That business of knowing how to approach people makes it sound as if everything I do and say is for a calculated effect. Actually, of course, when I like a person, the right words seem to come out just because I like him and feel at ease. The same thing happened last Sunday with your family. If I seemed to say particularly apt things then it's just because I'm getting to know and like your parents better as we get more used to each other.

    I object strongly that 99 percent of males would pick Jane in preference to you. You seem to forget that you are far from unattractive, my darling.

    Post's position doesn't seem so inconsistent to me. I think you tend to expect people to be conservative, liberal or communist but there are many gradations between. There are people who can be liberal in some ways and yet have blind spots.

    Afraid I have to stop now, tho I hate to. I'm hoping that you'll let me know the best time to call you this weekend. If not, I'll try 7 o'clock on Saturday nite, but don't let this interfere with any plans you have. If you're not in when I call, I'll try Sunday, same time.

Good nite, dearest. Take good care of my love—you've got all of it.

Danny

PS. if you'll devote your life to making me happy, I'll try my best to make your periods as comfortable as possible.

February 22, 1945

Dearest,

This is a novelty to be writing you at 8:30 A.M. but since I didn't write last nite and I feel at loose ends when I skip that, you wont get any mail today but I guess you'll get 2 somewhere along the line.

Was glad to hear the exam was easy and as usual I discount ½ your disparaging remarks on how poorly you did. WE ARE alike-except that my remarks are usually justified!

In your comments of the foreseeable future, when you put us as the main event, I felt a very definite pride. I still find it amazing that I can be that important to you. I want always be that important to you. And I shall work to hold my place of honor.

You mentioned that you once were blissfully contented, until I came along. And "how I hate blissful contentment". I'd just been thinking of that myself. I've always thought of myself as hating stasis, wanting change, thinking constant upward style as a good thing, admiring people with "drive" etc. And I've always thought I felt the same way about myself. Being honest, I find I'm not nearly that dynamic—that I really have an equal love for the calm and quiet. Perhaps it's due to certain laziness, a desire for an easy way out, or perhaps I'm reaching middle age prematurely!!!!I hate being insincere and I know that I'd like to consider myself the fight-tem-type but looking well within the shell of what is your fiancée, I hay me doots.

I guess it would have been better for you to read Howard's letter than for me to read it to you. You'd probably have gotten a better picture. I just thought of it when I was rereading YOUR letter and found certain phrases that were worded the way he would word them.

That was a good idea: of inviting Harry up here. If he

lets you know in time we could get him a date. Will try Amy if you give the OK tho it may not blossom into a great romance. I think she would be "diverting". I'd like to write him a note which, if you approve, you could send along to him-if you don't, you can tear it up. I've a funny feeling about that. When I knew someone thru someone else, like knowing Harry via you, I'd never feel right stepping in, without your OK first. It would be more understandable if Harry was a female but I feel just the same way about it. I guess it's partly a hang-over from the days Amy and I would go out with the same boy. It never never made for very good feeling (except when we both didn't like the boy . . . poor boy).

Studying the gold standard in Econ and all I can do is shake my head and mutter like my father does, "what a world!"

I'm getting worse and worse at bowling. Practice makes perfect may hold in SOME fields. Lord how I love you! (Pardon the interruption-just one of those outpouring of emotion. I don't have the curse any more . . . thought you'd be amused at my train of thought.)

That project that I mentioned has materialized in Soc into a reality and a more complex one than I imagined. We're each given certain territories in town- have to trace weird maps for assessment maps and go out and see how the land is used; how many families live in the residential houses, which are offices, factories, school buildings and auto repair shops but it ought to be fun.

If this letter has been factual, just read the spaces around the words for information concerning the present and future status of my love for you. The spaces are full of superlatives. All of me. Your fiancée

February 22, 1945—11:30 AM
Dearest Darling,
Quelle hectic life! Spent half the morning talking to Sirjemaki about my term paper. I said Frankly that I COULD manage to write a paper about our CT town conforming to the prescribed set of headings but that it would be fairly dull and incomplete seeing as I've been turned down by the local officials. I asked if there was something else I could do to make it better; given an inch he took a mile and suggested a colossal plan that was enough for a PhD and required doing field work on the spot. He threw out hundreds of ideas and told me to think them over which has left me one half to nowhere and distinctly confused. He thought I'd get more out of a more subjective paper using descriptions of people and attitudes I've actually discovered in the town, than a second hand factual report.

When I explained it would be very fragmentary, incomplete, he said he thought it would be but that I'd learn technique and evaluation and he was more interested in my learning something than in the finished product. At that I smiled and told him he was a rarity around here—at which he shut up like a clam. Am working on the theory that he's shy . . . tis rumored his wife is pregnant. We really had a very pleasant chat tho he's as cagey about his political opinions as anyone I've ever known. I keep giving him bait and he keeps ducking away, or rather encircling it. All in all it's left me a bit confused as to what to do next. I started making a list of all the people I knew and what social things I knew about them. I don't think I've got enuf data to really prove anything but from what he said I gather that's not important. So again I'm going around in circles.

I think I wrote you that we're studying more technique in Amer. Lit and will work in groups adapting a scene from the Portrait into a scenario. This afternoon I read "Mrs. Miniver" in script form. It was fascinating to see the parts they later cut and fun to be able to remember the scenes they describe.

Also did a poster for the Marxist Study Group which is being organized. There's to be a discussion on "The Philosophical and Psychological Aspects of The Class" by Venable, Lee (more conservative) and Lanier (Psych professor-liberal). Ought to be lively!

Tonight we listened to the Town Meeting: Agnes Smedley, Lin Yutang, Judd (Repub Representative) and Foreman on "Unity in China." It was exciting and the feeling was pro Smedley pretty much. Lin Yutang is a sly guy, isn't he?

A girl here asked if she could play a record she'd bought on our vic. When she played it, it turned out to be "I wanna get married" and there are a few phrases in it, besides the general subject matter, which will necessitate my learning the word and singing them to you.

Been thinking a good bit about Harry tho I didn't enclose the letter I thought I'd write. Have been trying to decide which would be better: Rosey or Amy. I think Rosey's a bigger gamble but Amy a better one. What do you think?

Writing this letter is a little like writing my term paper? I circle around the important point. I love you, darling . . . wholly. In fact I was thinking of it today: that I love you very much and trust you so much that I can't think of anything I wouldn't do for you if you wanted it. (Perhaps part of that faith is realization that what you want and I want is essentially the same.) At the same time I don't feel a loss of individualism. In fact, I AM beginning to feel middle-aged (see this morning's letter).

This weekend I study for three tests. (I must now convince myself of that fact) (No, I really have to study.) We've covered 8 weeks in Polit—13 cases to know and we only had 7 all last term and this is true/false which means "little things". Oh well, thinking about you and knowing you exist and for some unknown reason, want me, makes life very very worthwhile. (Don't mean to sound depressed. I'm not) Here's a terrific bear/kitten/tiger/sexy hug wrapped up all in my love.

Yours, V

P.S. Cig machine doing fine. I'm a speed demon and haven't wearied of it yet.

February 23, 1945

Dearest Darlingest,

By the time you get this I will have explained my stupidity about the paper and the research and I trust we will have spent a divine day together "escaping". I don't care a hoot about how much money it costs to come for only a day. I don't care if it means I don't do well in exams etc if

I can be with you even for a short time (without messing up your work schedule too much). Anything is worth it! Gee, Must be love! I somehow thought I'd never be so in love as to say to heck with practicality. I still don't quite throw it to the winds, but I certainly do more than I thought I would (The fact that I keep a little practicality now and then is not to be construed to mean I'm not completely in love with you, just means I give myself a wee bit of credit for a little common sense.)

Perhaps in the excitement of seeing you in the flesh (wow!) tomorrow, I'll forget to mention how I liked today's letter . . . the one explaining your evening hearing Dad speak etc.

I'm sure that the auricle/ventricle type of question is the kind of question Peter objected to and I think they're darn good questions- if you don't make a guy feel TOO silly when he realizes his own ignorance. Otherwise I think they're good in that they're obvious yet not obvious, make you think about accepting what seems obvious on face value. I should think it would be particularly good training for scientists.

I got a big kick out of your going to Dad's lecture. Not so much that it was Dad who was talking tho I know he'll be pleased you went but the fact that you sat with Mom and Mard, it makes things seem real (You can get German measles more than once).

I must leave you darling. So that I can go to sleep so that I wont yawn in your face tomorrow.

All my everything. V

February 25, 1945

Dearest Dopiest Darling,

What am I to say about a day that was by far the craziest looniest, funniest and wonderful day I've ever spent in my life. Lord, I love you!

I'm still far back from normal. This is the most solid cloud I've ever sailed on. After leaving you last nite, I caught the bus OK and got off in town for a leisurely sandwich and cup of coffee. Then I picked up P.M. (to my amazement) and wandered down to the station. It was about 12:30 when I got there and by 1 o'clock I decided to try to sleep. It really wasn't bad with the newspaper for a pillow. I staked out a claim to a sizeable hunk of bench and promptly went to sleep (after getting used to the snoring of a sailor on a nearby bench).

Woke up about 3 and they said the train was at least an hour late-it hadn't arrived at Albany yet-so back to sleep I went. The train finally pulled in at 5:30 when they were nice enuf to wake everybody up. Luckily I got a whole seat and went right to sleep again. Had breakfast at 8 and slept in my own bed (remember it?) till 11:30 so that all in all, I didn't miss much sleep-tho I was a couple of hours late to Dottie's. It certainly was a goofy day but I wouldn't have missed a minute of it, darling.

One funny thing is that my most vivid memory of us is of the last half hour of conversation that followed. I can't remember much of what we talked about, and yet I can still feel the mood-how close and completely one we were. There were so many high spots! Just standing with you at the station in the morning, feeling the well known flood of warmth from you envelope me as it does every time we are together . . . and which I always have to reassure myself when we first meet after an interval of separation... Us in NYC and at Churchill's and the conversation as we walked away . . . my little room . . . and us in bed, and then the knock and all that followed.

The funny things like your one-piece costume, seeing my brother in uniform right there, and foolishly blurting out asking how old he is! The rubbers dropping on the floor, and everything else together.

Later our second session which hit me so hard. The queer colored man in the subway and the nice guy viewing him with real "live and let live" understanding. Then the ride back with you back to college-the,conversation with the gruff conductor . . . then the bus ride-the last kiss and that last look which should last me for years but wont, greedy guy that I am.

Believe it or not, on the way home, I woke up at Yonkers and was terrifically ample right into 125th street. On the 3rd Ave el, it came back again and lasted til Fordham road! Fortunately between overcoat and everyone else's sleepiness, nobody knows but you. I love you so much darling, I ought to give some of it to people who need it. I've got enuf for a dozen-but considering that it's you, maybe I'll need it all not to get left behind.

Dottie and I went over the work today and then I took a nap while she did problems. After I'd slept a couple of hours, I woke up and helped her with the problems she was stuck on. It's now 9:15 and I've written this at her place so that it would get mailed earlier.

Good nite, my fiancé. I should put a million stamps on the envelope to take care of all the love that's going along with the written words. D.

February 25, 1945

Very Dearlingest Danny Mine,

All day I've been so overflowing with the most terrific warmth and love for you that, instead of yesterday seeming like a dream, today does. It was such a perfect day, full of talk, action, love and laughter . . . the kind of day that days should be.

Perhaps love makes you blind (I don't think so) but I just keep finding more wonderful things about you the more I know you . . . and the faults not only decrease but disappear! You're so wonderful, darling. The way you understand my moods, and me in general, and not only understand but saying the right things and doing the right things and looking the way you do. For example, the way you immediately thought of my reaction first at the sound of the knock on the door. There we were in bed with most of our clothes off. I was very touched at your concern for me-and the way you made it easy for me to meet Morrie. Ah gee! I can't even write all the instances, reasons I love you so much. I wont soon forget lying in the dark, snuggled in your arms, hearing your voice saying the things I wanted to hear as we lay in your little room.

And that you came all the way back to college with me!

I hope the trip back wasn't too gruesome. You certainly are spoiling me! And I love it! And appreciate it! And love you! And appreciate you!

Today I wrote my family mentioning having been in town yesterday, implying I'd gone to the museum, saying I'd seen you and met Morrie (for the record).

This has been "job" day. I did Nanette's job, my job, the corridor job, am now on message center working off my second hour of black list and this evening I do linen distribution. In between I've studied a good bit of Polit (I needed to!); went for a short walk with Barb after lunch and slept an hour before dinner. (I don't know about you, but yesterday's "activities" certainly wore me out! (How I love to be worn out!) And I'm stiff, too.

I've been thinking more concretely about announcing our "engagement". At present I figure it doesn't make any difference to me directly. I know what I want (you) and any decisions that Mom might feel to be the future, I think I, and we, have already settled. There certainly are no doubts in my mind. The problem is what's to be gained by announcing it. If I tell my family I want to announce it, they would probably ask why announce it now and I'd feel a little silly saying just to make you (my parents) feel better.

My idea now is to talk to Mom frankly when she comes up here next week telling her just what the score is all around and ask her which way she'd feel happier. In that way if all prefer to have it postponed, she'll still know just how settled I feel about it and the summer plans can go from there. It really doesn't make much difference to me if it's announced or not so I'll give my mother the questionable joy of letting her choose.

Thinking it thru I realize she would tell me she'd say to wait and being honest about it, now that I've got it into my brain, I realize I'd kind of like it known. Greedily I want the world to know I belong with you and you with me. But it isn't something I'd fight desperately for right now and if I see it really bothers her, I wont force it. But I DO love to talk to you about it . . . and to think of it.

While I've been trying to write the above, I must have been interrupted 15 times by fellow students who feel like talking and I jump from one mood to another. But the important moods and the only part of me that matters, is always with you.

Laughingly, lovingly, passionately, perpetually, increasingly, affectionately, adoringly.

Yours, V.

February 27, 1945
Dearest most unbelievable one,

I can't seem, to find my writing paper but this letter paper;-and all future ones should be on yellow paper anyway. It's drizzling outside, we got our exam papers back and I did worse than I had expected, and my mother writes in a very neglected tone. I should feel depressed by all this but am I? Hell no—I love you and you love me and I'm happy after all. It's drizzling, but it's warm. I messed up the exam, but I'm always coming from behind in every course I take, and I'll write my mother that I'll be in Philly in 3 weeks so she won't feel neglected. Yep. It's a wonderful world, and all our worries are trifles that are swept under the table when I think of you.

It seems to me he wasn't too fair in making our exams. We had 3 problems and a choice of either the 4th or 5th. Then he put up an extra credit one. Nearly everybody did them all, so he marked us on a basis of 140 counting each problem. I spent almost the whole time checking and rechecking the required ones and just took a flyer at the extras in the last few minutes. As a result, I got 5 out of 50 on the last two which he included as if they weren't extra. He's a nice guy and I don't think it occurred to him that it wasn't fair. Anyhow, I feel right at home, down near the bottom of the class (7th our of 10) and can now work my way up.

I'm a little bothered by my mother's attitude-that is I'm afraid she's very lonesome and has the feeling that the family is drifting from her. She's much too understanding to have any resentment about what is so natural, but instead of happy, contented years ahead with a loving husband, her whole life is rooted in us, her children, and it would be inhuman for her not to feel it being so as we get married and make our own ways one by one. I can understand this, and I'm sure you can too. What I want you to understand is that none of this feeling is even remotely connected to you. She's very happy that I've found you and just from my description is looking forward with a great deal of pleasure to meeting you.

Got a V-mail and a letter from Gene today. His description of Rose and his feeling toward her are rather baffling. From this distance it's impossible for me to have any opinion on the subject, and all I can say to him is-if you're sure you love her, and then go ahead. From what he writes, she's either very much in love with him or very very eager to get married. I hope it's the former. After all, I suppose to a 3rd person our relationship (what a cold word!) could be interpreted the same way, which you and I know is utterly absurd. He hasn't convinced me that he's in love with her, tho at times Gene is difficult to fathom since he'll objectively discuss all the pros and cons of their compatibility and never mention how she affects him emotionally.

There was so much fuss around the place when Morrie was looking for me that I thought it best to tell Mard that you had been in Saturday tho I thought it wisest if she didn't tell your parents, to which she agreed. She also thinks that it'll be a severe strain on your family ties if you come to the city just as they're leaving. You've probably already heard from them that they are going to the seashore first. You'll have to figure it out from there.

Not trusting the mail any more-. I kept your letter and opened it this morning. It was a certainly wonderful to have such a REAL communication from (and with) you. I wonder why we can't take an old letter and just pretend that it arrived this morning. It would be from you, I'll enjoy reading it and yet it couldn't take the place of a new one. I love you fiercely, darling and tenderly and passionately and possessively. I want you and I want all of you all the time and for all time. If this description of my feelings doesn't satisfy you, supply your own- the feelings are there; only the word are inadequate.

You are probably in the middle of your exams now (when this reaches you) and it is my turn to tell you that you're not taking them alone. The pin has always worked for me-it's now looking forward to our being together.

I've had time to read your last letters-the three that arrived Fri nite and Sat. I'm afraid I don't remember much of Howard's letter. I heard the words but was looking at you and listening to you and it didn't register very well. (If I ever had you for a teacher, I'd flunk the course cold).

You mentioned that "middle aged" feeling- a growing preference for calm and quiet. I've noticed it growing in me and have wondered about it quite a bit. It's easy to explain what's going on without too much damage to my ego, but it's hard to decide if my explanation is justified or is mostly rationalization. There comes a time when you don't feel like throwing your weight around as you once did. This may mean that the enthusiasm of youth isn't as strong as it once was. Then again, it may be a much saner evaluation of our powers. We can't fight every battle as we begin to discriminate between what is most important and what it is wiser to ignore rather than dissipate our energy in all directions. It isn't a conscious process, but I found that certain things began to be too small for me to get excited about. There are still plenty of large issues which can always get a rise out of me (sometimes they are small in the world's eyes but enormous to me).

Whether concentrating on things which you feel are

important is better than fighting everything that isn't the way you would like it to be, is good or bad, a sign of better adjustment to the world or growing love of ease, an indication of less energy or better judgment is a question I can't answer. At first I resented it and thought of maturity (your "middle age") disparagingly. Now it makes more sense. Still, I don't know whether it's a " good" or not. It happens to everyone, and no matter what the rationale, it would be hypocrisy to deny it. When a person goes overboard and no longer has anything he considers important he becomes dull and boring. That's a stage I don't think either of us will have to worry about (he said smugly). We'll tend to lean the other way.

You're lying flat; my arm is under your head, I hold you tight and we kiss-softly at first, then hard-hold on now. That'll be enuf now. Goodnite, my darling.

February 26, 1945
Dearest Darlingest,

Today has been a weird day in my thoughts although the actions were fairly ordinary. The news of a girl's marriage, a girl I have known since second grade, coupled with writing stacks of letters, has made me think of the past and at the same time the present and, as always, the future.

The girl who announced her engagement to a boy a year ahead of us in school is bright and tom-boyish and used to sneer at the more "social" girls in the class and had vowed she would have a career and maybe not marry for years. The sad part is if she marries him now, they will have only three weeks before he goes overseas for, maybe, 3 or 4 years. The difficulty that entails is almost overwhelming it seems to me. With many people, as you've pointed out, it takes a good deal longer than three weeks to make a really happy marriage, but one learns not to approve or disapprove such things. It's certainly something that no one can decide for anyone else.

I received an amusing letter today. It was written from the boy I met on the train last spring coming back from visiting Walt in North Carolina. He is now in France. But the amusing thing was that the censor had written quips throughout the letter and had even included his address, which is illegal but still amusing. (the ways people think up to increase their correspondence!) Hope he has better luck with other people he has undoubtedly done the same thing to.

Received an interesting letter all about politics in Belgium from the son of one of my parent's friends which I answered with clippings from the Times. He keeps complaining that he gets no news and that I'm his only source. So your girl friend has turned news commentator. (And what a lousy job I did of it!) Got another letter from Dave, who wants to know if you're good enough for me. To which I replied I felt the question could only be justified if worded in the opposite direction.

The Polit test was a poor one. First of all there was so much material to cover it could have been a three hour exam. Three large essay questions and 40 true false ones. Oh well . . .

Had fun in Sociology today. We were discussing

medical care and Sirjemaki kept mentioning the cultural lag in that the science itself is way ahead of the economic difficulties involved in getting people treated which created an anachronism. He kept stressing it as a problem to have to fit it into our capitalistic system. Little me, always the one to embarrass a teacher, innocently pipes up with maybe the system is an anachronism? He toyed with the idea while some of the class tittered, saying we had to be realistic. He said he didn't know whether it was better to keep patching up our present system (with insurance plans etc) or to make a clean sweep of it.

All in all, it's been a busy day and yet you've been upper most in my mind all the time—not even below the surface but upper most. Writing to people and seeing other people, I compare them to you and realize again how very extraordinarily wonderful you are and I miss you terribly. It's a different kind of missing than before:

Before seeing a box of cookies, being hungry but not being positive the box is full of all the cookies I like. Now it's seeing the cookies themselves, knowing they're my favorite kind and knowing that tho I can't eat them right now; they wont spoil if I have to wait a bit. GOD! What an analogy! You see I know for sure now, I've no doubts and that makes me so happy that at least the pains of doubt are gone, supplanted by an impatience and a greedy desire for more of your company, your smiles, your actions, your love, laughter and you in particular and in general.

Received a letter from Mom today which says Walt's life hangs in the balance of tests on next Tuesday and Friday.

If I believed in God I'd pray to let him pass them. This means so much to him-more that any other single thing has, that I do so want him to get it.

Can't wait to hear from you and to speak to you on Sat. and to marry you. All my important thoughts, my mind, and my body thou hast for the asking.
Love,from Me

February 27, 1945
D Darling,

Mmmm I loved the reminiscences of Saturday–not that I could forget them but they're now down in black and white for posterity and future chuckles. Almost died on reading of your continued amplenesses. What am I going to do with you? I guess all we'll need is a bed when we're married—no, a floor, and several handkerchiefs. (I can't hold ALL your amplenesses!)

Between life in general and your letter I can't concentrate on the Econ exam tomorrow. Studying for it has been more like last terms time-wasting, than anything else this term. When I'm supposedly learning about fiscal policies I find myself thinking the darndest thoughts: engagements rings, meeting you mother, clothes, sex, Mard and Howard, my parent's attitude toward us. Then there are vivid flashed of you-the smile on your face when I first saw you in the station; you jumping up and down in glee at having the whole day together–you surveying a menu and spotting a melted cheese and bacon-acting so beautifully at ease with Morrie et al with your leg slung over the rocker (you didn't think such an earthy picture would appeal to me?) It's things like that that makes the study of money and banking difficult!

Today has been cleaning day, but good! Clothes, the room, and me. Amer. Lit was weird, disorganized involving a preliminary discussion of "The Portrait" . . . forgot to mention the other day that when I'd written Mom that I'd been to the museum, I waited to mail it so you'd know that they knew before they knew it. (Tricky!)

Just decided I was starved and the only access to food was in the kitchen so Barb and I stole our way in with no qualms whatsoever (after the first time one loses ones social conscience. hmmm!)

So I'd just finished the last cigarette in my possession when I go to the mail box. And you, you cute (!) thing, send me what I wanted most that could be squeezed into box 436. Thank you, my darling. I can but repeat that I love to be spoiled and shall try to keep my feet on the ground by realizing this won't go on forever.

The discussion due Fri. by Venable, Lee and Lanier is cancelled because the dopes forgot to tell Lee and Venable about it! Also Venable said he'd never discuss Marx with Lee in a meeting. Apparently he's had an unfortunate experience doing so. It's a shame cause it would have been good.

Just ate five pieces of bread. God! Maybe it's a sign of ampleness! With that thought I leave you for the night, with the hope that you keep the bed in good condition, take care of our bathrobe and know that I love you terrifically . . . so terrifically. All of me. V.

February 28, 1945

My Darling,

(21 days till spring; 3 days till I talk with you and 9 days till I see you).

I can understand now why people write the kind of gushy salutations to letters that sometimes pop into print in breach of promise cases. When I try to think of variations in place of "dearest" or "darling", the things I think of are so revealing of the effect you have on my sentimental nature that I couldn't bear to see them in writing. The yellow paper continues, and so do the sentiments. Will you forgive me the indiscretion of saying that I love you very much?

Not seeing you on Sunday turned out to have a better effect than I expected as far as the incomplete feeling is concerned. In stead of rushing right into work as usual after our weekends, I had time to luxuriate in the warmth of the day together and really soak up all of the glow after glow. Then there was your letter to read Monday and one every day since so that my missing you hasn't yet reached that "how can I put up with it one day longer" stage, tho you're in my thoughts all the time. (If I'm incomplete when you're not here, just think of how incomplete I was before I knew enuf to feel incomplete without you!)

It's been a pretty rough week. Mrs. Wang had a baby girl on Monday and I took over Dr. Wang's lab for him. On Tuesday I took over Class's lab so she could study for her exam and today and tomorrow I have the dentals. Bill W has bitten off more than he can (or cares to)) chew in trying to run the whole course and I've found myself busily trying to pull loose ends together. I can't do much about the medicals but the dentals are going to get a good course or I'll burst. Today we gave them a demonstration on how to cannulate a cat and record its respiration. As usual I was all thumbs and did everything wrong, but I was glad to see that it didn't bother me at all and I could calmly explain to them what I had done wrong and set it right. I was also flattered to find that the fellows whom I hadn't had in conference yet were (or acted) glad to find that we rotate. We're now on what is considered the toughest chapter in Phys Chem-longest and toughest so that I have a long ways to go yet tonite, besides a conference to prepare for tomorrow. It's damn lucky that I like what I'm doing!

Now for some comments on your last letter which I liked exceedingly (not because it is filled with nice things you wrote about me). I wasn't terribly amused by that censor who put his two cents into the letter you got from France. a) I don't think the contents of a letters are any of his business except for security reasons and b) I don't think it's very fair for him to try to horn in on the friends of soldiers and possibly cut down the soldier's correspondence. (I'd never thought about it but I suppose even censors get mail!) What I object to mostly is that mail is a personal matter. If an outsider has to read it, he should have the good taste to be as unobtrusive about it as possible. Frankly, I think it's a stinking trick.

Dave's question as to whether I am good enuf for you was quite interesting. I've noticed in myself that after I had known a girl well and got to know her fairly intimately and respect her, I found myself wondering, when she fell in love, if the guy understood her and appreciated her real worth as much as I had. Looking at it analytically, I suppose it's natural for me in our egotism to think that we have gotten to know someone to a depth that others can't reach. After this happens a couple of times, the idea suddenly strikes you that the girl should be given some credit and be expected to fall in love with someone who understands her and whom she thinks is worthy of her. I don't know if girls have the same feeling about their ex's–it's tied up somehow with our vanity and our unwillingness to "give up" a tie we once had–but I suspect that fellows are more likely to expect a girl to fall in love "blindly" than a fellow. So is it that way with girls too?

Poor Surjemaki! Don't you have any sympathy with a fellow who will soon become a father and who, trying to get ahead in a conservative atmosphere, is trying his best to avoid having controversial opinions. I'm half kidding, darling, and I don't think he's really worried about expressing radical opinions if he holds them, considering Venable doesn't care.

It was interesting to notice that the idea of visual education for the public is only 40 years old. Forty years ago Physiology was just in its infancy-it's amazing how crude the experiments were in those days and how little was known about how the body works.

You are going to have an exciting week with your mother coming up for a visit and Venable to dinner on Thursday. I think your idea of talking to her about our engagement and asking her opinion is a good one. I'm sure she'll say to wait, but as long as you convince her that you're serious and it's a question of now or later, it'll be a step forward. I don't think it would be good to let her get the impression that you're just playing with the idea and can be too quickly dissuaded since the inference might be transferred to your feelings toward me.

If I hear anything about Walt, I'll let you know immediately. If you hear first, don't forget that I'm very much interested.

So long for now, darling. All of the love that you know I have for you plus all of my love that your modesty prevents from admitting to yourself, plus all the rest of the love of which I'm capable,-all of this and more-
Your fiance, D

February 28, 1945
D. dearest,

Yellow must be our good luck color for your letter on the yellow paper today was terrific. It made me feel so close to you, it was as if I could hear you talking-particularly the last page. I glow all over. I suppose each person thinks that the person they love writes the best "love letters" in existence and I'm no exception.

That sounds very silly about the marking of your exam but it will give you something to work towards: coming up the ladder. It's a shame that things worked out the way they did for your mother (does my making a statement like that bother you?) and I didn't really think she'd feel that way only because of me tho I thank you for taking care of that possibility with your reassurance. Those last few lines of description of us-interrupted by yourself have me feeling about us as ample as a female can—which is quite. In short, darling, I've now used all the realm of words in which I can describe my love for you, the joy I have when we're together. I leave it to unspoken signs or in the form of energy, force and electricity.

To get to less pleasant matters. The more I think of it, the more I think Mard is right about the weekend of the 10th. I've really felt it would be a tactful thing right along but wanted so to think it would be O.K. that I've sort of smoothed it over in my mind without solving it. I can't afford to take off two weekends in a row so I guess the only thing to do is to come in for a 2 day weekend on March 17. I hate like hell to have to put off seeing you for a week and to miss such a lovely opportunity but I guess it's for the best—and if you want to stay single, we'd better learn not to HAVE to see each other every two weeks. Gee, how I hate to have to write words like that. If I came in on the 17th, that would upset your Philly plans, wouldn't it? Would you want to go to Philly the 10th or am I making a complete mess of your plans?

The Econ test was pretty awful. Studying didn't help much. I didn't know why they were asking what they did. Usually you can figure out why a question is asked, what important points are wanted, but I definitely didn't have that feeling this time.

We had a required assembly today at which the head of

the Trustees explained their action to continue the three year plan—unnecessary and unhelpful. The point now is we've got the 3 year plan for 3 more years, let's get it to work. If it's an experiment instead of just cramming 4 years to 3. Throughout the assembly I sat next to a girl I'd never seen before who spent the whole time figuring an engagement ring. Its funny how once you get an idea into your head, you notice so many things that bear some relation to it that you'd probably never notice otherwise.

I've been sleeping with Fooless every nite but really, he's a lousy substitute. (Pardon me, Fooless, no insult intended, but I must be honest).

Finished taking notes for my American Lit paper so now I have to put it all together and speak my peace on what I think of it all . . . which shan't be too hard and ought to be accomplished this weekend.

What you do to me! I'm very tired and perpetually hungry. What would Freud say?

Had my picture taken this afternoon-a group picture of members of IRG for the yearbook. Had sense enough not to wear a sweater this time. Or wouldn't you call it sense?

Your sleepy in love fiancé must retire but first she would like to tickle the fuzz on your chest, say hello to an "old friend" and tell you, she's yours.

As always, V

March 1, 1945
D. darling,
Here I am listening to beautiful music "liebestod" midst

5 females in our living room, trying to imagine I'm hearing it with you, alone, somewhere far from civilization (I vant to take you out of ze verld). It's a beautiful piece and each person is busy with her own thoughts: Ann writing to her guy; Fizz, to hers, Barb to Johnny, Ray staring into space; Mary rolling a cigarette and Bunny just sitting. It's her record and I'm afraid it makes her think of her guy who is reported missing. Wouldn't it be fascinating to step into each person's mind, walk around a bit, and then slip out again?

Your letter was so wonderful today . . . and so long! Was interested in your comments re the censor. I realized after a while that it wasn't a very nice thing for him to do, though it didn't immediately strike me so. I guess I didn't think of it cause the letter itself was so impersonal and meant so little to me, but I can see how it would have hit me right away if I'd cared about the sender of the letter. The fact that he put his address on it might detract from the sender's correspondence was a good point which was partly why I wouldn't answer (the other being I have no desire to increase my correspondence, thank you). I was delighted you disliked it so heartily.

I honestly hadn't thought about Sirjemaki's reticence being due to fear of his job. I keep forgetting that—tho there have been several cases to act as a reminder. Since I became interested in "radical" ideas only moderately recently, I haven't had much first hand picture of the underground, and reticence etc needed. The freedom at my summer job at Spotlight and my home make me forget that not everyone feels free to say what they think. I forget that and should know better.

God! This music is beautiful stuff I'm hearing. There are few things that compare with the feeling of really moving music. Its beauty in one of its purest states and sometimes the richness of that purity is quite overpowering.

Tomorrow I have a test for which I'm not prepared too well—slept all afternoon (what's the matter with me? All I can do is sleep. When I'm away from you.) I can't worry about exams any more. There are so many nicer thoughts in the world and as long as one only has one life . . . it's a shame to have to waste time on such things as exams or regrets. How nice if I could act on that!

I want to spend this next year or so not cramming for tests but in growing, not up but "out" so that I'll be a fuller person by the time I'm your wife and in my muddling way, I think I can. With you as a guide and myself as agent and evaluator.

When I hear music like this or walk in a sunny day like today, I feel as I'm going to burst and "my heart sings". I'm a little speck on the horizon and a little gust of wind has pushed me toward you, another speck on the horizon and together we'll whirl and dance on the paths of a sunbeam.

Change of mood: Brahms 4th.

Do congratulate Dr. Wang for me. Gee, I just realized Clare' s exam is tomorrow, isn't it? Congratulate her too!

No, I haven't heard a thing about Walt. My guess is they haven't heard from him for a while and I guess the poor guy's pretty busy.

6 weeks from this Wed. Exams start and 7 weeks from then I'll be home. Oh how nice someday to say "home" and mean ours!

Pathetic thing happened tonite. Barb was standing near Nanette waiting for coffee after dinner when she asked if she could hold Barb's hand. Barb was quite embarrassed and said O.K. apparently not too enthusiastically. They did for 5 minutes. I suppose its people like Nanette who get led astray by more dominant females. Yes? Not that I know a darn thing about the subject, but that would be my guess . . . Or am I crazy?

What a note to end on! But at least you know I'm normal and that I miss you terrifically and love you twice as much as that.

All of me, always.

V

March 2, 1945

Dearest,

Last nite Barb and I had a discussion I felt was coming for quite some time. I forget now how we got into it but it involved sex and she somehow asked a question or something which could only substantiate my point of view if she knew I wasn't a virgin. So I told her and she was very good and intelligent about it. It makes it easier for me now not to have to make up all sorts of explanations for little incidental things and I thought it about time she knew considering the lack of practical experience she's had– and the fact that she's really come in contact with a loose woman like me, she was mighty good. Also told her the Morrie story of his surprising us when I was in your little room leaving out the precious bits of the broken rubber. She asked rather intelligent questions such as when the safest time was etc and I was only too pleased to impart information. I also gave sex a very high recommendation!

The Philosophy test was very fair and comprehensive. I knew the stuff but felt I wasn't expressing it very well. But it's over and so are all the tests for a while.

At 4:40 I went to a meeting on what to do about the college educational plan. Before the meeting I noticed that the students were in one section and the faculty in another. I went up to the girl who was chairing the meeting and suggested we mix up. I came back to my seat, meanwhile she announced the idea. Mr. Jackson was sitting behind me. (He's the head of the of the Zo dept. (Mard knew him well and we had spent time with him when she came up to visit).
He suggested I sit next to him and who was I to refuse? (Barb then sat next to the Dean). The discussion was good: no more 3 years vs. 4 years but how to change the system?

Miss Lockwood (brilliant dogmatic Eng. dept) gave a plan she and 3 other faculty members had worked on: a combination of fields all working together to give an integrated picture of the city: with field work, lab work in understanding the city- the part science plays, Soc. Sciences, English, Psych, etc. They're going to try it for the short spring term. The interest at the meeting was so great that something may come of it.

It was too late for dinner so Barb and I walked to the

drug with Jackson. He's a conservative, a disinterested conservative, who loves to talk. We talked about correlating courses and how you could with zoology. I asked him, (mainly to see his reaction), if he'd ever mentioned socialized medicine to any of his classes-those particularly who were going on to medical school-pointing out how Mard had noticed the indifference to social things among the medical students she now sees. He said he'd never thought about it, that he didn't know enough to give it a fair picture and that he'd be too biased. But even he realized that was a silly argument and I think I made an impression on him. There I go corrupting the faculty! I'm so sorry, darling, I can't help sticking a pin in things every so often.

Ate at the drug and came back to the dorm to find Mr. Lanier had eaten there (head of Psyc. and liberal). He believed it all lay in the confused idea of a college education today-trying to mimic graduate schools in giving whole courses in small fields, chopping up subjects into many departments. That there was a basic conflict in preparing for vocational training and trying to get a general liberal arts background. Went on from there to an interesting discussion of possible solutions and was glad to find he felt very much the way I do.

Among interesting side lights: Barb talked to the Dean for half an hour after the meeting at which time the eminent woman suggested a 2 week experiment that Barb and I should follow. Go to classes and learn only what you're interested in–don't take notes but just what you want.

Don't do assignments that don't appeal to you and use the time to do the things you want to do . . . which is all fine and dandy but highly impractical. So I'd get an incomplete for not writing my Polit paper, for instance. Seemed like an awfully unrealistic plan to me considering we still have marks etc. Oh well, this must be boring for you. I haven't given a good representation of all the discussion pro and con but it WAS fun.

All this talk, talk, talk but it's just the kind that I have when I first see you. Just an explosion of ideas that I want you to share. You're so much a part of me now that sometimes I have to convince myself that you weren't by my side right along.

Gee! Tomorrow I speak to you. How pleasant! What shall I say? Oh well, we can always talk about the weather. It IS getting spring-ish you know . . .

Wrote Bob today and had a terrific desire to write to him about you but decided to wait until it is official. I started creating an imaginary letter to him while sweeping the corridors and if I'd had a Dictaphone, it would have been interesting to keep a copy. (Your modesty wouldn't have allowed you to recognize yourself).

It's after the bewitching hour, my darlingest, so I will kiss you very passionately in my mind and wish that it wasn't in the world of thought but in the world of extension, as Descartes would say.
Your one and only, V.

March 2, 1945–11:45 AM

Hello Darling,

Back to white paper-not that my sentiments have changed at all, but I've found the paper again and I feel that yellow should be reserved for VERY special occasions, not just special ones like now.

I was going to write last nite after class, but a premonition told me to wait and see what your letter would say this morning. I'm not sure exactly what's what about the weekend of the 10th. If you need that weekend for your school work, than I'm all in favor of waiting till the 17th before seeing you again (even if I have to chew on my belt) but if the only reason for the change is because of the family situation, than a) you could come down either for Saturday or Sunday. If you feel you CAN use this weekend for study, then by all means let's make it the 17th. I would have agreed to the shift without any comment except that I sometimes get the feeling that you are afraid you are imposing on my work schedule, and I want you to know where I stand.

Harry was to come to Philly on the 17th. He would prefer to come to N.Y. or your college sometime when he has more time then just Sat and Sun off but a) I'd have no trouble convincing him to come to NY or b) there might be the possibility that we could go to Philly, so you needn't worry about messing up my plans. It would help tho if you'd let me know as soon as possible what you (and I) have decided to do.

Clare's exam starts in 15 minutes. She was in a state of complete nervous shock which was so infectious that both

Mard and I found that we were having trouble not to get in the same state.

Dr. Allison and I started going over my data which is now graphed and tabled. It's beginning to look as if it'll make sense. This is the last week of teaching the dentals for me until some time in April or May so that'll be able to get on with the paper and also get the reading done for the Chief's course. After a few drafts have been revised several times I may find it best to finish the blood flows but that'll be decided after the paper has begun to take shape.

What a day yesterday was! I missed both breakfast and dinner! Wednesday nite I was up with the Phys chem. Homework till 2. It was tough-just lots of graphs to draw, logs to look up and calculations. Then I had to read some physiology and prepare a conference. I don't know what time it was that I finally got to sleep, but the alarm woke me up and I arrived at 9:30 for a 9 o'clock class. Noble was to have 15 students but he was sick and so I found 30 of them quietly waiting. After 5 minutes to catch my breath, we settled down and had a nice session for a half an hour. They're awfully nice kids and took it all beautifully. It's hard to get the student's viewpoint, but I get the general impression that they don't mind my methods of teaching too much which is a good morale booster for me.

I missed dinner that nite because the watch which I did just got back for the jewelers is still up to its old tricks and when I thought it was 6 o'clock, it turned out to be 6:35 giving time enuf to rush to class.

But as jammed as my days are, I like what I'm doing so much that it's never burdensome and thoughts of you manage to fill in innumerable spaces during the day like sugar that is added to a glass that is already full of water (yours aren't the only fancy analogies!) It would be even more correct to compare it to syrup which gives body to the water, holds everything together and gives unity to the whole. (Top that one if you can).

Of course I don't mind you talking about my mother, tho it was thoughtful (typical) of you to let me know that you understand the personal nature of some things. My mother isn't markedly affected by the situation I described, but it never hurts to know what forces are working in a person's background or even subconscious.

This has been a very factual letter but I mustn't say things that keeps you ample all the time. I know I can't get any work done when you or thoughts of you get me in that state. But whether I say them or not, the thoughts are there often and amply.

I'll try to call about 7 or a quarter of 7 on Saturday, but if you have some thing to do at that time, I'll try the same time on Sunday.

I didn't mention something that happened Monday in lab which struck me as very funny tho I didn't let anyone know about it. In one experiment we have a fellow lie on his back and over-breathe for 5 minutes. They get up very dizzy from this and sometimes almost pass out. One of the guys was describing how he felt afterwards, and I couldn't resist mumbling in what I thought was an inaudible tone, "Now you know how a woman feels". One of the group unfortunately overheard me and asked "What do you mean?" I gave him a blank look and said "During childbirth, of course."

Well, that's about all for now, Darling, tho I want to repeat that what you decide about weekends of the 10th and 17th is entirely up to you. If you can use the 10th for study, I wont feel that you love me less if you stay at school that weekend, but I can come up if that is not the case.
All (my warm words, hr (energy), ma (force) and ww(electricity), Love D.

March 3, 1945
Darling,

You're in love with a fool! Honestly, I don't see why you bother at all. I was so miserable after talking to you-partly cause it was sort of a frustrating call, partly cause I felt you were somewhat down in the dumps, and partly because of the mess about this weekend. I won't go into the ins and outs of my reasoning processes but if you're still free next weekend, would you come up here? I've thought it thru (it's somewhat bigger than appears on the surface) and if you're not going to Philly or feel you can't for some reason, I'd love to have you here.

For the first time in weeks, I didn't feel "one" with you tonight. I guess it was a building up of circumstances but after the call I felt suddenly as if the bottom had dropped out of my stomach. So your stupid girl friend betook herself for a walk (the first fresh air of the day except to walk to the mail box this A.M.) in the starlight ending up by the brook. After getting dramatic and philosophic, I laughed and thought of my bottomless stomach feeling and decided to reinstate the invitation for you to come here next weekend. Though I've loved you terrifically all along, I feel now as if I love you even more. I can't directly put my finger on it except that perhaps it's a change in my feeling about giving up my freedom. I have known you came first in my mind. I've known it enough to say, to believe and yet I now realize, not enough to really FEEL all the way down deep. I now feel it and this weekend episode somehow symbolizes it. (Don't feel you HAVE to come, if you'd planned to go to Philly. The fact that I want you to come, at this moment is the important point.) Sometimes I wonder if I don't hurt you being as honest as I am about things and yet I can't help it; I've just got to be and I trust you prefer it so. At any rate, dearest darlingest, I'm back in the groove, feel fine about life and want you, miss you and love you terrifically. Don't forget to sock me hard for being such a dope, the next time you see me.

All of me, darling, even the bad parts are yours. God! What I wouldn't give to see you now. Hollywood would learn how a love scene should be played!
Your fiancée

March 4, 1945
Dear most hungrily missed Darling,

Damn long distance phone calls! I didn't call to talk to you about the future weekends or how school is; I wanted to hear your voice. I wanted to tell you that I love you

and that I miss you beyond description. I wanted to tell you how empty the bed is and how full my heart is. And I wanted to hear you say that you love me. Oh well, we know what our phone conversations are like. How I sympathize with people whose only contact for a long time had been unsatisfactory phone calls.

I left the phone feeling that I had said everything wrong and had left you with the impression that I wanted the change in our weekend plans. It surprised me that you hadn't answered the letter I mailed on Friday afternoon which explained how I do feel about it. I know you don't relish an extra week apart any more than I do, and you wouldn't have suggested it if it weren't necessary so please don't change your mind just because the phone conversation gave you the impression that I was disappointed. Of course I want to see you-every day if I could-and it's disappointing to have to wait another week, but as you said, we can't act like spoiled children. So stick to your studies with all of my approval and we'll look forward to March 16 with that much more anticipation.

Last nite I got to Andy's so late that there wasn't time even for a movie with everything closing up at 12. I didn't mind not spending the money a bit. She took me to see her new studio-a four room apartment that she shares with two other girls. It's in a "bare walls with one chair" state now, but they should be able to make it pleasant and it's a wonderful thing for her to have a place away from home since she gets along so poorly with her parents. We had a real talking session-when ever she paused for breath or to think of something new to say about her Howard. I'd burst in with something about you until I got interrupted. Next to being with you, the thing I like best to do is to talk to someone about you, so it turned out to be the least lonesome Saturday nite away from you that I've had in months. Unfortunately the incomplete feeling descended all the harder today. It's as tho my conscience accused me of running away last nite-that I should have stayed home and fought my loneliness without help. Of course, this is absurd–I might as well object to a moving picture if it helps to pass the time less completely and yet the feeling persists. I think I resent the idea of Andy or anyone else who is not us can even temporarily make me feel less lonesome for you. It must be a remnant of the "pure love" idea that Barb has, and I'm a bit surprised and ashamed to find it still in me.

Anyhow, after all that talking about you last nite, I miss you terrifically today and looking at your picture is no help-quite the contrary. God, how I love you, darling and how I'm going to love you . . .

Clare communicated as much today of her excitement to us, that I couldn't work at all yesterday. It was as if I had just taken an exam and wanted to relax and get away from books for a day. I suddenly remembered the idea for an improvement with cig machines that had occurred to me a couple of weeks ago and I spent the whole day in the shop working on it. It looks as if it'll work and will roll cigarettes in practically no time. I love working in the shop. When you get started in handcraft work some day, you're going to have a job keeping me out of your workshop. It reminded me of the old days when I had a car and used to take it apart and try to put it together again. It's fun to feel dirty and tired from the unaccustomed physical labor.

Andy said something yesterday which I didn't find too amusing. She said she's been thinking at times of the financial trouble she and her man will have. Altho he's brilliant, his talents don't lean toward money-making channels and she's afraid they'll have to get along on only $10,000 a year. Poor Andy!

I'm going to write Harry tomorrow about the revised schedule and see if he can come here the weekend of the 16th. If he can't, he'll probably make it the following weekend in Philly and I will meet him there. Andy mentioned that if Harry is desperate for a date, she would be glad to be it, and I'll mention it to him tho I think he'll have a better time with Amy. (I've kind of ruled out Rosey since it would take them a while to become friendly and his visits will be short and widely spaced. What do you think about it?

But to hell with everyone else. All I care about is that you'll be here in two weeks. You're making me selfish, darling. I hope I'm doing the same for you.

Theoretically I've finished teachings the dentals until some time in April but with the Chief and Root and Roughton going to California this week for at least a month, Ingrith is going to give the lectures and will run the labs. She has planned some beautiful experiments for the kids, but they'll take a lot of help and since I am one of the most persistent critics of the course around the place and am always trying to instill improvements when she asked me to help in the lab for two weeks, I had to agree. This will cut down on my freedom but I'll still be able to start on the first draft of my paper and can start reading on the chief's course. Ten times this term it's seemed to me that I have all the work that a person could possibly do in the next 6 months, and yet new things keep on adding in and yet they somehow get done. It's amazing how much time we don't really use in a day.

And with all this activity, I think of you more often and more persistently than ever. You are an integral part of me and all my thoughts. Despite what I said above, you've made me less selfish than I used to be. Instead of considering everything that happens in relation to it's being on me, I now think of everything in terms of us. Basically, I suppose it's just as selfish a viewpoint since you are now a part of me.

I'm thinking extremely ample thoughts at the moment. I can see your eyes and your lips–the smile in both–now it changes to a grave look, deep and warm and now it becomes hot and tender, as if your heart is beating up close to the surface. I kiss you, darling, a warm hard pent up kiss and I'd better end this letter before I become morbid.

So long, my most beloved darling. So long, and don't ever forget how much I love you.
Your fiancé, D.

March 5, 1945
Darling,

Maybe this letter should. never be mailed . I just reread your letter that you wrote on Sunday and my mind is filled with feelings and emotions. In a couple of days my thoughts will crystallize in a more rational manner, perhaps, it would be better if I waited till then before writing but I want you to see me as I am right now. Because you are—

I'm very sorry darling, but I was just interrupted by Nick who wanted to unburden his heart to me so I sat and listened and talked about his troubles, the faults of modern education and what not, for half an hour. I have only the vaguest idea what he or I said, but my train of thought with you is broken and I'll have to start over.

This time I'll start at the end. I'm not going to Philly this weekend and there's nothing to keep me here, but I haven't yet decided whether to come up to you, tho it would be a lie not to admit that every atom in my body is pulling me toward you or that I wont finally decide to go.

I'm terribly glad you ARE truthful with me since I knew something was wrong and it would have been worse if you hadn't been forthright. It is even more important that you be truthful with yourself and it is a matter that only you can decide.

Before going any further into my reactions, I want to tell you that I love you and want to marry you and I believe that you love me and want to be my wife. If it hadn't already happened before, I would have gone to see you yesterday after the phone call Sat. nite, but this time the response had to come from you. And you came thru magnificently. But I won't pull any Pollyannas as to the afterthoughts that are left in my mind. I want you to know about them, I want you to know that they don't in any way affect my love for you (if anything, they increase it) and I want you to know yourself-to know that all remnants of "holding back" in your love for me are completely gone, or if they be not, to face them squarely, see how much they mean and understand them as completely as possible. Don't give a damn about hurting me. I respect your feelings enuf to know when things aren't right, and it hurts much less if the fear of the unknown is turned to something concrete that we can evaluate.

As you know, we have felt that up until recently I loved you more completely than you did me-or to put it plainer—I was more aware of the full implications of loving you and prepared to accept them. After our new phase started a few weeks ago, we both hoped in our hearts that this was no longer so, since we ARE very much in love and these uncertainties are really only small things that as you realized even before I, will disappear in time. I know how it must have disturbed you when you realized Sat nite that there was still a difference in how we felt about each other. This time we were better prepared and you snapped out of it much sooner. It may have been the last time it'll happen-then again, it may not.

Your "bottomless stomach" was a realization that momentarily at least, you felt an inadequacy in your love for me. A few sentences later (after the walk) you say" The fact that I want you to come at this moment is the important point and as usual, you've put your finger on the crux of the matter.

Along with our love of each other, there is the strong feeling that we are right for each other-that we can be very happy together. This is true and important, but we must not let one hide the other. You feel a certain respect for me and following a moment of doubt, you whip yourself with contrition and feel how mean, small and unappreciated you are of big noble me. This is nonsense. You can like me all you please, respect me, admire me all you wish, but you must love me without feeling that you are unworthy in some way if you don't.

I was interrupted again. This time by Dr. Allison and Ingrith so I stopped to read over the first page. It surprises me how blunt I have been and I'm not sure that it was right. While your "undependability" is important, I feel strongly that it's not unusual-that we do love each other very much and that we'll start our marriage under even more favorable circumstances because we're so conscious of what we are willing to give up for each other-in fact the "giving up" process becomes a real pleasure, an ennobling experience. It doesn't give me any pleasure to remind you that you are young (19 and 2/3) but that fact is tied up with realizing and accepting things which you talk and think about but are only gradually coming to fully realize. I love you for the struggle, darling. I love you for placing a high value on your freedom, for having a strong social consciousness and I love you for writing to me so frankly and honestly (if you hadn't, my worries would be infinitely greater.)

Your mother will be coming up on Tuesday. She may be there when this arrives, and I know you were going to speak with her about us. All this discussion by me may have made a mountain out of a not as big a hill, and you may not feel in the mood to talk to her. I leave that entirely up to you. Just know, that I don't feel the uncertainty and I'm sure we're drawn closer than before.

Writing you this (plus the interruptions) has clarified my mind somewhat, and I know now that we should be together this weekend. You will be entertaining your mother Tuesday and Wednesday and Venable will be over for dinner Thursday, as you may find you need the weekend for study. In that case, let me know if I should make it Saturday or Sunday but it's going to be one of those days if you flunk a course on account of it.

So long, darling. Before I see you, we'll have exchanged several letters and all this will seem much less agitating. All my love, affection and admiration,

your finance.

P.S. I almost called right back on Saturday nite. I'm glad now that I didn't.

March 6, 1945
Hello Darling,

I decided to really pile on the work today after cleaning the corridors and distributing the linens. My Amer. Lit paper is signed, sealed and all but delivered. I think it shows a lot of work and some pretty fair conclusions.

Also made up some back work of last week incurred while studying for those exams. Started reading Locke in Philosophy and he's fun . . . the first really modern seeming one,

I guess cause he's the first empiricist. One part struck me as particularly apt, "That which thus hinders the approach of two bodies, when are moving one towards another, I call solidity. I will not dispute whether this acception of the word "solid" be nearer to its original signification than that which mathematicians use it in it suffices that, I think, it common notions of "Solidity" will allow, if not justify this use of it; but if any one think it better to call it impenetrability, he has my consent. From the Essay on Human Understanding." The things one learns at college!

I still feel a little strange after last nite. It's ok as far as I'm concerned but I do feel like seeing you or at least talking to you so as to get it all straight. I want to tell you how much I love you and I want to be spanked and kissed. (Guess you'll just have to dominate me!). I almost called you but I'm broke.

Can't wait to get a letter from you tomorrow even if it is only about mis-understandings of weekends. I'm going to work like a dog this week so I can see Mom while she's here and see you if you CAN come up. I miss you even more now, since last night and I feel absolutely weak in the knees when I think how much you mean to me.
XXX Me.

March 6, 1945
Dearest curly haired kitten,

Now that I've had time to mull over your letter, things have started back into their right perspective and this letter will sound lots different from yesterdays.

I think I've gotten thru my thick scull what this is all about, and knowing (or thinking I know) has dissolved the worry that I felt even before you wrote. (You guessed correctly that I was in the dumps when I called Saturday nite, tho I'm not sure if you knew that you had been the cause of it). I couldn't say anything because it might have been in my mind. But anyhow, I now feel much better about the episode. It wouldn't be true to say that it doesn't bother me at all, for it's impossible for me to love you as much as I do and not be disturbed by anything which draws us apart even if it is temporary and only a sign of growing awareness and maturity on your part. But understanding and being bothered is a far cry from being completely at sea and worrying. It's so difficult to put feelings into words and so easy to misunderstand a written thought that I'd prefer to drop the subject and if we feel in the mood, we can talk about it when we're together.

Mard surprised me today by saying your mother remarked that she expected you'd come in this next weekend. I'm going to feel damn silly if everyone expected you to come in and you didn't, just to be tactful! But I'm leaving our future (immediate, that is) plans up to you to work out as you see fit.

At times I must be getting complacent about you, for it amazed me how deeply I was affected by your letter-everyone asked me why I was so glum Monday morning and I had to plead tiredness but don't let it bother you.. That is all gone now!

So Barb hasn't cast you out with the snow drifts because

you've fallen! I suppose the idea wasn't entirely new to her. I count it amusing that you refer to yourself as a loose woman (I suppose you meant socially and not anatomically). To me you are the least loose mistress that's ever been (hope you're not too disappointed, my wanton wench.)

According to present plans, Harry is coming the weekend of the 17th. Only the Lord and my duchess know where we'll be then. If we are in New York, fine. If you're at college, I think he could be persuaded to come up and if you're at college and I am here, I'll probably go to Philly. Otherwise I'll go on the 24th to see the family. I've suggested Barb, Andy, Amy and Rosey as possible dates for him supplying a brief description and will see what he chooses.

I've been reading, preparing to start my paper and have spent a lot of time on Phys Chem. which is getting tough and time consuming. Sherwood, our instructor is nice and helpful but he's a very strict marker, knocking off points on our homework problems with gay unconcern.

This letter should reach you Wednesday or Thursday morning which will give you time for a hurried answer if anything important pops up.

Hope your mother enjoys her visit and I'm sure Venable will make Thursday exciting.

So long, darling.

Avec tous de mon Coeur. D

March 6, 1945–11 AM
Most Adored Cherished and Loved Man-o-Mine,

I've just read over your Monday letter three times and

am shaking form the impact. The appropriate and desired thing was to smoke one of your cigarettes (how you do time them!) and write to you that I'm so overwhelmed at you and us that I'm not fit for much for words. You certainly put it well and perfectly. We ARE right for each other; I do love you terrifically (and I am young). I guess even the most well-suited people have their crises but different from most–we solve them so beautifully! You understood me so well that sometimes you make me feel like something very delicate which is definitely a new emotion for me. But the most precious things are handled with care and love and are those we prize most highly and that's the way I feel about you. At this point I feel as if I could show you how much I loved you and how deeply I feel, by being with you rather than the two dimensional forms of pen and paper. You're right: our strange interludes do bring us even closer together afterwards, though sometimes I wonder how that's possible. We just get better and better reaching for some undefined, indefinable goal of perfection. And how I love the process of reaching!

Mom arrives in a few minutes. I had the infinite pleasure of reading your letter alone, undisturbed, with a little time to put back the outer shell that most people recognize as "me" and which you so beautifully melt away. I want even more than before to "talk things over" with her. Oh gee! I love you. Damn the inadequacy of words.

Please come up Saturday—as early as you can. I'll get my work done, don't worry. If one wants to badly enough, anything can be done. It's going to be a

wonderful weekend–whether it's spent in the basement or the dining room; whether it snows, sleets or hails. In any case, we'll be together and if we don't have the freedom of your room, you'll see how I feel by my eyes—and I'll be O.K. cause you'll be there. If I believed in God, I'd thank him for giving me the chance to know you and love you and for having you want me.
Yours, V.

March 7, 1945
Dearest Delicate Duchess,

    I don't see how you can like my letters. They're written on such unromantic paper.

    Last week passed fairly quickly but it's been a month since Sunday. I feel as if we should celebrate our first anniversary soon. But somehow or other the days pass and here it is Wednesday nite. Just two days to go! I'd given anything if I could have seen you sometime this week. I almost called several times but I was afraid you'd worry too much that I was worried and our phone calls never come off right and you would probably be out with your mother when I called. Anyhow, I'll take the 8:30 which pulls in about 10:15 Saturday morning. If you have something to do and aren't at the station I'll come to the dorm (Is Barb still talking to me?)

    Howard's letter was very interesting, now that I've read it. His theory is interesting but didn't your dissatisfaction with college come long before we met? I'll bring it up with me.

    If Locke wants to call it "solidity" or impenetrability" when something hinders the approach of two bodies, it makes no difference to me. There's nothing like that between us as we'll see Saturday (except for lack of opportunity).

Didn't mention Clare's exam as it is such a rarity that anyone flunks when they've come this far. She DID study like mad.

Got the watch back today and so far it's been working. Doris (the secretary) surprised me with a big clock for our room. I had mentioned it long ago and had long forgotten all about it.

What did you mean by not calling because you're broke! I'd be glad to pay triple charges anytime you feel like calling.

The Chief, Drs. Root and Roughton are going to California to do some experiments. Root and Roughton left today. The Chief will follow. By an odd coincidence I had a 4 o'clock coffee with Root on Monday and Mard on Tuesday. There was no significance and the conversation was routine tho I took the liberty of talking to Mard about you and the weekend. I had already decided what I thought about it all, but I was anxious to get a woman's point of view.

Your Mom has been and gone by now. I'm dying to know how she enjoyed her visit. You two probably talk about everything under the sun but us but still came to some agreement about the subject which wasn't mentioned.

Isn't it amazing how people of ill will can have no trouble recognizing their own kind while the "good" people often are mislead. (Just heard that Rankin proposed a note of congratulations for Congress to General Patten "who only a year ago was the object of the smear bund". There's going to be plenty of pressure on the returning servicemen to turn them to Fascist use.

Made a wonderful discovery today. You may wonder (but probably don't) that I started to study amino acids in the blood after hemorrhage because someone had reported he'd found they rose in rats after bleeding. Some guys at Rockefeller Institute also studied the same thing in dogs. We both discovered that the guy who worked with rats found a much bigger effect than we did in dogs. The Rockefeller boys dropped the subject, but I went on even tho the rise wasn't so great. Yesterday, while I was reading the original paper on rats, I discovered that they had used whole blood while the Rockefeller guys and I used plasma. The red blood cells contain 3 times as much amino acids as plasma so if a cc of blood is about one half cells and one half plasma, I've figured that my results check beautifully with the rat experiments. This means that different species probably react the same and my results can be transferred to man with some confidence. It also means that I don't have to try to explain dog vs. rat differences and it's going to make ears of the Rockefeller big shots just a bit scarlet.

I've heard that the little article that I wrote has appeared in print tho I don't know where I could get a copy. Do you really want one?

This'll probably be the last letter before Saturday but that's only 2 days away!
Good nite my syrupy siren, unofficially or otherwise,
Your Fiancé.

March 7, '45–12:AM

D. Darling,

Mom and I have had our little talk and it went exactly along the channels I had expected. I almost chimed in and said in chorus such phrases as "what's the rush?" I knew they were coming so well. And yet it did "good" and just along the lines we thought.

I thought the topic would come up when we got to talks about summer plans but planning such things never works and this was no exception. Barb, Mom and I were about to go out to eat when Mom brought up the subject of the summer and it just wasn't the proper time to bring the conversation to its logical goal. I did mention you figuring in my summer plans, your vacation and how nice it would be to spend part of it in the country, to which she readily assented. That left no indirect means of entry so after dinner when Barb had returned to the dorm, Mom and I were seated on the couch in the alumnae House library, I brought up the subject directly. There followed a 2 hour discussion-very friendly terms: no-shouldn't announce it. Why not? What's the rush? Are you sure? We don't know him very well . . . I made it very clear that part of my wanting to announce it was so that they'd realize I WAS sure. We got off the actual announcement angle fairly soon and a good deal of the time was spent convincing her how I knew we were right for each other. I think I convinced her that I'd thought a good deal about it and that I had pretty good reasons to be sure which is a definite step.

The two main problems were they didn't know you very well (Mom liked your suggestion to come over some evening when neither Mard nor I are around as diverting influences) and the financial mess. Frankly, tho I'm realizing its importance, I'm a little sick of discussing it. We cover the same ground each time, but repetition of my ideas will strengthen their realization that I mean what I say and think. Went thru the process of why Dad was worried about it, his financial back ground and ideas, my relations with Dad etc plus how much we (the family) spend, examples of people who spend a lot less etc. No new territory but the main thing is to get them used to the idea.

So while I shall have to postpone changing a silver ring for a gold one, for a while longer, the general over-all purpose was achieved or given a push in the right direction. And while it would be nice to have the world know how I feel about you and vice versa, it is enough and more important, if this has helped Mom realize it. P.S. She likes you very much. But as I said, I couldn't picture someone not liking you. And I, my darling, not only like you, but definitely am enamored of you, am ready to give you anything you desire me to, that I am capable of giving.

Right now, that's all my love.

V.

P.S. She should only know I've been your mistress for two and a half months now…"what's the rush?"

March 8, 1945
Hello Darlingest,

What a long and busy day and how I love you! Shall be systematic as best I can: 8:15 Econ. Got back tests a "C" as I deserved and expected but didn't particularly desire. 9:05 Met Mom who stayed at Alumnae House. Took her to Philosophy which she enjoyed and to Sirjemaki to get my project Ok'd and showed Mom the social museum . . . then to cleaning the corridors and to looking for a room for you. Very difficult due to a) freshman play to which they've invited dates b) the President's at Hyde Park and apparently detectives sleep in town. Haven't found one yet–will try again tomorrow. To Econ lecture by Miss Newcomer who was the only woman at the Bretton Woods Conference. She spoke about it. To lunch to talk with Mom. All day she kept bringing up points as if we'd just been discussing them. They came out logically from what she was thinking but often not from what was being said. More financial stuff, repetition. We each repeated hoping to impress the other one with our viewpoint and the strongest and importance of our convictions. Also felt she was sounding me out and carefully noting what I said . . . to be used later defending me against Dad's complaints. Mom, the moderator, she should be called. Thence to bowling with the highest score of the year 131.

Back with Mom to Alumnae House to drug for a soda. She left at 4 p.m. At 4:30 I went to the Dean who'd asked Barb and me to her office to discuss the faculty's decision on 4 courses or 5. It's an agreement, a vote of general feeling that each dept. should evaluate courses, perhaps change their scope. If all depts. do it, or enough do, you'll be able to take 4 point courses or 3 point ones. Etc. Will discuss its pros and cons when I see you. Too involved on paper. It's an advance in a very patchwork sort of way and better than nothing, but not perfect by any means. Thence to the dorm where there's great excitement over a very distinct case of anti–Semitism in the faculty toward a girl in our dorm. She's in a dither over it. Facts are in the Misc (newspaper); the consequences have been both good and bad. Will explain when I see you.

Went to dinner when Amy came over. Doubt if she'd want to make it on the 17th as she will want to see Peter whom she hasn't seen for a while but wont worry about that now. Did the Soc. Map, or most of it and started Econ trade problem. Decided I was too tired to make sense out of it to looking at back newspapers for Econ paper. Decided to do UMW strike possibilities as the most logical labor "problem". No one, not even the workers are Pro Lewis.

Ate a donut Mom had brought and now it is midnight with little to show for much effort. Oh yes! From 3:00 to 3:05 bought a bra! Last one in the store–no elastic for you to stretch!

Talking to Mom intermittently and more or less continuously was quite a strain but I think I convinced her that I know what I'm doing and think I convinced her to come around to my point of view.

Gee, I'm so anxious to see you and talk to you and look at you and love you "in person". So much to say, and do, I can't wait! But I also can't stay awake. Will be at the station at 11:14 unless I hear otherwise. that you're not taking that same train and haven't let me know, Don't phone just come back to the dorm I will wait for you there. I'd always wait for you darling, just as long as I knew there'd be an end to waiting. And there is . . . only 60 hours. All of my impatient self sends all my love to my future husband. Viv

March 8, 1945
Dearest,

Just a few hurried words before class in the hope this reaches you tomorrow.

Loved your account of the conversation with your mother. According to Mard, we have her complete support—her problem being to break things gently to your Pop and restrain you since that what he wants. I know I'll enjoy my visit with her (next week maybe) and hope her impression of me remains good. Wondered a little at the "we don't know him" as it's you I'll be marrying and the question is whether you know me well enuf, but I suppose that's her way of saying the same thing.

In just about a day and a half. I'll be on my way to the train and to you. I love you, darling, with all my heart and I'm all worn out from pushing the clock ahead.
See you soon,
All my love. D.
P.S. I once described you as my first and last Duchess. We can now make it Mistress.
P.P.S. Started on my paper today and finished the first draft of the introduction.

March 9, 1945

Dear Family,

It was lovely to have Mom come here and I certainly enjoyed it from the tales of the household, the general conversation to seeing her scribble notes in Polit. class. Glad she could see what I mean about Mr. V. and Philosophy class. I only hope her cold didn't get fostered by the weather and that she is O.K. now.

Having Mr. and Mrs. Venable to dinner at the dorm was as much fun as anticipated. Mrs. asked all about Mard who is very well remembered here. We had some good talk on politics, Russia at al and on anti-Semitism. The latter at the moment is a burning issue. A very unpleasant incident has brought it up. It's a long story but the gist of it is that Mr. Jackson showed his narrowness in no uncertain terms to a Jewish girl who wants to go to Med school. He told her in the presence of several witnesses, things that only a VERY prejudiced man would say. She published a letter describing the talk, not mentioning names and it has resulted in talk and action. I spoke to Miss Gleason about it and apparently it has come up before in regard to Mr. Jackson. The outcome is undecided but the faculty has been wonderful to the girl, calling her up to congratulate her on the tone of the letter, offering her help and generally being nice. Prexy called her into his office and was good too. This is definitely not to be publicized outside of the college. It has resulted in many discussions both good and bad. At the same time, I've been collecting the questionnaire that two are doing for Sociology class on; attitudes among Jewish kids at college. Most people have, when handing them to me, gotten into discussion about Judaism in general and there have been some good debates on the subject.

Amusing incident: Got the Polit test back and your youngest daughter got the highest mark in the class: an A…the first one on a big test since I've been at college. Now while this is most pleasant, it is also most ridiculous since I studied less, felt I knew less for it than on some other tests when I have felt I've really learned something and have shown improvement but which have not brought the "recognition".

A comic sidelight is that Jane Blodger (Mom met her) is crestfallen with a mere Bt and is gunning for me! I've had 2 people come up to me who don't even take the course but have heard all about my A from Jane who finds 2nd place hard to bear.

International Trade is a fascinating, strange and almost ludicrous business, I am discovering in Econ class. It's a little too mathematical to stay in my mind for long but its fun to see on what strange business trade functions.

My interview with the Dean was not to get my opinions. How could I have been idealistic enough to think she really wanted to know my views? What she DID want was to explain a plan the faculty had adopted which leaves the matter of evaluation of points per term up to each individual dept and endorses a program in which some courses will be given more point value so that it will be possible to take either 4 or 5 courses in one term. It isn't ideal since only certain courses will be given more credit and it doesn't help the correlation problem which apparently is being considered separately It's a step in the right direction if they mean to only patch up the system. The Dean said the petition had a lot to do with the action taken which is pleasant to hear in the sense that petitions aren't a hopeless waste of time.

Spent an enjoyable one and a half hours this evening seeing "Madame Bovary" in French, given on campus under the auspices of the faculty film club. French movies certainly have something that Hollywood can't get, tho some of it was over-acted.

It was so beautiful out today! The crocuses are out behind the Book shop; the snow patches are rapidly disappearing and the sun is really sunny.

I guess you're in Atlantic City now. I hope you'll be going to Quantico and that all goes well. If Walt comes back with you, maybe you could phone me some evening at about 6:45 as I'd love to say hello to him.

Keep well and I'll see you next weekend.

Love from your youngest.

March 12, 1945 (7 months and 2 days!)
Darling,

As usual you shall frame the weekend experience in more apt phrases than I. I always feel after getting your first letters that you said what I wanted to and didn't some how get across. But it was a wonderful weekend. Even if our minds kept coming back to forbidden, frustrating tho delightful thoughts. I'd had no doubts at all after getting your Monday letter (and really none after writing you Sat. eve) so it wasn't a reaffirmation or a getting used to anything weekend, just an appreciation of how wonderful we are . . . How much I love you and how I love to giggle, whisper, sigh, and play with you. (Take it or leave it, are you doing this for me?) (Barb has been working on a "newsreel" a la Dos Passos which is built like my Valentine with semi-connected phrases and that last was an unconscious influence of it.)

Don't really feel I have any right to miss you but as soon as we part, I feel like half a person-while when we are together I feel whole and terribly happy. Maybe you've noticed?

No doubts, no qualms, much happiness, much realization of my good luck, much love.

Got back to the dorm last night ten minutes late. Had completely forgotten that waiting for your train to come in would make me late-and if I'd remembered I would have waited anyhow.

I saw Amy in the library today: "He's so cute!" Saw Polly today: "He's so cute." Saw Rosey today: He's so cute." The ignorance of these college women is amazing.

Time out to stuff our bosoms full of bread. (We think there's more future in that than in the rear technique!)

This has been what ordinarily might be a lousy day but nothing can daunt me these days so here I am happy as a lark. 1) Mr. Venable decided we'd better have another Philosophy test this coming Monday . . . la di da. 2) New jobs posted and I've got "Lunch wait" which is sort of a nuisance but could be worse. 3) Exam schedules are up and what do you know? I have the last exam on campus. Not only that but I have two exams on the last day. April 11 thru April 17. Will try to get the Philosophy changed to the conflict exam on the 13th but tis a lonely schedule.

A girl suddenly noticed my ring today and asked if wearing it on my ring finger meant anything. Was I engaged? I had half a mind to say yes, but I suppressed that half and said "NO." People certainly are observant these days. Tonight a freshman in this dorm got a phone call, the next minute everyone knew that she was getting married this Saturday. The boy had come in from overseas. She saw him once last Wednesday. Hadn't spoken to him since five years ago when they had a fight (8th grade) after which they'd vowed not to talk to each other. So now the girl's getting married and her parents don't know a thing about it! Makes us seem like such conservatives!

Gee I'm so lucky to have a guy who is so ready, willing and ample . . . And for other reasons . . . Because we're so alike, only you're better, cause you handle me (no no not that way) and let me try to handle you and because you've got the nicest pair of eyes and nose and because you love to walk thru squishy mud and because . . . 15 minutes out for dreaming . . . mmmm!

Your loose and loving future wife.

V

March, 13, 1945

Dearest Earthiest one,

    Only three days to go—I'm starting to wonder if being married before you graduate and seeing you each weekend would be so bad after all. (The bed at alumnae House was very comfortable.)

    High spots for the past weekend for me: walking back across the golf course, feeling an irresistible wife to kiss every other step, and finding ourselves knee deep in mud; dinner Saturday nite (whether the people at the next table heard or not) and sitting in the dorm parlor with you later that nite trying not too successfully to get away from sex. I guess it would have been better to have called these EX-TRA high spots since I was high the whole weekend—not only in the way you're thinking either.

    You probably know by now, so I discovered yesterday that your Mom is slightly under the weather and hadn't gone away this past weekend. I understand it's distinctly minor and she may get to Quantico this week depending on how Walt's affairs turn out. I was toying with the idea of breaking the monotony of one of your Mom's evenings this week, but Sherwood (Phys Chem) is giving a make-up exam for those who missed the one in which I did so badly and is letting us take it if we think we can improve our marks, so should be as my evenings will be taken up pretty completely.

    Got a very interesting letter from Ruth on Monday. She and Steve are doing well, but as usual her letter had something meant for me to think about – life certainly is a complicated changing mess, and I'm more convinced than ever that we are unusual, ideally compatible and are going to be head and shoulders happier than anybody. Also had a pleasant surprise in a letter from a girl that I didn't expect. She's a very cute thing, but a bit tricky – goes to school upstate, has dark curly hair and lovely brows. I'm very much in love with her, and I'm sure you'll like her, too. She's coming down this Friday afternoon and I hope to show her what a bachelor's room looks like, tho I understand that she's not without some experience in such matters.

Gene also contributed to Monday's mail (4 letters in all!) with the wonderful news that he had completed his final missions. He expects to do some instructing in England for a few months and may return to the U.S. sometime this summer-possibly with Rose as his wife. They became engaged March 11th.

The last letter was from Mitzie, my brother Jerry's wife, who wants to know why I sent her a proof of you instead of a picture. She was afraid I didn't have any pictures of you and hadn't the money to have the proof developed. I'll explain to her that I have three pictures and the set you gave me for my birthday and sent her the proof because I didn't want to let any of the others get away from me. She very sweetly invited us to visit them in Camden explaining that they have an extra bedroom, but I could use the living room sofa if we're shy!

Haven't heard anything new about Howard or Walt and also haven't heard from Harry. Can't remember now what the situation was at the time I last wrote to him. As usual there's a lot of Phys Chem, teaching, writing and reading to do. We persuaded Sherwood to put off the phys Chem mid term until after Easter. Since I'll be here anyway and you'll be busy with exams, it'll give me a chance to prepare adequately for it. As you can probably sense, I'm reciting these facts, but my mind is elsewhere, and the elsewhere is where you are, and the weekend we've just had together. We've reached a depth of love and a degree of understanding that I thought would slip into a more or less "state" of happiness but instead you keep revealing new phrases of yourself that delight me even further and we share new degrees of intensity that make all of our future life an exciting anticipation.

I know that you are studying like mad and wondering impatiently why I don't get thru with this letter, so I'll continue . . . I've been told at the beginning of her latest picture Lana Turner is seen lying in a bed. A girl comes in and says, "Your lawyer is outside and wants to see you". Lana rolls over and says, "Tell him to go sue himself" (Do you think the world is catching up to us and will join us in the gutter?)
So long, darling. Study hard and in the pauses, remember that I'm terrifically in love with you.
Love, love, love.
Your fiance

March 13, 1945
Dearest,

If this letter sounds very strange, blame it on the lecture I have just attended. "Metaphor, Mainspring of Progress". I understood about a quarter of it and so I guess it will have no ill effects. I seem to have a blind spot when it comes to abstract stuff like that; using great terminology. It can, in turn, anger me, bore me, confuse me, but rarely enthuse me. I keep trying tho, knowing full well it must be my fault and there's lots there if I could only get it. I can take just so much and then suddenly I see it from Dad's angle and shake my head muttering "It's too much for me". Ah well. You'll just have to marry me for my cooking ability!

This has been a wonderful day (tho no mail from you but I still feel close to you from the weekend.) Firstly it was beautiful weather after blizzarding yesterday; today was like Sunday (tho I didn't get around to increasing my sun tan). A day like today makes everything good so much better; everything bad, unimportant.

At lunch time I received a phone call from my mother telling me Walt is graduating tomorrow! Dad went down to Washington to see it and bring Walt back for ten days before he goes to California (and from there we know not). Mom didn't go as she's sick since when she was here. It's a shame cause I know how she was looking forward to going to Atlantic City and to the graduation. You probably know about all this by now via Mard.

On the phone Mom asked when I was coming in. Without thinking said Friday. She wanted me to be with the family for dinner and the evening. I compromised and made it dinner saying I'd be seeing you after dinner, that maybe Walt and his date will go out somewhere afterwards. We left it at that.

I'll come in around 2 P.M. and if it pleases your honor, see you til 6:30. Then I fear I must leave you for dinner. I asked if you could come too but Mom seemed to want to keep it strictly family. (Perhaps I hadn't gained as big a victory as I'd thought. No, that isn't true, it's just she wants to see her brood alone, I guess.) I'm reluctant to do it– couldn't decide whether it was better to assert my independence or not. Finally, on the basis of its being Walt, I let it go. Am still awfully excited that he made it thru officer's school. Have been bubbling with joy ever since I heard

After lunch I went to get permission to take the landscape painting course (I haven't had the prerequisite) and spoke to the head of the practical art part of the dept. He and another man who teaches theory were awfully nice to me and together we figured our schedule and I got their OK. It's funny how modest I am when it comes to having to "sell myself" for a favor or a job application. I've noticed that I either forget to mention things (like being the art editor of the yearbook in high school) or don't mention them for fear they'll expect too much and be disappointed rather than pleasantly surprised.

Finished the Sociology paper which is only 10 pages; did an extra co-op job, went to the lecture and so it goes . . . Spoke to Amy telling her the whole set-up with Harry because I felt if he WAS coming this weekend, I'd have to let her know right away of the possibilities. I explained Rosey's part in the thing and we left it up to Harry, etc. She says she's not sure if she could/should make it. She invited Peter up but was going to cancel it because of work.

I'm working on her tho. Hope to hear from you about Harry's status soon.

If I had a cigarette, this would be one of those moments that I'd lean back and dream a bit; but since I haven't, I shall scratch at my finger nails instead. What a romantic girl loves you! But if this doesn't sound romantic, don't let this letter or anything else mislead you: our love is built on the most wonderful, stablest, bestest foundation possible and I don't think either of us will lose sight of that fact.

The week is going wonderfully fast: here it is almost Thursday which is almost Friday. Once Wednesday is over with its very long four classes in a row, I feel as if the weekdays are already over.

Have gotten so I hate not to write for one day. I feel sort of left hanging if I don't. Even when there's no news I love to babble on. (How well you know!) If I can't have sex, my next choice is conversation. But tonight I have a letter to answer from a certain professor you may know. I don't know how well you know him as he's full of contradictions. He's always cute; he's serious as a wise professor who calls med students "kids" and he's a little boy when he chuckles or produces proper gestures to the accompaniment of "Rum and Co-ca-cola." And he's an aggressive guy in a bedroom. Perhaps it would help if I told you I hope to see him in less than 48 hours at which time he will be allowed to be as superior or inferior as he wishes!

Got a kick out of your Monday's mail. Loved the idea of Mitzie suggesting we could use either the bedroom or the living room sofas. I wonder if I would be shy? It certainly is a new experience for me to have such things taken for granted! I gather your family is more "down to earth."

Worked in the "Retreat" this afternoon filling in for someone else, sucker that I am. No one else was working at the beginning and there was a big crowd waiting to get in, so I started doing it all by myself . . . with no change in the cash register. It was jolly! Never worked so fast in my life and prayed that my math was O.K. I came out one and a half hours later to find a discouraging note in my mail box. It seems I can't take the art course as I haven't taken the history of art course first . . . a stupid rule (and I DID have a history of art course in high school).

Went to hear a good lecture in connection with our forthcoming scenario project in Amer. Lit on "Hollywood, Today and Tomorrow," by the head of the Script Writers Guild, who was good, liberal and pleasant–really knew how to put over what he wanted to say.

Tonight had the pacifist friend of last year and her roommate to dinner. Jody ate with us and there followed an amusing discussion on the lack of privacy at college (and I didn't start the conversation, either!) One of the funniest things about the conversation was the background of each participant. One girl, who I recall from before, says you shouldn't do anything with a boy beyond kissing until you are married. Jody may believe in more than that but hasn't had any "practical" experience...then there was Barb and me...

Practically knocked my Soc. Professor off his feet when I said I had my term paper done. (Most kids haven't even started theirs.) But most kids don't have a guy who makes them get their work done and most kids aren't under the wonderful glowing spell that I am. I LOVE YOU…

That's wonderful about Gene and Rose and their coming to the States. Wonder if he gave you any new insights into his feelings for her.

Love, love, love, V.

March 14, 1945 (7 mo gone, 15 to go)
My very dearest darlingest most superior one,

Back to yellow paper which I once said could be reserved for special occasions–according to that criteria, I should use nothing but yellow.

This'll have to be a fairly brief hurried letter as I've got to study for tomorrow's make-up in Phys chem. Besides doing regular work.

Today's letter from you was the happiest bounciest most ebullient (put that in to maintain my professional dignity) one you've ever written and it makes me proud and pleased if I've had anything at all to do with it. I mentioned to Mard how happy you sound and she said it's probably because you're coming home this weekend. I said yes, it's amazing how fond you are of Bertha's cooking and hoped (inside of me) that wasn't the whole story. Your Mom's letter that you enclosed was extremely interesting and very nice and kind. I'll return it to you this weekend.

By now Walt's success is old news to you and it made me very happy (partly because I knew it made you happy). He'll be in this weekend, so if you want to arrange for either you or us to meet him Friday don't hesitate to do so.

Harry, that so and so, hasn't written so I don't know what his plans are which is just T.S. for him. I do know, via my sister Ruth, that he'll be in this weekend but don't know how he plans to partition his time between Philly and NY. Incidentally, Ruth's letter which followed quickly a rather depressing one that I got on Monday, was very cheery. The baby hadn't been eating well and had cried a lot till her and Ed's nerves were shot and they quarreled a bit, but the kid is fine now. They've both relaxed and everything is wonderful once more.

Gee, by the time you get this, the week will be about up. Umph, ahh, etc. You'll be amused to know that for some reason the muscles right under my shoulders were sore Monday. I don't remember squeezing you that much.

I wonder if it isn't about time Barb got a book on sex and read it straight through. There's not much point in picking it up piecemeal–especially from such a questionable authority. She's probably looked at the couch more than once and wondered what foul deeds were perpetuated thereon in her absence.

I've decided to do the Chief's and my own reading before going on with my paper so that by June 1st I can devote full time (at school) to the paper and French grammar.

You (and I) get the lousiest breaks on exams, tho it will give you days in between to study for the next ones (poor compensation). How are you managing to work in studying for your Monday's exam?

This letter is running on to much greater length than I had expected – what happens to my willpower where you are concerned?

Clare found out today that her contract called for $1500 starting July 1st. It had been made up before she got her PhD, but knowing the Chief, he let it stand at that figure. He hemmed and hawed but she left with the impression that something will be done about it. One of his arguments was that he tried to pay according to need, which is fine from my point of view. On the basis of Clare's contract, I can expect $1500 or a little more from July 1st until I get my degree at which time he's going to give me $2000 or else.

I just have to stop now . . . My frustration of last weekend indicated how much I love you only as the small bit of a whale that floats above the water is a poor indication of how much of it there really is. (My God, I'm comparing myself to a whale – well, look out when we get together.) See you soon in person. Amply and impatiently,
Love, D
P.S. Thought your description of the past weekend infinitely better than mine.

March 15, 1945
Dearest Kitten,

Mard has just extended to me from your mom an invitation to have dinner with you all on Friday. Mard will be with her in-laws and there will be enough to go around. I've accepted with the mental reservation that you must promise (between 6:30 and 8:30) to keep my mind off sex.

Walt has turned up with two tickets for "On the Town" for Friday nite, so I'm afraid we'll have to amuse ourselves –shall I pick up some comic books?

Harry, the ungrateful bounder, has kept me completely uninformed as to his plans. (I'm getting worried now whether I wrote him definitely what we'll be doing or if he is waiting for further info from us. If I don't hear from him before Sat – which I doubt – (I meant I think he'll write or wire by then) we're forced with the delightful possibility that he may drop in unannounced. Lord preserve us waifs!

I've rounded up a few packs of cigarettes and Mard said there are some at the house to which I casually (but carefully) commented that your Mom would get lots more if she knew how crucial they were to unmarried people at certain times. (Just call me the red herring kid.) Now I'll probably find out that she's known about us for a long time and is vastly amused at my feeble attempts to mislead her.

By this time tomorrow we'll be together!!! While listening to a lecture today, I suddenly got a picture of you in my bathrobe, which was partly open and my whole insides dropped down to my feet. What you do to me.

My watch hasn't stopped since that day with you. I've decided it was just empathy.

Between now and tomorrow I have an exam in Phys Chem, some homework to do, and some sleep to get caught up on. I'm glad we'll have dinner together – I'm sure we'll both have a good appetite!

Got an inspiration today – don't know yet how it'll work

out. I'm going to ask the Chief if I can read some sketches in German and French a) for his reading course and b) to prove I can read them. If he'd accept this as proof of my proficiency, I wouldn't have to memorize a thousand words in each language and take a test in them. He'll probably say no but I'm going to try it anyhow.

My thoughts keep on coming back to the same thing. So I'll wish you a successfully successful weekend and sign off. All my love, D.

> *Dear Diary: March 18, 1945*
> *Sex is amazing! How come I didn't know any of this before? Does everyone feel this way? Does it go away when time passes? Can't picture my parents... Maybe I could ask Mard.. Does she do it with Dr. Root? No, I can't ask her. No one mentions such things in our family.*

March 19, 1945

Dearest Darling,

Put all the possible giggles, the mmms and ahs sideward looks and sexiness together and you've got a fair facsimile of this weekend. Or perhaps you'd prefer me to say, "thank you so much for a perfectly delightful time." It was just what I wanted. I'm still very much in the mood of it, can't think of much else . . . but that isn't abnormal!

We've already mentioned the most significant advances of the past weekend but may I reiterate?

You were so wonderful with my family and it was so

perfect not feeling myself at all split between you and them. Everything just flowed along (lift up thy mind, my sweet!). It's not a case any more of feeling close to you at times, but of feeling close to you and closer still at very special yellow-paper or in-your-room times. How I love you! We're going to have the most wonderful life together. Every darn minute of it: if it's on the floor eating candy, fish, spinach or potatoes; if it's looking at monkey's rears at the zoo, sitting by a muddy lake watching boys fall in or sailors dash thru open cars; if it's giggling at landladies. We're just super wonderful and I won't let us forget it. But I know how you hate to discuss things like "us." After all, we must keep this on an intellectual plane, says she, while her foot wiggles a mile a minute.

Your future wife arrived at her dorm a very happy girl who talked over PARTS of the weekend with Barb. Awoke to study for the Philosophy exam, and it was not bad at all. Then to Sociology where I handed in my paper. He glanced thru it and seemed pleased and interested which was nice. Dull Polit lecture – went bowling after lunch and I think I inherited your curve! (we go so well together!) If you do come up next weekend you'll HAVE to just bowl a bit and see what I mean.

After bowling, tho dead, I biked madly over to (finally) get my clothes fixed, but the woman was out and I had to bike madly back so as to beat the rain which would play havoc with my skirts, which were conveniently bunched in my bike basket. Amy had Peter up and they had a picnic, but it t'weren't as good as our picnic, I'm sure.

Just got a letter from Dave and I quote with amusement: I'd said I wasn't good enuf for you . . . he, corrected saying perhaps it being the other way around. "You know damned well I wasn't kidding in my compliments, you just want me to say them again."

Wahoo, m' love! I love you and nothing else matters and I'm criminally happy. We are lucky, and not only 'cause we can see each other often but 'cause we're such nice people, who are so nice to each other, who appreciate others and ourselves. I still feel rather drunk from you. Between a nice family, sex being wonderful, seeing you so often, beautiful weather (can't forget that) I'm all bubbly, glowing and generally showing the signs of being very very happy. (As if the heavens were agreeing with me, I just heard a clap of thunder!)

You know we're both very loyal people, I've decided. You with Harry, Dave, Gene and me with Jane, Bob. It's funny, I feel a certain responsibility in friendships. If I once make a good friend, it's sort of decided that I am a good friend with them, always. I know lots of people make friends and then when they move away, or somehow get separated, that's the end of that. But neither of us do that. If it was just me I would think it was my love of the past but you don't have that and still you stick by your friends. I guess we're just nice people!

What does it show about us that you had doubts about my liking you enough sexually and not mentally and I had doubts exactly the opposite? But here we are with neither of us doubting at all. hmmmm.

Must get to work. Forgot Miss Miller of the history dept. is coming to dinner.

Bouncily, lovingly, sexily, your fiancé.

March 19, 1945

Dearest Sophisticated Darling,

Just finished talking to your Pop about dropping in for a chat tomorrow nite. I'm to call him on the phone at 7:30 and if nothing special has come up, tomorrow nite will be de tag. Your father had to think over his engagements – half talking to himself and half to me. Every once in a while he'd mention what a busy week it was with Walt in town –then I'd say, "Well, it doesn't have to be this week" and he'd say, "Now, just a minute" and I'd say, "O.K." and wait a minute.

God am I stiff! I can hardly move without groaning and Mard refuses to sympathize!

What a wonderful weekend it's been! Warm and continuous -- full of love and you. And such intellectual conversations! One more such weekend and I'll feel completely domesticated. The days when I was one step ahead of you are gone forever. We're together, eye to eye, shoulder to shoulder (to put it decently) and nothing is ever going to stop us or slow us down.

I felt very close to your family this time /spent enuf time with them and, even more important, I think they felt closer to me. It was also notable because we took less trouble to hide how we feel about each other in front of them.

There seemed to be something almost dreamlike about

Sunday. The walk down 5th Ave; thru the park and the train ride to Poughkeepsie. How I love that woman of mine! And how I love to curl her toes!

I wrote to Harry and suggested that if he wants to come up to Vassar, he should write directly to you. He will probably let me know at the same time.

The trip home was uneventful . . . I got a seat and slept all the way so I wasn't too tired today, tho it was a strenuous day in the lab. The Chief left for California leaving the dept. to the people who have been running it anyhow, except when he interfered.

You must be working your head off this week. How's the Econ paper going? A 20 minute quiz was hinted at for Phys Chem this Thursday and we're having our mid-term a week from next Monday after a one-week Easter vacation.

I talk about this and that, but my mind and my heart are full of love of you. How cute and wicked you look when you laugh and joke about sex . . . The way your eyes fill with the joy of living and your freckles set off that impish smile, and . . . well, just and . . .

Clare walked by the door this morning, popped her head in saying, "Wasn't the weather beautiful this weekend, or didn't you notice?" There's a girl who understands!

This letter was started at 9:30 and it is now 12:30. That's how much dreaming I've been doing between sentences. I hate like hell to say so long to you even in a letter, but I'd better let my mother know what's become of my plans and if I don't write tonite, it'll be a last minute notice to her.

SO . . . so long my dearest wife to be.
How I love you,
Danny

March 21, 1945
Dearest Toe Wiggler,

I'm feeling very sorry for myself – i.e., I planned to phone you today to say all the dopey things we do say on the phone and to hear how things, if things, worked out with my family and you last night. After hunting up change, waiting until what I thought would be a good time, 2:30 P.M., I phoned; but first it took ages to get the attention of the woman who answers to WA-3-2500 and then she rang and received no answer . . . so I guess you were busy or out. Will try to surprise you another time.

Got your Monday letter this A.M., but am now on message center duty and don't have it with me (tho I guess I know every word in it). As you know I am very eager to hear all the news about your "reassuring" encounter with my folks.

Rosey is going to be here this weekend, tho she says she has a terrific amount of work. She said she'd make it Sat Eve anyway tho she might not be able to see Harry on Sunday. (If she has a good enuf time on Sat nite, I guess she'll make time.) So now all that remains is for Harry to inform us that he's coming on another weekend or he prefers to stay in NYC.

Your comment about loving to make my toes wiggle seems to have caused a reflex action – every time I read it or think of it, my toes wiggle!

You're stiff! If we went bowling every two weeks or so, you'd know how I feel. But it's the sort of nice feeling . . . getting stiff, I mean . . . makes you feel so healthy!

Today we had to read the Communist Manifesto for Econ. (been studying comparative economies) and, together with a rather uninspiring teacher, a rainy morning and some people's natural reluctance to speak up, no one said anything in class. What should have been an exciting hour was a dull one.

The girl I sit next to, a nice, liberal kid and I decided to shoot off fireworks on Friday when we are supposed to be dealing specifically with Russia. We let the teacher in on it, just so she knew what we were trying to do. We also had a lecture by Miss Brown who stands about where you do, and she did a good job of it. I love to watch the reactions of everyone. The lecture was really very simple and nothing was new to me; but from the questions they asked afterwards, I can see it was to them.

Have been working this afternoon on the costumes for the scenes we're doing for "The Portrait of a Lady." (Just heard Mrs. Ellis has undulant fever . . . which may be just a rumor as a good friend of hers, also in the English Dept, has it. Is it catching? And what kind of a disease is it, Professor?)

The costume work is fun: looking up the period etc. and then explaining why you choose what you do — like the symbolism for the countess is described in adjectives which usually denote birds (chirps, twitters etc. and, luckily, feathers were in style then).

Can take the Philosophy exam earlier so will take the

3:23 local on April 17. If you still wish to make the date of my meeting your mother, April 21 is fine as far as I'm concerned. I won't have the curse then. I don't have it yet. I won't pretend I'm not worried, but I'm pretty sure everything's OK and I certainly don't want you to worry. I wasn't even going to mention it to you but since I have, I have. Will probably get it tomorrow. It isn't very late.

Tonight I'm going to hear the Pittsburg orchestra. They're playing Beethoven's 2nd among other things. Will think of you as I do all the time anyhow. Oh darling! I DO love you so over-poweringly, so unusually and so inexpressibly.

Eager to hear if I am to have the pleasure of your company this weekend, Mr. K. In any case, I shall be with you mentally the whole time.

All of me. Your wife to be...

March 21, 1945–Spring!
Darling,

It is 12:15 A.M. and I've just gotten back from a most interesting evening with your parents. But let me set the stage and fill in some background. About 7:30 I called up and your Pop said the road was clear. I said I'd be there in an hour – giving me fifteen minutes extra to think of anything I might have forgotten. I had already gotten a haircut (your style – an appeal to the part of your mother that is like you!) and the only use I could make of the time was to shine my shoes.

I arrived about 8:10 and ushered in by your Mom, who recognized me immediately (pardon my kind of humor).

There was a little to-do about Walt taking up all the hangers, but I finally put my coat on the settee and we went into the living room. Your Mom picked up a sweater she's knitting for Walt and settled herself on the couch. Your Dad sat facing the dining room and I sat on the other side of the table on which your Mom had thoughtfully placed some cigarettes and candy (tho I smoked my own).

We made conversation for a minute or two, then your father asked me to pull my speech out and start reading it. I explained I had not written out a speech with charts, references and graphs. But decided against, since my delivery would contrast too markedly with the smooth delivery of the talk he had given at the Academy – or words to that effect. We finally got down to the point and I started by making it clear how well we are suited to each other and how sure I am that we're far past the point where it would be infatuation or anything but the real thing, to which your Mom agreed on the basis of your conversation when she visited you at college.

I could see that they were waiting for my opinions about when, so I remarked casually that we didn't have any decisions to make that very night since I wouldn't think of supporting my wife till I had at least gotten my degree. Your Pop couldn't restrain himself any longer, and he burst in with how his principal worry had been that we'd rush off and get married on a shoestring. After this we talked a lot about marriage and how many people were rushing ahead after having seen each other only a few times.

Next we returned to financial matters, but just at this

point the phone rang and some woman wanted to know if she could have a cocktail with her pill. Your Pop said to tell her it was OK. Then I suggested bicarb to make sure her urine wasn't too acid (acid urine is bad with sulfa drugs) and your Pop rushed to the phone to tell her to take bicarb. Imagine me telling your Pop what to do! We all laughed at the incident and conversation flowed smoothly after that.

All this time your Mom sat quietly knitting, seeing that I had an ashtray handy etc. About finances, he said he had no opinions as to how much money was a minimum for two people to get along on, vaguely mentioning $3000 but in no way trying to set that as a figure. I told him about my plans and the possibilities of commercial work later and your Pop brought out a booklet by a commercial firm which was right down my alley – protein stuff written by physiologists.

By the time I had gained his confidence and we swapped stories (oh yes) I mentioned that the two possibilities that might lead to financial trouble was illness and having a baby; our ideas at that moment were, I think, along slightly different lines.

We also talked quite a bit about you and what we think you'd like to do. At this, your Mom joined in and we agreed very well on that point too.

I liked your Pop for coming right out bluntly that I shouldn't be fooled by their fancy apartment address and expect that all my financial burdens will be lifted by marrying you. He was so frank that I felt a bit hurt by the thought, but at the same time I know he didn't think I had any such idea in mind. I flatly said that, when we married, I felt their financial responsibilities to you were ended. Your Dad said, no; he felt it was his duty to give me a fully educated daughter and if you wanted to go to art school after marriage, this was his affair. For a minute we nearly quarreled over that, amiably, the way people fight over the check.

Any tension that had existed was completely gone by this time and we tried to find something on which we could disagree but didn't have much luck. We thought we'd found something when I said I don't want you to work, but it wasn't a disagreement, after all, when I made it clear only until you'd taken any art courses you want and had found something you really liked. I had thought he'd meant that you'd have to "go out and get a job" in order for us to get along and he thought when I objected to this, that I wanted a wife to sit around all day.

To wind up the evening, we called Mard in and had something to drink amid anecdotes, laughter and much good feeling. Your Pop told about an uncle or someone who was an authority in the family when he courted your mother and whose OK he had to get much to his resentment. He said he wished there was such a person in this case just so that he could be called in to give his OK. At that, I turned the tables on your Pop and protested that I wasn't engaged to you and hadn't given him my permission to speak to anyone but US, as if everything was completely settled! Mard got a big kick out of this turn of events (and I suspect your Mom did, too).

That was all there was to the evening. I hope I haven't

bored you with such a long, detailed recital. Your Mom and Pop gave us their blessing and good wishes and I went home.

So that's where we stand now, darling, if you still love me . . . and you'd better!

I succeeded to some extent whenever I got on the subject of you. I think I surprised and pleased your Pop by remarking on traces of him I see in you, especially evident in certain pictures – traces in the pictures he likes best! He thought Mard was a lot like him, but he thought you were almost completely like your mother. (We were alone at the time.) Do you agree with me on this? I meant it and wasn't trying to please him.

Got a long letter from Gene today which doesn't please me a bit. He intends to marry Rose in June even tho he feels that she loves him more than vice versa and says he expects to become devoted to her. He's old enuf to know what he's doing. And I hope it works out, as he feels sure it will (after all, you knew how you'd feel about me before the real feelings arrived). He still hasn't filled in any details about her and I'm a little afraid that he hasn't 'cause he really doesn't know her. He sent a couple of small snapshots which don't show much other than a girl who appears to me, anyway, to one who knows her own mind . . . shall I say, a very practical woman.

Harry hasn't had time to write yet. Otherwise all is quiet on this front.

Being with your family has been, in a way, being with you (tho not nearly as satisfying!). It's now 1:25 and I'm tired as hell but full of love of you and wishing that I could have told you all about this instead of writing it, but we'll undoubtedly re-hash it when I see you.

Good nite, my lovely one. Practically your fiancé, Practically your husband. And always your lover. D.

March 21, 1945

Darling curly-head (and toes),

Back again with you. Your first letter of the week came this morning and, as usual, it gave me a lift (not that I need any). The strange colored ink puzzled me at first, and I had to look to make sure it was from you, but one look at the contents took care of that.

I haven't heard from Harry yet. As much as I like the guy and even tho we're friends of 12 years standing, I think it'll take physical force to keep me away from you this weekend. It just occurred to me that you'll get this on Friday, so I'd better call you Friday nite about 6:45 to get the weekend straight – unless he writes that he has already written to you. Of course, I wouldn't be looking for a good reason to call you up!

I'm at a loss what to say in this letter. It's been a very ordinary day since I wrote to you this AM and there's nothing new except that I love you and think of you and us all the time, which is old but is always new.

While talking to your parents yesterday, it became clear that it would be a mistake for us to get married right now, but I want to save all this till I see you. If we can't have any privacy at school, the next best thing is to talk with you about the future.

I've been trying to think of a good compromise between calling your folks Dr. and Mrs. Bass and Murray and Agnes. I don't really feel so familiar as to call your parent by their first names but after the warmth of yesterday's talk with them, I don't feel like staying to the formal Dr. and Mrs. Any suggestions?

I found myself really looking at your father for the first time yesterday. He's had a tough, hardening life and is naturally cautious and conservative by inclination; but when he spoke of you and our future, there was much love and concern and also keen understanding of both your strong and weak points (the former necessary in a wife and mother, the latter the strongest reasons why I love you), that I was quite touched. And he was far more reasonable than I had expected. For instance, I don't think he has many objections at all to our getting married before you finish school. I believe I've won his confidence which is the main thing.

Peter today asked me if he could go out and have something removed from his eye. I said OK and asked if picnics always affected him that way. He was so startled that it wasn't til a half hour later that he came around and asked how I knew about it! I assured him that the news wasn't all around your college but had come directly from Amy via you. (The fellow at his table seem to think that he's got quite an eye for the women.)

One of the kids in the class came to me with tears in his eyes and showed me our last quiz in which he'd got a D-. I talked it over later with Monica Reynolds (don't know if you've met her, but it was she who had marked the paper). It seems she divided the answers into 3 parts. If one part was wrong, (in her opinion) she took off 33% which reduced the grade to 67 or D- with nothing in between! Ingrith, Bill, Clare and I went into a quick huddle and, as a result, all the papers were called back, and I'm to mark them all so that they'll be standard. It seems to me that this is a perfect example of pedagogy as an absurd extreme.

If on reading a paper thru you're sure that the person should pass, its crazy to give him a D- because he didn't explain one part to your satisfaction. There are often cases where a guy indicated that he probably knows what he means but doesn't explain it well. When she slashed them unmercilessly, I'd have given him practically full credit. I may be too soft, but Clare and Ingrid agreed with me and I don't think anybody should get a bad mark on a question that he knows the answer to, but has got mixed up a bit in explaining.

We're having quite a time with Monica, who is studying here for the first time. So far she has kept things under control, but I will have to tell her a few things instead of asking. If I can do this without having her get "mad" at me, I'll really feel good.

I don't know why I ramble on about school for such a time. The big thing in my whole life is you and everything else is secondary. I think of you, things we've done, things we're going to do, and there are thoughts that make up my day with everything else momentarily appearing and disappearing from my consciousness. I'm not neglecting my work to the contrary, but I'd be a liar and a damn fool

if I didn't admit that nothing I do is nearly as important as one word in a letter from you.
Goodnight my darling.
love and kisses, D.

March 22, 1945
Dear Mom and Pop,

   Your very nice letters arrived this morning and I've been all aglow ever since. I'm so happy that you like Danny; that you all saw eye-to-eye regarding the future of your youngest child. I know how much I like him, and why; but it is always nice to know that other people agree with you, or at least understand why you feel the way you do. As usual, you both came thru as I would have expected of my favorite parents, beautifully and I thank you (or God if I really believed there was one) for being you.

   Last night was an unexpected surprise. Barb and I went to a concert given in the chapel here at Vassar by the Pittsburgh symphony orchestra. As soon as we'd arrived and settled back to watch the orchestra file in, I let out a shriek: "Terry!" Yep, there sat Terry playing first cello!!! In the intermission, Barb and I raced around to the side entrance and knocked on the door, feeling very much like "stage door Johnnys." We were admitted with the accompaniment of wolfish whistles. When I asked for Terry, one of the men said, "That guy sure has a following" and disappeared in search of him. Pretty soon Terry appeared and we had a pleasant chat. He looks the same as when we knew him from Walt's camp. He's been with Fritz Reiner and the orchestra for almost a year. He says it's sort of exciting but they play practically the same thing each time while on tour which is rather dull. He asked about everyone and sends his love to you all.

That's the main news from here. Homework calls.

Love from your youngest.

March 22, 1945

Dearest Freckles,

 Just heard "And I Could cook Too" from "On the Town" – also Beethoven's 8^{th,} which went well with my light-hearted happy mood. And why shouldn't I be happy with such a perfect future to look forward to?

 The letter you wrote Tuesday arrived today and as I read about summery weather and spring fever, large wet snowflakes sailed against the window pane. But the weather bureau promises fair and warmer tomorrow and much warmer Saturday…We may picnic yet…

 Haven't heard a word from Harry yet. He seems to be having trouble getting away from his job – or he may have written you directly by the time you read this. I'll probably have talked to you on the phone and we'll know where we stand. I've spent part of this evening packing a few clothes since I may go right to Philly from the lab and then directly to you. As of now, I expect to spend Fri. Nite and Sat. afternoon in Philly and arrive at your college sometime Sat. evening, but I can't make anything definite until I know where Harry fits in.

 Mard tells me that your Pop every so often says ,"Such

a nice fellow," which is nice. She had a talk with Walt – more than they had talked to each other all their lives up to now. Apparently, she was surprised at how well Walt knows himself and how much he had thought about his future and the world in general. Judging from his similarity to my friend Gene, I'd say that it's easy to understand him. It may take some time but he figures things out for himself and eventually knows pretty well where he stands.

I've succumbed to your trick and found myself picturing us getting off the train in Philly, taking the subway, then the trolley and finally arriving at the birthplace of my home. I even pictured us walking in and meeting my mother. And I was so proud of you and your sophisticated suit!

Got another quiz in Phys Chem tonite and did O.K. Guess I won't worry about it anymore till I flunk another exam.

In just a couple of days I'll be seeing you. Guess we won't be alone much, but we should be able to get a few words about the events of the past week and maybe kiss or two. Gosh! I feel daring!
Good nite, my love. Keep them wriggling til I get there.
All my oomph, Your fiance,
P.S. Nancy Walker is now singing "You got me and it's all free." There's also a line about how ample her love is!!!

March 22, 1945
My darling,

Lord, I love you! I have just received 3 letters. After glancing at the handwritings, I rushed home to the dorm to be alone when I read them. One was from Dad, one from Mom and the best one from you. I'll enclose the other 2 so that you may blush in private. Don't feel like kidding right now. I'm so proud of you and so happy for us and so pleased and terribly in love and glad that it is you! I knew they'd think you're wonderful, I never had any doubts about it; but it still is pleasant to hear them say it or read them write it. If they think well of you, what do you think I do? My eyes are glowing having been recently filled with tears of extreme happiness and if you were here, I'd give a performance of love-making that would make Hedy Lamar seem like a block of wood…Maybe she'd be petrified?

    I love your description of the evening, too. I could visualize every minute of it and felt as if I'd been right there, at least for the drinks. I can think of nothing pleasanter than getting high on other occasions. I could just see Mom knitting quietly while Dad sat cross-legged, elbow rested on the arm of the chair, hand against his forehead and you watching it all. You wearing your brown suit and, let me guess, one of your green ties?

    I can picture all the expressions on your face . . . The phone ringing . . . pop answering it . . . You laughing with your head thrown back. Oh darling, how I love you, want you, miss you, need you, desire you. And how nice it is to know that other people can see why!

    Suddenly remembered that last month was Feb. and that it only had 28 days, so the curse isn't so terribly late. Still haven't gotten it, but when I do I'll be so completely happy – that's all I need to make this a perfect day.

March 20, 1945
From Dad,

    It's 12 M. and we have just spent a very pleasant even with Danny. We talked things over thoroughly and found that we completely agreed on the important points. I am sure it will all work out very well and that you will both be very happy and have a really harmonious life together.

    He certainly has a lot of common sense, knows what he wants and has taken the time to work out how to attain what he is after. He certainly gives me a feeling of real confidence and a sense of trustworthiness that is very reassuring.

    I was sorry that you had already left on Sunday when I came back from the party, but I just missed you. We just had remarkable news that Micky's original work will be played next year by the N.Y. Philharmonic orchestra! And to think we have all known him since he was a little boy.

With this piece of news I leave you.
Good night and lots of love (the paternal variety).
from Dad

March 21, 1945
Dearest Pussy, (From Mom),

    As Dad wrote you last night, we had a very pleasant evening talking, at last; just he and us as he had the good sense to suggest. I can describe it as the meeting of two exceptionally nice men who seemed to understand each other perfectly . . . Dad's worries seem to subside if not all melt away in the warmth of D's sureness, and so we are very happy, most of all in your happiness, the happiness of both of you. It was also a good pleasure to be able to talk about you.

Lots of love, from Mummy

March 23,'45,10:30 AM
Hello, m' Love,

Life is lervly and at tomorrow at this time I'll be with you... mmmmm. That, incidentally, was one of the nicest phone calls we've had. Somehow, more natural, or rather more like "us" or didn't you think so?

Not much point in writing the little news that there is as you'll have heard it all by the time you read this. I wish I could do what you do – say there's no news and then spin out a beautiful 3 page letter.

Harry's letter was most amusing, both meaningfully and otherwise, and I'm awfully anxious to see him and Rosey together. Of course I'm a good deal more anxious to see you and me together. Pause for a long delicious daydream.

Wrote Bob last night – a 6 page letter – all about you. I thought it about time I told him and it was both fun and hard to write. I wasn't (and amn't) sure how he'd take the news, so I figured it had to be both gentle and firm. It's always a pleasure to write about you and the way I feel about you (not literally, you understand) and this time was no exception. Writing to him was a kind of milestone. I've often thought in the past, of how someday I'd tell him

I'd really fallen in love. (We've known each other well for years and years, you understand.) Of course I hadn't pictured it would be with a serious intellectual professor-to-be or that Bob would be in uniform, enjoying the mists of England. But then tis hard to predict such things.

Also finally answered Howard's letter about "us," so I'm almost caught up on correspondence.

I write a way and yet my mind is ahead of my pen: 21 and 1/2 hours ahead, to be exact. And how I love you! Always, always and ever increasingly.
And how proud and happy I'll be when I no longer sign this fiancée but rather your wife! V

March 26, 1945
Dearest Rabbit,

If you now wish to frustrate me, just keep me around you and other people. As, Lord, I do love other people but I love us together better. Aside from people and minor incidents, it was wonderful. When I think back on it, this time we proved we can be with other people and enjoy it, too. Rosey thought we were wonderful together – so much in love, so we can do it when we have to, but I still am going to prefer a desert island for a long while to come. It's funny how intimate we were even among other people, like when we were caught having a conversation at supper last night just with our eyes.

I was rather disappointed in what happened before I came out dressed for dinner Sunday night at the dorm. I went to leave a message for Walt and accidentally overheard

Rosey telling a bunch of girls, first Harry's name, then someone asked if she had a good time and she said with great glee "no" and then something about it being dull. I guess I was hurt, firstly because we've gone to some trouble to arrange the date and it was rather an insult to my friends, but it was more than that. I was disappointed that she wasn't more mature.

If you recall she didn't say anything when the four of us were together, except when you asked very nicely about something or when you worked Harry into the conversation and she directly answered. She might find she would have a better time if she wasn't so ready to sit back with that "I dare you to amuse me" look. Yes, darling, I was sore. The glee with which she was telling those kids also shows how unsure of herself she is.

We're prophetic, Jane and Don are in a mess! Amy came up to tell her she wasn't coming to her party and Jane told her there wasn't going to be a party(!) partly because it's Sunday, Don's last weekend and they're going to the country and partly because they're very sorry they announced the engagement as they didn't realize what it would mean. It's only considered a pre-engagement so that they'll both be free to go out with other people and when so doing people won't talk. Why the heck they had to put it in the newspaper then change their mind three days later, I don't know. Thinking about it I suppose if one is an idealist, one must get disillusioned about people or maybe it's partly that I come from a family where people really do give and take and understand each other and make the best of it. Things like Jane and Don always confuse me and I wonder how people like to hurt each other. I remember hearing at a party a guy said he enjoyed fighting with his wife; it made life interesting. I wonder if people like that really want a peaceful world after all. Fighting among individuals is like fighting among nations. It may not show the bodily harm but you can kill parts of them destroy things. And so my darling because I think we're peaceful loving people for this and other reasons I foresee one hell of a wonderful lifetime ahead for us. People might think we're crazy the way we get our fun.

Love you darling terrifically much . . .

Don't forget it or doubt it.

Your fiancee

March 26, 1945
My very dearest Darling,

It's been such a strange, wonderful and fearfully important week-talking to your parents, the hasty trip to Philly and then seeing you. Events seem to kaleidoscope into a whirling pattern; with you always at the center and others approaching and receding like shadows. I almost feel that it's unfair of the world to ask anything of two such perfectly suited people as us except that we enjoy each other, but we're grown people and our mutual headaches perhaps even more than our pleasures will bring us ever closer together.

Those hours in the garden and the "picnic" with Harry were so beautiful-I'm filled with love for you. How I ache for you just remembering you kicking off your shoes high in the air, biting me and thoroughly charming Harry.

Got lots of letters today. Your Sunday nite letter about Terry and your parent's letters were here. I was extremely pleased (and blushed in private) at what both your mom and pop had to say. This morning there was another warm letter from you, and from my sister Ruth and one from Dave. Neither of them said anything new and both asked us to visit.

Also found a communication from your Pop in the form of a reprint of his that Mard left on my desk at the lab. I had a pretty tough day today and was really tired by 5:30 but there was no class tonite, and I was in such a glow from seeing you that my spirits weren't dented a bit.

I'd give anything if I could be with you and reassure you that the curse will come (according to my guess, I don't expect it has happened yet). I've known of so many cases of my friends who have gone thru the same business that I'm not really worried about the delay, but it must be tough for you (a watched pot never boils) especially because you miscalculated and have been expecting it much too soon so that you were looking for it the past week instead of just for 3 or 4 days.

Harry had a very good time with Rosey and will probably write her one of his fantastic letters when he gets home. I felt rather sorry for him being with us as much in his lonely state, but I'm hoping he's started to meet some girls and do something for himself.

You'll have to send me full details about this weekend.

Where I'm to go and when. Whether I should ride up to the country with your family etc. tho I shouldn't be surprised to get a message relating to the above from Mard. It would seem a shame if the curse were to hold off till then and spoil the weekend.

You're constantly with me, darling. I sit here and look at your picture and don't even see it—seeing instead a laughing animated you-warm and alive and reflecting all the love that is radiating from you. You and your love for me are, and will always be somehow real and at the same time unbelievable. Good nite, my very dearest darling . . .
I end this letter as I began it.
Your fiance, D.

March 28, 1945
Hello Darling,

I've just basked (basqued?) in the sun letting my freckles run as they wish, whacked and cropped my hair, put on a clean dress, smoked a cigarette, taken a long cool drink of water and now I feel wonderful. (I know what Barb means when she wished Johnny was around when she wears a new dress. Maybe it's a strictly feminine feeling.)

Got your first-of –the- week letter and laughed a devilish laugh in the middle of Philosophy class when I read that "a watched pot never boils". As a matter of fact, darling, I'm not really worried about it. It surprises me now how little I have worried about this all week. There was a day or so there last week when I sort of felt panicky but not now. So don't you worry.

I'm glad Harry had a good time since the whole thing didn't work out ideally. I felt as if I got to know him somewhat better and found that tho nice and tho I liked him, he nowhere near measures up to you (I'm not prejudiced?) Rosey agreed on this. I felt you are much more able in handling conversations and in knowing generally how to handle yourself. I guess it's the word "poise" that I'm looking for. I felt Harry lacked it and lacked the proper psychology to bring out his own good points. Maybe he needs a woman somewhat older than either Rosey or Amy. Anyway, it showed me how lucky I am to have you!

I guess you know by now that Jane's party is off. I received a note from her mother saying it had been called off cause Don couldn't get leave- a good excuse, I guess. It still seems rather disappointing to think of the whole mess but I'm waiting not to draw too many conclusions until I hear directly from Jane what the score is.

Mom sent a postal saying I should come to NY and that we'd go to the country after lunch and that we could either pick you up at your place or at school. Imagine a whole weekend together . . . except for sleeping . . . my family being so different from yours!

Dreamt about you last night-first time in a long time. I was taking a course just so I'd sound intelligent when talking to you. Then I found that the teacher of the course had done the same thing when she had been in love with you! and you were sitting there thru out this whole revelation!

Nice that you finally heard from Dave. Did he mention how married life agreed with him? Or was he so used to it?

Can Connie live off campus with him? Or is it only on weekends?

Gee! Just remembered your mid-term is next Monday. Maybe you'd rather not come for the weekend?

Been dreaming of the country weekend and us and the dream is most appealing—damn my toes always a dead give-away!

So long til the day after the day after tomorrow . . . and only tomorrow by the time you get this.
Love love love, from me.

March 27, 1945
Dearest most darling, darling,
What a pleasant surprise to get a letter from you today. And such a warm bubbling one! Though I can't understand why you felt frustrated much. I think we felt so intimate even tho other people were around because the other people were friends and, at least, I didn't have to hide my feelings at any time tho I can't say I wasn't
restrained in other ways. I'm so very much in love with you, darling. It seems to be crowding my entire consciousness.

I'm not surprised at Rosey's reaction and it doesn't bother me particularly. It didn't bother Harry either. He remarked that Rosey is probably quite immature socially and sexually. I think she feels that she should pretend to be intellectually superior to such a childish thing as a mere date-which is my interpretation of the glee in her voice when she told the girls that she hadn't enjoyed the date. The fact that she had breakfast with us Sunday morning seems to belie her words.

After all, she is quite young and takes pride in her supposed independence-give her time, she'll learn.

Jane and Don certainly have twisted themselves into a knot. I think they're better off not making the engagement final at this time. I'm not sure who does the deciding for them, but I've got some ideas on the subject.

I guess Walt's fate is pretty much in his own hands now (or possibly hers) but many things can happen before he gets back. It may be better for him to go away with a girl to come home to even if he some day gets a " dear John" letter Besides, I've got a feeling that given time, Walt can figure out a situation pretty well and doesn't kid himself or let himself be kidded too far. Seeing how fellows like Walt and Gene respond to warmth from a reasonably attractive female, I'm wondering how any girl who wants to get married ever fails to catch a husband. By the way, what was the method you used on me? I've always thought that I would take more than a lot of flirting to get me hooked.

That remark about men like to fight sounded to me at the time like a bit of bravado. People like to feel that they're not dull and commonplace. We manage not to be without having to fight. Some people find release (demonstrate their individuality) by drinking, or fighting but we don't seem to need artificial stimulants! I don't think you can carry the analogy over between nations. There's a vast difference between a verbal fight with your wife and wanting to shoulder a gun and possibly get shot yourself.

I've passed a beautiful warm spring day marking lab reports, studying Phys Chem and reading Claude Bernard in the original French. The French reads very easily and after I've learned the biological words and recalled a couple of verbs, I don't think I'll have any trouble with it at all. It reads almost like English.

Had a little chat with Clare today-she very kindly said she thought it was worse to be separated from the person you love for short times as we are, than for her not seeing her husband for a year or more. She says she has got sort of numb-like suspended animation-while we are constantly reminded of each other-but I wouldn't change with her, I'm sure she'd rather see him as often as I see you.

If the curse hasn't come by this weekend, I guess you're going to miss it entirely this month. In that way it would be better for us to arrange a Friedman Test so you won't be worried till next month. Considering that you started to get it the last time you were in N.Y. I think it's impossible that anything can have gone wrong, but we'll be better off once our minds are set at rest. I'm afraid of what this worrying may do to your studying for finals.

It seems as if one by one our friends have indicated that in some way we're ahead of them. We've said this to each other so often and yet it's such a nice thought to know—that we're happy together. To be your husband and know that we belong to each other has become my driving ambition and final goal. I love you so much and not patiently.
Good nite, my sweet. I wont ever forget that you love me if you'll remember that that's only half the story.
LOVE, D.

March 28, 1945
Hello Darling,

Another beautiful day. I hope it continues over the weekend. I walked down Fordham road tonite for the first time (in the evening) in months and was amazed to see the mob milling around. It may be the balmy weather, or perhaps it's like this every nite, but it made me realize I've lost touch with the outside during my subway, work-subway home routine.

It also made me reflect on what an enormous change you've made in my life and outlook. Without you I'd be driving myself for the sake of my interest in Physiology alone-and deep down inside, I'd have felt incomplete. I'd be going out with various girls, feeling that I didn't belong to, or with them, nor they to me. You've slipped so smoothly into my scheme of things that it takes an effort to remember how pointless my previous social life was-like the effort it takes to recall that you've been away from home after you've been back for a while.

It came to me because I'd had an uneventful day and the summery feeling of the evening put me into a reflective mood. I thought of how you first as an interest, than as an idea and finally as a part of me which has come to mean so much to me. In a quiet way I felt my love for you running all thru me, reaching to the farthest corners of my mind and body and soul.

I felt grateful that we feel so much the same about so many things. Instead of upsetting my life, falling in love with you and having you reciprocate has deepened and hardened it, making it more tranquil and giving more reason and purpose to everything I do. I'm so thankful, for instance, that you're above such immature feelings as wanting to hurt me or make me feel jealous. Darling, I love you so warmly and strongly. It's such a meaningful love that even tho every other pair of lovers have felt that theirs was different, I still feel that ours IS special-it's mature and understanding and at the same time young and exciting.

Today was an ordinary day. Worked hard all afternoon in the lab and succeeded in destroying a nice clean lab coat, getting tired and proving to myself that I can do the experiment 6 times in the course of an afternoon. I'll spend tonite doing Phys Chem problems and thinking of you.

I don't know what your family's plans are for the weekend. I may call them up tomorrow to see if there isn't something I can help with. You'll probably get this; on Friday, so it may be the last you'll hear from me till Saturday. But that's only 2 and half days away. Figuring that, I'll sleep at least 18 hours between now and then, that makes only a little over a day and a half of before I see you!

If you feel that in the last month you've begun to love me completely and without reservation, the same applies to me for I can now see that there was a little bit of me that was holding back waiting til I was absolutely sure of you. You mean everything that life means to me, fuzzy head. You own me as completely as I own my hair or teeth or any part of me. Good nite, darling . . . for just a couple of days . . . Your fiancé and future husband. D.

April 1, 1945

Dearest,

Altho I'm sitting here writing this note, it's really only an illusion. Actually I'm with you on a train between NY and college. I'm squeezing your hand except the ring finger and the sore one, and looking at your steady eyes that break so swiftly into a wicked dancing laugh.

It's been a warm, close, mellow week and , darling, and I've been very happy being with you and at your country home. How many times this summer are we going to romp and love and tie our lives completely together! I love you so much darling even in your sexy shorts!

There's just a chance this will reach you some time tomorrow, so here goes.

Rushed home today as I had hoped there were two delicious letters from you. Didn't get one yesterday and missed it enormously. Talk about being spoiled!

I don't think I know yet whether I can meet you at 125th St but I think I'll have Phys Chem. under control by then. as I've been working on it all week. Also I took over some labs this week for Ingrith as she was lecturing and I will probably be able to study all day Monday.

Helped a couple of kids do an experiment, leisurely-in 2 and ½ hours instead of the normal 8! And they did practically all the work which proves, if they know ahead of time what it is all about, they would get a heck of a lot more out of it and they bombarded me with questions. The exam is tomorrow from 9-10. Some of them cut this lab to study which I'm afraid will have been a mistake as there are some questions pertaining to it.

Got a letter today from one of my aunts who I missed last weekend. She has invited me to sleep over at her place Saturday nite! Just have to let the family fight among themselves but they are all mighty anxious to meet you (poor you). She said after the talk (we two) and I quote" the talk we had when you were here a few weeks ago, I feel as if I know her already and love her as much as you do. Or don't you want to share her with anyone?" I seem to have done a pretty good job selling myself to your parents, just imagine how I've done selling you whom I'm really enthusiastic about!

I think you're right about Harry needing a mature woman to bring out the best in him but you seem to think he didn't have a good time. Which wasn't true. Rosey intrigued him even if she wasn't an ideal companion..

I'll be seeing you so soon that I hate to describe how much I will be missing you this week. Just give me a little time alone in the country and I'll show you what I mean. A Bientot ma Cherie. D.

April 3, 1945
Dearest, Freckled, Fuzzy headed Fiancé,

What a pig I am! After having a whole weekend with you, it's only Monday nite, and already I'm counting the days til Saturday. It seems a little futile to describe our weekends anymore cause my feelings are so obviously written all over my face while we're together-or has it been along time since you've looked at my upper nose?. If you'll forgive my boldness, darling, I love you enormously dressed or undressed, hot or cold, freckled or unfreckled. I'm so completely gone that I like whatever you do or say before it happens. I'll tuck (TUCK) you into the hollow of my arms, now, and tell the trivialities that happened today.

We had a tough day in the lab-it's a grueling experiment and tomorrow will be the same. Then came Phys Chem exam which was middling tough. Four problems which I knew how to do but probably got the wrong answers in and one problem that as far as I could see nobody in the class knew how to do. I'm not worried about the result.

The ride home was typical N.Y. subway ride. A crowd of colored soldiers in very high humor welcomed everybody who got on at one of the doors and tried to talk to people on the platform into getting on the train. A blind man then walked thru rattling a cup, ignored by half the people and solicitously helped by the other half. A little later there was a scream from one end of the car. All the people at my end rushed over and all the people at the other end came and took their seats. Nobody could see anything, but the word "fainted" buzzed around the car. As I got off somebody was pointing to a half opened (from the top) window saying, "He jumped outa here." Another mystery I'll never solve.

At home there was a letter from my Mom. She knew Mitzie's invitation and also Aunt Cele's. I guess we're in the hands of the family and will have to resign ourselves to being "looked at" for the best part of the weekend (tho it wont be as bad as it sounds). As of now the plans are: spend Sat. afternoon at home and meet my parents; Sat nite at my aunt's and meet various aunts and uncles; Sunday noon at

Sylvia's and meet Jess and his wife. Don't know where Jerry and Mitzie fit into the picture. She has to appear in a play for the benefit of a hospital the Saturday nite we were supposed to be at her place. She had forgotten about it. I also don't know where we'll sleep that nite, but since it's not at Jerry and Mitz', don't undress for me.

All this may sound confusing and worrisome for you, tho you really wont be as uncomfortable as it sounds. My family collects so rarely that they use occasions to talk to each other, and the guest of the evening usually falls asleep in a corner. This arrangement also has the advantage that we won't meet everyone at once and you'll be good friends with my mother before we meet the crowd. Of course, the final say on our trip belongs entirely to you and if you have any preferences or opinions as to what we do, that doesn't include meeting so many people in one short weekend, they'll just have to wait.

That's the sum total of My Day except for the numerous times when I added in your impish grin or your freckled face to a column of figures showing how much urine the dog had made. I actually had to shake my head several times to pull my mind back from 80 miles away.

As usual I'm expecting to hear from you on Wednesday but hoping for a letter tomorrow. Since I'll be taking up all of the next weekend, I'll understand if you have to study more and write less this week.

Good nite, my love, from the bottom of my toes to the top of my head.

D.

April 4, 1945

Dearest sunburned Wobbit, after the Country visit,

   A Monday letter as we've agreed is easy to write. It usually consists of words such as "wonderful" and "perfect" and this one is no exception. I've got a lervly sunburn and memories to continuously remind me of it. Guess the outstanding thing will be: You dancing to "Rum and Coke Cola"; you leaning over to put out a cigarette while the car mysteriously swerves; us sitting by the river and in the field; waking you up Sunday A.M.; all of us eating breakfast, cooking lunch and lying in the sun together. By the way," Goodbye". I somehow lost you in the shuffle to make the train. I did make it with about one minute to spare—long enough to get kidded by two conductors who asked in response to my question on whether the train had already left. The train was practically empty, amazingly enough. I ate my sandwiches in sunburned peace and quiet and read "Until the Day We Die", tears streaming down my face and I grabbed for my Easter hanky. Really a very moving play . . . one of the best in the collection.

   The bus back to college was jammed and I stood by the driver. He asked me if I'd had a good time in N.Y. and I sheepishly said yes. Then he asked about the Easter parade and I was too lazy to explain I hadn't seen it. He told me he's been in NYC once—on New Year's Eve. A cop had told him to "keep moving" (and he certainly was a beautiful example of American individualism) "ME! He told ME to keep moving. I aint going to be shoved around by no cop. So he raised his club and I punched him in the stomach and ran." So I guess he doesn't like New York! He was so engrossed in his dissertation that he forgot to let half the people off at the correct stop and thus ends a perfect weekend. Full of pleasant sighs and delicious musings.

The weekend was also eventful in that you were even more accepted by the family than ever. Perhaps they realize we're not "rushing things" in comparison with certain other members of the family (Didn't mean that to sound nasty, if it does).

Had two good classes this A.M. Philos and Soc . . . Polit lecture was dull. (I guess an introductory course is a hard thing to make very interesting. Facts is facts and until you learn them, there's not much you can do about it.)

This afternoon went for my gym physical exam. We had one last year and this is to be compared with it. It consists of donning white angel costumes as they're called, which are white soft squares with a hole in the center which you put your head thru. They cover the strategic area in length, are open at the sides and feel most chilly. You then proceed to do some strength measuring things, pushing on things as hard as possible, blowing into things as much as possible etc. the funniest is one in which you bend your knees, keep your back straight and pull up on a handle attached to what you've been standing on which also has a recording apparatus.. With legs bent, angel robe haphazardly draped and anguished, pushing face, it's quite a picture! Found I'm a good deal stronger in everything than last year and a deal smaller in girth, height at now officially 5'3, 3/8 tall and 124 pounds. What you do to me, darling! (Only fault is that my right shoulder is lower than my left. (We'll have to change positions, dear).

It's a very quiet message center and I'm lonesome for you and the weekend. But there will be others (weekends, I mean).

Hope your exam isn't too bad and that you could study for it Sunday eve-or did all the fresh air put you to sleep?

Just been dreaming about whether we'd serve iced tea or iced coffee to the party for OUR friends when we announce our engagement, Didn't realize I thought about it so much! Also think of life AFTER all the ceremonies are over. How nice to come "home", locking the door, standing nude, brushing teeth, sleeping, eating, talking, laughing, playing, living with you. It just seems too good to be true . . . but it is true, it really is.

Will mail this now and maybe you'll get it tomorrow. Your funny faced future wife. V

April 3, 1945 (Gee, It's my 19 and 3/4 birthday)
Dearest Danny mine,

What a lovely surprise to find a letter awaiting me this morning. You DO treat me well, darling and I love it. And I love you too, Mr. K . . . so terribly much. I catch myself thinking the darndest most wonderful thoughts–like snatches of scenes, conversation, and actions of the past and the future. They jump out of the Econ books or the salad dressing with equal ease and I must admit I don't try to squelch them. I love you more every day and my logical mind (?) doesn't see how that's possible, but it is–it must be cause it's happening.

Your c.t. (curly toes) has spent a lovely day. She's forgotten how to work tho somehow the work gets done and there's extra time for other things. Had Polit class outside! Then went to Amer Lit class where Miss Read tried to teach T.S .Elliot. It was pathetic. I almost wept in embarrassment and pity for her. She is really too old to teach anyhow but it became apparent when she tried to teach us about modern poetry. There were long, terribly long pauses, vague fumbling for words. It was really an awful teaching of the works and a waste of time. At the half way mark of the two hour session, she let us go out to smoke and Barb persuaded me not to go back in. Many people left and I felt guilty and still do, at the rudeness of it. But honestly, we would have gotten much more out of a cut and it would have been less humiliating for her.

Went to the libe to do some Econ-part of the assignment on post war problems: read Hayek's "The Road to Serfdom" Have you perchance read it? or seen any reviews of it? It distinctly annoyed the daylights out of me and I can't understand what possessed the Econ dept. unless they thought by now we'd become too radical!
Enuf for now. Know that I love you sooooo much. V

April 4, 1945
Darling Monkey,

I know Monkey is Mard's name for you but I like it too and she'll have to share it with me. I had a hunch last nite

that I'd hear from you today-and it worked. Many of the events of the weekend seemed to belong more to you than to me tho I remember them and enjoyed them equally with you. So I left their description to you-and you did them justice (I'm thinking of the way you drove or didn't drive when I leaned over to knock off some ashes.

One thing the weekend convinced me of, is that we couldn't possibly have gotten secretly married and kept it from your family. As it is, we acted almost as if we are-in broad daylight! Just think of how we'd have to dissemble if we were actually married. Twould be impossible.

It's funny but tho I hardly thought at all of our weekend in Philly, now I've mentioned it to your Mom it has suddenly become very real in my mind. I picture you meeting my mother and I can see myself tossing you a wink in the middle of meeting with my aunts and uncles session. And how they'll love you! And how I love you! And how!

It's a shame I won't be able to see you in a nightgown yet, and I still look forward to the thrill of curling up next to you and falling asleep and finding you there in the morning...ummm (time out while I straighten my trousers and you uncurl your toes).

Had a wonderful day in the lab. For once everything turned out as it should. The kids seemed to enjoy the whole experiment and thought the dept. had done a good job of organizing and getting everything setup-which we had done. It was a nice feeling to walk out and feel an air of general approval radiating from the students We'll have a tough time making a really good course out of it with the present set-up, but there are so many of us "youngsters" around that I think in future years it should improve enormously.

    I've got to write my mother, that aunt, Dave and Gene, Leon and Morrie yet tonite and do some laundry and study for tomorrow's classes so I have to say good nite now. Sleep well, my darling, you won't get much of the stuff after we're married. All my love, Danny

April 6, 1945
Hello Darling,

    I was about to start this letter with the appellation "Chile Concarney (spelt phonetically) so I could get in Spanish rice and then stopped to wonder whether the 2 always go together or if they only did in a camp cheer of the 1930's.

    Am feeling full of energy. I consider your face or your knee or any other extremity affectionately fit in an outburst of my enthusiasm) and tres gay. I love life and I love you even more. I can't wait until you come up so that I can show you what I mean:

    I'm a soap bubble

    I'm a carrot, I'm a message center

    Or a sparrow.

    I'm an ingrown toe nail, I'm a sugar spoon,

    I'm Eric Johnson

    I'm feeling rather foolish and I don't know WHAT I am.

    (With profuse apologies to A A Milne (and you).

    So here I sit feeling very foolish and loving you very much.

    Maybe if I turn the page I'll feel more sober (seel more fober?) (Oh shut up!!!)

So this is the kind of piece I'm marrying, he says, dubiously, searching madly for some escape. Can I really introduce "that" to my family. They won't respect my judgment any more if I do. Oh well, what's to be done can't be undone (who says?). Life is so peaceful in the country. How about a round of golf? Nope, too cold. Well, come inside. Thanks, guess I will. Well, you don't HAVE to. Well sure, sure I'm a comin. Toes, STAY STILL. If I had a wash stand and a tooth brush I'd stand on it (stand not the brush) all nude and chillish—childish.
The way I write, you'd think my voice would go up at the end of each line…enuf of this nonsense…Hello darling. I'll try again to suppress it . . . sober up)

Went to the campus movies last night. The first thing on the bill was a Disney short on corn "Grain in this hemisphere" which was an educational film about on the 4th grade level but was interesting to me for its pictorial techniques. Then there was a long short entitled "Here is China" put out by United China Relief and narrated by Clifton Fadiman which was amusing and sad after reading Foreman. They didn't even mention Red China and ignored most of the politics completely except for a picture of Chiang as the "leader" of the government.

Then came "The Negro Soldier" which I thought both good and bad. It was good in that it showed how the Negro was like other people (as someone with us said. It could have been any soldier) and in the historical part explained how the Negro had been in all the American wars etc. But while it's good to show that the Negro is like everyone else, you never had the least idea there was such a thing as a problem: segregation or discrimination.

It made the U.S. look like heaven, even misleadingly so such as showing a negro graduating from West Point where, if I remember rightly, only one has graduated and his stay there made almost unbearable. For the people who think Negroes are very different from whites, I guess it's good, but for those who don't understand "the problems" or don't think one exists, I shouldn't think it would help them much.

Read Kant this A.M. and am completely in a fog over him.

Had a pleasant surprise at lunch time when I saw Jean Ramon (the girl who graduated in Dec. who doesn't want to get married and is interested in anthropology/Econ major). She looked so changed I hardly recognized her. I hadn't seen her since her graduation. She'd just gotten a job in town so will be living near by. The job upstate which she had gotten fell thru and she'd just come up today for the interview. She's so happy; it's just wonderful to see. She'd hated college and then that business when her two best friends had so unceremoniously left school upset her terribly. Now she's all smiles, looks better and is generally amazing to behold.

Another curious thing:she told me: 6 months after she came to college she stopped getting the curse. Didn't have it for the all of the time she was here (over three years). I'm sure that was part of her pessimism about marriage, too. Last week she got it again! Certainly shows how closely it's tied with mental conditions (and vice versa, I guess).

I wonder which causes which, tho it sounds as if the mental strain came first.)

She took us up to the Pub (after I'd rushed my tables thru lunch) and treated us to Manhattans. I finished one half of mine which may account for the first part of this letter. Got to Polit class 20 minutes late. At the last minute I decided to go for the good of my soul . . . and my marks.

Came back and read the articles you sent me which were good. It must have killed you to have to wait a week in between them. Each seems to have some accusations unanswered but the first articles seems to hit the hardest. I guess as always, neither side is wholly right but I'd still rather believe Snow if I have to choose all of one or the other. Particularly after Foreman's account –who was actually in Yemen and did live with the peasants there. Thought the Spanish poem rather good and of course got the point.

Sure, do bring up sneakers if you can fit them into your suitcase without breaking the hinges. Don't bother about tennis balls. We have some. Not sure whether I'll feel like playing or not . . . Been feeling distinctly strange of late but don't worry about it. I'm sure its nothing that time won't cure. Just hope things don't start happening (getting the curse, I mean) during exams or the weekend when I'm with your family. But shant think of that.

Day after tomorrow . . . How pleasant! What an understatement! And how I love you. Hey! Maybe in 9 months and a few days we'll be married! Gee, gosh, mmmm All of me, curseish or otherwise, sends its love to

you straightened trousers or otherwise.
Your ghoulish girlish fiancée.

April 9, 1945
Hello My Juicy One,

Here tis Monday at message center after a weekend with you. And I'm already counting the minutes until the next one . . . guess we'll remember this last weekend as picnic number 2 (or is it number 3? O.K. show up my ignorance) Anyway, a nude French extended picnic. T'was divine, darling and I got a real shock when I woke up this morning and found it was Monday. I somehow thought it was Sunday again and that you were still here. Felt very lonely to find it not true.

Have had all but one class (I'm not going to Amer Lit tomorrow. The Philos this A.M. was terrific; he read thru half of Kant and then cheerily said of course we understood him! Got back the exam taken several weeks ago, a B... I'm in a rut. Post gave us the last lecture in Polit and he chose the subject of "Wills" as being appropriate. He said he often speaks on marriage and divorce the last class but this year since it was a sunny day he thought he'd speak on wills.

So now I know all about wills . . . or at least enough to know to "ask my lawyer."

Stupid mix-up in spring sports choices and had to try to get that settled for one hour this afternoon. Will know about that tomorrow.

Got a letter from Mom written in Westport. She said all

that was needed was "Danny and you and Walt to make it complete"…hmmm. Have you been bribing her or only hypnotizing her? How DO you win your women?

My physical state is just the same and I've given up hope or thought of change. Amy is out of the infirmary having been told she had an attack of appendicitis and that she ought to have it out this summer. I think when the infirmary diagnosis one thing wrong (they had skipped one appendectomy) they think everyone has it . . . or are afraid to make the same mistake twice.

Come hell or high water this week will pass and I'll soon be with you..which is after all, all that matters to me. I can't think of anything I'd rather do than spend my life right next to yours–or maybe on tops of yours? Or underneath? I don't care if we live in a cave or a mansion (as long as our children have a womb to play in and you as a father to play with. I don't care if we starve or freeze, life with you will definitely be fun and adventurous and I'm looking forward to it with great happiness, impatience and expectancy.
Best had better goeth to bedeth.
Your finance, Viv

April 10, 1945–6 p.m.
My Darling Crampy Co-ed
You're probably mystified by the hurried note I sneaked off this Mon. I wrote it because I had a sudden vision of you not getting this letter till Thursday and I know what that let-down can be like-especially during exam week.

The trip home was rapid and uneventful and I decided

to write to you Monday nite-the crazy letter hadn't arrived yet (and boy was it nutty-and I loved every word of it!) towards Monday nite I began feeling grippy-stuffed nose and a queasy feeling in my stomach. Also felt droopy around 9:30. I promptly fell asleep till morning. Whatever I was getting has disappeared completely. This week I'll be teaching every hour from 9-5 Monday thru Thursday except for one hour tomorrow morning-so I began to worry about you're not hearing from me before Thursday and dashed off that note.

Lots of things have been happening. First of all Ruth got that bladder trouble that I think I mentioned to you and Mother went down to Washington to help out. When she had to rush off, Father in his characteristic way, decided to write to me to postpone our visit. Of course Ruth is O.K. now and my mother is back home and wrote today NOT to postpone the trip. It seems Father had the wrong weekend in mind! Now that Ruth is better, Ed ate something and got the Washington version of the plague. He is coming up for a physical soon and decided to be operated on for piles which were aggravated by the plague. So –we won't see them this trip.

Got a letter from friend Billie today. She is now a WAVE at Hunter College and asked me to buy some notebook paper for her. It's not sold at the Navy store and they can't leave campus. She also invited us to visit her some weekend.

Had a talk with Mard yesterday-decided to tell her our story and get the benefit of her advice and experience. I told her about your continuous cramps and she said it certainly doesn't sound as if you're pregnant. All cramps and pain disappear during pregnancy. She also said there were several times when her period was 3 or 4 weeks late for no reason that they could figure out.

Do you think (if the curse hasn't come by now) that we should arrange a test as soon as you finish your exams or would you rather wait till after the Philly trip? Remember, darling, all signs point to the other way but we might as well look at all the angles.

I can't say that I've any particular appeal that I have for women in general, if your mother likes me, it's only evidence that you two are very much alike and it also looks as if I'm getting some of the radiation of her love for you. Anyhow, since I've always been certain that you and my mother will get along perfectly,. it looks as if we have not only wont fight but we won't even have in-law troubles.

And for our weekend: We didn't do anything special and went nowhere; there were no remarkable events and yet I loved every minute of it. I suppose the picnic could be counted a high spot with you in your playsuit (much sexier than the picture) eating sandwiches, a dog as usual and trying not too hard (mentally) to read French while you entertained our friend. It was lovely-all of it and I'm convinced just being with you is enuf to make me supremely ridiculously happy. And your French maid dress! Ah me and Mommie!

Tomorrow you'll be right in the middle of your exams and I'll be with you every moment. I remember having written a poem during the last final week about "Who the hell cares" and those sentiments haven't changed. I know who you are and what you're worth and I love you because of (not despite) it. Let other people look at your marks–I know this girl who is going to be my wife.

On looking over the teaching schedule, I discovered the happy news that after this Thursday I have practically no more labs or conferences. I'll give one demonstration some time in May and have one week of labs at the end of the term which Ingrith will take over to repay for the ones I took for her. This gives me full time to concentrate on Phys Chem and the Chiefs reading course so I'll probably get them done by June and maybe even work in a couple of blood flows too. The tie up will come when I try to write up my paper during the summer and nobody is around to help me whip it into final form but I hope that I can have it in such good shape that there wont be too much whipping" to do. This would put my exam around the end of September-just 2 ½ years after my first course here.

Well, that's about all the news from here for today. If it's news that I love you, and then I want to add that too. If it's news that I miss you ALL the time (even when you are a few feet away waiting on tables) than I'll say it again. And if it's news that I'm only half living till the day we are married and can be together all the time, then I must tell you that too. News or not, everything that I am; everything that I hope to be revolves about you-with you, I'm happy without you I'm not. It's as simple and profound as that.

Good nite, my dearest darling.

All of my sunburned self,

Danny.

April 11, 1945

Dear Supersexed Darling,

    Your "positively not Thursday nite letter" came today and met an enthusiastic reception. By tomorrow nite 4 out of the 8 days apart will have passed. I've been extremely busy every day which helps the time to move along, and your exams, I guess will work the same way.

    I miss you so much these days, and you seem to feel the same way that I'm beginning to think your parents are right: we should admit to ourselves that we're serious about each other and start to plan our future. It'll be hard, but I think you should be getting over this what's the rush idea. As your father said-and your Mom tacitly agreed- if we're sure that we are sure, then why NOT rush? (Pardon darling, I'm just dreaming).

    Is my family all mixed up! Just got a letter from Ruth saying that there's still a chance that they may make it-it seems that Ed doesn't need an operation (as of today). But don't let these events bother you. The family is still expecting us on the 21st and looking forward to meeting you.

    Had another chat with Mard today, I figured that she might have gotten new ideas after a couple of days to think it over. The outcome of our talk was somewhat like this: by all processes of reasoning it is practically impossible that everything won't turn out all right. But the cramps you are going thru certainly isn't normal and good and you should see a Dr. about it a soon as possible. We figured that the most sensible thing to do would be to have an A-Z test done while you are in N.Y. Then when we're positive that you are O.K. as far as that is concerned, you should see a doctor about the cramps.

Maybe it would have been wise for me not to have brought all this up during your exams. (The curse may even come before you get here) but I think you know that it is extremely unlikely that anything could have gone wrong and wont be worried because I'm thinking about it and trying to plan what we should do if the curse doesn't come.

We had quite a day with the kids. The Chief arrived in the A.M. especially to attend a seminar at which the students described the experiments we did on water balance so the other groups which did something else could get a complete picture. One of the students got up and gave a very breezy and extremely impudent talk. He was obviously trying to impress everybody with how smart and witty he is, but he stepped far over the bounds of common decency and respect for the Chief and the rest of the dept. At one point the Chief asked him to explain how the experiment was performed so that everybody would know what was going on. The kid dismissed him with an airy wave of the hand and said, "Take it easy. I'll get around to that". I don't know how the Chief kept his temper
(I wouldn't have) but he did. Then later the Chief asked him about a very important point that he had left out and then said, "I don't know why you want to drag that in, but I'll explain it," very condescendingly.

After the student had finished, the Chief and Ingrith managed to let the class know that it was an extremely important experiment, much used clinically, and despite the guy's breeziness about its errors, it was a very reliable technique. I don't mind seeing some spirit in a student, but when his talk wanders all over the place and doesn't say anything, when he gives the impression that the errors in the method (not HIS errors) make it very uncertain, and when he as much as tells the Chief to shut up, I'm all in favor of making life a little more real and less of a stage for him in the future. I suppose the Chief was wise in saying nothing because the rest of the students felt acutely embarrassed and came up later (at least 15% of them) and apologized for the class so that he'll probably learn via popular pressure.

Here's a new book that I haven't read but which got interesting reviews. You may come across it. It's written in the James style and sounds intriguing from the two reviews that I've come across. "The Ballad and the Source" by Rosamond Lehmann.

It certainly hit me with a bang when you described going to the Shakespeare garden with Barb. As much (or almost as much) as thinking a lot of your new attitude-don't worry too much about day to day details-and trying to figure out what it means. In some ways it's good, because you did chew over things more than was necessary but I still don't know if you are swinging into a more mature attitude of saving your introspective worries for bigger things, or are merely transferring your fretting over me (mentally). I'm inclined to think that it's most the former-that is-that we have become important enuf so that these other things like exams shrinking to the proportions they should have.

The funny thing is that I know that no matter how you may go from one point of view to another, you'll always come out where I would want you to . . . You may think that I'm prejudiced or are just trying to bolster your morale, but I meant every word of it, and I've really tried to understand you objectively because no matter how you do come out, I love you now and I will love every development that comes from you in the maturing process-so that I'm more concerned with understanding where you are at any moment than in trying to "shape" you.

You still say you can't understand why I love you. In some ways you can and in others you can't—That's exactly how I feel about your love for me, and I can't think of a better basis on which to build a happy marriage. We both have a lot of what the Bible calls "humility" and in its true meaning it is a quality which we each had to find in the other before we really fell in love.

Good nite, my lyrical darling-don't ever forget even for a minute that this Physiology instructor is very much
in love with a certain college junior.
All my love, Danny

April 11, 1945
Hello Darling,

I guess many people feel the way I do tonight: very sad and feeling a personal loss in the death of the only President I've ever known. I won't go into eulogies of him: you can read them in newspapers or make them up yourself. He's such a terrible loss to the world and tho it shouldn't be that one man is indispensable, I just don't see how anyone can come near him in filling his shoes. It's such a God damned shame and terrifying to think of the consequences-to think of only a few: the San Francisco conference, the Democratic Party, the leadership in Washington.

Willkie, Wallace being kicked around and now this, is a lot to have to bear in one year, and tho many say Wallace is too much of an idealist, I'd rather see him as president than Truman. I'd somehow trust his mistakes more than Truman's.

What kind of a world are we going to be bringing children into? But I suppose women have been saying that since caveman days. And they continue to bring forth and hope for the best. But how long will it take before people know hoping isn't enough? From the different, but I must say, varied response that the news was received here, I'm afraid it's a long way off. Some girls here actually cheered on hearing the news!

We heard about it at 6 P.M. Barb burst into tears, partly I think due to the strain of these last couple of days- (She's thru exams tomorrow) After she'd subsided we decided not to eat in the dining room, both of us felt a great desire to get away from lots of giggling women. We went for a long and quite silent walk. It seemed strange that the leaves and flowers should be so beautiful. I somehow expected them to wilt. Ate a sandwich at the drug and returned to try to study. Wasn't very successful.

Well, let us try to talk of more cheerful things.

Don't sling your physiological jargon at me. What is an "A-2" test? The idea of a Dr. afterwards is a good one, only if it takes several days to know the results of the test-or doesn't it?

The Philosophy amazes me at the ease it runs in and out of my head tho I liked the course. I was interested in it and understand it as we go along. When reviewing, I find everyone and everything merges together or I leave great gaps of theories and proofs.

Is the Chief back for good? That certainly sounded like a fresh kid!

Guess I'll go to bed. Today has worn me out and saddened me muchly. It's still a wonderful world; I love you greatly and am selfishly and greedily very happy but I can't help feeling it's a terrible blow to us.

Forgive the morbidity of this letter. It should definitely not indicate anything concerning the state of my affections toward you . . . unless in terms of contrast.

All of my lanpy crove and impatience,

Your wife-to-be, V.

April 11, 1945

Darlingest, Danny-mine,

You do treat me well and I love you so awfully much. And I miss you almost equally so. I received your note in the early mail this A.M. Was slightly mystified but glad you sent it. I hope to hear from you further tomorrow. Then after lunch, I went to the noon mail and found a thick letter from you. I couldn't decide whether to "save" it until after the exam at 2:30 or to read it first to cheer me up. Decided on the latter and read it thru several times.

I still feel just the same way with recurrent cramps but/and I think you're right, we might a well be sure so that it's settled once and for all. I'd rather have it before Philly so that we can get the results before I go back to college, on Monday, if possible. Do you know where I go? Does one make an appointment? Are they open on both mornings and afternoons? Is it free if it's a clinic? I show you my ignorance. You see, dear, I've never had to do this before!!!! If they're open in the afternoon I think I could go on Wednesday since Mom had originally planned to take me to a matinee but had to call it off since there was a meeting she wanted to go to. That would leave me free, I suspect. If it's possible in the mornings, WED. A.M. would be as good as any, I guess. I'll have to think of some innocuous excuse to leave my mother's eager arms. Would Mard know about details? Is it just a matter of getting a sample of blood...from anywhere? It's not that I'm scared, darling, just want to know what I'm in for. And by-the-way, you're not to think you have to come with me.

Unless Mard thinks I'm crazy, I'd like to be honest, give my right name and address and the fact that I'm not married. I'd naturally prefer that Dad didn't know and would bear that in mind in choosing a hospital. Do you think you could find out the detail either thru Mard or calling a clinic so that we could know and if possible do it on Wednesday? Maybe after all this, I'll get the curse by then, wouldn't that be nice?

That's a shame about Ruth and Ed—that they've been sick and that we won't see them. I somehow thought I remembered Ed in a navy officer's uniform in one of the pictures, but I guess he isn't in service since you mentioned a physical coming up??

I hope the oncoming grippe really disappeared for good and I'm not breaking down your resistance!

So I'm getting competition in the form of a WAVE eh? See that you restrict your gift to notebook paper, I'm jealous of those in uniform.

Your description of the weekend far outdid mine and I loved you for remembering to mention the play suit and the French maid dress. Oh gee! I love you. Consider yourself kissed rapidly 10 times, hit energetically and affectionately on the cheek 5 times and kissed lengthily at least once.

I also loved your consolation paragraph about exams. It certainly hit the spot. You're so sweet, darling, and I get so speechless with love of you that I want to weep—out of sheer excess emotion. I love you, I love you, I love you, so there too.

Today's exam was pretty darn silly. Everyone agreed that to give an exam in Amer. Lit was sort of a dumb since the 3 sections had done such different things and even each person's reading had greatly varied. I guess the teachers found it hard to make out the exam too. and left it up to us. We received regular mimeographed papers telling us the exam questions: to tell why making up this set of questions was a good examination for us; to list which questions we could do and which we could find hard and why…and answer one of our own questions. It wasn't really as dumb as it sounds but I'm certainly sore I spent any time worrying about it! Oh well, as you say, who the hell cares! Barb and I found we'd made up practically the same questions. As a result of having discussed the course and the essential points in it... and even answered the same one question. I should think an exam such as that would be difficult to grade but that's not my worry. Haven't gotten our term papers back yet either which is all she has to mark us on.

In a few minutes I'm about to go over some of the Econ questions with another girl. Tomorrow I study Philosophy. Friday I take the exam. I am already annoyed at the idea of having to spend such beautiful weather days away from you and shut up studying these things which I shall promptly forget–but such is life.

A little freshman just came in to borrow my Polit syllabus. She'd lost hers. I cheerfully gave it to her and only realized after she'd walked out the door that it's full of your name and nude females (thank God I spared the males!)

You were an angel to send the Lady Hamiltons and I am diligently saving them for the last few days when things get most desperate.

Must get back to work. You are going to the country, aren't you?

All my humblest and most passionate love, darling, V.

April 14, 1945–Saturday A.M.
Dear Family,
I feel as if I should write condolence notes to everyone I know, for I feel that Roosevelt's death is a personal loss to everyone. It certainly is for me. I've been so lucky in not having any personal deaths in my whole lifetime but I

really feel that this one is…All of us said at election time that one man shouldn't be indispensable and we claimed Roosevelt wasn't, that he was only the best qualified person to help win the war and the peace, as being one of the few people big enough to hold his own and win the respect of Churchill and Stalin but also the rest of the world. But underneath it all I think we felt he was indispensable and now his loss is a terrific and terrifying one. Everything seemed to crumble after hearing the news. The optimism we'd been feeling with the wonderful military successes and the coming Conference were swept away for me by future un-seeable and unoptimistic events. He certainly had a wonderful life and has made a great difference to history, if we attribute any credit to the "great man" theory. Tolstoy believed that no one man changes history, that it is a process of inevitable trends caused by innumerable little events. But a far seeing leader certainly is terribly important and Roosevelt was all of that. Besides his wonderful accomplishments, I felt a real love for him . . . particularly after this election when I had the lucky opportunity, the unforgettable time on election eve at Hyde Park and the preceding one here in Poughkeepsie.

The story of Truman's rise to fame is an astounding one. I only wish I could have more faith in him. But expecting anyone to fill such big shoes isn't quite fair, I guess.

    Exams are still in process. They haven't been bad. The American Lit. was the most fun to take as we were told to make up our own exam, give some data about why we'd chosen the questions and then answer one of them.

The Philosophy was fairly difficult but fair and interesting. I've just come from the Polit one which was very general and quite boring to take.

Monday morning I take the Sociology one; Tuesday the Economics and then I'm home for a hurried but welcome vacation.

Barb finished her exams yesterday and I have the three rooms to myself which is quite lonely, but nice for her.

Have you planted anything yet? Guess I'll get answers to any questions when I see you Tuesday.
Loads of love and impatience, Viv

April 13, 1945
Dearest most thoughtful and wonderful Sweetheart,

That was a terrific letter about Mard and you and we and your exams. It has probably never occurred to you that you're a wonderful person to think of Mard and her troubles and to be so noble about wanting to spare me any possible embarrassment, at a time when you are bogged down with exams and have every reason to be thinking selfish thoughts.

Mard talked to me about her present desire to have a baby and her plans to check up and find out as much as possible whether or not an operation might be needed. It is biting irony that we're always getting the things we want at the wrong time-but on second thought, I guess it all evens out—for instance, our meeting could hardly have been better timed.

As far as your "test" is concerned, it has all been made

very easy because Mard knows the people who run the tests for the hospital. They'll need only a sample of urine which Mard can bring over with her Wednesday morning. No hospitals or Drs. are involved. They don't know who it is for and you don't have to go anywhere, do anything or give anybody any explanations. We'll have a report before your return to school tho I'm still bothered by the idea of your going on with continual cramps. You should see a doctor as soon as we're positive you're not pregnant. Just for the record, I didn't talk to Mard just to be able to talk to someone-it isn't weighing on my mind to that extent. I simply wanted her advice and ideas and she has already been helpful with that. But it was very typical of you to not mind my talking with her even if it were just to relieve my mind-Gee, how I love you. I have yet to find anything that you've liked about me that I haven't found in you, so whenever you want to know how much or why I love you, just look at your feelings for me-and there are lots of things about you that I love which are not in me.

    I and many of us around here have been feeling depressed all day about the President's death. As I said yesterday, the feeling of personal loss is extremely strong.

    To keep the record straight on Ruth and Ed, the present status is that they may come in. Ed is a Lt. in the navy and they are subjected to periodic physicals, which explains a point you raised.

    Harry has just written to me one of his very amusing but pathetic and touching letters. The girl he met didn't please him-for this to happen (please Harry) she would have to be quite extraordinary. His extremely high standard makes it doubly hard for him, because he is not too poised or (in the conventional sense) socially attractive. But that's the way it is, and despite his present loneliness, I admire him for maintaining his standards and I'm sure eventually he'll meet the girl he's looking for-and he'll be what she wants. What makes the whole thing doubly difficult is that the kind of girl he admires is least likely to be fascinated by him-she would like him, admire him but fall in love with someone else. Of course, eventually, he'll meet one who will love him and she'll find him to be a devoted husband.

You'd better start worrying about your Wave competition. I just found out that if I was married to one, I could claim $2500 exemption on my State Income Tax and her salary isn't taxable. What have you got to offer, other than that I'm in love with you, wouldn't be happy unless I were with you and wouldn't consider marrying a Wave (unless you became one)?

My next letter will probably come from Westport (am I cruel to mention it?) tho you wont actually be there, you'll be the uppermost thought in all of our minds-the unifying force that ties us all together.

Your struggling over Philosophy right now, but don't draw up any philosophy of life that doesn't include me or I'll make you sleep in a twin bed!

Harry forwards the story that Col. McCormack started a campaign to have an airport named after Gen. Marshall til he realized that it would be called Marshall Field.

**So long for now, my-wife-to-be . . . just three more days
All of my completest admiration and love,
Lucky me, Danny**

April 14, 1945
Dearest Most loved one,

 Just received your letter written after hearing the news of Roosevelt's death. Was again amazed at our similar reactions. Even to the "well, to more cheerful thoughts" transition. Maybe the answer is that we're so alike that we're really one person, with on mind and one train of thoughts. How does the idea strike you?

 Right now you're on the train to my favorite country spot and you're probably about at Stamford. You're sitting with mother. Mom has as usual brought up a lot of gush . . . No, she's left it for Dad to bring up in the car tonight and you shall unload it.

 For a brief wild minute I thought of taking the bus over to Danbury and coming back tomorrow nite but I thought (rational me) of too many reasons against it. Not the least being that I've got to do 5 co-op jobs between now and tomorrow afternoon—to say nothing of doing a term's reading for Monday's exam.

 Have just come back from the Polit exam but since I didn't write yesterday you haven't heard about the Philosophy one yet. The latter was quite stiff but fair and "a good exam" on the whole. The Polit was too general and terribly dull to take. Don't know as I did brilliantly although I knew the stuff. Was too darn bored to write it out, having been given no incentive by the questions.

Barb left this afternoon and I was really glad for her. She's had a rather a tough term of it particularly seeing me make such good use of my weekends. She took the exams more seriously and nervously than I. I guess one does where there's nothing else immediately more important around.

The room feels lonely, I'm feeling leisurely and I still haven't recovered my good spirits since the news of Thursday nite. The Friday paper (the Times) was really a beautiful fascinating thing to read, and something I want to keep.

In three days I shall be seeing you, darling, and no one shall be happier at the ending of this term than I.

Mom asked in a postal if I'd be home to dinner. They're having a buffet and 2 of the people who were at Mard's party are coming. (one who was the plain, pretty girl recently married to Nick the doctor who arrived late and talked food to Mom). I just didn't answer about dinner cause I want to be with you. I also know I won't be terribly hungry!

It was nice coming out of the exam and finding a letter from you waiting for me. I do love you, you know, my sunburned one.

But much as I love you, I must now wash my hands, eat my lunch, wait on table, reset lunch, go to the library, work, eat supper, reset tables, work and finally go to bed— alone—without even a roommate.

This will reach you Monday I suspect and tomorrow and tomorrow and tomorrow shall be creeping in its petty pace until I'm with you—

Shall I be obvious and wish you an infinity of those terrific kisses? Of course I shall . . .

Your still curse-less but ever loving fiancée.

I dreamt we got engaged over vacation (this vacation) and that the vacation was extended ten days.

I think I'll go back to sleep.

Love, V

April 15, 1945–10:15 p.m.

Most missed Darling,

(8 mo.plus I day/8 mo and 2 days til Xmas vacation and ?)

Altho I'll see you for a few minutes tomorrow we wont have time for more than a hurried hello, so this will have to be my report on the weekend till I see you again on Tuesday nite.

It was as nice a weekend as I could possibly have had considering that you weren't there. It was hot during the day and cool at nite. I went down on the 10:50 with your mom Sat. morning. We sat around talked of you and many other (general) things and I raked up part of the tennis court. Mard and Clare came about 7. Your Pop had to go to Cedarhurst and arrived with most of the dinner at 8:30. He and I clicked beautifully-he almost embarrassed me by winking happily at me almost continually! We had started dinner just before he arrived. He sat down, tasted the meat and said, "Um, this is so good, I'm not going to say a word but just eat." I immediately said, "I'll take bets on that" and was surprised how much Mard and your mother (and your Dad too) laughed. After that we all got along famously. We raked leaves, burned caterpillars, sawed off dead branches and raked, rolled and taped the tennis court. It was work and fun and I missed you terribly. There were so many reminders.

Your mother showed me thru the house (I had never been upstairs) and I saw your room with the figures pasted (or painted?) on the bed, the white rug and the little chair you used when you were small. I also noticed twin beds in the room???

Mard, Clare and I discussed my distrust of American Communists and tho Clare couldn't see the point I was trying to make, Mard was honest enuf (or open minded enuf) to admit that I had a point she couldn't answer. Clare never did see the point. I guess she's been defending her position so long that she refuses to admit that the communists are even (or were even) wrong-that's an idea that is uncomfortable with every human or group I know and she has yet to convince me that they are Gods. I'm afraid my verdict must be that while she is radical she is not liberal-that is, she doesn't start from facts and go to conclusion, but is already set in her conclusions and tried to make every fact fit into a pre-existing rigid framework. I was glad to see Mard argue less dogmatically.

That was about the sum and substance of the weekend, but it was lonesome, darling. I missed you so much. You kept coming into the conversation; you were at the tennis court, and you were with me in the fields-and yet you weren't there. I had your last letter along and read it at least 5 times during the two days. I love you so very very much, darling. More and more without a let-up.

I'll probably be able to explain about the sudden trip tomorrow morning when I see you. If I haven't time, Saturday's letter will help (you'll get it tomorrow). We're lucky to be able to arrange it with a minimum fuss. I'm quite concerned about your continual cramps and want you to see a Dr. as soon as possible after we get the report back. You'll probably have to tell him the whole story but he'll keep it confidential.

We're going to have wonderful times together, darling at Westport or anywhere. This weekend has reminded me once again how happy I am with you and how incomplete I am without you.

My love is aching for you thru out these pages and if I don't write well enuf to express it, you'll see it on my sun burned face tomorrow and every tomorrow forever.
Good nite, my dearest most precious darling.
Until Tuesday nite—Every fiber of me is aching for you'
All my deepest love, Danny

April 15,'45
Dearest Darling,

I seem to miss you most at evening time—that dusky atmosphere seems to affect me and God, how I've missed you! Last nite I started feeling sorry for myself and wanted like anything to hop a magic carpet to Westport—to walk in the front door, to find your arms welcoming and surrounding me. I started to phone but I somehow thought it would make me feel even lonelier, so one of the girls suggested a movie which helped a lot. It was "Hanover

Square" a psychopathic murderer and a (really!) bitch with George Sanders, one of my favorites, playing a small "good" lead. Most absorbing, fairly obviously done, but it did the trick.

Came home and she stayed to talk while in my room. She went to Catholic boarding school at the age of ten when her parents were getting a divorce and the routine and nonsense!!! I'm amazed she's "turned out" as well and progressive as she has.

Did some studying this A.M. Washed my hair, then after went over to Main and spent most of the afternoon in delightful inconsequential talk with a couple of girls there. Came back to a party given by 4 seniors who are leaving (graduating) Wednesday. One of them is Ellie (Connie's friend). She finally received a letter from Dave enclosing a batch of half started, half finished letters to her!

It's now 7:15 and I'm sick of studying so here I sit writing my favorite correspondent, my favorite man, my favorite human being.

I'm cold and I'm sleepy and devilishly impatient to have started counting the hours.

Do you remember that Thursday nite we go to theater with Mard et al? Will you get done your exam in time?

I'll phone you at school when I arrive. Will probably go to 42nd Street so that we can stay a while at the Commodore. I hope you get this Tues. A.M. at which time it wont be long before I'm there to tell you all this (and more too) in person.

Did I ever tell you I love you, Mr. K? If you answer

"yes," I'll be only to happy to repeat myself. If you answer "no" you'll be a liar but I shall then pretend you've told the truth and have the pleasure of telling you for the first time. No one could possibly know how much I love unless they too were in love and even then, it would have to be a very special type of person who was in love the way I'm in love. Perhaps some day when I'm physically normal again I'll show you what I mean. Until then, you shall have to believe me by my mental and exterior physical actions.

Every exam I study for, I find your name scribbled all over everything. I guess, darling, you'll just have to resign yourself to the fact that you're in my thoughts, subconscious and conscious.

Oceans loophole, Lakes of love, Livers of rove.

Your one and only, Viv

> *Dear Diary;   April 27, 1945*
> *What a few days this has been! I won't ever forget them but I'll give a feeble attempt to record them anyway. The test came back positive. I am pregnant! I'm still numb and stunned by that news. And still feel sick thinking about the evening we had to tell my parents.*
>
> *I absolutely HATE to remember the look on my father's face. He is so beloved all over New York for being this wonderful ethical man and now his daughter has disgraced him. Not sure we'll ever have a good relationship with him again.*

Danny told him in one room and I told Mom in another. She looked serious but did say they would love to have a grand child and mine would be the first (or maybe only?) So that wasn't too bad. . . . but I still can't bear to think of the look on my father's face when he came back in the living room.

I myself have been kinda numb ever since getting the news. What will it be like to be mother? At least no more college exams!!!! But Danny hasn't finished his degree . . . He says he's perfectly happy to be a father tho we both agree it has come somewhat sooner than we had planned (not planned!).

I am so numb that I just obeyed Dad who kinda took over. He said no to an abortion tho none of us had even mentioned it as yet as a possibility. And that I should get married and go back to college for the spring ten week semester . . . A bit weird, but we just followed orders not really having any alternative ideas.

Danny's mother was told to come to a wedding and came by train from Philly for the wedding in a judge's office...a man Dad knew. Mum and Mom and Dad were the only others present in a small room with a short ceremony. My Mom had called close relatives to come in afterwards to the apartment for tea and cake and they had been told what the occasion was.

The morning of, she and I went to shop for something new to celebrate. I got a new blouse and what I really wanted: a black night gown. That part was funny. My mother hid behind a pillar in the dept. store as I bought it! Dare devil me! I think she was afraid she'd know someone and they would see what I was buying! But I wore it on our wedding nite which we celebrated at the Brevort, an old elegant hotel downtown. Even tho all this has happened to us, we had a wonderful time giggling and knowing we were now really together. As soon as we knew we were getting married, Mom wanted us to go to Tiffany for a wedding ring. We went and got the cheapest gold ring they had and it is now on my left hand which I stretch out to show off wherever I go.

So April 25, 1945 is our wedding anniversary day and I will have a baby in December! Wow!

April 27, 1945
Darling, darling WIFE!

It is now 57 hours since IT happened and I find it still almost impossible to believe. (Tho all I have to do is relax for a second, and I'm flooded by the memories of these past few days. Warm, delicious, over-powering memories: The wedding, your cutting the cake, a smorgasbord dinner, the Brevort and the funny step down from the john, early to bed, a sheer, slinky sexy black nightgown and alone at last in the dark with you. Wanting to hold you- hold you so close that I wouldn't tell where one of us ended and the other began-and waking up in the middle of the night to find you there . . . mmm.

There are so many things to remember with you: getting the license and the ring before and breakfast and the trip back to Vassar the day after. How beautiful you looked all the time and how proud I was and am and always will be to know that you are my wife. There are all these things to talk over with you and I hate to write about them in inadequate black and white words. I love you with all my heart and soul, darling-Love you utterly and completely and so far beyond anything I could describe.

Last nite I got as far as writing to Harry, my sister Ruth. Then complete weariness overcame me and I went to sleep-alone-damn it! Tonite I hope to write to Leon and Ruth, Gene, Morrie and my father. That'll dispose of the most urgent ones and I can write to more over the weekend. How are you doing?

The news burst like a block buster in the Dept. Mard had to tell somebody, so I didn't have the pleasure of seeing Dr. Root surprised. I waited til Clare came in so that we could see (and hear) her reaction, and then let out the secret. P.S. We weren't disappointed–she just opened her mouth and screamed! Everyone was taken by surprise and all who knew you told me how lucky I am-as if I had to be told! The Chief was goggle-eyed for five minutes and then went up and down the halls, kissing all the girls as if he was the groom. And how those wolves howled because they'd been cheated out of kissing the bride! I got so excited all over again that it was impossible to study, but they wouldn't have let me anyhow. I had to promise that those who hadn't met you yet would be given the opportunity soon. But I suppose all this is mild compared to the reception you got at Vassar. How did you make out about the missed classes and leaves? Was everybody surprised? Tell me all. You have to now: you're my WIFE!!!

Root has already hinted broadly that this may cause a change to be made in my new contract. As he put it, somebody might get the idea of giving me a salary boost, but not to get too excited as taxes would take most of it-"that's how marriage works out" he said. But he was very nice about the whole thing. Nobody spoke of premonitions but everybody recalled suspicious things I had done and said that last week. And should have seen Wang's face! He slapped me on the back and in an excited falsetto exclaimed, "Good for you. That fast work!"

I've resolved to work hard from now on; even tho I couldn't concentrate today. So far the cold you promised me hasn't appeared. How is yours getting along? I wish I were with you to get you to bed early. That's the way to treat a cold-and your wife-and me.

Barb was wonderfully nice. Thank her for me and tell her I love her dearly tho not in the same way I love you. (Also let me know what you've decided to tell her).

Got a letter from Gene today. He says he hopes he's not setting too fast a pace for me, but he's moved up his wedding day to May 20th! I'll relieve his mind on that point in a hurry. The Army is sending soldiers and their wives back on transports. He will be able to come home that way with her soon after their marriage unless V.E. day comes first in which case the transports will undoubtedly be used to bring just the men back.

It must seem funny to you to sit in a classroom and finger your ring. I'm hoping we'll be able to settle down soon and get a reasonable amount of work done.

Oh yes, I told my landlord and his wife about us. The unassimilated one, after congratulating me said "So fast! But that's the way in America".

There are millions more things I'd like to talk to you about but there is still a formidable list of people to be written to. And the sooner I finish with them, the sooner I can relax and think some more about you and us, and the thousands of wonderful days we're going to have together- and all the things we're going to do' and how much I love you, your mind, your body and all of you.

So long for a little while-not my fiance, not my wife-to-be but my wife. My own dearest, darling lovely wonderful unbelievable wife.
Your loving, honoring and cherishing husband.
P.S. Say hello to my mind for me. I left it with you when I got on the bus.
P.P.S. Just addressed the envelope. What a queer feeling!

April 27, 1945–W. Day plus 2,
Dearest darlingest husband-o-mine,

We knew this letter would be a tough one to write and it is. I'm so overflowing with love for you and
pride (and prejudice) that it's even hard to write how

hard it is to write! If you know what I mean.

Usually after we've seen each other we both write summaries of the important moments to try to recapture them for the other. I don't even think I'd dare try to do it for this vacation for even the calmest moments. And our wedding night! I'll never forget a minute of it—wanting to wake you up-being glad you were right there beside me, showing you my black nightery, singing in the dark etc etc. I'll never forget.

Best wedding night I've ever spent! And the fun we had over breakfast. Gee, it's so clear and ever present in my mind. And I'm so darned happy and I love you so superactively much. We're going to have one terrific life together. Perhaps even richer by some of our "problems". It was Hawthorne who believed that people became real people only after they'd suffered some and I can see his point. But marriage to you, my darling, is no hardship and I certainly don't feel sorry for myself!

What a silly inadequate letter this it! And how I miss you! I want to bury myself next to you, laugh with you and live with you.

Everyone has been just wonderful up here. The news spread like wild fire and everyone was properly shocked, amazed, delighted and very nice. The whole house sang congratulation while I stood blushing.

Tried to see Amy to tell her but she got in late last night. I'd left her a note and upon reading it the poor girl apparently burst into tears. Saw her for dinner tonite and she sends you her best.

Venable was very cute about it. I told him before class. He was really excited. When he went thru the role (he's trying to learn everyone's name) his lips moved to say my name then he smiled and amended it in a whisper.

Last nite a crowd of freshmen were all grouped together several yards away from me and they all just stared—not saying anything in fact their mouths were wide open. Feeling distinctly self conscious, I stared back and said in a loud voice, "Stop staring at me. I'm still the same" someone picked up the cue to say "Are you?" and everyone laughed while I turned bride's pink. It's even funnier knowing the whole story, ne-ce pas?

Classes are O.K. Didn't really get interested in any except mechanical drawing which is loads of fun so far. Social Psyc OK, Anthropology couldn't concentrate, so not fair to judge yet and Philos. As usual…but I actually was caught up by Mr. V. in the middle of a yawn.

Everyone thinks I'm crazy to have come back this term and are very impressed with the fact that you've got to work and I can't distract you too much, and that I plan to get a degree eventually.

Jane phoned last night having called me back and spoken to my mother. She was very pleased and envious.

Gee, I miss you. When I'm busy as I have been all day, buying books, seeing people, going to classes etc it isn't quite so bad but as soon as I have a moment to think, I'm overwhelmed at us and love and marriage and life in general.

This is a funny letter written with long pauses between

words, phrases and sentences, but every pause or every word says the same thing.

I haven't thought about the little fish. I did tell Barb. She had pretty much guessed. She was very nice and fairly silent about it except to encourage me to eat which I still find difficult to do. Upon telling this to people I've received many stories of sisters and friends who lost 10 pounds after marriage etc so I'm not too worried.

My cold is coldy but I expect to have it gone by the time I see you again. Everyone envies me and I envy myself. I've got the best husband any woman can possibly ask for and don't think for a second I don't know it! I must begin those eleven letters, darn it. I haven't written any and I'm not really relishing the thought except that I love to write about you.

Your adoring wife sends her love and hundreds of kisses.
Mrs. Danny K.

April 30, 1945
Dearest burpy, yawny, one and only wife,

With all due respect to pride and prejudice, the first letter I got from my wife was as tender and touching and wonderful as any wife has ever written to any husband. Of course I'm starved for the sight of any thing that pertains to you, but it was a beautiful lovely letter, darling, and after the fifth reading, it still leaves me limp (mentally!) and warm. If there is any further way for me to show you how much I love you other than by my words, expressions and actions, I'm going to discover it and do that too. At the same time that our love has made me feel more "adequate" with respect to the rest of the world, I feel less adequate when I want to express all that you mean to me. When you burp, when they sing your name, and you blush as I do. What you do, I do, and what you feel becomes a part of me.

Harry wrote today (I had to tell him the truth as he knew you were overdue) and it was a warm, tumbling letter, filled with his generous heart and enormously relieved and happy for us. These past few weeks he had become family for us but wouldn't write for fear of upsetting us. He dropped in on Ruth in the hopes that he'd get a clue from them but from the sound of his letter, must have been near nervous exhaustion when my letter arrived. He rejoices that we acted as we did, feeling as we did, that we have what we want, we'll be happy and to hell with the uproar it may cause. He said "It seems that conventions couldn't keep you two apart and now the law can't either." He also puts in his bid in for an early opportunity to kiss the bride. I was touched by a) the evident envy in his tone and our having found each other and b) right after he said he wants a simple ceremony too; he added "No grandiose wedding, if ever".

His letter set off a train of thought which ended in my appreciating more than ever how wonderful you are. During all our trouble, we stood shoulder to shoulder, never bickering, regretting or criticizing whatever happened or might have happened. I know that we'd stand together and face what ever comes as on a mutual front and we know it's going to be like that always God, I'm a lucky guy!

Harry says to tell you and Barb not to worry about his attitude toward Rosey. He had written only because I made him promise he would (before I knew the inside dope) and he'd have been surprised if she had answered.

Ruth also wrote-not too surprised after Ed's report on us and said she couldn't think of a couple that has less need of good luck wishes! (If only she knew!) Ed goes to California so Ruth is now in Philly with Steve and expects to be there for a month. She wants to know if we could come down.

Mitzie also sent her best wishes and want us to let them know if there is anything they can do for us (meaning financially).

Peter surprised me today with his congratulation. He has a lot of common sense and discretion. He was thoughtful enuf to realize that I'd rather not be the subject of student gossip and said nothing to the rest of the class.

Had an ordinary day today-as usual my vacation from teaching was interrupted when I had to give a quiz to the dentals tomorrow. I have to operate on 4 cats in preparation for a demonstration and so it goes. We're now in the last chapter of Phys Chem. I like the subject but it's a wonderful feeling that it will soon end.

By the way, I think I got the cannibal puzzle. If I have dinner at your house this week, I'll see if your Dad has solved it yet.

Tonite is half way mark in our 8 days apart. I'll come up Saturday and arrive at 10–meet you at the dorm. Now I've got to uncurl my toes, write to Harry, and try not to think of you while I read Phys Chem.

Good nite from your loving, desiring, missing you, terribly in love, husband.

May 1, 1945

Dearest unbelieving Mrs. K.,

 And two letters from you today~ We act so much alike, I sometimes feel as if we're puppets on separate strings, but operated by the same mind. But I'm sure it shouldn't be as much fun having a puppet for a wife! I've been acting like an elevator all week even when I read the parts of your letters that isn't directly concerned with sex. Look out for the salesman who'll come calling on you this weekend with his ample samples!

 Your first letter sounded like the way I felt before I got your Monday letter and your second one sounded the way I felt after it. It isn't that I felt in any way distant- everything just seemed not quite real and I had no ring on my finger, tho I have a small twig given to me during the night that serves the same purpose. I don't think we're really going to feel married until we're living to- gether regularly (am I repeating myself?) If I had to leave the country and we had to leave things as they are, (as so many have done) that wouldn't have done at all but it's only a matter of a short time when we'll get straightened out-and every weekend will help. Meanwhile, since it's impossible for me to support you here in NY we might as well decide that what we've got is better than what we had and let it go at that. I'm practically dying of impatience for this weekend to come, but it won't be so bad from now on if there aren't too many week-ends between our visits.

At one time I thought that if we were married, we could go on as before except that we'd be together on our weekends (that was before all the mess started) but now it's plain that every new step we make moves us closer and makes the next step seem that much more logical. It's the same story mentally with us that it was physically-we are so tied up together that neither one of us is going to be satisfied until we are completely husband and wife. I'll agree with your father that I was stupid about the sex angle, but that's as far as I can go with him. Everything we did followed logically and inevitably from what had come before, and if we had done anything else, it would have been unnatural and harmful.

It seemed to cut the week in half when you said I could come up on Friday night instead of Saturday.
I had counted four days to visit-but now its only two days (at times I find it easy to not count half days!) I can catch the 6 P.M. I'll look for you on the platform at 7:40 and if I don't see you will proceed to the dorm. OK? Gee, you'll get this on Thursday, so I'll see you tomorrow. Hmmmm!

Now that you've lost your taste for cigarettes, what will we do during our intermishes? Looks as if our mutual friend is in for lots of attention (goody!)

I feel kind of bad about your having to drop the art course. There are going to be a number of things you and I and both of us will miss for a couple of years but we're going to eventually get everything that's coming to us-like with our wedding day, the meal may start with dessert and end in the middle, but it's going to be a full and complete meal by the time we're thru.

On another subject: In the talks you girls have about the qualifications you look for in men. Does it ever occur to the girls (you and I are excluded form this discussion!) to look at themselves and see if they are what a fellow looks for-and if not, to do something about it? I've come across girls who wax sarcastic in comparing the guys they know with their latest hero out of True Stories, but fail to realize that they don't bear much resemblance to the heroine either! I remember especially talking to girls who sighed for a romantic dashing young man in place of the clerks they know but it never occurs to them that if such a man came along, they'd have nothing to interest him.

It seems funny to think of girls and fellows in a detached way-I guess I AM married! One change I've already noticed is that while I still admire a pretty girl in the subway, etc. I find myself thinking, "She's OK for some guy" instead of the former, "There's something I'd like to meet"

The other nite I had a mild-very mild-repetition of that scary dream I once had in which you didn't love me. This time we were married and you were you, but at the same time I thought you had once been the girl I went to my high school senior prom with. If I've ever spoken about her, you'll remember that she was a hateful puss. In this dream I kept thinking that you were perfect now, but I couldn't reconcile it with the girl you had once been (the prom girl). I kept on thinking of how you had acted that nite and what my friends had thought of you, then I realized that you weren't like that anymore-it was completely baffling, but when I woke up there weren't any after effects like I had after that bittersweet dream. All I can figure out is that my subconscious, too, is happy that you are you and not anybody else!!

 I'm afraid I wont be able to make you happy, if I've got to say that I love you half as much as you love me-or maybe I can make you twice as happy by saying it twice and adding them up! If you love me twice as much as I love you, then Christ had better step down-he met his superior when it comes to love for your fellow man! I presume that you were only giving me an indicator of how much you love me-if you have any foolish notions that you love me more than I love you; you are in for a rude awakening Friday nite! Or perhaps you think I'm superman and have always been ample so continuously with every girl I've known-just to mention the sexual angle only for the time being. (I know you know that I'm proud of my virility and love me for being such a school boy about it.)

 My God! I've answered only one of your two letters so far! Guess I'll have to save the other one for tomorrow nite or this week-end. Still have to answer why you want the Chief to repeat his kissing act while you are there (remember I didn't kiss any of your girl friends!); why I didn't mention how many socks I have, modest me (I've always t mended my own and expect to continue doing so); why I hink we're ready to fight the next depression harder than we fought this war; etc etc. And if there is any question in your mind how much I love you, I'll take care of that this weekend. All I can say now is that I love you with everything that makes up my mind, body and soul. If that isn't enuf for you, you're hitched to the wrong guy and I'll never believe that as long as I live.

Guess you saw Mussolinni died. Good riddance. Good nite, my darling wife. How I'd love to be caressing your hair, putting my arm around you just when you want me to, and squeezing you close to me-right now!!! Indefatably, indestructibly, indescribably, but not indiscriminately.

Love, from your husband,

Danny.

May 2, 1945

Dearest Darlingest Danny,

It's the ungodly hour of 7 AM and I've arisen to write my wonderful husband. I missed you so much yesterday that I almost took the next train from here straight to NYC but after calling myself all sorts of unpleasant names and realizing what a spoilt wife I am, I felt better and resolved to be a good girl. But gosh! I'd so much rather be with you than anywhere else under the sun and I keep wondering what foolishness keeps us apart now when we're finally and absolutely a married couple belonging emotionally and LEGALLY to each other. But I know it's best this way; it's just that I want you, simple as that.

Being married has all sorts of advantages, like yester

day receiving 6 letters in one mail! Congratulation notes-from relatives mostly . . . all of whom want to meet you and one card came from Camden N.J. and was signed Phil and Frieda. I trust you know them!? One envelope from an aunt and uncle of mine sweetly contained a check for $25 saying we'd probably know best what we wanted. Such a lovely idea! Now we can buy a bed!

Marks came yesterday and if I ever doubted the worth of them, I certainly lose complete faith in them now. I was so surprised at one mark that I went up to the recorder to see if there hadn't been a mistake. There hadn't been. Amer. Lit B; Phil B; Econ, B; Soc B; and Polit C!!! Polit was the one I thought I might get an A in. Member I got the highest mark in the class on the big test and a "good" on my paper when most people got bad comments. Well I've always said marks are stupid things.

Dinner with Barb's mother was very pleasant the other night. She was very cute and surprised and nice. I showed her your pictures and she made nice comments which for her may have been mere stabs in the dark but happened to be true! She's very eager to see you (as am I!)

Today's my big day with 3 hours of Mechanical drawing. It is also a certain anniversary of a certain marriage of a certain couple—one week ago! Happy anniversary, darling and may we have oodles and oodles more and all of them together.

Jody was reading me some of Dorothy Parker last night while I was doing drawing homework and I'm so glad I'm not a cynic (cinic? Scenic? no looks worse and worse).

Anyway I'm glad I'm not one. I DO like to read the stuff tho, particularly now, it makes me realize how wonderful life is.

So now Germany surrenders and we just have the war in the far East … then maybe peace?

I've never seen anything go as slowly as this week, have you? I hope it hasn't for you, too, that would be too much.

My cold is better: don't worry about me. I miss you greatly and I love you infinitely more…And I must get up and start another day which, when it is ended, will be one day nearer to you.
All of me, Thy wife.!!!!

May 4, 1945
Dear Family,

The week has been busy and a long one with everyone being very nice to me. Received many notes from friends and relatives who've heard via Mom's phone calls and in various grape vines. Al and Florence sent a check and a few others have asked what we wanted which has left me slightly non-plused.

Work has started in earnest. I decided it was a little too much so I regretfully dropped the landscape painting which I was taking for 5 hours a week for no credit. Mechanical drawing is fun but hard on the eyes. Anthropology too is good and Philosophy is as usual.

Last night Mrs. Ellis gave me a surprise party! At least I didn't know the party was for me until I arrived. There were seven of us and we had a wonderful time aided by champagne!

In five hours I am going to see a certain husband of mine whom I haven't seen for 8 days which may not seem long to most people but when it is 8 days since one has taken vows of matrimony and the unseen person is the newly acquired husband, it IS long.

Received a very nice letter from Walt today which doesn't say anything new as far as his activates are concerned but left me with the general impression that he is enjoying himself immensely.

Danny wrote to me of the momentous moment when the first wedding present arrived and was opened. I think he called it a Burmese begging bowl. Do you think there's significance in that?

I'm fine tho I get tired and seem to require mountains of sleep. The cold acquired has practically disappeared. I'm drinking plenty of milk, enjoying playing tennis. Been making good use of the trousseau umbrella.

The news continues terribly exciting. It won't be long now. Have been writing this while at message center.
Must go to class now.
Best to all, love, Viv

May 8, 1945
Dearest Tiger Lily Wife,

I hope this gets to you tomorrow. I'm starting to think that either we've got the same thing, or that I just share whatever is affecting you at the moment. Anyhow, I came home from Phys Chem last nite and promptly went to sleep. I'll make this just a brief hello and write again tonite. Meanwhile, I'm hoping to get you on the phone tonite so the delay won't seem so bad.

The week-end was so absolutely perfect that it seems a shame to water it down with feeble words. Besides the overall wonderful-ness of being with you, the things which struck me most were a) how closely we're drawing together and how well we understand and try to anticipate each other's wishes and b) the realization that we are rich in time-that we can spend time with people we like and don't have to feel that every minute we are not alone is wasted. Now that we have our nites together, there'll never be a time when we won't have a chance to shut out the rest of the world and just be us.

Please excuse the hasty note-but I couldn't have you wait three days without hearing that I love you, that I'm still awed that you love me and that we are especially nice people and are going to have (and are having) the kind of married life that other people will use as a standard. And I couldn't wait another hour to sit down to tell you this. Pride and Prejudice-call it what you want-being your husband has made my past, present and future everything that I had always hoped it would be.
Only three days to go.
All my love from a very lonesome husband. Danny

May 8, 1945–V-E Day
Dearest Darling,

I'm still in a glow from our Vassar honeymoon week-end. It certainly was perfect! Meeting you in the rain, going to Talbot's and toe wiggling, having "later" talks and agreeing and comparing opinions people and things. The Pines which shall always by synonymous in my mind with sex…steak, feeling proud of you, you eating soft eggs so nobly, me being told my figure was as good as the hula dancers; the Nelson house coffee shop, but most of all just you, looking at you, feeling you, being with you and knowing I'm your wife and you're my husband for ever and ever and that someday we wont be limited to weekends! In other words, Mr. K., I sorta enjoyed myself and hope you did too.

It's Tuesday A.M. and we've just learned that there are no classes this morning; that we're all assembling in the chapel to hear Truman speak at 9 A.M. After finally fumbling around with surrenders and non-surrenders, everything seems to be straight and all agree that today is V-E Day. We've been glued to the radio (uncomfortable?) and it's so exciting hearing the descriptions of the reception of the news received around the world. So now it's two wars down (if you can manage to count Italy separately) and One to go! If Roosevelt only could have seen it!

I received an extremely moving and saddening letter today from the boy I met on the train last spring. You may remember my saying he was extremely idealistic, wanting a house with a white picket fence and 6 kids etc. Yesterday's letter was written after he'd been to see the German prison camps. His description was factual and very vivid. Then there was a paragraph dealing with the freeing of some P.W. Americans which his unit had done the night before.

Both had obviously made a terrific impression on the guy and he ended the letter with a fairly vague analogy and the line, "There will always be misery as long as human nature exists".

It was such a touching, pathetic letter in the sense that all of a sudden this kid had grown up, but it had happened so fast that his ideals and ideologies had gotten rather confused and he was drawing conclusions that wouldn't help him in life any more that his previous romantic one did. I showed the letter to Venable as a study in philosophy. He was very interested by it and wanted to keep it overnight to show his wife. I'll bring it this weekend.

Yesterday afternoon Canada Lee spoke on the "Negro and the Peace" which turned out to be very moving, dramatic but honest appeal for tolerance. It was very good since many people, who wouldn't attend an inter-racial group meeting, came to see the famous actor and thus we reached more people than ever before.

There's a Negro girl, Della, on campus who's a freshman and apparently a mixed up disillusioned girl. She asked questions at the end: "Mr.. Lee, don't you get bored giving speeches when you know it won't do any good?" He answered her very well, I thought, and the whole audience was with him…He who was much more idealistic; she who was both more mature and less idealistic than he.

Went to see Miss Newcomer. I'm sure she thinks I'm a dope. She saw me make a fool of myself when I thought I might switch to Sarah Lawrence and now here I am married and dropping out of college. I'm sure she thinks I got married so that I wouldn't finish college..altho I did tell her I would finish some day.

I'm now back from chapel and hearing Truman for the first time now that he is our President. He struck me as a very simple and unsubtle individual. To compare his delivery with that of FDR would be cruel. He seemed to say everything with the wrong intonation or no intonation at all. But what he said was O.K. I thought. We could have done with a little less religion (I've heard he is quite a religious person) but I guess most people don't feel that way about it.

Prexy then spoke for entirely too long and included Jesus Christ entirely too much especially since all in the audience aren't Christian. But so it goes . . .

Have done practically nothing for an anthropology paper due tomorrow and shall now get busy on that. If I don't get this in the mail, you'll not get it before I see you! The post office seems to be closed for at least part of the day so don't know WHEN you'll get this.
It includes all my love and many kisses from your one and only WIFE.

May 8, 1945
Dearest Curly (head and toes) Wife;

I've just finished talking to my favorite wife-and I'm still excited and tingling. Just to hear your voice (I can see your face as if you're right here when I talk to you) does things to me that would be very difficult for any physiologist but me to understand. Any day now MY toes are going to begin curling.

The letter from Howard sounded exactly as I thought it would. It was brief but very nice and showed him as a sensitive but direct person. As is everyone else who knows you, he also revealed a great affection for you which of course, anyone with any sense must feel. It made me feel all over again how terrific it is that while so many people respect and admire and love you, I and only I am your husband. And don't try to claim that I'm putting you on a pedestal, you know exactly what I mean, my "nice" person.

It's too bad that we can't go to Philly the weekend Harry will be there, but I agree completely with the decision. He has met you twice already and we'll be able to see him later. I don't know if I would have agreed so readily if it wasn't for the peculiarities of the situation with your family. After all, sooner or later, we've got to realize that we're a new unit and can't expect to keep up exactly the same relationship with our families as we had before–not that I expect or want you to become less close and intimate with your mother–it may just become impossible for us to drop in on them or spend a whole weekend with them every other week. But you know what I mean and how I feel about your parents, so I doubt if this will ever be more than an academic objection. (I'll probably be pulling you over to 1112 more than you'll want to go there).

On rereading the above paragraph, I decided that it wasn't clear that I entirely agree with you about this weekend and would have made the same choice if it had been left up to me. In fact, we'll see so much of your parents till Sept. anyhow and from then on physical considerations will be our main consideration, so that I'm almost sorry I dragged up the point at all, but the idea did cross my mind and you may as well know about it.

We celebrated V-E day rather calmly (if not soberly) at the place. Our celebration came off a day early as Doris heard the news Monday morning and promptly ordered a keg of beer. It was all so expected and stretched out that there was no sudden burst of excitement-and there's still the war in Japan-so we mostly went about our work until the beer and pretzels were hauled out at 4.

I've got a lead–a very slim one on an apartment that may be available in a few months. Dottie (the girl from Phys Chem) lives in an apt. with two other girls only two of them signed the lease and since an old lady downstairs complained that they made too much noise, the landlord has ordered them to move. According to the O.P.A., they have 3 months time which will make it around August first. Of course, the landlady may already have promised the apt to someone else or two of the girls may stay on, but we have a fair chance. It is at 60th St and Columbus Ave–one block from Columbus Circle. The neighborhood isn't wonderful but it is one block from Central Park West and according to Dottie she's never had any kind of trouble no matter what hour she's come home. If we have time on Saturday we could go have a look at it. What do you think?

Got a letter from my Aunt Cele with a check for $10…I've been plugging away at my work when ever I can tear myself away from thoughts of you. Last nite we were given a terrific Phys Chem problem to be handed in next

Thursday. It's not very difficult but involves a lot of complicated and tedious math, and it's the kind of problem where one small mistake near the beginning will make everything that follows unrecognizable. Fortunately I had done this week's homework right after class last Thursday, so I'll have lots of time to work on it.

I've finished reading Claude Bernard and have started another book. Yesterday the Chief walked by and suggested that I read Sherrington which happened to be the very book that I was reading when he walked in! For some reason he seems to have the idea that I should do a lot of background reading that he didn't insist on with anybody else. It may be that he thinks I should read it (though he has no way of judging) or he may expect more of me or what is most likely, he has always wanted to read these things himself and is expressing his desire through me. The books he's recommended are very good and make fascinating reading.

That disagreement that I mentioned to you is being resolved in favor of the Chief. The "people at the other end of the hall" have decided they haven't clear cut enuf evidence to oppose such a well established theory and are going to hold up publication until they have proven their point more decisively or turn up additional evidence that forces them to agree with the Chief. It sounds as if they've been bullied into their decision, but actually they have only one or two good points on their side against much evidence on the other, but never the less one good experiment that goes against a theory means that nobody knows the whole story and some day it will have to be explained. It's my opinion that the whole subject should be thrown wide open until the discrepancies are ironed out, but I think it will take an entirely new line of approach to do this. The experiments on both sides are still too inconclusive.

Meanwhile I've been talking with Mard, and Clare about the method of measuring blood flow and was surprised to find that none look at it the way I do. Either they didn't realize what the guy was driving at or I somehow came out with the idea that he hadn't had in his talk. Anyhow, I can't start on the work until I'm thru with the PhD and there are lots of tough nuts to crack in the method so it'll have to be stored away for a few months. Forgive me, darling, I've been talking shop for pages.

I happened to be walking down the street at 9 AM. this morning and looked around to see what was happening at that momentous time. It wasn't inspiring. One guy across the street was picking his nose in a most industrious manner while on my side of the street another man waited patiently while his dog paid its respects to a pole. Perhaps some day the whole world will be as uninterested in starting wars as these two were at the end of this one.

A very heartening letter arrived yesterday from a Bishop McConnell of the Methodist Church. He asked for donations to help the Workers Defense League which is fighting a new, vicious practice that has appeared in the South. Sheriffs pick up a colored man and fine them $35 for vagrancy-without trial-even tho they are employed and have union cards to show. I know thru the chaplain here that the Methodists are very enlightened socially and are fighting for the under dog. Clare, Mard and Ingrith and I are chipping in modest amounts-do I have your permission to spend one of our dollars for this cause?

    I still can't help feeling that you are luckier than I am. (I have three more days to wait, but when you read this you'll have only two or less. But each weekend bring us closer to the end of June when you'll be nearby all the time. I'll never get used to being any place where you aren't and as much as it hurts, I never want to.
Good nite, my darling wife-you know that I love you-don't ever forget how much I do.
All my everything. Danny

May 9, 1945–two-week's anniversary
Hello my most adorable wife,

    Just had dinner and spent the evening with a beautiful charming and most gracious woman-and we were alone! Mard was out and your Dad had a dinner meeting so that your Mom and I could enjoy each other's company without interruption. She amazes me by how cheerfully she looks at our situation, and I don't think she's pretending either for y (our) benefit or hers In the first place she seems to feel that there's a lot to be said for early marriages, especially in your case. She seems to think that you'll get a lot more out of future studying that you do than you are now or getting before we met. She is also highly optimistic about how you'll take to domesticity and how the stabilizing effect it will have on you.

I mentioned how it will be tough for us to have to give up trips that we had vaguely planned but she pointed out that Mard was born only ten months after their marriage, and yet they found time for many short trips and later lengthy long vacations in Europe, etc. And since they had no trouble finding an aunt to take care of Mard, we shouldn't have any either since out baby will be irresistibly cute.

I got a preliminary report of some of her brothers I'll meet Friday. Let see, there's Al, Will (has a daughter engaged) Frank (her favorite) and Fred, married 3 years. Then there will be Elliott and Eleanor Sanger who met at their parents wedding. No that can't be..must have been somebody else's parents.

Spent a busy day at the place tho I didn't get much done. Out of the six cats we had prepared for demonstration two of them died, so I had to prepare two more. The first was easy but in the middle of the second operation, the cat suddenly began choking. I was afraid he was choking on his tongue, so I pulled his jaws apart and grabbed for it. Just at that moment, the darn cat gulped and clamped down his teeth down tight. It's amazing the force they get into such an unconscious reflex. One tooth went right thru my finger nail. Luckily the others missed entirely. It didn't bleed much and appears to be well on the way to healing, but is my finger sore! And when I walked into the lunch room the first thing the Chief said was "hello Danny. Did you learn anything today?"!!

During the afternoon Wang, Clare and I ran through the experiment and the results came out just the opposite of what should have happened. This usually happens in front of the class. Maybe our luck will be reversed this year for a change.

Your mother said she'd like to go with you to the Dr. Saturday morning. I think this would be better than if I went along. I'll work Sat. A.M.; then join you, if we have time for a quick look at that apartment I mentioned or if not we'll go right to Westport with your Pop and Mard.

It's going to be a wonderful weekend and it'll start just 48 hours from now. At 7 o'clock Friday nite, I'll be sitting at your folks waiting for you to come in! Please, time, stop your eternal marching and start running!

Good nite, my darling wife. We'll be seeing each other soon! A lucky husband sends his wonderful wife all of his Love, Danny.

May 14, 1945 (10 months since we met)
Dearest most loved husband,

Twilight is the time when I always miss you the most and tonight is no exception. All is quiet, I've got the radio on playing soft music to keep me company and to prevent my thoughts from making too much noise in the silence. This weekend wasn't as obviously full of love and wonderful. We'll always get on darling, come what may (and it will). And it is nice to know. It would have been nice to be alone a little more but our times will come and I guess it's the least we can do to honor people with our company. Some time this summer, we'll have to go somewhere completely incognito for a weekend at least. How about it?

Today has been a non-working day. At 9:05 went to Anthropology where she asked if there were any questions. I brought up what I thought was a fallacy in her theory and we discussed it for the whole period. We even continued it for all of chapel...fascinating. As usual I thought up some very good arguments after the discussion!

She and her husband were here for dinner tonight as guest of some freshmen so I told her I had thought up a lot more points for my side and we agreed to continue it after class tomorrow. As I understand her ideas, they would logically lead to a great deal of mysticism and greater "trust" in emotions than science. There's so much wrong with it that I keep feeling I must convince her how wrong she is, to save her soul, so to speak, and I'm sure she feels just the same about me! It's fun and good to get a new approach which, while you may disagree with it, helps one clarify one's ideas.

After class went to the drug store and got the calcium and acid stuff. Decided to get only the 4 oz bottle since it might look suspicious. After lunch I felt a sleep coming on so went outside and decided to do so in the sun. I apparently faced to one side in my slumber and the result is most strange. My right side is rosy. I trust I can even myself out by the weekend! Came inside and for two hours wrote thank you notes. Went to the mail of which there was none. Ate an ice-cream cone came back and washed my hair and cut my hair! Slept another half hour before dinner then reset dinner and here I am. Not a strenuous day but a full one. Or wouldn't you call sleeping a "full" day?

Barb had showed the letter I had gotten from Dick, the innocent boy who saw things in the war that has made him less innocent, to a liberal friend who asked my permission to use it on the radio as an example of a typical American boy and what he saw, hoping to make people realize it isn't all propaganda and "our boys have seen these things too".

I'd love to be curled up next to you even if I don't get an "A" in sex these days. I deserve that grade in the amount of love I have for you.

Your wife loves you A-ish-ly. V

May 13, 1945
My dearest dearest Darling,
(Please read this some time when you're alone)

This weekend I learned again something that I already knew. I learned that when you're happy and when I'm with you, then I'm as happy as I've ever been or ever want to be. When we walked down the road holding hands and you were a saucy school girl, my heart sang as it only does when I'm with you. And when we sat on the grass and I teased you, and you called me a provocateur, I wanted to smother you with kisses and say things that can't be put into words. Sometimes in the future there will no doubt, be times-short times-when we wont be as happy as we were at that moment. Don't ever forget that if I'm with you, you can make me as happy as it's possible to be.

Good night my darling wife. Thank you for being you.
All my love with all my heart.
Danny.

May 15, 1945

Hello Darling;

    I guess I'm married to a wonderful guy. How did that happen? Ask me no questions…Your wife is a saucy school girl. Wishing like hell I was with you and not 80 miles away.

    It's always about Tuesday afternoon when I feel the week will never end and that I'll just hop into NYC and into your arms for a nice little vacation (?). By Wednesday nite I figure the longest part of the week is over and it's only a matter of terrific impatience. Before that there is a strong element of "homesickness", home being where I hang my hat.(!)

    The afternoon was spent doing mechanical drawing. I'm very good at it. drawing it wrong, that is. Over and over again. Have been working at it this evening too while listening to Beethoven's 7th and Prokofiev 2nd Concerto on someone else's Vic. typical Vassar scene…7 females in various stages of undress. But it's nice to be married!

    Oh! last night I wore Ruth's blue night gown. As long as I don't seem to wear it when I'm with you, I might let someone else see it: my good ol room mate! Does look great so I'll have to give you a viewing sometime.

    Am now sitting in Philosophy class…seem to be having trouble getting this written. Tried to after breakfast but had to clean up the room instead. Then to Anthro and now here.

    Two amusing things to tell you about I.O.T.F. (infant of the future) Gee, even mentioning it and I still don't believe it. I think I forgot to tell you about it: I received a note from Miss Ball of the physiology dept addressed to Miss Bass about experiments she was doing. Would I be a subject and get 50 cents an hour? It all sounded good until I read that the experiment's concern, of all things, the menstrual cycle!

So sleepy! That seems to be all I do these days! Love you muchly tho. Viv

May 15, 1945
Hello my Saucy Wife!

This seems like an afternoonish sort of letter tho it's 7 o'clock. The sun is out and it's warm and balmy. Looks as if you can get your freckles back into shape.

The past weekend was a rather strange one. We were alone so little. Not so oddly, the outstanding events in my mind all seem to have happened when we were practically alone-you reading Winnie-the-Pooh to me (and rolling off the sofa in unholy glee) our walk down the road, sharing your room at Westport, opening a joint bank account and as always us in bed. One thing tickled my fancy happened when we were very much not alone. That was when your Dad invited the Wolfsons to see the pictures of China, and you said, "And how about the Klines?" Sometimes I think you are getting to like the idea of your being my wife!

Howard sent us a note to accompany their check. I left it up at the place-I'll try to remember it and enclose it in the next letter.

Harry didn't' get my card till Monday. He is coming to Philly next week so it'll work out right after all. He's so set up about being accepted by the army that he's trying to get into Radar School with the Navy!

Sylvia sent a cute letter and $75 to add to our account. She says Steve, her nephew is so cute she's wondering about her decision not to have any children! Guess I'll enclose it too as it may give you a more human picture of her. I wrote to her that we are coming to Washington next weekend so you don't have to write to her too.

It's been a medium hard day at the place. Spent the morning correcting lab reports. I think I've finished with my share for the year now. In the afternoon Clare gave a demonstration of the liberation of adrenalin (in the cat not in her!) while I assisted. Thursday we'll reverse the roles. At one point she was stimulating one nerve while I stimulated another (to get more adrenalin released). I couldn't see what I was doing because the guts closed over the electrode and when the cat moved a little, the electrode came off the nerve. In her typical Clare misuse of language, Clare turned to the class and said blithely, "We'll try this over again because Mr. Kline fell off the nerve" As you can imagine, it brought down the house. She has a habit of personalizing things people do-it took me months to get over recurrent hysterics after she asked Walcott "Can I get into the Centrifuge with you?" Bill nonchalantly answered "Just for the ride?"

I learned today that marks for the chiefs reading course don't go in til June 7th so I'll have an extra week to work on it-two weeks after Phys Chem ends. I don't know how many books he expects me to read-don't think he does either-but they're not light fiction and he can't insist on too much more.

I called Andy last night; the last time I had talked to her, her boy friend was on the verge of going to the South Pacific. Since then, he's been miraculously transferred from unit to unit, ending up a few weeks ago with an assignment in Times Square! He was polling the men's preferences for the point system of discharging men from the army. He is now in Washington DC and it appears he will be there for some time. Andy is thinking of marrying him and going there but she has no experience at anything that will earn money and they have none between them. After this discussion, she asked me how we are. I said, "Mrs. Kline is all right." There was a gasp, a shriek and an outpouring of congratulations. She wanted to know why I hadn't let her know sooner but quickly forgot in her excitement. Poor kid, she couldn't help contrasting my happiness with her troubles, but at least her man isn't overseas which is something.

The back of my thighs were stiff as the devil yesterday and still aren't back to normal (from rolling the tennis court). I made the mistake of admitting this to members of the dept. and got only leers in return.

I know I can't depend on you to let me know how you feel, but I'll try to convince myself that you're O.K. though I can't help wondering at this end of the line.

So long darling. Take good care of that woman who means so much to me. I love her very much. Will you tell her that? So long 1/2 my bank account and 3/4 of my life. All of your husband's love, Danny.

May 16, 1945(3 weeks minus 1)
Dearest Darling,

Here it is Wednesday nite and I've just had dinner chez Bass again. Looks like this is getting to be a habit. As usual, I had quite an interesting time at your parent's place. Your unbelievably wonderful mother said that she thought that we should have a honeymoon soon after you get out of school and that we should spend it alone. Maybe you've already spoken to her about it, if not, her understanding is amazing.

After dinner I had another interesting talk, this time with your Father. The subject was finances and it's much too detailed to describe in a letter. He wants to give us some money as a wedding gift a) so that you'll have the best of everything b) so that I can work free of worry and c) so that we can keep the $5000 in reserve which he feels we ought to have as a cushion in case of illness or anything else unexpected. I made it clear to him that there were certain principles involved that there wasn't anything personal involved but that I wanted time to talk to you and think it over.

We ended in high good humor with him saying that there's no decision for us to make-that the money would be deposited for us and we could use it or not as we pleased. I suggested that we could shift banks and then he wouldn't know where to deposit it. We laughed and he said nobody had ever heard of such a thing-changing banks so that someone couldn't put a deposit into our account! We'll have time to discuss this over Saturday which will be the first time I'll be able to talk to you.

Your letter to the Dept. arrived today and received

much comment–all very favorable. It also appears that a couple of other letters you've written have made a hit. A Mr. Rosen is so pleased that he is saving it to show your parents, Mard said. I was so proud of you that I wanted to put up a notice pointing to your letter on the bulletin board, saying "this is my wife, signed DK"

Mard got a letter from Howard today saying he got letters from both Klines. Apparently he hopes to get home in the not too distant future.

Spent most of today interviewing the kids (individually) who had missed a question in the last quiz. It took all afternoon, and I ended up hoarse. I used every device for explaining the idea I'd ever heard of or could dream up. Packages of plasma were running around with stuff inside of them; urine flowed all over the blackboard-men dropped nickels into slots and my sweat flowed like wine. Even after such a concentrated dose, I still feel a couple of fellows don't understand it. One guy in particular squirmed until I let him go. How he ever got into dental school, I'll never know. I hope someday he finds a job like moving a pile of sand from here to there.

Peter who did well on the quiz and is doing O.K. with the course in general, came up and very nicely offered to drive me up to school if I was going to the big dance.

Tomorrow I give the demonstration. Hope my voice holds out. (The cold is just about gone). I've been so busy with other things that I'll have to talk almost spontaneously but I feel so much at home with the dentals that I have no qualms . . . Mard is giving an hour's lecture tomorrow on the cerebellum. I know it's going to be good, if her conferences, when I took the course, are any indication. It's going to be a full day in the Physiology department for our family!

I haven't said anything so far about us. Frankly I'm worried at not having heard from you since Sunday. I know you're busy writing letters and get tired and "not in the mood" in the evening. I don't feel at all neglected but am wondering if you are all right. I would have called tonite, but I didn't know whether or not there'd be letter when I got home, and by then it was too late. There'll probably be a letter in the morning's mail, and this worry will all be seen as foolish.

As you can easily see, I'm missing you terribly. It won't be so bad now the Wednesday hump is passed-by tomorrow nite I can start to count the hours.

I've run out of events to tell you about and I would like to look over my notes for tomorrow so I'll stop now. I could go on and tell you how much I love you and miss you and wish you were here, but that'll have to wait till Saturday. Good nite, my darling wife.

All of my love, Danny

P.S. Just remembered something else your father said (don't know whether he was being honest or expedient). According to him, after the talk I had with your parents (our first one) he had told your mother that if finances were the only drawback, he would "stake us to our first baby" and the events which have happened since then haven't changed his mind about that.

This came up as part of his reasoning why we shouldn't refuse their wedding gift to us.

May 18, 1945
Dearest Darling, or My Favorite Husband,

    Gee, I'm a terrible correspondent these days. I never seem to learn that waiting to write to you till the evening means I won't write to you until the following morning.. Now maybe you won't get this before you see me tomorrow nite.

    The phone call was a lovely idea. I came into the dining room ready to re-set the dinner with a terrific smile on my face; everyone of course knew why and got a vicarious pleasure and the job was done at record speed.

    Yesterday I spoke to Mr.Lanier about dropping Psychology and he was very cute about it commenting, "A married woman and taking such a heavy load!" And signed the paper. So now I have three courses which is most pleasant.

    I cut philosophy for the first time in ages to get some work done. Oh yes: Tuesday nite and yesterday I managed to finish the Anthropology paper. If anyone had told me I would get it in on time…I'll be interested to see what she says about it as I directly attack her ideology. She'll either respect me for my nerve or flunk me cold.(or more likely give me a "C")

    At 4:30 I played a tennis match defending my position on the team (I haven't even decided whether I want to stay on it and here I am defending it!) I beat the girl 6-0, 6-3 but it was closer than it sounds and a fairly good game.

Got home in time for dinner and was just about to write to you and climb into bed when I had a phone call and it was Mr. Venable asking if I'd take care of his kids while they went to a movie. Being a soft hearted sucker and very fond of him, I went...thinking I'd get back at 10:30. It's a long story and better told than written but at any rate there went last evening.

So here it is almost 9 AM and I've got to quick cram some Philos. into my head so that I can say something on a 15 minute quiz on Schopenhauer whom I have read. See you in less than 36 hours, my darling, and until then you have all my thoughts and love.
XXX Your Wife.

May 17, 1945
Darling,

It gave me a terrific lift to know that you'll be here tomorrow nite instead of Saturday. Last weekend left me feeling unsatisfied (mentally) and your first letter today didn't sound as chipper as you usually do. But now everything is OK-I'll be seeing you in 17 hours instead of 38 that it had been before.

Don't worry about whether I can spare the time as I couldn't work Saturday morning anyhow and I'm studying for a Phys Chem Exam on Monday and 3 hours more on Sat. morning wouldn't make any difference and right now I'd have to be crazy to prefer 3 hours extra study to 21 hours and a whole nite with you

Bring your black night gown or don't bring anything but

come. I love you and always agree with your decisions-but on this one, I agree most.

In just 37 hours and 50 minutes I'll be seeing you at 125th St. Love, love, love, Danny

May 21, 1945–9:45 p.m.
My darling darlingest,

I'm still feeling very glowing, warm and wonderful after the weekend. As you said, it was one of the nicest ones we've had. There are so many highlights this time: creeping up on you from the back and surprising you at the station; discussing values over tuna fish salads, wine, cigars and foreigners combined with being so glad to be your spouse…and the rest of the night. Macbeth, Caesar, sleeping on your lap on the sofa, the squeaking bed, beautiful day watching all the children under the age of five…iced coffee, the train ride back. It sounds so colorless just to list things. If I could describe how I feel and felt at the same time it might be worth something. I liked the weekend partly cause we were alone more than at other times and I love being selfishly and completely with you. I love you so darned much!

Eight Vassar girls on the train made me not so proud of going to that institution but I managed to get a little sleep on the ride up here…I seem to need endless amounts of sleep! Got to the dorm at 11;20 sleepy but happy.

Got my anthropology paper back. The one in which I attacked the initial theories etc. a B+! Much amused.

Venable's book came out today and I got a copy and his

signature. Now I'll have to read it! I can picture reading it leisurely some time this summer.

Then at 11:30 I took my psychological tests. The first was working with syllogisms. The subject was asked to estimate how well, compared with other Vassar girls, you thought you would do on the first group of syllogisms. You then did them, was timed etc and asked after how well you thought you'd done on them, then you were told what you had actually done on them; then you were told what you actually did do. And had to guess another time for next set.

There were about 15 sheets of syllogisms all the same. In fact they all dealt with Smith, Jones and Brown and whether they were taller or shorter than each other. I guessed originally 60%. I received a 30% (in other words 30 people did less well than I) by the end I was told afterwards it was a trick, which actually I had guessed at one point. The test is for seeing how people work under success and how they do under thinking they have failed and ultimately testing whether you get depressed easily.

The scores told to you that you do, 30%, 80% are all fictitious and standard subjects were doing less and less well and other increased. I had the former variety and finally came out slightly more tended toward depression than average. Robey came out very depressible.

Other tests were on personality and needs. One on creative imagination which was sort of tricky. A boy gazing at a violin; his expression just vague enough to be interpreted as longing, boredom etc. You were asked to state the subject of the picture in one sentence-say what the boy would do etc. Finally what would happen to the boy in the future? I laughingly said he be on Wall Street. Apparently others have said that too!

Slept this afternoon and read some more about the Arapesh. Have just come back from the bond rally where I proudly pledged part of our wedding present. Different objects and privileges were auctioned off: nylon stockings brought $1000; Bramer sweater $325; carton of cigarettes $1,400 etc. some by individuals some by groups. Our dorm pledging 12,000 got the privilege of smoking at dinner for a week. It's funny: the ones with the most money are often the ones too broke to buy bonds and it's the poorer ones who scrimp enough together.

Looking forward to speaking to you. Don't call after 7:45 on Wed. will be at a lecture…but any other night. All my love, Your wife

May 21, 1945
Dearest wonderful Peanut,

Such a lovely lovely weekend. It was wonderful being alone with you here and the episode with my landlord added just the right piquant touch. I'm so happy when I'm with you that it's almost unbearable to think of the days when we'll be together all the time.

I'll admit that I was a little worried because your letters hadn't sounded so chipper last week but from the moment your impish face popped up behind me at the station, everything became all right. Every minute that we're alone had a dreamy quality that is still very real and delicious.

Lying in the sun and watching the kids play in their little oversize pants and beanies, making iced coffee with ice cream . . . and just being overwhelmed every so often by the realization of how much I love you and that you're my wife . . . ummm it's so good.

Wrote to the hotel in Wildwood and to Syl about the book but that's starting the day at the end . . .

A very nice letter from Harry today. It's addressed to us but I'd like to hold it a day or two until I can answer. So you think the picture of me looks gangsterish. I think that's a charitable way to describe it!

Didn't do much work today, but studied Phys Chem, finished the first "book report" and got a good hunk of the second one underway. I'll divide my time between P. Chem and the books until this weekend. By that time, hope to have the first 3 books finished and will then have two uninterrupted weeks to read and write up the last four. These first three are the most important and I'm covering them in some detail but I'll move a lot more rapidly after this week.

Somehow I got on the list to teach the dentals this week but the lab will consist of demonstrations by Wang and Root which I can skip and I got out of the conferences. They certainly were liberal with my time in making up this year's schedules

The next event of the day was a discussion with Clare about the advisability of having babies soon after marriage! I don't know if she'll find out the true story or not and I don't much care, but taking advantage of her grapevine abilities, I let the hint drop that considering the instability of things today, we didn't much like delaying since we both are very anxious to have children. Don't worry about my overplaying it–I won't bring up the subject again. (O.K. so I'm tricky!)

I called your mother from a pay station near school to tell her that I couldn't come for dinner Wednesday on account of my final the next day. We tentatively changed it to Friday nite. A couple more presents have arrived. I guess she'll write you about them.

Today's exam turned out to be surprisingly easy. I'm usually cautious about deciding how I made out in an exam, but after comparing answers with others in the class, I think I did all right. Thursday's final has been cut to an hour and a quarter and should be pretty easy since it means a lot of little problems. There just isn't time for long tough ones.

And so I come to an end of another Monday. The glow from the weekend hasn't faded as yet, tho the struggle to get over the hump of Wednesday will soon begin. It's funny that I get terrifically lonesome for you and miss you abysmally as soon as you get on the train. (That's why Sunday nite is my favorite movie nite, tho I didn't indulge myself this week).Then I'm O.K. again till right now. I'll be all right tomorrow till I get home from work-but this time I'll talk to you on the phone which should help.

Maybe we ought to shake ourselves out of this state of affairs. After all, it's a form of self pity and we can at least fight it. I'll see you in just 4 ½ days. What reason to I have to complain?

Mard said she had a very nice time in Croton with your aunt Floss. Have you ever been there? She raved about the beauty of the place. By the way, what clothes should I take along? Just how casually can we loaf around or is there much work to be done?

There is the story of a med student who has an old rattle trap of a car which he calls "Plymouth Rock" because it's the place where all the pilgrims "come across". The fellow who told the story announced in advance that it was a risqué tale and as soon as he said "Plymouth rock" knowing that that's the name of a hen, I leaped to the wrong conclusion and wondered at his daring to tell it in mixed company.

I'll probably talk to you before this letter arrives but I never get around to telling you that I love you, how much I miss you and what a wonderful wife and sweetheart you are. The only person in the world that I envy is me!
Good nite, darling, oodles of love, Danny

May 23, 1945–2:10 A.M.
Dearest Most Adored Man 0 Mine,

I now feel wonderful after getting your first letter which was nice and newsy. I hope you didn't feel too badly after last night's phone call and I guess I'll explain all. When you phoned I was in the midst of feeling pretty lousy. Between my cold which is a juicy one and what ever happens to me in the evenings, I'd just left the dining room without eating and was lying down in hopes of recuperating, when you called. Naturally I was VERY glad to hear from you but couldn't make myself very articulate. In fact I don't even remember what I said! Later in the evening I got rid of the supper I didn't eat and felt better. Am still a bit shaky this A.M. so am staying in bed until the afternoon when I'll go to Mechanical drawing.

So now you have a full account of how I feel, something which I hate to make letters full of, but which I figure will explain my lack of spontaneity over the phone.

By the way, while on the subject of illness: I should warn you I'm a terrible patient. I'm not a hypochondriac but I seem to feel delightfully sorry for myself when I'm sick. So slap me swiftly on my "character" whenever I act in said manner and maybe I shall improve.

The dept certainly has it in for you to teach the dentals! Maybe they'd change their minds if your wife came up and told them a thing or two. (Lovely picture of me browbeating the department!)

Yes, I agree. I miss you most in the evenings, too. Just about sunset time Altho I wouldn't put that down as a hard and fast rule: sometimes I feel like that all day.

Just got a letter from Walt enclosing a wedding present check for $35. The presents which await us at home are: a Mexican tin tray from "the Baroness" ½ dozen attractive old wine glasses (quoted from Mom's description) from Aunt Flora (the old woman who was there that Fri eve who I introduced wrong). A beautiful lunch set white with green vine embroidery from Jensen's from a friend of my parents.

We're going to be might busy eating and drinking!
Much as I love you, and I do, I think I should get to work.
All my love, all my life, Your wife.

May 24, 1945
A-day–1 (this letter will probably arrive on our anniversary instead of yesterday's)
Dearest,

Today's letter from you certainly cheered me up (I hope you weren't trying to deceive me). I knew from the phone call that all wasn't well, but I didn't know how "not well" you were. You're still up to your old trick of telling me all, after the worst is over but I'm getting resigned to it.

This husband of yours has certainly pulled some dopey tricks this week (more than the usual). The worst of all was in thinking that yesterday was Thursday, the 24th. This isn't the first time that I've thought Wed was Thurs. Either I'm going nuts or I count days and look toward the weekends so wishfully, that my subconscious desires get the better of me. You can take your choice as to which reason is the right one, but one evidence in my favor is that it only happens toward the end of the week just before it's close enuf to start counting the hours (43 from now).

The second boner is that I forgot to mention the check to Harry and Syl. I had intended to write a letter but sent a postcard instead and forgot to mention to thank for the check! I've since written and I hope you'll forgive me enuf not to call off seeing me this weekend.

My mother wrote today that she has bought 4 sheets

and 4 pillowcases for us–pre-war stuff and good. Turkish towels are impossible to find. She's mailing them up to me and I'll send her a check when the sales slip arrives. From what I hear, it was a darn lucky buy.

I haven't said much about your physical troubles-you know that anything that happens to you is my concern and don't hesitate to tell me about it even if it take 4 pages. I would rather read that you're feeling fine but if not, I'd rather hear about it than just be left to imagine the worst. Incidentally, you'll have all my sympathy but I wont hesitate to spank you anytime I think it'll do us good.

You conceited woman! So you thought Howard answered your letter sooner than mine!

Clare's voice is now resounding down the hall-probably from 4 floors away. She rather favored early babies" with things as upset as they are today, tho I don't think she regrets what she did since she wanted to go on to get a degree.

As for my lovely dirty mind in connection with Plymouth Rock, I was thinking of the laying habits of hens. Thursday afternoon! I'm dying to see you, darling. Somehow these hours will pass.

All my love, Peanut,

Danny (who loves peanuts).

May 28, 1945
Darling Wife;

Last nite will rank among the most memorable of all the wonderful nites we've spent together, for me. I don't know exactly why it was so special, but I think I had something to do with the feeling that we were really alone. Whenever there's no one else around, I feel more strongly than usual that we're really husband and wife. And then there was something so family like when I got up in the morning and went to work. You looked so small and protectable with the covers pulled up to your chin and only your nut brown face dotted with freckles that I love so much showing against the pillow. I liked the feeling of rising from OUR bed and going off but I wanted so badly to come back and kiss you and climb back into bed alongside of your warm body and just stay there . . .

With cooperation from all sides, I managed to catch the train and get a newspaper to read on the way. The bus driver said he was scheduled to reach the river at 7:38. When I told him I was trying to catch the 7:37 he sped up and got there a couple of minutes early. Then the train man promised to hold the train while I ran upstairs for a newspaper. Poughkeepsie was very kind to me today (It seems such a long time ago instead of this morning).

There were two big boxes from my mother waiting for me tonite. Look at the stuff that was in them!

6 sheet and pillow cases

4 Turkish towels (small)

2 wash clothes

1 large Turkish towel (looks as if it might be a bath mat, it's so big and heavy)

2 yards of toweling (looks like dish toweling, though it may be to make hand towels)

6 large dish towels

It all totals up to $25. I'm sure it's worth it. The slip that came with each sheet intrigued me so much that I tore one off so you could see it.

Got a long letter from Leon today in which he congratulates us and sends you regards. He wasn't at all surprised and said "I knew from the tone of your letters that you were sure of your feelings". He wants some pictures of us and asked me to induce you to drop him a few lines. I'll leave this entirely up to you as to whether you have the time and feel like writing to him or whether it would just be a bother. (and don't think it's a duty- his wife never wrote all the time Harry and I were at Purdue and we knew her well!!)

Robert E Sherwood, for the Nation wants to know if we'd care to attend a dinner in honor of Thomas Mann, Henry A Wallace, Albert Einstein, Marshal Field, Carl Sandburg, Pearl Buck etc etc who will be there. As you can see it is only $25 per plate. It should be a wonderful meal! On second thought, I just noticed it's to take place June 25th and you have your finals then. Guess the etc won't include us. Even if you didn't have finals, it would interfere too seriously with our bedtime to consider going.

Spent the day reading about the status of Physiology in 1838. It really makes fascinating reading. A still unsettled problem was whether or not living things started spontaneously from rotting material. He also speaks of a vital force which makes the difference between inert chemicals and living things. One effect of the book so far was to strengthen my belief that you were right in our discussion.

I still haven't completely shaken off the egotistical notion that we are anything but a collection of molecules. It is unscientific in the extreme to try to invent a raison d'etre. Does it surprise you that you've already made a contribution to my work as a scientist? It doesn't me–I've always known that you not only have the intelligence to reason clearly (which is good but not rare) but also the courage and honesty to follow your reasoning to a logical conclusion no matter where it leads (which is very rare-and for which I thank not only you but both your parents as well).

Another interesting thing about the book is that many of his explanations are exactly what we think today-if you change certain words. Of course, the words he uses indicate that his concepts were basically different from ours, but his reasoning processes and his ultimate faith only in experimental proof are just as sound now as they were then. The book was written at a peculiarly fascinating time. Belief was still prevalent in mysterious vital forces that inhabited living things and Darwin's theory had not yet come out.

The experimental method was not yet established as the only method to be used on living things, and yet the progressive men of the day (he was one) had already groped to the threshold of all of these new concepts and methods of approach.

It's really a fascinating book that I could go on for pages and bore you indefinitely-it just occurred to me that what I've written to you about it is very much the same as what I'll write the Chief. Do you think he'll mind if I quoted him some of our personal correspondence? Poor you, you had to go and marry a scientist!

Mard and Nick engaged me and Wang in a doubles match today. It was very windy and we kept hitting the ball off balance and then there was little rallying.

I spoke to our mother over the phone. She and Pop expect to arrive at Poughkeepsie around lunch time on Sunday. They'll have lots of room in the car to take the vic and your winter clothes that you can pack up. Shall I bring my large overnite bag?

My molecules! It's 1:30 AM. Guess I'd better get to bed even if it is lonesome. Don't worry, Darling, I'll look first thing in the morning to see how "I am".
All of the love, your terribly in love husband can send.
Danny

May 24, 1945
Dearest Wonderful One,

Gee, you're so nice, so cute, so terrific and I love you terribly much.

The flowers came this afternoon and I was so pleased! It was the first time anyone had seen me bubbling over except as weekends approach, in just ages. I finally wangled the conspiracy out of Barb who with very good taste and judgment had made them roses–12 beautiful red ones! But it was the idea even more than the flowers that I loved, and the person even more than the idea that I'm really crazy about! And then the cut-out card arrived appropriately about a half hour later also. All was complete.

In case you're interested in the dull subject of my

health: I'm much better and back to my normal burping etc. Cold is still coldy and tis sad as I can't smell the roses! But am definitely on the road to recovery.

Tomorrow I have a test in Anthropology, on the Arapesh, and also a test in Philosophy. I haven't done all the reading for either and I trust in the powers that be and happily leave it at that.

I received a screwy letter from Len, Barb's father, concerning our marriage which I'll bring along if I remember it.

Only another day and then it will be a weekend once again. And only another 5 weeks and we won't have to live by weekends at all! Oh God, won't that be heavenly though. It makes my mouth water and my toes curl to even think!

One thing I'm still puzzled about. Why did you have the flowers come today? I've figured two reasons: one being you were thinking it was Thursday as you did once before. But the probable reason was to make it a compromise between 4 weeks which was yesterday and one month which will be tomorrow—so you made it today—or a third reason: you really thought it was today?

In any case, you put me to shame: I did at least remember it was 4 weeks yesterday but my weakened condition didn't do anything much about it. So as usual, I think again how much more wonderful you are than I...not with any jealousy, envy or what-have-you but with pride and the usual amazement that you see anything in me (can you? so soon?)

Like most nites: I must go to bed now . . . while the sun shines happily in my window, your wife retires for the evening. With many thoughts and kisses for her husband whom she misses and loves muchly.

All my everything, eternally. The weenut Peanut with a jelly-like belly (How unattractive!) take it or leave it. I'm talking of your wife! V.

May 23, 1945

Darling,

Don't be upset if my month anniversary plans come out on the 24th instead of Friday. I started a day early because I don't trust the mail, but I KNOW it is the 25th.

So long from your dopey but loving husband,

Danny

May 30, 1945

My Darling Peanut,

In a half an hour I've got to go down and help Clare with a demonstration, so this letter will probably be interrupted in the middle.

Not much new has happened since I last wrote. I've been reading most of the time and have now finished the four books. I'll finish the 5th by Friday which will leave two more for next week.

Last nite I went into town and much to my amazement got tickets for a)"On the town" and b) "the Glass Menagerie." I figured it would be better not to get them for the same week so we'll see "On the Town" July 6th and the "Glass Menagerie during the week of August 25th.

Somehow staying with you till Monday morning and seeing you Friday has made my week seem very short.

The hump didn't really arrive at all and today is only two days till I'll see you again. I don't know how your work and plans are set up but as far as I'm concerned we could break all our previous records and spend Friday, Sat. and Sunday nites together this weekend. That's almost half the nites of the week! The Pines will soon be called our home away from home!

It would be foolish to ask how your cold is coming along as I'll see for myself before you could answer. I hope it is going away. I haven't picked up even a trace of it

When I spoke to your mother Monday, she reminded me that we should be sure there is no conflict between your doctor's appointment and our honeymoon.

So much of my time has been spent reading that there hasn't been much for me to talk about in this letter. When I'm not reading (and a lot of the time when I am) I think mostly of you and count the days and hours till Friday afternoon. So much of my time is spent in thinking about us that I wonder what will happen when we're together all the time. But I have no fear of being bored!
All my thoughts, and all my love, Danny

June 5, 1945
Darling,

"Intercourse with the dead is as casual as with the living." Yip! Believe it or not, that's what I've just been told. As you may have gathered I'm in anthropology and to keep from exploding, I'm writing to you. "We are a culture that values change" . . . "There is in human nature a craving for sameness." "That is part of the conflict, as individuals when they grow older want to remain as they are"…Oh nuts! It's a mess and as usual I need you to straighten me out and to curl me up.

Since I saw you last, 24 long hours ago, I've been mighty busy. Of these 24, 14 of them have been spent in semi consciousness in that lovely state of sleep. That leaves 10 hours spent: one hour in class; part of one hour waiting for Philos. and Mr. V., who didn't come; one hour in the library; one hour at message center; time to eat, wash clothes and do some Mechanical drawing. Such a busy wife!

It was a lovely weekend, wasn't it? So nice and long, too…With minimum obligations to others…mmmm

I dreamt about the cutest baby last nite. It was half a baby and half a doll, I think. And it had red hair! And it was very vague as to whether it belonged to us or to the Venables!

Am now engrossed in reading about the Manus, a tribe "infesting' the Admiralty Islands.

We got another cut in Philosophy today. Apparently he isn't' very healthy or maybe I put a curse on him by dreaming about him.

Much excitement about the prom this weekend. A common sight is to see two juniors at a distance, gesticulating, hands on shoulders or waist-probably saying: "It's very sophisticated!" "It's my sister's;" or "the date is my uncle but anyway the shoes are divine!" Or some facsimile of said conversation.

My mail for two days consisted of a bill for 85 cents from the bike place which I hadn't paid last month; a bill from the Bookshop for $3 for Venable's book and the receipt for the $20 I sent to the hospital and a request that I pay 25 cents for a class meeting I missed. Everyone's so mercenary!

Will get Mard some tennis balls for an extra addition to the note paper for her birthday. A "tricky" extra as you'll probably use them too! Gee, I want this weekend to come! And bring with it sunshine, for Pete's sake! I feel as soggy as the grahams crackers in my drawer.

Another engagement in the dorm accompanied by more cries of frustration by non-engaged members.

That dream last night about the red haired baby has made me more pro "it" than I have been so far. Watch out: I might begin to believe in the power of dreams!

I've just been a greedy pig and eaten a huge amount of coleslaw and the results are so noisy that Prexy came running to see what was the matter. When I told him all, we had a long talk about sex and he told me as he had told Robey that he wished it took only one day!

Your wife is mad, wacky, and thoroughly in love with her husband. In such a condition, she leaves you to return to the gay life of the Manus.

XXXXXXXXX Thy wife

June 5, 1945
Dearest Bunny,

It wouldn't surprise me if this letter had to be delivered to you at the Pines: you looked so cozy and comfortable in bed it wouldn't surprise me if you just decided to stay there! (But don't forget to get up by Friday!)

The trip home was uneventful. I even had enuf time to get some coffee at the station. I must have got up way after 7 that first time.

There was some interesting mail when I got home. A letter from my Ma—there seems to be a terrific demand for seashore places this year. One of my aunts had to pay over $500 for a small place for the season. Neither they nor Mitzie will go down till the end of the month so we'll a) have to take the Sheldon b) write to the chamber of commerce and then apply somewhere sight unseen or c) go somewhere else. There was also another package from her containing two large bath towels and two wash cloths.

I had the darndest luck in the library yesterday. They couldn't find the German book that the Chief wanted me to read. It's a rare old book and for a while I had hoped it wouldn't turn up, but they found it. It's only 42 pages and I've slogged thru 22 so far so that I should finish it tomorrow. So far I've read 4 books and half of each of two more and have typed up two of them with two more ready to be typed.

The Chief stopped me in the hall yesterday and wanted to know if I'll accept a fellowship. As far as I can gather, all it means is that I'll have the honor of being on a sort of scholarship- no change in salary. I'm holding up my O.K. till I see if there are any strings attached (such as fixing my salary for the next year).

The news these days has us all walking around glum. Churchill spouting medieval stuff, Russia insisting on the right to veto even the discussions of a dispute, and Canada apparently going very conservative.

But there'll always be the weekend and I'll be with you again.

A picnic dinner in bed, a walk, a talk after a movie, a discussion of democracy, and I'm ready to fight the world single handed.

Just noticed this morning that the hair around my ears is growing in again and I don't look scalped any more. You have a lot to look forward to this weekend.

So long, Peanut. Keep those freckles toasting. Having dinner at your parents' tonite so there may be some news tomorrow. By the way, would you rather stay at my place or at 1112 Friday nite?
Love from your very lonesome husband,
Danny.

June 6, 1945
Darling Mrs. K.,

Just read your delightfully nutty letter-better stay away from coleslaw and Prexy. Funny that you dreamt about a red-head. This afternoon we happened to be talking about hair and Clare remarked that our kids would have curly hair but we could be reasonably sure that they wont be red heads! I'm curious (jealous) about your dream. Weren't you sure if it was Venable's or did you think he was the father, the cad.

Had an interesting and pleasant evening at 1112 yesterday. Michael and Nina Heidelberg were there and your father was in rare form and the conversation was fast and furious. I brought Pop one of these paragraph-long, involved German sentences that I came across in my reading.

And he got stuck on one part of it, insisting that there was a word missing. (There wasn't).

This inspired him to a harangue a la Hitler in garbled German which I'm sure you've heard many times, but it had your mother and me laughing til we cried. The Heidelbergs are awfully nice–especially he. I was delighted to find him a liberal and completely unassuming for a man of his prominence.

Your Mom appeared in fine fettle. She hadn't decided yet whether to go to Westport Friday or Saturday but I think she wants to go with you to Dr. Goff on Saturday. They wont be going to theater Friday nite-we're to have dinner there. Mard is home but is willing to sleep on the sofa if we want to sleep over there.

I pretty much played the truant today after 4 o'clock (while my wife was slaving away at school) Nick and I played Wang and Bill- 3 tough sets and the best tennis I've ever been in the middle of. Bill is almost as good as Nick and with me to drag down our side, it was very even. We lost 4-6, 6-1, 6-4 mostly because Nick got tired covering the whole court.

I just looked up and was reminded of the new picture of you that your mother gave me last nite. It was taken in Westport and shows you about to cut a birthday cake. I counted ten candles- was that right? It's a very cute picture of you and has already become one of my favorites.

One of the doctors at P. and S., a rather limpid guy, is rumored to take daily shots of sex hormone. The 4th year classes having its party tomorrow and for it one of the kids made up a song to the tune of Accentuate the Positive. The first lines go: You've got to accentuate the androgen. Eliminate the estrogen etc. I hope the Dr. in question doesn't show up!

Mard, Cliss and I had dinner together and then went to see an oldie, "The Stars Look Down." It ranks with my 10 best of all time. Did you ever see it? The story of a coal mining town. All the people in it are real and human and the story works out naturally and mentally toward a tragic finish. There's also an impersonal plea in it to nationalize the coal mines.

My work is coming along OK. By tomorrow I'll have the last book read and just two to write up. The German one is a stinker. There are just a few points that the guy has difficulty fitting into his theory and how he squirms! Its easy reading till he comes to one of these corners that won't fit in right. Then he dives into a tortuous long sentence and by the time he comes out, the difficulty is overcome–for him.

I haven't yet spoken to the chief about the fellowship, but Mard tells me he has also offered her one at a good salary, so it doesn't look as if he'll try to use mine to limit my salary.

There are several small things I want to talk over with you-about my work and us-but they'd take too long to write about. I hope we get at least a little time alone this weekend tho I suspect our only chance will be at nite or at A.M. in the morning.

Gee, a whole letter and I haven't told you how much I love you. It (my love, not our mutual friend) is still in the growing stage, I've had the feeling lately that it's been tougher going for you than you admit to me. Tough enuf so that you haven't been getting as much enjoyment out of things as you used to and will again. But it's not much comfort to think of a year from now and I want so much to be with you all the time. to let you know that every atom of me is with you all the time. In just 43 hours I'll be with you again-then only two more weekends!

God, you were cute at ten! That picture looks more like you than any young one of you that I've seen.
Good nite, darling. Think of me, thinking of you.
Thy loving breadwinner.

June 6, 1945
Dear Darling,

Here I slouch again on message center, ready willing and interruptedly able to write to you. Of course I forgot to bring today's letter from you with me but I think I recall what was in it

The summer plans do sound up in the air. There is a possibility: Barb's father Len (of New Year's Eve fame) has a place on Long Island that he has offered to folks almost free. It is by the shore and I'm sure would be lovely. Let's see about it, Yes?

Your mother is really doing wonders on the towel situation. Are you being snowed under in that little room? Will ask more about your "scholarship" when we see each other.

In ten minutes I have to go to my jolly little 3 hour Mechanical drawing class but with the lovely thought that there are only two more of them and that in three weeks from this minute I shall be on my way to you for good and all.

Got a riotous letter from Phil this A.M. so beautifully typical of them that I couldn't stop laughing over it. ½ page in red ink written upon receiving my letter saying I was married-ending practically in the middle of a sentence. 2nd page one half filled saying he just found the first page which he thought he'd mailed and finished. Didn't have time to finish it but was sending it unfinished. ALSO encloses two pictures of himself. Really, it was so wonderfully typical that if I'd been paraphrasing his character and making up what he'd do or say, it would have been exactly that!

It's sunny! For the first time in five days..and it would be the one day I have class til 4:30. Ah well, you must take your wife on the whitish hue for the present….and I shall be pleased to take you shorn, unshaven or sexless—
All of me until I give it to you in person the day after tomorrow. V

June 11, 1945
Most Wonderful Wife;

This letter is being written by a very weary husband. It was such a hot anniversary day that we just couldn't stay indoors-result was 4 hard sets of tennis. Boy, did we sweat! Nick and I got soundly beaten in all four sets tho the games were close. Bill celebrated his new station in life (he got his degree Saturday) by playing a whale of a game.

Last nite after I left you, I realized that your train didn't leave til 7:40 and I was sorry we didn't use the extra ten minutes.

Summer is here-insects are starting to fly around the lamp.

Believe it or not, seven hours have passed since that last sentence. I suddenly got so tired that I fell asleep, woke up at 3 and staggered to bed. Guess I'm getting old!

After I left you I went to your folks and had a most entertaining evening. I had a piece of Mard's birthday cake and chatted with your mother, then your Pop came in and hauled out the projector to find a good picture of Howard's father to enlarge and to select some of his best to take with him to the guy who's going to teach him photography. He pulled up the screen, and then it suddenly snapped out of his hands, rolled ¾ shut and then tore almost into two pieces. We grabbed it before it disappeared into the container and then began a series of "How could I do such a stupid thing?" etc. etc while he was reconciling himself to the fact that this isn't the best of all possible worlds and that sometimes, terrible, terrible, maybe stupid things happen to the best of us, your Mom got some metal fasteners and we patched up the damage. Then we sewed the torn edges together and tho it doesn't look pretty, it'll show pictures almost as well as before. I loved the way your mother had to thread the needle for us, describing it as a "Process of chewing" I know you would have hugely enjoyed watching your Pop and me on opposite sides of the screen passing the needle back and forth trying to follow the ups and downs of the tear.

He found a marvelous picture of Howard's father and some excellent ones to show the guy. (There was one of you and Mard-poor of her but one of the best, I thought, of you. I suggested that he should show the guy some of his bad ones along with his best. He agreed to the idea but didn't do anything about it.

Then I discovered I'd left my razor at Westport. I had brought it downstairs but when you put my stuff in the lunch basket, I forgot to tell you that the razor and shaving cream were in another place. Your Mom dug up a Rolls razor that someone had given your father which he never used and we fiddled around till we learned how it worked. It comes in what looks like a sardine can and is one those tricky gadgets I love.

We finally decided to reward ourselves with some more of Mard's cake, but there was only a small piece left and since I'd already had some (and wasn't really hungry-just being sociable) I withdrew. I suppose time in itself is a great healer, but I felt more genuinely friendly terms with your Father that nite than before.

A new package arrived from my Mother with two Turkish towels and 3 dish towels. I'll send her a check for the works today. There was also a surprise letter from my Pop containing $50. Quel Surprise!

Got a letter from Harry this morning. He's all mixed up about his draft status. They accepted him, then deferred him and now they may revoke the deferment. He sounds very lonesome for mail, so I'll write to him tonite. If you have any time and are in the mood, I know he'd love to hear from you, but he knows you are busy and not in the best shape yourself so he'll understand if you don't feel like writing.

Now that classes are finished, things are beginning to liven up around here. Cliss and Bill are getting material together for a new set of experiments and bottles are starting to crash on the floor as of old. I've written the first very crude copy of the method for my paper and have polished up the introduction a bit more. The introduction and discussion are the only really creative parts of the paper. Method and results and summary are pretty cut and dried.

I picked up the Venable Philosophy book and read the first page. It's amazing how he thinks philosophy should directly connect with our everyday lives and not consist of abstract ideas. To me, what you get out of philosophy depends on how deeply you look into life. On a bread and butter plane, it merges into economics and political theory which is fine in itself, but doesn't probe into the more abstract concepts that you've been debating at school and with me.

So all of these things happen and yet the big thing is that it's now Tuesday and just about two weeks and then this waiting for weekends will be over forever. Last weekend was all mixed up, but I'll never forget Saturday nite lying in bed with you and feeling our love for each other flowing all around us.

Tomorrow will be seven weeks for us; the beginning of 7, 000 even happier ones. It's going to be unbelievable to realize that there doesn't have to be a week in between every time I see you. Almost as unbelievable as that I'm married to you!
So long, my favorite wife.
Always and forever your very much in love husband,
Danny

June 11, 1945

Dearest Wabbit,

    Here I sit midst a most lovely sight: a bare bookcase and a bare floor. It is a lovely sight because it means the end of this rather crazy existence is near—and that is good. No more of this foolish 7:40 ish feeling; no Wednesday humps, no more waiting impatiently, no more lonely beds. Twill be nice is an understated way of putting it.

    Today has been a pleasantly lazy sort of day-or at least I haven't done much work..tho I DID'NT sleep; for a change. Did some Anthro; went to two classes, to message center, sunned and wrote letters. I wrote 4 latest present-thank you notes and my conscience bothered me on the trunk and plates ones since we returned one and will return the other. But I raved ecstatically anyway. Wrote to Len about the possibility of spending our two week honeymoon at his place at the shore. Also got our $100 bond but I don't know quite what to do with it…and a statement from the bank which somehow figures that I've got $11 less, when I thought I had $9. Haven't gone over the stubs yet. I fear me life may get a bit strained and I may have to draw some $ out of our precious account…or could YOU maybe bring up about $20 to last me. I've got $6 now and I'm about $1.30 below the $200 at the bank–and there are such things as $6 for the rug, shipping the bicycle and trunk still to go. Gee, do I feel like a wife!

    I had one letter from Frank (I had written that I was married) which was quite amusing. I had one date with him at which time he impressed me as very intelligent,